War In Peace

Volume 12

War In Peace

The Marshall Cavendish Illustrated Encyclopedia of Postwar Conflict

Editors-in-Chief
Ashley Brown
Dr. John Pimlott

Editorial Board
Brig-Gen. James Collins Jr (USA Retd.)
Vice-Admiral Sir Louis Le Bailly KBE CB
Ian V Hogg; David Floyd
Professor Laurence Martin
Air-Vice Marshal SWB Menaul CB CBE DFC AFC

MARSHALL CAVENDISH
NEW YORK, LONDON, TORONTO

Reference Edition Published 1985

Published by Marshall Cavendish Corporation
147 West Merrick Road
Freeport, Long Island
N.Y. 11520

Printed and Bound in Italy by L.E.G.O. S.p.a. Vicenza.

© Marshall Cavendish Limited 1985
© Orbis Publishing 1983, 1984

British Library Cataloguing in Publication Data

Brown, Ashley
    War in peace : the Marshall Cavendish
    illustrated encyclopaedia of post-war conflict.
    1. History, Modern—1945- 2. War—History
    —20th century
    I. Title   II. Dartford, Mark
    909.82   D842

    ISBN 0-86307-293-3
        0 86307 305 0   vol. 12

Library of Congress Cataloging in Publication Data

Main entry under title:

War in peace.

    Includes bibliographies and index.
    1. Military history, Modern—20th century. 2. Military
art and science—History—20th century. 3. World politics—1945-
I. Marshall Cavendish Corporation.
U42.W373 1984   355'.009'04   84-19386
ISBN 0-86307-293-3
        0 86307 305 0   vol. 12

Editorial Staff

Editor	Ashley Brown
Editorial Director	Brian Innes
Editorial Manager	Clare Byatt
Editorial Editors	Sam Elder
	Adrian Gilbert
Sub Editors	Sue Leonard
	Simon Innes
Artwork Editor	Jonathan Reed
Artwork Buyer	Jean Morley
Picture Editor	Carina Dvorak
Picture Consultant	Robert Hunt
Design	EDC

Reference Edition Staff

Editor	Mark Dartford
Designer	Graham Beehag
Consultant	Robert Paulley
Indexers	F & K Gill
Creation	DPM Services

Editorial Board

Contributors

David Blue served with the CIA in various countries of Southeast Asia, including Laos, and is a writer on and a student of small wars.

Gordon Brook-Shepherd spent 15 years in Vienna, first as lieutenant-colonel on the staff of the British High Commission and then as a foreign correspondent for the *Daily Telegraph*. A graduate in history from Cambridge, he is currently Chief Assistant Editor of the *Sunday Telegraph*.

Jeffrey J. Clarke is an expert on recent military history, particularly the Vietnam War, and has written for the American Center of Military History.

Major-General Richard Clutterbuck OBE has been Senior Lecturer in politics at Exeter University since his retirement from the army in 1972. His works include *Protest and the Urban Guerrilla*, *Guerrillas and Terrorists* and *Kidnap and Ransom*.

Alexander S. Cochran Jr is a historian whose area of research is modern Indochinese affairs with particular reference to the war in Vietnam since 1945. He is at present working in the Southeast Asia Branch of the Center of Military History, Department of the Army.

Colonel Peter M. Dunn is a serving officer in the USAF. His doctoral thesis is on the history of Indochina during the mid-1940s.

John B. Dwyer served both with the infantry and with armoured units in Vietnam. He was editor and publisher of the Vietnam veteran's newsletter *Perimeter* and has been a writer and correspondent for *National Vietnam Veteran's Review* for the past few years. His particular interest are Special Forces and Special Operations.

Brenda Ralph Lewis has specialised in political and military history since 1964. She s a regular contributor to military and historical magazines in both Britain and the United States.

Hugh Lunghi served in Moscow in the British Military Mission and the British Embassy for six years during and after World War II. He was interpreter for the British Chiefs of Staff at the Teheran, Yalta and Potsdam conferences, and also interpreted for Churchill and Anthony Eden. He subsequently worked in the BBC External Services and is a former editor of *Index on Censorship*.

Charles Messenger retired from the army in 1980 to become a fulltime military writer after 21 years service in the Royal Tank Regiment. Over the past 10 years he has written several books on 20th century warfare, as well as contributing articles to a number of defence and historical journals. He is currently a Research Associate at the Royal United Services Institute for Defence Studies in London.

Billy C. Mossman is a well-known American writer and historian. He is currently working on a volume on the Korean War for the US Army Center of Military History.

Bryan Perrett served in the Royal Armoured Corps from 1952 to 1971. He contributes regularly to a number of established military journals and acted as Defence Correspondent to the *Liverpool Echo* during the Falklands War. His recent books include *Weapons of the Falklands Conflict* and *A History of Blitzkrieg*.

Chapman Pincher is one of England's leading authorities on international espionage and counter-intelligence. He is the author of political novels and books on spying, the most recent of which is *Their Trade is Treachery*, which deals with the penetration of Britain's secret services by the Russian secret police.

Yehoshua Porath is a noted scholar at the Hebrew University in Jerusalem. He has made a special study of the Palestinian problem and is the author of two books on the subject, the most recent of which is *The Palestinian Arab National Movement 1929—39*, which was published in Britain in 1977.

Contributors

Antony Preston is Naval Editor of the military magazine *Defence* and author of numerous publications including *Battleships, Aircraft Carriers* and *Submarines*.

Brigadier-General Edwin H. Simmons, US Marine Corps, Retired, is the Director of Marine Corps History and Museums. At the time of the Inchon operation and the Chosin Reservoir campaign, he, as a major, commanded Weapons Company, 3rd Battalion, 1st Marines. Widely published, he is the author of *The United States Marines*.

Ronald Spector is an expert on Vietnam and has recently completed a book on that subject for the Center of Military History in the United States.

Andres Suarez served in the Cuban ministry of education from 1948—1951, took part in the Cuban revolution, and served in the ministry of housing from 1959. From 1965, he has been Professor of Latin American Studies at the University of Florida. Other publications include *Cuba and the Sino—Soviet Rift*.

Sir Robert Thompson KBE, CMG, DSO, MC is a world authority on guerrilla warfare, on which he has written extensively. He was directly involved in the Emergency in Malaya in the 1950s and rose to become permanent Secretary for Defence. From 1961 to 1965 he headed the British Advisory Mission to Vietnam and since then he has advised several governments, including the United States, on counter-insurgency operations Sir Robert Thompson is a Council member of the Institute for the Study of Conflict, London. His books include *Defeating Communist Insurgency and Revolutionary War in World Strategy, 1945—69.*

Patrick Turnbull commanded 'D' Force, Burma during World War II. His 29 published works include a history of the Foreign Legion.

Contents of Volume

Aerial challenge

The battle of San Carlos Water

On 21 May British soldiers began to come ashore at San Carlos on East Falkland; the choice of time and place for the landing caught the Argentinian commanders unawares. It took General Menendez' headquarters in Port Stanley several hours to digest what had happened at San Carlos, and it took Buenos Aires even longer. At Puerto Belgrano, Rear-Admiral Juan Lombardo, responsible for the overall conduct of operations around the Falklands, received the first news of the British landing at around 0800 hours, and army headquarters was informed at about the same time. Incredible as it may seem, the air force was not told for a further two hours, allowing the British forces landing at San Carlos crucial breathing space to establish a secure bridgehead.

The rivalry between the Argentinian services had re-emerged when the surface fleet had retired to its bases after the sinking of the *General Belgrano*. The army and air force had until then accepted that what was seen as an essentially naval campaign should be conducted under the command of a naval officer, but all three services were subsequently inclined to plan and execute operations without reference to each other. Ironically, it was the air force, which had been

a less than willing partner in the original invasion of the islands, which was to sustain the Argentinian national sense of honour in the weeks to come.

The mainland-based Dagger, Mirage and Skyhawk squadrons were already aware that they were about to enter this particular fray suffering from a number of serious disadvantages. Fear of the Royal Navy's medium-to-high altitude surface-to-air missile (SAM) umbrella meant that attacks could only be delivered at low level, yet the British choice of an anchorage surrounded by hills made Argentinian target acquisition difficult, a factor still further complicated by limited fuel endurance, which only permitted sufficient time for a single pass. That the British submarines lying off the Argentinian coast would observe and report the passage of sorties was beyond reasonable doubt, and ever since a British troop-carrying Sea King had been found abandoned near Punta Arenas in Chile, it had to be assumed that SAS and SBS teams now had the Argentinian mainland air bases under direct surveillance and were doing likewise. Knowing the aircrafts' estimated time of arrival over the target area, the British had simply to position their combat air patrols

Above: Sea Harriers played a vital role in defeating the Argentinian air offensive against the landings of supplies and troops in San Carlos Water. They provided three combat air patrols around the Falklands, destroying 12 Argentinian aeroplanes during 21-25 May. This Sea Harrier, flown by Lieutenant-Commander Mike Blissett, is landing on HMS *Hermes* shortly after he had shot down a Skyhawk with his left-hand Sidewinder. Flight-Lieutenant David Morgan (inset) was the most successful British pilot during the conflict, credited with four-and-a-half victories.

Below: On 24 May, HMS *Antelope* lies broken-backed and sinking; an unexploded bomb in its engine room blew up on the day before while attempts were being made to defuse it. Nine ships of the Royal Navy were sunk or damaged by Argentinian aeroplanes in San Carlos Water. Despite these losses, the British defence of the Task Force, based on a complementary mix of electronics, surface-to-air missiles, anti-aircraft guns and Sea Harriers, was successful in imposing an unacceptable rate of attrition on the Argentinian air forces.

(CAPs) and wait. To allow for this, Argentinian sorties were ordered to fly at high altitude to conserve fuel, then dip below the British radar horizon and fly at sea level for the last 80km (50 miles), thereby exploiting to the full the Task Force's lack of an AWACS aircraft as well as using the land mass itself as a defence against detection.

The first air attacks on the British amphibious group were made by Falklands-based aircraft shortly after 1000 hours. They increased in intensity with the arrival of the high-performance jets from the mainland within the next hour, and reached a crescendo of fury during the afternoon. During the short periods that the Daggers, Mirages, Skyhawks, Aermacchis and Pucarás were above the target area, the sky was filled with tracer and SAM trails, and the howl of jet engines was accompanied by the whoosh of missiles, the steady thump of Bofors, the rattle of Oerlikons and the continuous clatter of hundreds of general-purpose machine guns (GPMGs). The determination and courage of the Argentinian pilots in pressing home their attacks earned the sincere admiration of their adversaries, yet the very nature of those attacks revealed grave tactical weaknesses.

Given that the object of their mission was to eliminate any chance of success the British landing might have, the targets selected by the Argentinian pilots should have been the logistic ships, the transports, the landing-craft, the troops already ashore, supply dumps, vehicles and equipment. Yet these went virtually unmolested while the aircraft expended their munitions on the escort warships. Totally committed to scoring a hit, the pilots bored straight in at their targets, releasing their bombs at the

last possible second. This meant that the majority of bombs were not in free flight long enough to become armed, so that when they struck home comparatively few exploded. As the day wore on, it also became clear that the higher direction of the Argentinian air offensive was extremely poor. For example, there was no attempt to swamp the defences by coordinating the arrival of sorties above San Carlos Water, nor were the defenders compelled to split their fire to meet simultaneous attacks from different directions.

Carnage in the air

Running the gauntlet of fire at San Carlos was only part of the Argentinian pilots' ordeal. They had also to brave the Harrier CAPs, one of which was positioned north of the islands, another over West Falkland and a third at the southern entrance to Falkland Sound, a favourite exit route for Argentinian pilots who had completed their mission. The carnage inflicted by the Harriers was frightful – three Skyhawks and four Daggers were blown apart by the deadly Sidewinder AIM-9L air-to-air missiles, while one Skyhawk and a Pucará were shot down by 30mm cannon fire. Harrier cannon fire also administered the *coup de grâce* to another Skyhawk which had already been crippled by HMS *Ardent*'s automatic weapons. In addition, Sea Cat SAMs launched by *Argonaut* and *Plymouth* downed a Dagger, and the SAS destroyed a second Pucará over Sussex Mountain with a Stinger SAM. Most aircraft which succeeded in returning to their bases on the mainland bore scars of the encounter, and with growing horror senior Argentinian officers realised that the loss ratio for the day's fighting amounted to about 50 per cent.

For the Royal Navy, the price had also been high. *Ardent*, which had begun the day bombarding Goose Green in support of a diversionary SAS raid, became a particular target and was hit repeatedly by bombs, rockets and cannon fire. Blazing fiercely aft, she went down fighting, taking her 22 dead with her – the survivors being taken off by HMS *Yarmouth* and helicopters. *Antrim* was also hit by several rockets and bombs – the latter failed to explode but one smashed its way through her after magazine, and lodged in the heads, where it took 10 hours work before it could be defused and tossed overboard.

Her place in the gunline was taken by *Argonaut*, which was later hit by two bombs. Neither exploded but one penetrated the engine room, putting the engines and steering gear out of action; the second ploughed through a fuel tank and into the forward magazine, starting a fire which was brought under control with difficulty. *Argonaut* signalled that she could still float and fight but not steam, and during the late afternoon, *Plymouth* towed her into San Carlos Water where she remained for the rest of the battle, disposing of her unexploded bombs and completing the repairs which enabled her to limp home at 10 knots. *Broadsword* and *Brilliant* also sustained varying degrees of damage, but by last light 4000 men and 1000 tonnes of equipment had been safely put ashore. The liner *Canberra* left during the night, having disembarked the last of her troops.

Ashore, the process of consolidation and expansion continued without interruption during 22 May. The Argentinian aircraft might have been expected to mount an all-out effort against the British lodgement, but failed to appear until evening, and then only in token numbers and without result. It seemed probable that the Argentinians were reorganising after the mauling they had received – a process prolonged by unimaginative staff work, while bad weather closed the southern bases to operational flying for much of the day.

On 23 May, however, the Argentinian pilots returned with a vengeance, displaying the same brand of desperate courage. *Antelope* was hit twice with bombs that did not explode, but one of these had been incorrectly fused by its Argentinian armourer and detonated while it was being dealt with. Uncontrollable fire spread throughout the ship, which had to be abandoned. After dark, the flames reached the magazine and *Antelope* was engulfed in a tremendous explosion which broke her back and sank her.

Left: An Argentinian Skyhawk of Grupo 5 has HMS *Brilliant*'s profile painted on the nose; in fact, the ship was not damaged although the bomb intended for it smashed through the hull of HMS *Glasgow*. The Argentinian attacks were carried out at such a low level that the bombs often failed to arm in time to explode in the British ships and for the Argentinians to use a shorter delay on the fuze would have endangered the attacking planes.

Argentinian losses amounted to one Skyhawk struck simultaneously by several weapon systems, including *Antelope's* Sea Cat SAMs, and four Daggers knocked down by the Harriers' Sidewinders. Four more Argentinian helicopters – an Agusta 109 and three Pumas – were destroyed by Harriers with 30mm cannon fire near Shag Bay on West Falkland. When subsequently asked why he had made no move against the British beachhead, Menendez pointed to the serious losses inflicted on his helicopter fleet, commenting that these seriously curtailed his mobility. That his troops might have solved the problem by personal effort, as did the British when faced with a similar dilemma only days later, does not seem to have occurred to him.

Although the Argentinians continued their air attacks on San Carlos for some time to come, these lacked the venom displayed during the earlier sorties. On 24 May they changed their tactics and the Royal Fleet Auxiliaries *Sir Galahad*, *Sir Lancelot* and *Sir Bedivere* were all damaged. Three Daggers were destroyed by Sidewinders and a Skyhawk was so seriously damaged by the combined defence that it plunged into the sea during its return flight.

25 May is Argentina's national day and the British expected the Argentinian airmen to make a special effort, although they took surprisingly few additional precautions. Shortly after 1400 hours *Broadsword* and *Coventry*, on radar-picket north of Pebble Island, were hit by a formation of Skyhawks. This time luck was with the Argentinians, who pressed home a model attack which benefited from a number of tactical errors made by their opponents. One bomb bounced off the water, through *Broadsword*'s hull and out via the destroyer's flight deck, wrecking her Lynx helicopter in the process. Three more smashed through *Coventry*'s plating and exploded, blowing a huge hole in her port side. On fire, she rolled over and

sank with the loss of 19 lives.

Later that afternoon, two Super Etendards approached Admiral Woodward's carrier group from the north and each launched an Exocet AM 39 missile, hoping to hit *Hermes* or *Invincible*. Both missiles were decoyed by chaff and helicopters, but while one sped harmlessly on to end its flight in the sea, the other selected a fresh target in the form of the *Atlantic Conveyor*, a requisitioned container vessel, and impacted with fatal consequences. Despite the gaping hole that had been blown in her hull, the ship did not sink for several days, but 12 lives were lost and fires raged through her interior, destroying everything aboard. She had been carrying Harrier reinforcements, but these had already flown off, as had a single Chinook helicopter. Three more Chinooks, six Wessex and a Lynx were gutted by the inferno, however, and since total reliance had been

Top: Super Etendards like these sank the *Atlantic Conveyor* as it sailed towards San Carlos Water to unload its valuable cargo of helicopters. Above: Argentinian Mirages of Grupo 8 in flight over Argentina.

Above right: The Skyhawk was the main attack aeroplane used by the Argentinian Air Force for operations over San Carlos Water. Right: An Argentinian Dagger on its bombing run passes over the *Sir Bedivere*.

placed on the lifting capacity of these machines when the time came for 3 Commando Brigade to advance inland from its beachhead, the enemy had clearly scored a notable success, despite the loss of two Skyhawks over San Carlos and a third shot down by the Argentinians' own AA guns at Goose Green.

Although there would be further air attacks on ships lying off the beachheads, the loss of the *Atlantic Conveyor* signalled the end of the battle of San Carlos Water. The result was a strategic defeat for Argentina, despite the tactical victory gained by her airmen on 25 May, for by that evening the British had 5500 troops and 5000 tonnes of supplies ashore. The logistic build-up had been extremely difficult and just what Argentina might have achieved was graphically demonstrated when 12 bombs were dropped on the brigade maintenance area at Ajax Bay, killing six, wounding 27 and setting off explosions in an ammunition dump which erupted for an entire night. Of the Argentinian Army, however, there was no sign at all, and the strategic initiative on the ground in the Falklands was soon to pass decisively to the British. **Bryan Perrett**

Argentinian airpower

The Argentinian aircraft involved in the Falklands War came from every service, including the air force (Fuerza Aérea Argentina – FAA), naval air arm (Aeronaval Argentina – AA), the coast guard (Prefectura Naval Argentina – PNA), and the 601 Combat Aviation Battalion of the Argentinian Army (Ejército Argentina), which was based on the islands themselves.

Argentina enjoyed overwhelming numerical superiority in the air (some 112 combat aircraft capable of operating over the Falklands from bases on the mainland, against the 20 Sea Harriers initially available to the British), and concentrated all its available aircraft at the six airbases of Comodoro Rivadavia, Trelew, Rio Gallegos, Santa Cruz, San Julian and Rio Grande along the southern and central Argentinian coast – even then, however, they were operating at extreme range when they flew missions against the Task Force.

The key Argentinian unit was the 2nd Naval Fighter and Attack Squadron, based at Rio Grande and equipped with four operational Super Etendards armed with Exocet missiles. As well as sinking the *Atlantic Conveyor* and *Sheffield*, the threat posed by the Exocets forced the British aircraft carriers to stay well to the east of the

Falklands, reducing their ability to provide air cover to the other Task Force vessels. The Exocet threat was limited, however, by the small number of the missiles available to the Argentinians – only five at the start of the conflict. The embargo imposed by the French government on further arms deliveries prevented the Argentinians restocking the weapon.

The 20 A-4C Skyhawks of the FAA Grupo 4, based at Rio Gallegos, and the 26 A-4B Skyhawks of Grupo 5, stationed at both Rio Gallegos and Santa Cruz, along with the 11 A-4Qs of the 3rd Naval Fighter and Attack Squadron flying first from the aircraft carrier *25 de Mayo* and then from Rio Grande, and the 34 IAI Daggers of Grupo 6, operating from San Julian, Rio Grande and Rio Gallegos, provided the mainland-based hitting power which struck the Task Force repeatedly in a series of courageous and determined raids, particularly against the vessels anchored in San Carlos Water.

The 601 Combat Aviation Battalion on the Falklands was composed of helicopters, but the garrison also included 25 Pucarás of FAA Grupo 3, stationed at Port Stanley, Goose Green and Pebble Island; five Aermacchi MB 339s of the Ist Naval Attack Squadron, flying from Port Stanley; and four Beech T-34C Turbo-Mentors based on Pebble Island.

Goose Green

2 Para triumph against the odds

On the windswept high ground of Sussex Mountain at the southern extremity of the San Carlos bridgehead, the men of the 2nd Battalion, the Parachute Regiment (2 Para), commanded by Lieutenant-Colonel Herbert Jones ('Colonel H'), had joined in the combined defence against the Argentinian air attacks, but after several days of being particularly wet and cold, a sense of restlessness began to grow within the battalion, born of the instinct that wars are not won by standing still.

On 23 May, 2 Para were detailed to carry out a raid on Argentinian positions around Darwin and Goose Green, lying on the isthmus connecting the northern and southern halves of East Falkland, but they were stood down. Then, at about 1400 hours on 26 May, it was decided to proceed with the attack after all and Colonel Jones was ordered to report to HQ 3 Commando Brigade for briefing. There he was told that the whole battalion would be employed, with the support of a Marine Blowpipe troop, three 105mm light guns belonging to 29th Commando Regiment Royal Artillery, naval gunfire provided by HMS *Arrow* and, if possible, Harrier strikes after first light on the 28th, the day of the attack. A request for a troop of the Blues and Royals' Scorpion and Scimitar light tanks was denied, partly because of a fuel shortage and partly because these vehicles had yet to demonstrate their astonishing ability to cope with the atrocious going. A request for BV Snowcats to move 2 Para's heavy weapons was also denied for similar reasons, but in the event two such vehicles and their drivers were later hijacked and employed hauling urgently needed ammunition forward.

The object of the operation was to be the capture of the settlements, which were believed to be garrisoned by a single weak battalion. This intelligence was provided by D Squadron, 22nd Special Air Service Regiment (22 SAS), whose patrols had been operating on the isthmus for some time.

At 2000 hours on 26 May, 2 Para commenced its long approach march to Camilla Creek House, where it would lie up throughout the following day. The battalion possessed twice the normal complement of machine guns as well as a dozen M79 grenade-launchers. As the men were marching in battle order every single weapon and piece of ammunition had to be carried, and for this reason their loads were cut to a minimum. The rifle platoons' two-inch mortars were left behind on Sussex Mountain, while 2 Para's Support Company was reduced to two 81mm mortars, three Milan firing posts with 17 missiles, and six machine guns.

Camilla Creek House was reached during the early hours of 27 May. The companies crammed themselves into the buildings and snatched what sleep they could. Morning revealed that the farm lay inside a hollow which sheltered it both from the wind and the enemy's view. C (Patrol) Company moved out to observe and identify the enemy's positions on the isthmus. The radios were tuned to the BBC World Service which announced blandly that 'a parachute battalion is poised and ready to assault Darwin and Goose Green.' Complete incredulity turned to savage anger as the implications sank in. Colonel Jones threatened to sue the secretary of state for defence and the BBC for manslaughter if any of his men were killed during the battle to come. The Argentinians, too, had heard the broadcast and after dusk began lifting reinforcements into Goose Green by helicopter, as well as alerting their forward defences. In the meantime, the Para outposts snapped up a civilian Land Rover containing an officer and two men from an Argentinian reconnaissance platoon who, during interrogation, disclosed that the enemy's strength was already well in excess of the SAS estimate.

Jones held his Orders Group during the afternoon,

Bottom: The road to Goose Green. It was here and in the surrounding hills that the men of 2 Para came up against heavy opposition from well dug-in Argentinian troops. The Paras had marched, carrying all their ammunition and equipment on their backs, from the bridgehead at San Carlos. Assaulting the Argentinian positions under cover of darkness, they incurred heavy losses, including Colonel Herbert 'H' Jones (below), who died while storming an enemy trench.

Left: An Argentinian dug-out at Goose Green, built from turf cut from the soft, waterlogged ground in the area which prevented the use of trenches.

briefing his senior officers on the six-phase plan of attack, according to which companies would go into the lead by rotation as each objective was secured in turn. After nightfall, helicopters clattered across Sussex Mountain and down to the selected artillery gun position to the east of Camilla Creek House, where they deposited the three 105mm guns of 29 Regiment's 8th (Alma) Battery.

At 1800 hours C Company moved off to initiate phase one of the attack by securing the start-lines for the A and B Company attacks, which lay beyond the Camilla Creek and Ceritos Arroyo bridges and across the neck of the isthmus, at this point subdivided into two narrow corridors of land by Burntside Pond. The isthmus itself is a little over 8km (5 miles) long and 2.5km (1.5 miles) wide, with a low spine running down its centre, intersected by a belt of gorse running from the ruined Boca House to Darwin Hill. Muddy tracks meander along a broadly north-south axis from both settlements, which are located on the east coast. The only cover available is provided by the contours themselves.

C Company, under Major Roger Jenner, completed its task without incident and then provided guides which led A and B Companies onto their start-lines. Major Dair Farrar-Hockley's A Company went in at 0235 hours, making for Burntside House, with gunfire support provided by HMS *Arrow*. After a brief exchange of fire the Argentinians dug in around the house fled, leaving two dead behind. B Company, under Major John Crosland, moved off at 0320 hours to secure the enemy's positions between Camilla Creek and the spine of the

isthmus, and at once became involved in a protracted soldiers' battle in which the Paras' high standard of junior leadership proved decisive. One by one, those trenches which offered resistance were eliminated by a long-familiar drill: first, their occupants were pinned down by sustained automatic fire, then they were neutralised by a phosphorus grenade or a 66mm LAW round. Fiercely engaged, Crosland's platoons pushed steadily south and even secured the objective which should have been taken by Major Philip Neame's D Company in phase three. This, in fact, proved to be no bad thing, for in the darkness B Company had inevitably missed several positions and D Company promptly dealt with these when they opened fire into the rear of the British advance. As the light increased, however, B Company was exposed to intense fire from a strong enemy position around Boca House and forced to go to ground.

On the opposite flank A Company had made a similarly dramatic advance and by 0530 hours had secured its second objective, Coronation Point, without opposition. Farrar-Hockley asked for permission to press on. Such is the confused nature of

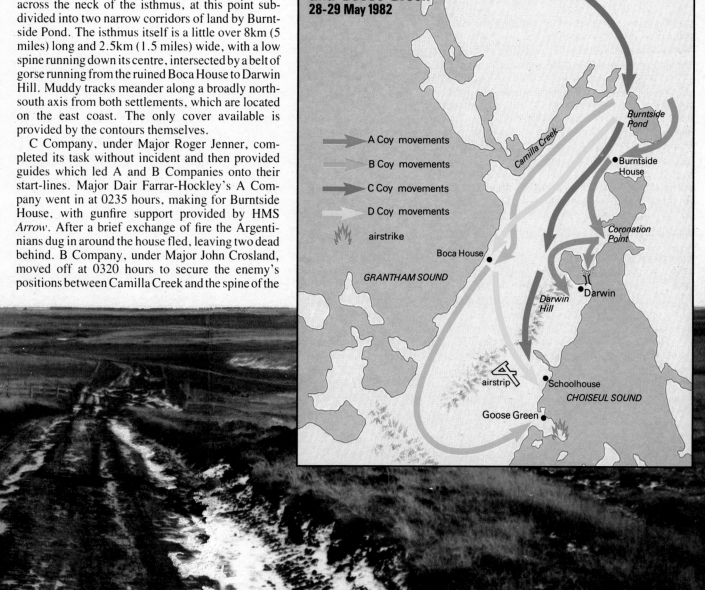

The battle for Darwin and Goose Green
28-29 May 1982

A Coy movements
B Coy movements
C Coy movements
D Coy movements
airstrike

Camilla Creek House

Camilla Creek

Burntside Pond

Burntside House

Coronation Point

Boca House

GRANTHAM SOUND

Darwin Hill

Darwin

airstrip

Schoolhouse

CHOISEUL SOUND

Goose Green

night fighting that Colonel Jones understandably doubted whether A Company had got as far as it claimed and decided to go forward and see for himself. This cost 30 priceless minutes during which the remaining darkness ebbed steadily away.

Farrar-Hockley decided to leave his 3 Platoon on the eastern shore of Darwin Bay, across which it would give fire support to 1 and 2 Platoons as they moved round to attack Darwin Hill, followed by the battalion's tactical HQ. The light was now much stronger and suddenly the assault groups were pinned down by heavy fire from bunkers and trenches on a spur at the northern end of the hill.

Thus, with the coming of dawn, the fortunes of war had undeniably swung in the Argentinians' favour. All of 2 Para's companies were halted in their tracks and subjected to a growing volume of artillery, mortar and machine-gun fire. Fortunately, the soft peaty ground minimised the effect of the enemy's rounds, but the same was true of the Paras' own support weapons, ammunition for which was strictly limited. HMS *Arrow* withdrew just before the dawn deadline laid down in the agreed plan, and bad weather at sea prevented the launch of Harrier strikes. The same considerations did not apply to the Argentinian aircraft based on the Falklands, which mounted a series of attacks on 8 Battery's gun line and the British helicopters which were ferrying ammunition and wounded, shooting one down and killing its crew. The enemy aircraft were engaged by the attached Royal Artillery and Royal Marine Blowpipe teams and a naval Aermacchi 339 attack trainer was destroyed by this means; an air force Pucará failed to return to its base at Port Stanley and is believed to have crashed in cloud among the hills.

Beyond the call of duty

Both Colonel Jones and his second-in-command, Major Chris Keeble, shared a belief that a determined attack by a few men, delivered promptly, could achieve what a much larger number of men might fail to do later in the battle, and it was with this in mind that he ordered Farrar-Hockley and A Company to maintain their fierce pressure against the enemy on Darwin Hill. 'It was,' as the citation for Colonel Jones' posthumous award of the Victoria Cross comments, 'a time for personal leadership and action. Colonel Jones immediately seized a submachine gun and, calling on those around him and with total disregard for his own safety, charged the nearest enemy position. This action exposed him to fire from a number of trenches. As he charged up a short slope at the enemy position he was seen to fall and roll backward downhill. He immediately picked himself up and again charged the enemy trench, firing his sub-machine gun and seemingly oblivious to the intense fire directed at him. He was hit by fire from another trench and fell dying only a few feet from the enemy he had assaulted.'

This, psychologically, was the turning-point of the battle. The Paras swarmed up the hill and this time they were not to be stopped. Trench after trench fell to grenade, machine-gun or LAW attack. The enemy began to surrender and the firing died down. The Argentinians had held Darwin Hill with 92 men, of whom 18 were now dead and 39 wounded; significantly, among the prisoners were six officers, and these were the only Argentinian officers encountered by 2 Para in the front line. The battalion's own

losses were six dead and 12 wounded.

Major Keeble was advised of Colonel Jones' death by radio and came forward at once to assume control of the battle. Support Company, which had originally been positioned west of Camilla Creek, had also arrived in the forward area and its Milan missiles were winging across the heathland with pinpoint accuracy to blast apart the Argentinian bunkers in the Boca House area. Under cover of this and the fire of B Company, D Company moved south along the shore, sheltered by a shallow cliff, until they were parallel with Boca House, which they then assaulted. The enemy surrendered at once and the entire Argentinian defence line had thus fallen.

It was now approximately 1515 hours and Major Keeble made his dispositions for the final advance on Goose Green. B Company would move south and then swing east to block the southern exit from the settlement; D Company would advance directly along the axis Boca House-Goose Green, with C Company (reinforced by A Company's 3 Platoon) on its left; the remainder of A Company would consolidate its gains at Darwin.

Throughout the afternoon the advance continued steadily, despite the volume of fire produced by every weapon in the enemy's arsenal, including automatic 35mm anti-aircraft weapons employed in the ground-support role. It was now becoming apparent that many Argentinians had lost heart as surrenders became more numerous; but others were willing to go on fighting. In a very confused situation, Lieutenant Jim Barry and two men were killed while going forward to accept the surrender of an Argentinian unit which had shown the white flag, almost certainly because of a misunderstanding. Following this, a hard-fought action took place for positions around the blazing schoolhouse, from which none of its defenders emerged alive.

Towards evening, Argentinian aircraft again attempted to intervene in the ground fighting. After an unsuccessful bombing run by a pair of Skyhawks,

Above: Men of 2 Para's A Company on Darwin Hill, shortly after its capture from the Argentinians. Shocked by the death of Colonel Jones, the Paras stormed the enemy defences trench by trench, clearing them with grenades, rockets and automatic weapons in bitter close-quarters fighting. Above right: Paras and men of the Marine artillery support company inspect an Argentinian anti-aircraft gun which had been used against the British troops during the battle for Goose Green.

two Pucarás attacked with napalm and rocket fire, but failed to strike their targets; one Pucará was downed by a Blowpipe, the other by concentrated smallarms fire. Improved weather conditions at sea now permitted the Harriers to take a hand and at 1925 hours the enemy's artillery and AA gun positions on Goose Green Point were struck by three in succession, using cluster bombs. The Argentinians were already virtually confined to the peninsula on which the settlement is built and the effect of this airstrike on their morale was considerable. At last light an Argentinian Chinook and six Huey helicopters attempted to land reinforcements at the southern edge of the battle area, but took off rapidly when engaged by B Company and the British artillery.

During the night, Brigadier Thompson reinforced 2 Para with J Company, 42 Commando, three more guns and the battalion's own mortars, to be used should it prove necessary to storm the settlement next day. In the event, the enemy commanders at Goose Green, Air Vice-Commodore Wilson Pedroza and Lieutenant-Colonel Italo Pioggi, agreed to Keeble's suggestion for a parley, and to surrender unconditionally after a face-saving ceremony. To the Paras' astonishment, some 150 air force personnel and approximately 1000 soldiers laid down their arms during 29 May; the captured equipment included four 105mm howitzers, two 35mm AA guns, six 20mm AA guns, six 120mm mortars and two Pucarás. Argentinian casualties were estimated at 250 killed and about the same number wounded.

The capture of Darwin and Goose Green by 2 Para was a remarkable infantry battle. At a cost of 17 killed and 35 wounded, a 450-strong battlegroup had pitched a force four times its size out of carefully prepared positions and utterly defeated it. For the Argentinian junta, it was a graphic and deeply depressing demonstration of British resolve to recover the islands; for the British, the result of the first major clash between land forces provided a striking victory when it was needed most. **Bryan Perrett**

Above: Some of the 1200 Argentinian prisoners taken at Goose Green under British guard. After their victory, the Paras were amazed to see how many enemy troops they had been up against. Their capture of Goose Green was the first successful battle of the British land campaign in the Falklands, but it was not achieved without cost. Left: The 17 dead of 2 Para being buried near where they had fallen at Darwin.

The long march

Yomping and tabbing to Port Stanley

Despite the extravagant claims of the Buenos Aires media that the British were surrounded at San Carlos and facing a second Dunkirk, the total lack of contact with the Argentinian Army convinced Brigadier Julian Thompson, in command of 3 Commando Brigade, that Major-General Menendez had already developed a siege mentality and would passively await events inside his defences. This assessment was remarkably accurate, for Menendez was later to reveal his belief that the harsh Falklands terrain inhibited the use of military wheeled vehicles and that this, coupled with an inadequate helicopter lift, would prevent the British from mounting an offensive against Port Stanley.

Back in London, the politicians seemed to have no conception of the problems involved, particularly in the area of logistics, yet had placed Thompson under intolerable pressure to break out of his beachhead from the moment he set foot ashore. Whatever plans he may have made were discounted when the greater part of his helicopter lift was destroyed aboard the *Atlantic Conveyor* on 25 May. But this event in itself raised the need to break out to the level of a political necessity. Having been ordered to proceed, Thompson briefed his unit commanders on 26 May.

The salient fact to emerge at the briefing was that the medium-lift helicopter capacity possessed by the Task Force amounted to one Chinook, 20 Sea Kings and 17 Wessex, of which only a portion would be available to 3 Commando Brigade at any one time. These helicopters would be fully engaged hauling guns, ammunition and heavy equipment; the troops themselves would march, carrying all of their weapons, ammunition, personal equipment and rations – the load in some cases amounting to 65kg (140lb). On the southern flank, 2 Para would advance against the enemy positions at Darwin and Goose Green. 3 Para, supported by a composite Scorpion/Scimitar troop of the Blues and Royals, would advance due east from Port San Carlos with Teal Inlet as its objective, some assistance being provided by local farmers who loaned tractors and trailers to transport some of the heavier equipment. 45 Commando, after being ferried across San Carlos Water, would head north to Douglas settlement with the support of a Blues and Royals troop and their heavily-laden Volvo BV202 Snowcats. 42 Commando was to remain in immediate reserve and 40 Commando, to the disgust of its members, was detailed to assume responsibility for the security of the beachhead.

The advance began on 27 May. Much of the Royal Marines' and the Parachute Regiment's initial training takes place, respectively, on Dartmoor and the Brecon Beacons, both of which provide a harsh upland environment very similar to that of the Falklands. The training is extremely tough and in itself forms part of the selection process which eliminates all but the most determined recruits. To

Above: Marines loaded with heavy backpacks and equipment in the rough terrain through which they 'tabbed' from San Carlos to the hills surrounding Port Stanley. After the loss of *Atlantic Conveyor*, which had been carrying most of the Task Force's transport helicopters, the British faced serious problems in moving men and supplies. Only the passivity of the Argentinians allowed 3 Commando Brigade to stage its march across East Falkland unopposed.

Right: Marines of 45 Commando advancing through an Argentinian minefield with one of the few cross-country vehicles, a Volvo BV202, available to the British land forces in the Falklands.

Below right: Members of a Marine air defence troop (ADT) digging in at Teal Inlet. Armed with Blowpipe missile launchers, the ADT was responsible for protecting 3 Para from enemy air attack during its rapid cross-country advance on Port Stanley.

the Commandos, this style of marching is known as 'yomping', and to the Paras it is 'tabbing'. Both were convinced that only the best infantry in the world could undertake the task they had been given, and the rivalry between them added an edge to their will to succeed. Despite sprained ankles caused by tussock grass and feet perpetually wet and frozen, very few men fell out from the steadily trudging files. The Volvo BVs performed well, while the Blues and Royals' Scorpions and Scimitars coped superbly with every kind of unpleasant going that was encountered. 3 Para reached Teal Inlet after dusk on 29 May and rested the next day, resuming its march at last light. Its epic march ended at Estancia House, on the lower slopes of Mount Kent, during the evening of 31 May. 45 Commando had reached Douglas on the 29th and arrived at Teal Inlet on 30 May. Both units were extremely proud of their achievement and had been greatly encouraged by the news of 2 Para's tremendous fight at Goose Green.

On the main axis of the advance, however, there had been virtually no contact with the enemy and it seemed very much as though Menendez had no intention of contesting the considerable spaces of no man's land lying between the two armies. On 26

May, the Royal Marine Mountain and Arctic Warfare Cadre – another elite within an elite like the Special Boat Squadron – had detected an Argentinian special forces' unit of similar size at Top Malo House and eliminated it in a fast-moving attack which killed four of the enemy, wounded seven and captured the remaining five at a cost of three Marines wounded. SAS patrols had been operating on the 460m (1500 foot) Mount Kent since early May and by the end of the month were established in strength on the upper slopes. They were able to confirm that the Argentinians were no longer holding the summit. They had, in fact, been despatched by helicopter to reinforce Goose Green and thus far no replacements had arrived. This was a blunder on the part of the Argentinians, for not only did the line Teal Inlet-Mount Kent-Mount Challenger-Bluff Cove provide an ideal outer rampart for the concentric scheme of defence devised by General Menendez, but Mount Kent also gave the attacker an overview of Port Stanley and all the intervening features. Brigadier Thompson responded to this priceless piece of intelligence by despatching K Company, 42 Commando, in helicopters to occupy the vacant ground. When the Marines touched down during the afternoon of 31 May a firefight was in progress between D Squadron, SAS and an enemy patrol; this was quickly resolved in favour of the SAS. Two hours later a Chinook lifted in three 105mm light guns. Next morning the gunners fired several rounds into the distant Moody Brook barracks, believed to be an enemy headquarters, to advise its new tenants that the battle for Port Stanley had begun.

The final assault on the Argentinian garrison concentrated around Port Stanley depended upon the arrival of 5 Infantry Brigade, however, which was to advance along the southern flank through Darwin and Fitzroy. But on the day 3 Commando Brigade were seizing the heights of Mount Kent, 5 Infantry Brigade was still on board its transports moving towards the bridgehead at San Carlos Water.

Bryan Perrett

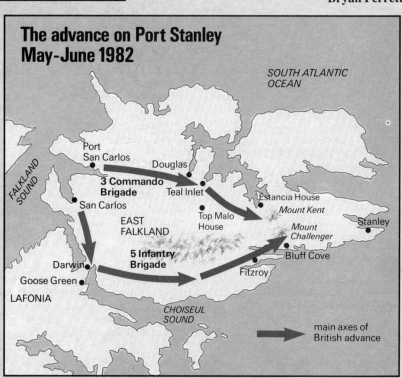

The advance on Port Stanley
May-June 1982

The conscript army

The Argentinians in the Falklands

In April 1982, the Argentinian Army had not fought a foreign war for over 100 years, and had never faced the forces of a major power such as Britain. In spite of a number of long-standing territorial disputes with neighbouring Chile, the fundamental role of the Argentinian Army had been the preservation of internal security. This task often brought the armed forces to the forefront of the political stage, and there was a long tradition of military intervention in the political life of the country.

During the 1970s, this tendency towards intervention prompted the armed forces to overthrow the weak and incompetent government of Isabel Perón, wife of the former Argentinian leader President Juan Perón, in March 1976. The country was at that time racked by deep internal conflicts which contained all the ingredients for an open and bitter civil war between left-wing and Peronist guerrillas on one side and the deeply entrenched forces of the ultra-right on the other. With the establishment of a military junta after the March 1976 coup, the armed forces declared all-out war on the Peronist Montenero guerrillas and the Trotskyist Ejército Revolucionario del Pueblo (People's Revolutionary Army-ERP) in what became notorious as the 'Dirty War', during which

thousands of opponents of the military regime were kidnapped, tortured and murdered. Many simply 'disappeared' in what was one of the darkest episodes of modern Latin American history. All sections of the Argentinian armed services were expected to take an active part in this campaign of political terror, and many officers and NCOs were deeply implicated in the excesses which occurred.

The subsequent political and economic problems which beset the Argentinian military junta were the prime reason for its decision to invade the Falkland Islands, and their capture was welcomed with wildly happy demonstrations throughout the country. The public display of nationalist enthusiasm for the reconquest of the Malvinas does not seem to have found universal reflection amongst the ranks of the young, confused conscripts, however, who found themselves being mobilised and shipped to the southern Argentinian military base of Rio Gallegos, from which they were flown by air force C-130 Hercules transports to the airport at Stanley (renamed Puerto Argentino) on the Falklands. Although the initial Argentinian invasion of the Falkland Islands had been carried out by members of the elite Buzo Tactico, a Marine unit similiar to the

Above: Argentinian soldiers man a 7·62mm FN machine-gun outside Port Stanley. Though their equipment was in many respects comparable to or even better than that supplied to their British opponents, the Argentinian troops who garrisoned the Falklands were hampered by inadequate training, poor leadership and badly organised logistics.

Left: Major-General Mario Benjamin Menendez, Argentinian military governor of the Falkland Islands and commander of the troops stationed there. Responsible for preparing the islands' defence against the British Task Force, Menendez concentrated the bulk of his mainly conscript troops around the capital, Port Stanley, and failed to react aggressively to either the landing of British troops at San Carlos, or their subsequent march across the island towards his positions.

British Special Boat Service (SBS) or the US Navy SEAL teams, the overwhelming majority of the garrison which was subsequently stationed there consisted of poorly trained conscripts. Many of these had already completed their 12 months compulsory military service and had returned to civilian life, only to be recalled to their units at the beginning of April 1982.

While proud to fight for their country, once on the Falklands, most seemed to succumb rapidly to a debilitating and infectious form of fatalism which grew worse as the British Task Force drew nearer to the islands during April and early May. The junta had gambled everything upon Britain accepting the Argentinian seizure of the islands without a fight. Once the Task Force had been despatched and war appeared increasingly inevitable, morale amongst the troops on the islands slumped dramatically.

Scattered positions

Few of the Argentinian troops had any clear idea of where they were, or where the front line would be when the inevitable British counter-blow fell. Most units were stationed in and around Port Stanley, but there was little planning or mutual support between the scattered positions. There seem to have been very few maps of the islands available to the Argentinian troops, and many expressed surprise after their capture by the British to see how well informed they were, not only about their situation, but also about the positions occupied by the Argentinians themselves. While the Argentinian commander on the islands, Major-General Mario Benjamin Menendez, had correctly identified Port Stanley as the key to the defence of the islands and had made his dispositions accordingly, the basic lack of strategic insight of the Argentinian high command filtered down to the troops on the ground in the form of extreme passivity and lack of aggressive patrolling and intelligence-gathering. Rumours of the presence of British Special Air Service (SAS) and SBS infiltration teams on the islands, operating in the midst of the Argentinian garrison, contributed further to demoralisation, and the Argentinian conscripts became even jumpier when they began to hear stories that the SAS and SBS were dressed in Argentinian uniforms and spoke perfect Spanish. Trigger-happy soldiers on guard duty tried to identify friend from foe by asking questions about the strip colours of famous Argentinian football teams.

The three basic problems affecting Argentinian morale, however, were food, climate, and the poor relations between officers and men. By far the most serious of these was the last, and many conscripts complained bitterly of their treatment by superiors. Officers took little part in the construction of defensive positions and had only the slightest contact with the ordinary troops, who were left largely without leadership or explanation of their tactical situation.

Isolated in the front line, the Argentinian conscripts suffered severely from the harsh conditions of the South Atlantic winter in which the war was to be fought. The clothing with which they had been supplied was inadequate to protect them from either the freezing cold or the penetrating rain. The water-logged nature of the ground into which they had to dig their trenches and dug-outs was also a serious hazard, and even where troops were relatively warmly dressed, their permanently soaking feet left them

---

'Why did they lie to us?'

Flown into Stanley airport from Rio Gallegos on 15 April 1982, Guillermo, an Argentinian conscript, spent the war in the hills around Port Stanley, eventually serving in the crew of a 105mm gun.

'We arrived at Puerto Argentino airport to be greeted by foul weather. It was raining and very cold. Many people have said that the clothes we had were inadequate; I think they were adequate for the first few days when it was still autumn, but later in the winter, wearing those clothes on sentry duty, you just froze solid. It was summer clothing; it wasn't right for the mountains or snow...

'At first we tried to sleep in tents and build fortifications to shoot from, foxholes, like the ones we dug in our training in Buenos Aires Province. But the soil on the islands was terrible; you dug a hole and within two days it was full of water... We built caves, stone fortifications. We put them together as best we could, using big stones weighing as much as 40 pounds. We took ages to finish them but we were lucky; they were ready before the attacks began. Once the naval and air attacks began, we learned as we went

along. The boys from other positions hit during the first attacks told you how they'd got on... So bit by bit we were learning to make war...

'When we began to miss out on meals, we realised that the food dump was down at Moody Brook and we began to go down...to tell the truth, we went down to steal, that's the right word...

'I'd only done five shooting tests during my entire military service... I met a group of kids from the Tablada Regiment... They taught me to shoot PDF rifle-launched grenades, they showed me how to use mortars, a cannon, masses of things I didn't know. I think I should have been taught those things during training if only to have the basics. But I had to learn them there in the middle of the war and I had to learn them from another conscript...

'When they landed in San Carlos we knew we were in direct contact, by land, and we didn't like it at all... At first they told us that there were only 200 English ashore and that they were surrounded. But later we found out the truth, there were more than 200. And the troops' morale plummeted. "Why did they lie to us?" we asked ourselves.'

cold and depressed. Frostbite was also a major problem, and many lost toes and fingers.

Even though the bulk of the Argentinian forces were stationed within reach of Port Stanley, there were continual problems in supplying the forward positions with the food which the dejected and defeated troops later discovered was stockpiled in sheds near Stanley airport. As they heard the Hercules transports fly regularly in, laden with supplies from the mainland, the conscripts wondered when they would see their next square meal. Many were reduced to shooting, skinning and eating the sheep which grazed around them, while others, emboldened by hunger, took to stealing food from army stores in the rear areas. Scavenging, stealing and barter took up much of the time of the troops, and the collapse of discipline led to the disintegration of military units into mutually supportive groups of friends and comrades, who did not, however, feel any greater loyalty to officers or regiments.

The brutal methods used by NCOs and officers to

Below: Argentinian conscripts on the Falklands parade below their national flag. Their initial enthusiasm for the war against Britain soon evaporated in the harsh physical conditions of the South Atlantic colony. Bottom: A tent encampment, where Argentinian troops awaited the arrival of the British Task Force with sinking morale, until by the time of the San Carlos landings they were already psychologically a beaten army.

impose discipline on the resentful troops indicated just how deep the corrosive influence of the 'Dirty War' had gone into the Argentinian armed forces; it merely served to deepen the divide between leaders and led. Caught stealing food or deserting their positions, young conscripts were beaten or tied spread-eagled on the ground in the freezing cold.

After the British landings at San Carlos, the morale of the Argentinian garrison slumped even further, and as the British troops advanced across East Falkland, the Argentinians remained paralysed in their defensive positions, allowing their opponents to advance unmolested to the heights overlooking Port Stanley. The initial fighting at Goose Green and Darwin showed that the Argentinian soldiers were capable of offering a determined resistance when fighting from strong positions, but the battles around Stanley resulted in a swift disintegration of the ordinary conscript's will to resist, and many fell back into the town where they waited resignedly to be taken prisoner. Although some units of professional troops, such as the 5th Marine Battalion, did fight fiercely and courageously, they were soon isolated and forced in their turn to retreat to Stanley.

In the confusion of the final rout and surrender, there were many instances of looting and vandalism by Argentinian troops in Stanley, but on the whole they seem to have behaved remarkably well towards the islands' civilian population throughout their occupation, considering how utterly miserable their own conditions were at the time. Their experience of war on the Falklands totally shattered their confidence in both their military superiors and in the military government in Buenos Aires, and contributed to the dramatic decline of the popularity in which the junta had temporarily basked after the invasion. Returning home, they found that they were an embarrassing reminder of a humiliating military defeat, and many had difficulty in readapting to normal civilian life. For the young Argentinians who went to fight for their country on the Falklands, the scars of war would be a long time in healing.

Robin Corbett

BUCCANEER

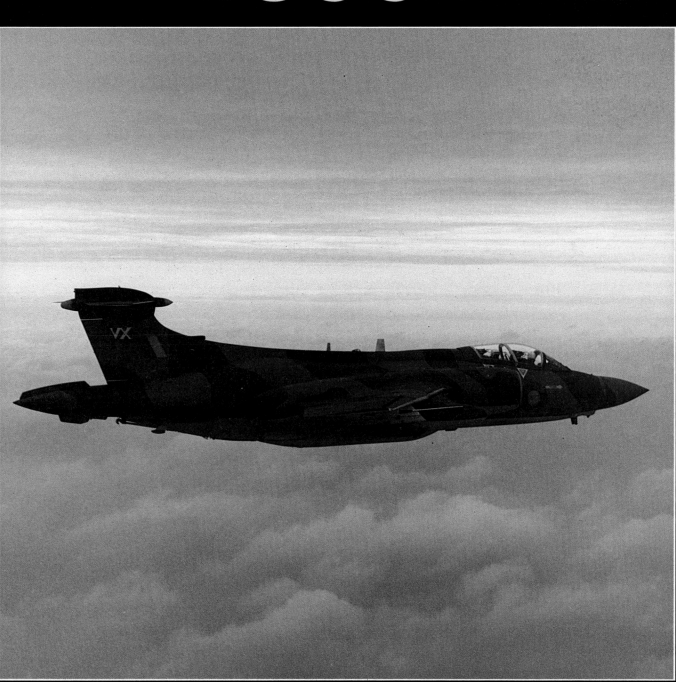

The Blackburn Buccaneer began as Royal Navy Requirement NA 39 issued by the Admiralty in June 1952. This document called for a carrier-based strike aircraft capable of delivering a nuclear weapons load against major units of enemy surface fleets while flying at very low levels to avoid radar detection; provision for the carriage of a wide range of conventional weapons was also requested. Specifically, the new aircraft was to be capable of speeds in the order of Mach 0.85 at an altitude of 61m (200ft) over a combat radius of 740km (460 miles) with a nuclear store carried internally. Such a specification was extremely demanding for the period and to achieve it required the application of the most advanced aerodynamic theory. Several manufacturers produced NA 39 designs but, as work progressed, it became apparent that the Blackburn submission was the most promising. Accordingly, the company was awarded a contract for 20 development and pre-production aircraft during July 1955 with the rider that a prototype should be available by April 1958.

Despite the advanced nature of the aircraft, Blackburn managed to keep to the specified timetable and the first NA 39 (the name Buccaneer was not to be applied to the type until 3 August 1960) made its maiden flight on 30 April 1958. The new aeroplane was powered by a pair of de Havilland Gyron Junior turbojets offering a combined thrust of 6440kg (14,200lbs) and, in order to achieve the required performance, its design showed careful attention to aerodynamics. The fuselage was shaped in such a way as to ease the drag at speeds close to that of sound, while the wings were optimised for service at high speeds, a consideration which resulted in a relatively small overall area. In order to achieve an acceptable performance at low speeds, Blackburn incorporated a 'blown air' system into the wings to increase the lift available during take-off and landing, the areas of flight at which the chosen wing-design was least efficient. Overall, the NA 39's structure was made immensely strong to cope with the demands of maritime low-level operations and the general stress of carrier operations. Provision was made for a crew of two and the most up-to-date navigation/attack avionics, together with a spacious internal weapons bay to house the nuclear store, covered by an ingenious rotary door that reduced

drag when the bay was opened. The NA 39 was an extremely elegant solution to the problems posed by the specification and it says much for the basic design that, apart from its avionics system, the Buccaneer remained one of the best low-level strike aircraft available a quarter of a century after its maiden flight.

Deck landing trials began in June 1959 aboard HMS *Victorious* and in October of the same year, Blackburn was granted a production contract for 40 Buccaneer SMk1 aircraft. The SMk1 featured a number of refinements over the original NA 39, especially in the shape of the nose radome and the geometry of the tail fin. The first six aircraft were delivered to No 700Z Flight (soon to become No 809 Squadron) at Lossiemouth in March 1961 for trials work and the type became operational with No 801 Squadron during the following July.

No 801 Squadron was also formed at Lossiemouth and spent most of 1962 getting to grips with its new equipment. The Buccaneer's nuclear role was emphasised in the early days by its overall 'anti-flash' white finish, amended in 1964 to white undersurfaces only. On 20 February 1963, No 801 Squadron took the aircraft aboard HMS *Ark Royal* for its first tour of duty at sea and thereafter the Royal Navy's Buccaneer force began to increase rapidly, eventually encompassing aircraft operated by Nos 800, 801, 803 and 809 Squadrons and Nos 700 and 736 Training Squadrons. The last Buccaneer SMk1 rolled off the production line in December 1963 and the type remained in frontline service until 1965, by which time it had played an important part in the enforcement of oil sanctions against Rhodesia, with No 800 Squadron's aeroplanes flying intensive anti-blockade runner patrols in the Indian Ocean.

In service, the Buccaneer SMk1's Gyron Junior turbojets proved to have a heavy fuel consumption and a thrust which was too modest to exploit the aircraft's full potential. Accordingly, Blackburn modified two of the pre-production machines to take the Rolls Royce Spey engine in the hope of improving general performance. Offering a thrust of 5080kg (11,200lb), the Spey proved ideal for the Buccaneer and aircraft with such engines were ordered into production as the SMk2. No 801 Squadron was the first operational unit to receive the new model, taking delivery of its first aircraft during

Previous page: A Buccaneer SMk2B of No 15 Squadron which used these aeroplanes until their replacement by Tornadoes in 1983. Above: Two Buccaneers are refuelled by a Victor tanker; in-flight refuelling would allow Buccaneers operating from bases in eastern Britain to reach targets in Poland.

Below: The 18th pre-production model of the Buccaneer in the anti-flash colour scheme and the markings of No 700Z Squadron. The SMk1 model, like this aeroplane, had the less powerful Gyron Junior engines with smaller air intakes than later models' Rolls-Royce Spey turbofans.

April 1965. The SMk2 could be distinguished from its predecessor by virtue of its larger air intakes and the installation of a fixed refuelling probe forward of the cockpit. In service, the model showed a 30 per cent increase in available thrust over the SMk1 and considerably better fuel consumption figures.

The Buccaneer SMk2 remained in service with the Royal Navy until November 1978, by which time Nos 800, 801, 803 and 809 Squadrons and No 736 Training Squadron had all flown the type. During the period, the SMk2 had flown from most of the fleet's carriers. Aircraft from Nos 736 and 800 Squadrons were involved in the sinking of the tanker *Torrey Canyon* after she had run aground off Land's End in March 1967 causing massive oil pollution along the adjacent coastline. The Buccaneer's demise as a naval aircraft was brought about by the 1966 Defence White Paper which effectively put an end to the Royal Navy's conventional carrier force and directed future aviation towards the 'through deck cruiser' concept; these vessels could not operate large fixed-wing aircraft. With no carriers to operate from, development of an advanced Buccaneer model, the 'Two Star', with improved avionics was shelved but the SMk2 modification programme to enable it to carry the AJ168 Martel air-to-surface missile (ASM) was allowed to proceed, resulting in the redesignation of the Royal Navy's aircraft as SMk2Cs or SMk2Ds, the latter having the Martel capacity. Additionally, the SMk2C could be equipped for tanker operations with a Mk 20 refuelling pod carried on one of the wing pylons. In this role, the SMk2C carried a total of 13,730 litres (3020 gallons) of fuel. No 809 Squadron was the navy's last

Above: The Buccaneer was provided with folding wings to facilitate storage on aircraft carriers. Below: A Royal Navy Buccaneer in flight over Norway during an exercise. This aeroplane belongs to the Fleet Air Arm's No 809 Squadron, at this time (early 1970s) based on HMS *Ark Royal*.

Buccaneer SMk2B

Type Two-seat strike/reconnaissance aircraft
Dimensions Span 13.41m (44ft); length 19.33m (63ft 5in); height 4.95m (16ft 3in)
Weight Empty 13,610kg (30,000lb); maximum loaded 28,123kg (62,000lb)
Powerplant Two 5080kg (11,200lb) thrust Rolls Royce Spey Mk101 turbofans

Performance Maximum speed 1040km/h (645mph) at 75m (250ft); typical cruising speed 917km/h (570mph) at 915m (3000ft)
Range Typical tactical radius 805-966km (500-600 miles) with stores load and standard fuel
Ceiling Over 12,192m (40,000ft)

Armament 1814kg (4000lb) capacity internal weapons bay and four wing stations each with a maximum capacity of 1360kg (3000lb). Stores carried include the Martel ASM, the Sidewinder AAM, the Paveway 'smart' bomb, rocket pods and a range of general-purpose 'iron' bombs

Below: A Buccaneer shows its low-level flying capability; the shaping of the fuselage to decrease drag is noticeable, as is the thinness of the wings.

Above: A Buccaneer of No 809 Squadron with its split tailcone airbrake open and arresting hook lowered for landing. Right: The landing of a Buccaneer on HMS *Ark Royal*, the last Royal Navy aircraft carrier to operate the aeroplane. Below: A Blackburn NA 39 undergoing deck trials on HMS *Victorious* in 1959, its wings and nose folded for storage.

Buccaneer squadron and its 10 SMk2D and four SMk2C tanker aircraft were paid off when HMS *Ark Royal* docked for the last time on 27 November 1978.

This event did not mark the end of the Buccaneer's career, however, as it had by then long been in service with the RAF. In July 1968, the RAF had announced an order for 26 SMk2 aircraft. This rather surprising turn of events was prompted by the cancellation of the F-111K in January 1968 and the need for an interim strike aircraft to fill the gap until the introduction of the Tornado. The newly-built RAF aircraft differed from their naval counterparts in having the weapons bay door modified to house an additional 2046 litres (450 gallons) of fuel. Because the Buccaneer was considered a stop-gap measure, no attempt was made to update the navigation/attack avionics. Delays in the Tornado programme have meant that the Buccaneer has served and will continue to serve the RAF for much longer than originally envisaged, which will result in the 1950s-era electronics becoming a major handicap.

The first Buccaneer was delivered to the RAF at Honington in October 1969. Like the naval SMk2s, the RAF's aircraft designation is based on possession of the Martel capability, which SMk2A aircraft do not have, while SMk2Bs do. During 1971, a further 19 aircraft were ordered and a number of the 84 SMk2 aircraft built for the Royal Navy have been transferred to the RAF, giving a total inventory of 60-65 aircraft at the beginning of 1984. The number of aircraft available to the RAF received a hard knock in February 1980 when a Buccaneer flying a 'Red Flag' training sortie shed a wing. Subsequent investigations revealed a number of aircraft with fatigue cracks in their wing spars and the entire fleet was grounded while appropriate modifications were undertaken. In the end, the problem was found to be severe enough to result in the writing-off of a number of airframes.

With the RAF, the Buccaneer has served with Nos 12, 15, 16, 208 and 216 Squadrons and No 237 Operational Conversion Unit (OCU). Of these, No 216 Squadron has been disbanded while Nos 15 and 16, assigned to RAF Germany, have been re-equipped with the Tornado. This leaves a current force of Nos 12 and 208 Squadrons flying SMk2B aircraft from Lossiemouth in the anti-shipping role, backed up by No 237 OCU flying a mixture of SMk2As and SMk2Bs. As currently operated, the RAF's Buccaneer SMk2B aircraft are equipped with the Ferran-

ti Blue Parrot radar, the ARI/18228 radar-warning receiver system and a single American AN/ALQ-101-10 jamming pod. As noted earlier, the SMk2B is 'plumbed' to carry the AJ168 TV-guided Martel ASM and its associated data-link pod. In addition, the aircraft can carry a wide range of 'iron' (unguided conventional) bombs and rocket pods together with the AIM-9L Sidewinder air-to-air missile for self-defence and the Paveway I and II 'smart' weapons.

After some initial scepticism, the RAF has come

Top: A Buccaneer SMk2 with some typical loads, including flight refuelling pods at the centre. Munitions can be carried in either the bomb bay or on four wing pylons. Above: A Buccaneer fitted with AJ168 Martel air-to-surface electro-optically guided missiles.

to appreciate the Buccaneer's qualities and many of the aircraft's crews have expressed doubts as to whether there is an adequate replacement available for it in the low-level strike role. In an attempt to prolong the type's usefulness, the RAF has issued Air Staff Target (AST) 1012 which calls for a major update to 32 Buccaneers to optimise them for low-level anti-shipping operations in the current European combat environment. The document calls for a complete overhaul of the mission avionics including the provision of an inertial navigation system, a completely redesigned cockpit layout with head-up displays (HUDs) and refinements of the existing Blue Parrot attack radar. Equally, the AST 1012 calls for the introduction of the BAe (British Aerospace) Sea Eagle ASM to supplement the existing Martel/Sidewinder/Paveway capability and provision for the Marconi Skyshadow ECM pod, a new radar-warning system and the American AN/ALE-40 chaff/flare dispenser.

Desirable as this update appears, AST 1012 has proved to be abortive; during the course of 1984, BAe's estimate of the programme costs was revised upwards to the point where it seems unlikely that the full conversion will be funded. While it is beyond doubt that the Buccaneer will remain in RAF service until at least the 1990s, it now seems probable that only the Sea Eagle capability and improved avionics will be introduced prior to its withdrawal from service.

To complete the Buccaneer story, mention should be made of the attempts to sell the aircraft abroad. Strenuous efforts were made to promote the type in West Germany, Canada, Australia and India, all without result. This was no reflection on the Buccaneer's design or capabilities but rather a response to the initial lack of interest shown by the RAF in the type as a land-based strike aircraft. In the event, only the South African Air Force (SAAF) purchased the type, a direct result of the 1955 Simonstown Agreement between the UK and South Africa covering the defence of the sea routes around the Cape. A total of 16 Buccaneer SMk50s were supplied, forming the equipment of No 24 Squadron which was formally commissioned at Waterkloof airbase in July 1966. The SMk50 was based on the Spey-powered SMk2 model with the addition of two Bristol Siddeley BS605 rocket motors installed in the rear fuselage to boost take-off performance from 'hot and high' airfields on the veldt.

No 24 Squadron actually formed at Lossiemouth during 1965 and the South African crews were trained for the type by the Royal Navy. At the end of the year, the crews began ferrying their aircraft back to the Republic, and during the operation one SMk50 was lost. The SAAF attempted to obtain further aircraft but their export was blocked by Britain's adherence to the UN resolution banning arms sales to the country. Consequently, the South African Buccaneer force has been gradually whittled down by attrition over the years until only some six aircraft remained serviceable in 1984.

Below: A Buccaneer SMk50 of the South African Air Force (the sole export customer for the aeroplane) makes a rocket-assisted take-off. Below centre: Two RAF Buccaneers in flight; the aircraft has become popular with the RAF despite initial scepticism. Bottom: Wingflaps lowered, a Buccaneer of No 809 Squadron takes off from HMS Ark Royal.

Sitting targets

Tragic losses for the Welsh Guards at Fitzroy

Above: British troops engaged in the unloading of supplies on the beach at Fitzroy, rush towards the shoreline as the *Sir Galahad* burns offshore. Many survivors from the crippled vessel were helped ashore at Fitzroy shocked and suffering from severe burns. The lack of air-defences to protect the Fitzroy bridgehead had left the Welsh Guards aboard *Sir Galahad* and her sister-ship *Sir Tristram* dangerously vulnerable to Argentinian air attack.

On 1 June 1982, 5 Infantry Brigade, commanded by Brigadier Tony Wilson, began to disembark at San Carlos. The brigade, consisting of the 2nd Battalion, the Scots Guards, 1st Battalion, the Welsh Guards and 1/7 Gurkha Rifles, had sailed from Southampton on board the *QE2* on 12 May, transferring to *Canberra* and *Norland* at South Georgia on 28 May. The commander of the British land forces for the Falklands operation, Major-General Jeremy Moore, had travelled with them, and he now set about positioning 5 Brigade on the southern axis to Port Stanley, which passed through Darwin and Fitzroy.

Events now began to move swiftly. Having set up his headquarters in Darwin, Brigadier Wilson discovered that the telephone link between Swan Inlet House and Fitzroy settlement was still working. The settlement manager at Fitzroy informed the British that the Argentinians had withdrawn towards Port Stanley the previous day, destroying the bridge to Bluff Cove as they left. Wilson took immediate

advantage of the situation. The 2nd Battalion, the Parachute Regiment (2 Para), now attached to 5 Brigade, had been resting at Goose Green since the battle there; Wilson used the surviving Chinook helicopter to ferry the Paras onto the high ground above Bluff Cove, 50km (30 miles) distant. There they remained in isolation from 2 to 6 June, while the rest of the brigade moved forward by various means to join them.

2 Para had been relieved at Goose Green by 1/7 Gurkha Rifles, who were now engaged in eliminating enemy outposts on the high ground overlooking the Darwin-Fitzroy track, and in rounding up those Argentinians who had fled south into Lafonia after the battle. While this series of minor operations was in progress, it was decided that the most efficient method of moving the two Guards battalions from San Carlos to Bluff Cove was by sea around the southern coast of the island. The Scots Guards sailed aboard HMS *Intrepid* on 5 June, transferring to landing craft off Lively Island during the night. This last leg of the voyage was carried out in the teeth of a gale, so that when the Guardsmen finally made their way ashore after seven hours in the open craft, all were exhausted and some were suffering from exposure; the fact that they had come within a hair's breadth of being sunk by a patrolling British frigate had further contributed to their low morale. On 6 June, the Welsh Guards made a similar voyage aboard *Fearless*, an amphibious transport dock, capable of accommodating four tank-carrying landing-craft and up to a battalion of troops, and armed with four quadruple Sea Cat launchers and two 40mm guns. The aim was to disembark the Welsh Guards off Fitzroy with the assistance of the four landing-craft left behind there by *Intrepid*, but these were prevented from putting to sea by the bad weather conditions. After setting ashore two Guards companies in its own landing-craft, *Fearless* turned back to San Carlos with the remaining 300 troops still below in its tank decks.

The decision was now taken in London that *Fearless* was far too valuable to risk in the Bluff Cove operation. The Cabinet feared the political repercussions which its loss would entail, while the Admiralty wished to preserve what was one of the most important vessels in the Task Force. It was agreed that Sir Lancelot-class landing-ships should be employed to land the rest of the Welsh Guards at Bluff Cove. These vessels were operated by the Royal Fleet Auxiliary and were manned by mainly civilian crews, in this case largely Hong Kong Chinese. In principle unarmed, the assault ships attached to the

Falklands Task Force had been equipped with two 40mm Bofors guns.

On 6 June, the landing-ship *Sir Tristram* arrived at Fitzroy carrying artillery ammunition which it began to unload by landing-craft. As there were still no Rapier air-defence missile batteries to defend the beachhead, *Sir Tristram* was in an extremely vulnerable position. The lack of direct communication with San Carlos was another weakness, which explained the surprise which greeted the arrival of *Sir Galahad* at around 0700 hours on the morning of 8 June. On board were the elements of the Welsh Guards which had been unable to land at Bluff Cove on 7 June, including the Prince of Wales's Company, 3 Company, a mortar platoon and support echelon, as well as 16 Field Ambulance. Because the Argentinians had demolished the bridge linking Fitzroy with Bluff Cove settlement, the Guards were reluctant to land at Fitzroy as this would mean a 20km (12-mile) march to reach their positions. Since their landing-ship could not negotiate the narrow channel to the beachhead at Bluff Cove, they decided to remain aboard *Sir Galahad* off Fitzroy until landing-craft arrived from the shore to take them off.

Potential for danger

Major Ewen Southby-Tailyour, who was in command of the landing-craft at the beachhead, then busily engaged in unloading the ammunition from *Sir Tristram*, realised the extreme danger to the troops aboard *Sir Galahad* should there be an enemy air attack, and took out a landing-craft, still half-laden with ammunition, to try and persuade the Welsh Guards officers to land their men immediately. Perhaps because they had not been present during the Argentinian raids on the ships in San Carlos Water, the Guards preferred to remain on *Sir Galahad*, unaware of the risk they ran. They also quoted the

Left: Lifeboats from *Sir Tristram*, herself badly damaged by the attacking Argentinian Skyhawks, pick up survivors from *Sir Galahad* out of the icy waters of the South Atlantic.

Below left: A Royal Navy Sea King helicopter winches men aboard from one of *Sir Galahad*'s life-rafts as thick banks of smoke pour from the stricken vessel. As well as lifting many to safety, the helicopters were able to use the draught from their rotors to blow the life-rafts away from the burning ship and towards the shore. Below: The white-hot plates of *Sir Galahad* show the intensity of the fires which blazed inside.

regulation which stated that troops were not to be transported along with ammunition. The ambulance unit did decide to unload its equipment, however, and this now occupied all the available landing-craft. Meanwhile, a Harrier patrol, flying cover over the Bluff Cove beachhead, was called off to deal with an Argentinian air attack on HMS *Plymouth* in Falkland Sound.

At 1310 hours, five aircraft appeared over the beachhead. Some of the troops on shore began to fire at them with their SLRs and GPMGs, but were ordered to stop when the intruders were identified as Harriers. These were not Harriers, however – they were Argentinian Skyhawks of the FAA Grupo 5 based at Rio Gallegos. While two of the raiders peeled off to attack *Sir Tristram*, the others made straight for *Sir Galahad*. Without the hazard of British Rapiers and heavy groundfire which they had faced at San Carlos, the Skyhawks concentrated on accurate bombing before breaking off and racing for home, leaving *Sir Galahad* a crippled wreck, with an intense fire blazing amidships.

The scramble to safety

The first bomb to hit *Sir Galahad* detonated amidships, setting alight petrol stored there and causing heavy casualties among troops in the cafeteria. The fire inflicted horrendous wounds upon the troops and crew, and as they began to abandon ship, shore-based helicopters arrived to help in the rescue operation. Winching men to safety from rafts and life-boats, the helicopter pilots tried to blow the survivors away from the mortally damaged *Sir Galahad* with the wind of their rotors, and many men were dragged from the sea by soldiers along the shore.

Sir Tristram had also been hit, though not so seriously, and as her crew fought to control the damage, her life-boats were launched to help in the rescue of the *Sir Galahad* survivors. In all, the Argentinian air attack had cost the British 51 dead and some 46 injured – but the real cost was even greater.

The effect of this disaster on the morale and combat potential of the Welsh Guards was catastrophic. Not only had they suffered heavy casualties, but their equipment and weapons were also lost. The survivors were transported back to San Carlos, while two companies of 40 Commando, which had been defending the San Carlos bridgehead, were moved in to strengthen the troops at Bluff Cove for the coming offensive against Port Stanley.

Though the original decision to move 5 Brigade to Bluff Cove by sea had been made because it was felt necessary to concentrate all available helicopter resources for the supply of 3 Commando Brigade in the north, helicopters were swiftly diverted to lift out casualties and lift in reinforcements once the operation had gone tragically wrong. The decision of the Welsh Guards officers to leave their men on board *Sir Galahad* merely to avoid a 20km (12-mile) march must be criticised, as must the decision to send in the two Sir Lancelot-class ships without the protection of Rapier missiles or supporting naval units.

The tragic events at Bluff Cove had little influence upon the eventual outcome of the war with Argentina, however, and the British noose continued to tighten inexorably around the Argentinian garrison at Port Stanley.

Anthony Mockler and Bryan Perrett

Victory in the mountains

The decisive battles and the Argentinian surrender

In making his plans for the final offensive to recapture Port Stanley, Major-General Moore could not afford to leave anything to chance, least of all the enemy's will to fight, which remained an unknown quantity. It did not necessarily follow that because the Argentinian land forces had neither interfered with the build-up within the San Carlos beachhead nor attempted to harass the British brigades during their move across the island, they would not fight well from inside the defences they had been manning for weeks. Indeed, one had only to remember the fierce resistance encountered by 2 Para's A Company at Darwin Hill to recognise that, properly led, the Argentinians were quite capable of holding their own until physically overwhelmed.

Nor did Moore possess the numerical superiority of three-to-one theoretically required for a successful assault on prepared positions. For the defence of Port Stanley the Argentinians could deploy five infantry regiments and a battalion of Marines, whereas the British could field the equivalent of seven-and-a-half infantry battalions. The Argentinian artillery amounted to 30 Italian Model 36 105mm pack howitzers, plus four French Model 50 155mm medium howitzers. The British possessed 30 helicopter-portable 105mm Light Guns, 12 being manned by 4th Field Regiment, Royal Artillery (RA), and 18 by 29th Commando Regiment, RA. This could be impressively supplemented by naval gunfire, which could now reach every corner of the battlefield – the output per minute of a single 4.5in naval gun equals that of an entire 105mm Light Gun battery, although it lacks the land artillery's pinpoint accuracy. The Argentinians also had a squadron of Panhard AML-90 armoured cars, of which they made little use, in contrast to the Blues and Royals' half-squadron of Scorpion and Scimitar light tanks, which proved their versatility repeatedly and were kept constantly employed. The 81mm mortar was common to both sides and the Argentinians also possessed recoilless rifles of various calibres. For bunker-busting, the British used the Milan ATGW, the 84mm MAW, the 66mm LAW and the M79 grenade-launcher.

The Argentinian defences can best be visualised as three concentric rings based on Port Stanley. The outermost ring – and potentially the most formidable – followed the line Mount Estancia-Mount Kent-Mount Challenger-Bluff Cove, and was abandoned without any serious attempt being made to hold it. The second line ran from the Murrell River through Mount Longdon, Two Sisters and Mount Harriet to

Above: A mortar-crew of 1/7 Gurkha Rifles establish radio contact from a position on Mount Kent. The Gurkhas were not involved in any of the major battles of the campaign, but their presence on the islands terrified many of the young Argentinian conscripts. Below: Men of the Scots Guards taste the pleasure of victory on the crest of Mount Tumbledown.

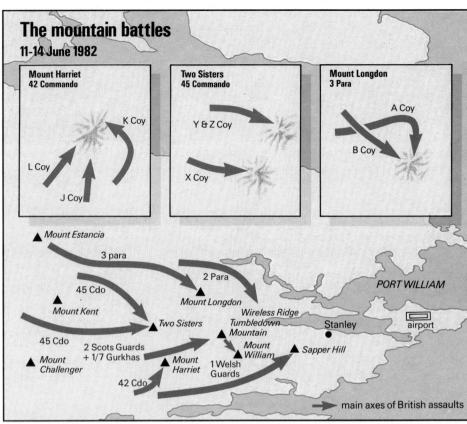

The mountain battles
11-14 June 1982

Mount Harriet
42 Commando

K Coy
L Coy
J Coy

Two Sisters
45 Commando

Y & Z Coy
X Coy

Mount Longdon
3 Para

A Coy
B Coy

▲ Mount Estancia

3 para

45 Cdo
2 Para

▲ Mount Kent

Mount Longdon

PORT WILLIAM

45 Cdo
2 Scots Guards
+ 1/7 Gurkhas

Two Sisters

Wireless Ridge
Tumbledown
Mountain

Stanley

airport

▲ Mount
Challenger

▲ Mount
Harriet

Mount
William

1 Welsh
Guards

▲ *Sapper Hill*

42 Cdo

→ main axes of British assaults

Port Harriet. The inner line included Wireless Ridge, Tumbledown Mountain, Mount William and Sapper Hill, beyond which lay only Port Stanley and its airfield. The nature of the virtually trackless terrain, which consisted of rocky outcrops, boulder-strewn slopes, semi-arctic upland tundra and peat bog, meant that the coming offensive would have more in common with a World War II infantry battle than almost anything which had taken place since 1945. There was, in fact, a comparison to be made with certain aspects of the Italian campaign of 1943-45, and veterans of this would have rated Moore's chances of success as being slim, given the very limited amount of artillery and armoured support at his disposal.

Moore and his staff would have been delighted to learn that the degree of demoralisation within the enemy's ranks went well beyond their expectations. The truth was that the Argentinian Army was essentially a counter-insurgency force which had never expected to fight a full-scale battle against a professional enemy and was as profoundly shocked as the rest of the nation by the British response to the seizure of the Malvinas. Major-General Menendez has been sharply criticised for his passive response to the San Carlos landing and for permitting the British to advance unhindered to within 16km (10 miles) of the capital, and at one stage senior Argentinian officers in the Falklands were seriously considering a coup which would remove the military governor from office. In fact, Menendez probably doubted the ability of his conscript soldiers to do more than man their trenches, and it would certainly have been in the forefront of his mind that however impressive the defence of Darwin Hill might have been, it had still proved inadequate. It must also have been deeply depressing to know that whatever supply difficulties the British laboured under, his own internal logistic

arrangements had broken down completely. After the war, it emerged that many of the regimental officers and NCOs, the professionals who formed the nucleus of the Argentinian Army, had not only failed to provide the necessary leadership, but had also been conspicuous by their absence at critical moments, leaving the wretched conscripts to fend for themselves. The latter were also totally inexperienced and, as the British predicted, were seriously unsettled by shellfire, particularly from artillery weapons accurately directed by an observer. All in all, it seems that despite the strident urgings of Buenos Aires to resist to the last man and last round, Menendez took a pragmatic view of his army's abilities and had already decided to fight only as long as honour demanded; in practical terms, that meant until the high ground overlooking the approaches to Port Stanley was in British hands.

There was some disagreement among General

Below: A group of Argentinian soldiers seeks shelter from the biting cold behind a windswept ridge. Waiting passively in their bunkers and trenches as the British swept towards them across East Falkland, the Argentinians' morale slumped dramatically as a result of the harsh climatic conditions and the poor organisation of supplies.

Moore's staff over which plan to adopt for the final offensive against the Argentinian garrison entrenched around Port Stanley. Deputy land force commander Brigadier John Waters argued for an advance across a narrow front, bypassing and outflanking the strong Argentinian positions around Two Sisters and Mount Longdon, and concentrating the full weight of the British attack against Mount Harriet and Mount Tumbledown. General Moore at first favoured this proposal, but he was eventually persuaded by Brigadier Thompson to adopt a second plan which called for a more systematic advance across a much broader front. Thompson argued that it was vital to ensure the security of the advancing British forces' lines of communication, both in order to safeguard supply routes and to be able to evacuate casualties rapidly from the front line. It was therefore decided that the attack would be across a front stretching from Wireless Ridge in the north to Mount Tumbledown and Mount William in the south.

By 9 June the Argentinian troops on East Falkland were confined to their enclave around Port Stanley and in a series of aggressive patrol actions the British established complete domination of no man's land. For the next two days helicopters clattered back and forth across the windswept moorland, bringing up thousands of rounds of 105mm gun ammunition. Intelligence officers marked their maps with the location of minefields and other information supplied by SAS and SBS patrols, while unit commanding officers were briefed by brigade headquarters and passed on their own orders to their company commanders. What General Moore envisaged was a series of attacks made alternately by 3 Commando Brigade and 5 Infantry Brigade, to be carried out at night to obtain maximum advantage. The offensive would open on the night of 11 June with an attack by 3 Commando Brigade. 42 Commando would capture Mount Harriet, 45 Commando Two Sisters and 3 Para Mount Longdon, with naval gunfire support (NGS) provided respectively by HMS *Yarmouth*, HMS *Glamorgan* and HMS *Avenger*, plus the fire of both artillery regiments. Simultaneously, HMS *Arrow* would provide NGS for an SAS operation in the Murrell Hills.

Mount Harriet lay at the southern end of the enemy line and in Brigadier Thompson's opinion was potentially the most formidable of his brigade's objectives. Lieutenant-Colonel Nick Vaux, the commanding officer of 42 Commando, had studied the approaches to Mount Harriet carefully and had also sent out patrols to examine them. His plan required K Company to outflank the enemy and assault them from the rear. Next, L Company would overrun the forward positions and finally J Company would come forward to consolidate the captured

Left: A wounded Para is carried to a casualty evacuation (Casevac) assembly point during the Mount Longdon fighting. Main picture: Helicopters lift supplies in and the injured out at Goat Ridge.

Top: The crew of a British 105mm gun dig in on the slopes of Mount Kent. Above: Argentinian gunners fire a 105mm Model 56 pack howitzer at British positions during the battle for the mountains.

ground. All went exactly as intended. The start line was secured by 1st Battalion, the Welsh Guards, reinforced by two companies of 40 Commando. As the Marines began to pick their way across the minefields of no man's land, the summit was blanketed by artillery fire, NGS and bursting mortar bombs, while the Welsh Guards' Reconnaissance Platoon and Milan teams of J Company staged a diversionary attack against the western slopes. K Company got to within 90m (100 yards) of the crest before being detected and thereafter systematically fought its way to the top using 84mm and 66mm anti-tank rounds and grenades to blast the enemy out of their positions among the rocks. L Company's attack made similar progress, but when a hut on the summit was set ablaze both companies came under fire from the Argentinian artillery, although without incurring serious loss. By first light, Mount Harriet was firmly in 42 Commando's possession at a cost of one killed and a dozen wounded. Many of the enemy had fled and others offered no resistance. Some even came in from nearby positions to surrender rather than undergo the sort of assault they had witnessed, so that eventually J Company, which included the original Falkland Islands garrison, found itself marshalling no less than 300 prisoners.

Taking Two Sisters

Mount Harriet had been held by elements of the Argentinian 4th Infantry Regiment, the remainder of which was located on Two Sisters, for whose capture 45 Commando had been allocated. The plan was for 45 Commando's X Company to initiate an assault from the west on Two Sisters' southern peak, while Y and Z Companies would approach the Argentinian positions from the rear. The difficulty of moving across the broken terrain in total darkness delayed the arrival of X Company at the start line by two hours, but it was able to advance to within 450m (500 yards) of the summit before coming under intense fire from the ridge's Argentinian defenders.

45 Commando's commanding officer, Lieutenant-Colonel Andrew Whitehead, soon realised that the force defending Two Sisters was far stronger than

'Someone's got to go …'

Corporal Steve Newland of 42 Commando, the Royal Marines, was awarded the Military Medal for his contribution to the assault on Mount Harriet. Here he describes part of the fierce night-fighting:

'All the time we were lying there rounds were ricocheting off the rocks at us and the cold was freezing our bollocks off. On the radio I heard Sharkie talking to his boss. He said "We're pinned down by a sniper and we can't move." I thought "Right, someone's got to go for this bastard." So I took off my 66 [LIAI] shells, got on the radio to our boss and said "Wait there and I'll see what I can do" …

'I crawled around this mega-size boulder, climbed up a little steep bit, went over the top on my stomach, rolled into cover, crawled a bit further and looked around the corner of this rock, thinking that the sniper had to be there somewhere. There was more than a sniper – there was half a troop! About 10 of them were lying on a nice, flat, table-top rock overlooking our positions. It was perfect for them. They had a machine gun on the left and the rest of them were lined out with rifles. Every time one of ours tried to move forward, one of them would shoot at him, so to us it looked as if there was only one sniper who was keeping on the move. They were waiting for us to break cover and try and clear this one sniper – then they would just waste us with their machine gun.

'I sat back behind this rock and whispered down my throat-mike to Sharkie about what I'd found. I told him to keep the lads there and I'd see what we could do … Then having made up my mind I picked up my SLR, changed the magazine and put a fresh one on and slipped the safety catch. I then looped the pin of one grenade onto one finger of my left hand and did the same with another. I was ready. So I thought "Well, you've got to do something." I pulled one grenade, whack – straight onto the machine gun. Pulled the other, whack – straight at the Spics. I dodged back around the rock and heard the two bangs. As soon as they'd gone off I went in and anything that moved got three rounds. I don't know how many I shot, but they got a whole mag. I went back round the corner of the rock, changed the mag and I was about to go back and sort out anyone who was left, when Sharkie called on the net: "Get out. We're putting two 66s in" … So I ran back down the hill, dived into this little hollow I'd seen on the way up. Over the net I told him to "Let it go!" The 66s exploded and the next thing I heard was Sharkie on the radio again. He said "It's clear. They've given up. Go back to where you were and make sure they don't get out the back." I went up by a different route and as I rounded this rock, I saw one of the guys that I'd hit. I'd only got him in the shoulder but he'd gone down like the rest of them and in the dark, I'd automatically thought he was dead. But he was far from that, because as I came back round the corner, he just squeezed off a burst from his automatic. He must've realised he was going to die unless he got me first. I felt the bullets go into both my legs, I thought "Shit, the fucker's got me". I was so angry, I fired 15 rounds into his head …'

he had expected, and swiftly adapted his plan accordingly. As the Argentinian troops poured mortar shells, rifle-grenades and automatic fire down from dug-outs constructed from large slabs of rock, all three Marine companies mounted a joint attack on the twin peaks of Two Sisters. The Marines, supported by artillery and mortar-fire, fought on through the night, finally occupying their objective early on the morning of 12 June. When daylight revealed the full extent of the Argentinians' well prepared and formidable defences, Whitehead commented that given a company, he could have died of old age holding them.

Four Marines were killed and 11 wounded taking Two Sisters, but to these must be added the 13 dead and numerous injured aboard HMS *Glamorgan*, which was struck by a shore-launched Exocet missile while providing NGS for 45 Commando. The missile was detected in flight, and damage was minimised by turning the ship stern-on, so that the explosion was confined to the hangar and galley areas. The ensuing fires were brought under control, and after temporary repairs had been effected, *Glamorgan* was able to remain on station until ordered to return home. She was the fourteenth, but also the last, British vessel to be damaged during the war.

Meanwhile, to the north of Two Sisters, 3 Para, under Lieutenant-Colonel Hew Pike, fought the bitterest battle of the night, and the costliest of the whole land campaign in the Falklands. 3 Para's objective was Mount Longdon, but here the Argentinian troops were to prove much better led and more highly motivated than those at either Mount Harriet or Two Sisters. The fighting began shortly after 2300 hours, when a corporal from B Company stepped on a mine. The Argentinians opened fire at once, pinning down A Company which had been advancing along a ridge to the north.

Instead of the relatively light opposition which the Paras had expected to encounter, Mount Longdon was in fact held by a company of the 7th Infantry Regiment, supported by Special Forces Unit 601 and men of the Marines, as well as elements of a second infantry company which arrived during the battle. These units had excellent night-vision equipment, far superior to that supplied to the British troops. This enabled the Argentinians to subject the attacking Paras to deadly-accurate sniper fire, which further slowed their advance.

The result was a soldier's battle in the manner of Goose Green, in which the leadership qualities of junior officers and NCOs were critical. Even the Paras' Milan teams found themselves coming under intense fire, and one was eliminated by a direct hit from a recoilless rifle. Eventually, the initial impetus of the assault was lost – a common problem in night

Wireless Ridge

In the early hours of 14 June 1982, 2nd Battalion, the Parachute Regiment (2 Para), commanded by Lieutenant-Colonel D.R. Chaundler, crossed the start lines for their part in the final battle for Port Stanley. Wireless Ridge was one of the last bastions of Argentinian resistance. The assault was planned as a four-phase night operation with artillery, light tank and naval gunfire support. Initially D Company was to take an enemy position on the western spur. This would be followed by A and B Companies assaulting from the north, while C Company would take ground to the east. Once these positions were secured, D Company would sweep eastwards across the ridge clearing the ground, with A and B Companies giving fire support. At approximately 0015 hours an artillery and mortar bombardment of the enemy positions began. At 0045 hours D Company crossed their start line and launched the battle; well supported by Scimitar and Scorpion light tanks with excellent night-vision equipment and the battalion machine-gun units, it overran its objective in record time.

Following the success of phase one, A and B Companies prepared to move. Once again good support was provided from tanks and artillery, with starshell illumination clearly showing the enemy positions. In extended line formation, the two companies moved up the hill. Counter-battery fire virtually eliminated the threat from enemy artillery and the accuracy of the armour's guns destroyed Argentinian morale. The two companies quickly closed on the objective, consolidated their positions and wiped out the sporadic enemy resistance encountered at some of the defensive trenches. Most of the enemy had fled, and those that remained were either dead or taken prisoner. Bunkers were cleared and reinhabited by A and B Companies as Argentinian artillery zeroed in on the positions.

To the east, C Company initiated phase three. During the battle there had been no activity from C Company's objective and they pushed quickly and confidently round the edge of an identified minefield onto the knoll. Their approach remained unchallenged. They secured the knoll without incurring casualties and discovered evidence of a hasty enemy retreat in the form of scattered equipment and tents. The company consolidated and then pushed up onto the hill where they dug in, awaiting the final phase of the operation.

D Company began to advance onto the western end of Wireless Ridge. Tanks and support weapons (including mortars and machine-gun sections) moved up to join A and B Companies on their position which overlooked the D Company objective, also coming under fire from Argentinian artillery. At the same time, British artillery bombardments pounded the remaining enemy positions along the ridge. D Company advanced with 11 Platoon to the left, 12 Platoon to the right and 10 Platoon in reserve. The first part of the ridge was taken reasonably quickly with no enemy encountered. Further east, three enemy machine-gun positions remained. These were heavily engaged by A and B Companies and supporting arms. As D Company advanced, the Argentinian positions continued to harass it despite the withering fire being provided by the support units. The advance continued with enemy positions under flare illumination. To the left, 11 Platoon pushed forward into a minefield which temporarily slowed its advance. 10 and 12 Platoons pushed on in order to maintain the momentum of the assault. 12 Platoon engaged enemy units to the right of the feature, while 10 Platoon cleared bunkers as the Argentinians conducted a fighting retreat. As 12 Platoon finally reached the telegraph wires and consolidated, 11 Platoon moved up alongside 10 Platoon. Despite increasingly heavy enemy artillery bombardments, the company retained the feature and easily drove off a scattered and ill-organised counter-attack. With 12 Platoon dug-in at the telegraph poles, 10 and 11 deployed on the reverse slopes of the ridge. Throughout the night, 12 Platoon was the constant object of sniper fire but no attacks in strength were launched against the D Company positions. Orders not to exploit beyond the ridge line inevitably meant that some enemy might still hold positions. By first light the situation was clear. The enemy was retreating in large numbers.

In the final stages of the battle, A and B Companies were now ordered to move onto the ridge, accompanied by the Blues and Royals. B Company pushed on to Moody Brook and high ground to the south. A Company advanced at speed towards Stanley, the advance covered by tanks; C and D Companies brought up the rear. As the battalion continued its relentless advance in pursuit of the fleeing enemy, a ceasefire was announced. The Falklands War had been won.

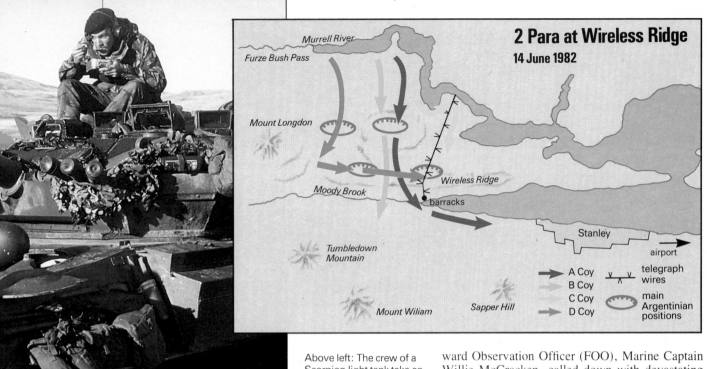

2 Para at Wireless Ridge
14 June 1982

Murrell River

Furze Bush Pass

Mount Longdon

Moody Brook

Wireless Ridge

barracks

Tumbledown
Mountain

Stanley

airport

Mount Wiliam

Sapper Hill

	A Coy	telegraph wires
	B Coy	
	C Coy	main Argentinian positions
	D Coy	

fighting. B Company's 4 Platoon was pinned down by fire from an Argentinian bunker, and its commander, Lieutenant Andrew Bickerdike, was severely wounded in the leg.

While Platoon Sergeant Ian McKay regrouped his men for an assault on the bunker, Corporal Ian Bailey charged forward, firing as he went. Reaching the enemy position, he was hit in the legs and stomach, and fell into the bunker, still firing. Sergeant McKay had meanwhile worked round to the rear of the bunker, upon which he now led a desperate attack. As he reached the Argentinian position, McKay lobbed in two grenades before falling dead into the bunker. For this act of exemplary courage and leadership under fire, Sergeant McKay was later awarded a posthumous Victoria Cross.

Its momentum restored, B Company now moved on to eliminate one Argentinian strongpoint after another under cover of artillery fire which the For-

Above left: The crew of a Scorpion light tank take an opportunity to relax and eat some hot food. The excellent cross-country capability of the Scorpions and Scimitars surprised even their crews, and gave the advancing British troops an added advantage over the Argentinians, whose own wheeled armoured cars were confined to the streets of Port Stanley. Below: An advance patrol of 2 Para moves warily into Port Stanley. Below right: British Marines search Argentinian prisoners of war after the final surrender.

ward Observation Officer (FOO), Marine Captain Willie McCracken, called down with devastating accuracy only 45m (50 yards) ahead of the advancing Paras. The Argentinian artillery responded with pre-registered defensive fire which, together with the still considerable volume of machine-gun and sniper fire coming from uncleared positions, compelled A Company to approach the hill by an alternative route to that originally chosen. Passing through the positions of the embattled B Company, A Company delivered the final assault with fixed bayonets just before first light, the surviving defenders escaping under cover of mist.

The battle for Mount Longdon had lasted some 10

The battle for Tumbledown Mountain
13-14 June 1982

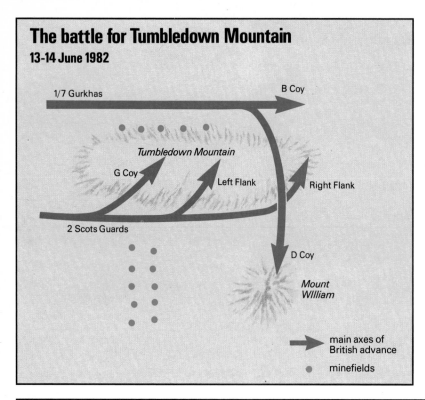

1/7 Gurkhas — B Coy

Tumbledown Mountain

G Coy

Left Flank

Right Flank

2 Scots Guards

D Coy

Mount William

main axes of British advance

minefields

Mount Tumbledown

Whatever criticisms might be levelled at the performance of the Argentinian Army during the Falklands War, particularly its lack of initiative and failure firmly to defend strong positions, the battle fought on the slopes of Mount Tumbledown during the night of 13/14 June demonstrated that well-trained professional Argentinian troops could prove formidable opponents if they had the right kind of leadership.

Brigadier Julian Thompson's original plan called for Mount Tumbledown to be attacked by 2nd Battalion, the Scots Guards on 12 June; the operation would coincide with 2 Para's assault on Wireless Ridge. Problems in moving the Guards by helicopter up to their assembly point behind Goat Ridge and their desire to be able to carry out a preliminary reconnaissance, led to a postponement of the operations until the following night. During the morning of 13 June, the Guards were heli-lifted to the assembly point, while the enemy positions which were to be their objective were closely scrutinised through binoculars.

The Scots Guards' plan was for G Company to lead the initial advance through the enemy minefield and against the Argentinian positions on Mount Tumbledown, then for Left Flank Company, commanded by Major John Kiszeley, to move through G Company for a final assault on the northern sector of the summit, supported by Right Flank Company moving parallel but along a lower line of advance. HQ Company, under Major Richard Bethell, and supported by a Scorpion troop of the Blues and Royals, was to stage a diversionary attack southeast of Mount Harriet.

The diversionary attack began at around 2030 hours, and proceeded initially without encountering any signs of resistance, but the 30 men of Bethell's detachment suddenly found themselves in the midst of an Argentinian unit firmly entrenched and pouring automatic fire at them. What was to have been a minor manoeuvre was suddenly transformed into a pitched battle, with the Guards clearing trench after Argentinian trench before being forced to withdraw after suffering heavy casualties.

Meanwhile, the main Scots Guards force was moving forward through the darkness towards the Argentinian lines around the foot of Mount Tumbledown. Having negotiated the enemy minefield, G Company reached its first objectives without any sign of the enemy, but as Left Flank Company moved through G Company's positions to continue the advance, it came under heavy Argentinian fire, and an intense firefight broke out. Soon three British soldiers were dead and several wounded, while the Argentinian complex of bunkers, carved out of the rock of Mount Tumbledown, protected them from even the 66mm and 84mm rockets which the Guards fired at them. The battlefield was criss-crossed by streams of tracer rounds and illuminated by flares fired from Argentinian mortars, while the sound of British and Argentinian artillery filled the night and drowned the cries of the wounded and the dying.

The Argentinian positions were defended by men of the 5th Marine Battalion, the best regular Argentinian unit on the Falklands. They were determined to repulse the British attack and held their ground courageously, incurring severe losses as the Scots Guards fought their way slowly and methodically up the slope. Major Kiszeley himself killed an Argentinian soldier with his bayonet when he was surprised with an empty magazine, but the Guards too took casualties, particularly from Argentinian snipers who continued to resist from positions which had been bypassed by the British advance.

As well as its dead and wounded, Left Flank Company was forced to leave many men behind in order to guard the prisoners who had been captured, so that only seven men finally saw the startling sight of Stanley, fully illuminated below, as they crested the ridge which had been their objective. Three of these men immediately fell to an enemy machine gun, however, leaving only four to hold the summit until the arrival of reinforcements.

The battle continued into the morning of 14 June, with Argentinian troops stubbornly holding on to positions on the slopes of Mount Tumbledown until cleared by Right Flank Company. It was not until 0815 hours that the British force finally secured its objectives. The battle had cost the Scots Guards nine men killed and 43 wounded, some of the heaviest British losses of the land campaign, while the Argentinians had lost an estimated 30 killed and numerous captured. The remaining troops who had defended Mount Tumbledown retreated to Sapper Hill or Port Stanley, where they joined their comrades in waiting for the arrival of the British and the inevitable final surrender.

Above: Royal Marine Naval Party 8901, composed of the original Falklands garrison which had faced the Argentinian invasion, prepare to raise the Falkland Islands' flag over Government House.

Below: Major-General Jeremy Moore (foreground), the victor of the Falklands campaign, surveys the scene of one of the war's tragedies – the burnt-out hulk of *Sir Galahad* off Fitzroy.

hours, and was the bloodiest victory for the British of the entire campaign, costing 3 Para 23 men killed and 47 wounded. The Argentinian casualties were estimated to be approximately twice this figure. The Argentinians had clearly been shaken by the loss of Mount Longdon and shelled it heavily during 12 June, killing a further six paratroopers, but there was no attempt to counter-attack.

The night of 13 June witnessed the concluding phase of the British offensive. On 5 Infantry Brigade sector this would consist of two phases, the first of which was the capture of Mount Tumbledown by 2nd Battalion, the Scots Guards, and the second the capture of Mount William and Sapper Hill by, respectively, 1st Battalion, the 7th Duke of Edinburgh's Own Gurkha Rifles, and 1 Welsh Guards. Simultaneously 2 Para, operating once more under the command of 3 Commando Brigade, would take Wireless Ridge, supported by the mortars and heavy weapons of 3 Para from Mount Longdon. Once these objectives had been secured, the road into Port Stanley would lie open.

The battle for Mount Tumbledown began at 2030 hours with a diversionary attack by personnel of the Scots Guards' HQ Company and the Blues and Royals' 4 Troop, the intention being to convince the enemy that the main British thrust would be made along the axis Port Harriet-Port Stanley. This resulted in several Guardsmen being wounded and the party was lifted out by 4 Troop, one of whose vehicles sustained mine damage; the weight of the Argentinian response clearly indicated just how sensitive they were about this sector. At 2100 hours the remainder of the battalion, commanded by Lieutenant-Colonel Mike Scott, assaulted the main defences of Mount Tumbledown, supported by the fire of five artillery batteries, the guns of HMS *Active* and *Yarmouth*, and the mortars of 42 Commando and 1/7 Gurkha Rifles. Even with so much firepower available the struggle was as intense as that for Mount Longdon and ended in the same way, at the point of the bayonet. Nine of the Scots Guards died and 43 were wounded, but the 5th Battalion Marine Corps, the best troops Menendez possessed, had been driven off this vitally important feature.

To the north, 2 Para's attack was accompanied by a diversion carried out by the Royal Marines' Rigid Raider Squadron, in company with an SBS team and the Boat Troop of D Squadron, SAS. This consisted of a landing at the eastern end of Wireless Ridge and immediately attracted much of the enemy's attention, including that of his automatic AA weapons. 2 Para, commanded by Lieutenant-Colonel David Chaundler, had thoroughly digested the lessons of Goose Green and took special precautions to ensure that its ammunition supply would remain adequate for the task in hand. The capture of Wireless Ridge was the only all-arms battle of the campaign, for the Blues and Royals' 3 Troop had been placed under Chaundler's command, the Paras benefiting not only from the direct and accurate firepower provided by the light tanks, but also from the latter's night-vision devices, which were superior to anything the British infantry possessed. The attack itself began at 0045 hours with the support of two artillery batteries and NGS provided by HMS *Ambuscade*. Whenever resistance was encountered, tracer ammunition focused relentlessly on its source until the position was silenced. By first light the ridge had been taken, 100 of the enemy being killed and 17 captured at a cost to 2 Para of three dead and 11 wounded.

The dying moments of war

During the morning 1 Welsh Guards and 1/7 Gurkha Rifles closed up to their objectives, encountering only half-hearted opposition. The RAF's Harrier GR3s had been flying ground-attack missions for some time in support of the land battle and were now using Paveway laser-guided bombs to take out specific targets with clinical precision. Moore sensed that the enemy had reached breaking point and ordered the artillery to increase their rate of fire. Observers watched the ridges opposite erupt in gouts of peat and rock splinters under the sustained impact of hundreds of shells. Then, quite suddenly, the Argentinians abandoned their remaining positions and bolted for Port Stanley. White flags began to appear in the town at once and at 1225 hours a Harrier strike was cancelled with seconds to spare. The British units closed in with instructions only to fire in self-defence, but it was quite clear that the enemy had had enough. Moore had balanced his equation very neatly, for in some batteries the ammunition was down to six rounds per gun, despite helicopter resupply during the night.

A link with the Argentinians existed via the islands' medical radio network and representatives of the two sides met to discuss terms. These were ratified that evening when Moore flew into Port Stanley, and amounted to the unconditional surrender of the Argentinians and all their equipment, although Menendez deleted the word unconditional from the surrender document.

The sheer size of the Port Stanley garrison came as a shock to the British, and it was obvious that many of the Argentinians had never been near the front. For a while the conscripts were out of hand, but eventually they were rounded up, marched to the airfield and disarmed; it took some days longer to assemble the outlying garrisons on West Falkland. The prisoners were then shipped back to the Argentinian mainland, mostly aboard British vessels, and the impression received by their captors was that they were glad to be going.
Bryan Perrett

Falklands aftermath

The effects of the war on British defence policy

The Falklands War of April-June 1982 highlighted what appeared to be a basic flaw in British defence priorities. The defence review of June 1981, introduced by Secretary of State for Defence John Nott under the title *The Way Forward*, had endeavoured to stave off a financial crisis by cutting the Royal Navy's global capability and by tying Britain's overall defence effort firmly to Europe. As many commentators were quick to point out, it was perhaps fortunate that the Argentinians did not delay their attack for a few more months. As it was, despite being included in the projected reduction, the aircraft carriers HMS *Invincible* and *Hermes* were still available, the ice-patrol ship HMS *Endurance* had not yet returned home from the South Atlantic and the assault ships HMS *Fearless* and *Intrepid* could be made ready for service with the Task Force. Even so, the navy was stretched by the campaign, eventually deploying nearly two-thirds of its surface fleet 'beyond the Nato area' and making heavy demands on its support facilities. Such a commitment implied a need for global capability which Nott had apparently neglected to take into account.

But this is a superficial analysis, ignoring long-term effects of the campaign which served to reinforce rather than undermine the basic trends of *The Way Forward*. As always, these revolved around the question of cost. According to government figures issued in early 1983, the Falklands operation and its immediate aftermath was an expensive affair. The war itself cost £750 million, and although this was to be paid from a special Treasury contingency fund, the rest of the bill, at least until 1985-86, had to be met from within the defence budget. A significant proportion of the total would arise from the need to maintain a 4000-man garrison in the Falklands, together with a 12,870km (8000 mile) supply line back to the UK. This, it was estimated, would cost at least £232 million a year, even after the construction of a new airport at Port Stanley: according to press reports in early 1983, it was already costing a million pounds a week just to keep the air route open.

In addition, there was the cost of replacing lost equipment, estimated to total about £1000 million, spread over the next few years. Six major naval vessels had been lost in the South Atlantic – two Type 42 destroyers (HMS *Sheffield* and *Coventry*), two Type 21 frigates (HMS *Ardent* and *Antelope*), one

Above: The *Canberra*, packed with troops, returns to Southampton after the conclusion of the Falklands campaign, receiving a hero's welcome. Argentina's refusal to declare an official end to hostilities made it necessary to station a strong garrison on the islands. Fortress Falklands was hugely expensive to maintain, and diverted vital military resources from Britain's Nato commitments, but the enormous popularity of the British government's conduct of the Falklands War helped it to victory in the June 1983 general election, and allowed it to maintain a hard line on the future of the islands.

logistic landing ship (RFA *Sir Galahad*) and one roll-on/roll-off general cargo ship (MS *Atlantic Conveyor*). The latter was, of course, a chartered merchant ship but, in common with the Royal Navy and Royal Fleet Auxiliary vessels, its replacement still had to be paid for by the government. At the same time, eight naval vessels had been badly damaged, requiring costly repairs, and many others, both civilian and naval, needed comprehensive refits, all at public expense. Nor were the losses confined to the fleet: 10 Harriers and 24 helicopters were destroyed and a large amount of more basic kit, such as the tents on board *Atlantic Conveyor*, had been lost. Taken together, the Falklands conflict and garrison were likely to cost the staggering total of £2610 million up to 1985-86, and although the first £750 million had been found from elsewhere, this still left £1860 million to be found from an already squeezed defence budget.

Maintaining the garrison

Cost was not the only ramification of the war, however, for in its immediate aftermath a series of defence changes had to be introduced to cater for the sudden emergence of a substantial and unforeseen 'out-of-area' commitment. In December 1982, on the eve of his retirement from politics, Nott presented a new defence paper to parliament, entitled *The Falklands Campaign: The Lessons*. Dealing principally with a short history of the war, the paper nevertheless contained details of certain unavoidable policy refinements. Among these was the decision to maintain the 4000-man garrison on the Falklands, backed by rapid reinforcement capability on a strategic scale. New wide-bodied tankers were to be provided for the RAF and both 3 Commando and 5 Infantry Brigades (the latter soon to be retitled 5 Airborne Brigade) were to be maintained for non-Nato commitment in the event of a future crisis. More importantly, the projected naval reductions were halted and Britain was henceforth to retain, in the short-term at least, three aircraft carriers and a destroyer/frigate fleet of 55 vessels. *Invincible* was not to be sold, *Fearless* and *Intrepid* were to be maintained and *Endurance* was to remain on station.

In strategic terms, this looked like a return to the global 'maritime' policy rejected by Nott in June 1981, but it would be wrong to draw that conclusion. Throughout the paper of December 1982 Nott stressed that Britain's interests were best served by a continued emphasis upon Europe, and although he had no choice but to accept that global capability of some description was essential so long as Britain retained overseas possessions that required protection, this would remain a secondary and subordinate role for forces geared primarily to 'continental' defence. What he seemed to be advocating was a strategic 'mix' of regional with some global capabilities, and there is no doubt that this would represent an 'ideal' solution to Britain's basic defence dilemma. Unfortunately, it is unlikely to be put into effect, chiefly because of the continuing problem of cost.

This becomes apparent when the subsequent development of defence policy is examined, for although there have been signs of a gradual economic recovery in Britain, there can be no escaping the fact that defence has cost more and more each year merely to maintain existing force and equipment levels. On 6 July 1983 Nott's replacement as Secretary of State for Defence, Michael Heseltine, presented estimates for the financial year 1983-84

Below: British troops begin to clear some of the huge amounts of arms and equipment abandoned by the Falklands Argentinian garrison after the final surrender. The Argentinian armed forces soon began to re-equip, however, with aircraft supplied by France and Israel and naval vessels built in West Germany. Bottom: Britain, meanwhile, attempted to revitalise the Falklands economy with a number of projects, such as the construction of a new airport. Here, heavy construction machinery is being landed from a merchant ship near the site of the new airport.

Losses of the Falklands War

	Britain	Argentina
Casualties	killed 255 wounded 777	killed approx 1000 wounded unknown
Aircraft lost	fixed wing 10 helicopters 24	fixed wing 76 helicopters 26
Ships lost	destroyers 2 frigates 2 Royal Fleet Auxiliary 1 container ships 1	cruisers 1 submarines 1 patrol boats 1 freighters 2 trawlers 1
Ships damaged	frigates 3 destroyers 3 Royal Fleet Auxiliary 2	patrol boats 2

and, despite the absence of significant alterations to the size or capabilities of the armed forces, the total bill had risen by £1500 million to £15,973 million. This pattern was repeated a year later, with estimates of £17,033 million, implying that the services were, to all intents and purposes, 'standing still', even though defence expenditure was constantly rising. This suggests that any attempt to shift defence priorities permanently, or even temporarily, from the regional framework of *The Way Forward* to the global implications of the Falklands War was not likely to meet with success, creating expenditure that Britain just could not afford.

Nor is this the only factor to be considered, for one of the major reasons behind Nott's 1981 review – the need to cater for projected costs of new weapons – remained in force. The government was still firmly committed to the Trident missile programme – by late 1984 officially estimated at around £9000 million over the next 10-12 years – and the essential process of up-dating conventional equipment could not be halted. The army would soon need a new main battle tank and the issue of the 5.56mm Individual Weapon System as a replacement to the 7.62mm Self Loading Rifle was long overdue; the navy was demanding new classes of surface ship and the air force was already talking about the next generation of attack aircraft. At the same time, in the age of Emerging Technology (ET), no armed forces could hope to retain credibility without all the latest robotics, computers and other 'hi-tech' equipment, while the existence of such sophisticated kit would require a new class of highly educated recruits who would be unlikely to join the armed services unless rates of pay were at least comparable to those in civilian life.

All this suggested that the financial crisis in defence that Nott tried so desperately to forestall in 1981 was still a distinct possibility, made more likely now that the Falklands War and its ramifications had to be absorbed. Indeed, even if that conflict had not occurred, it was conceivable that the twin pressures of rising cost and weapons modernisation would have forced a revision of Nott's review sometime in the late 1980s. The events of April-June 1982 merely accelerated this process, creating a squeeze on the defence budget which, taken in conjunction with

Trident and other new developments, threatened to affect the central core of Britain's defence effort – her commitment to the conventional defence of Europe. This appeared to have been recognised by the government in late 1984, as remaining overseas commitments were progressively rationalised in an effort to restore strategic balance. An agreement with China over the future of Hong Kong ensured the release of British forces from that commitment by the late 1990s; Prime Minister Margaret Thatcher had already spoken of a withdrawal of troops from Belize, subject to local guarantees of security; and although success was elusive, diplomatic channels with Argentina were being explored, aiming eventually towards a rapprochement which would enable the Falklands garrison to be reduced.

Even if this occurs, however, the evidence suggests an impending crisis, described by press reports in late 1984 as 'the biggest ... since the Second World War'. Amid rumours of secret demands for cuts of £10,000 million over the next 10 years and the preparation of another radical defence review (strenuously denied by the Ministry of Defence), it would seem that Britain has yet to find a settled defence policy, free from the pressures of finance and strategic dilemma. The long and tortuous process of realignment from global to regional power has yet to be completed.

Ashley Brown

Above: British troops wait on a jetty in Port Stanley as they prepare to leave after a four-month tour of duty on the Falklands. The presence of a large military garrison excited mixed feelings in many islanders, who were eager to deter a further Argentinian invasion, but feared that their traditional way of life was being destroyed.

Below: The aircraft carrier *Illustrious* takes over from her sister-ship *Invincible* on station off the Falklands. The continued failure of Britain and Argentina to arrive at a negotiated settlement of the Falklands dispute left Britain with no alternative but to maintain a large and expensive force for the defence of the islands.

Key Weapons

THE ENGLISH ELECTRIC LIGHTNING

Assured of a place in aviation history both as the last wholly British designed and built interceptor to enter service with the RAF and as the first British fighter capable of exceeding the speed of sound in level flight, the Lightning originated in a contract for a Mach 1.5 research aeroplane awarded to English Electric's Aviation Division in May 1947. As work on this project progressed, the original specification (coded ER103) was superseded by a later requirement, F23/49, which called for a similar speed performance combined with an airframe strong enough to take the stress of 7g manoeuvres and carrying a gun armament and related sighting system.

Designated the English Electric P1, the F23/49 design was handled by a team led by W.E.W. 'Teddy' Petter, the creator of the innovative and best-selling Canberra jet bomber. While this experience with jet aircraft design was invaluable to the P1 project, the problems in achieving the required performance were extremely daunting. At the time, the conventional wisdom was that supersonic flight using turbojets was impossible without the additional thrust of afterburning. The two most powerful engines available to Petter were the Armstrong Siddeley Sapphire and the Rolls Royce Avon, both of which were 'dry', that is non-afterburning. It is to the designer's great credit that he managed to achieve what both the United States and the Soviet Union found impossible; the Lightning remains one of the few fighters in the world capable of supersonic flight on dry thrust alone.

In designing the P1, Petter's main considerations were the maximising of the available thrust and the minimising of airframe drag. The latter factor resulted in the twin engines necessary to provide enough thrust for supersonic flight being vertically stacked; it also caused the use of the highest possible degree of wing sweepback to minimise the drag build-up at the supersonic boundary. The P1's aerodynamics were the subject of considerable dispute between the design team and the Royal Aircraft Establishment at Farnborough, which resulted in the construction of the subsonic Short SB5 test aeroplane to evaluate the benefits or otherwise of various degrees of wing sweep and their relationship to the position of the tailplanes. The SB5 made its maiden flight on 2 December 1952 and provided practical proof of the basic English Electric concepts. In its final form, the P1 achieved the performance asked of it, but at a price. As a developed fighter, it offered an outstanding rate of climb, an impressive level speed and excellent handling characteristics. Against this, the uncompromising nature of the design left little room for fuel or anything other than the most limited of weapons loads. While these factors were of little consequence to the RAF, the Lightning's lack of load flexibility was to kill any hopes of wide-scale export sales.

The soundness of the basic concept resulted in English Electric being awarded a contract for a structural test airframe and two Sapphire-powered flying prototypes (to be known as the P1 and the P1A, the latter aircraft having provision for two 30mm Aden cannon) during 1949. Some five years were to elapse before the P1 (serial number WG760) was completed, and the aircraft made its first flight on 4 August 1954, going supersonic for the first time a week later on the 11th. The success of the P1 resulted

in the company being given the go-ahead to build three prototypes of a true fighter variant, the P1B, which was to be powered by afterburning Avon 200 series turbojets (suitable equipment had been developed for the original dry engine in the intervening years since the inception of the P1 project), to carry a Ferranti AI-23 'Airpass' radar and to have a basic armament of two 30mm Adens and two de Havilland Blue Jay (later Firestreak) AAMs (air-to-air missiles), or four cannon, or two cannon and two 24-round 5cm (2in) unguided rocket packs instead of the AAMs.

The programme continued with the first flight of the P1A (WG763) on 18 July 1955; contracts were issued for 20 pre-series and 20 production P1Bs in November 1956. The prototype P1B (XA847) took to the air for the first time on 4 April 1957, powered by two Avon 200 engines, each offering 5105kg (11,250lb) of thrust dry or 6545kg (14,430lb) with afterburning. The performance potential of the type was amply demonstrated seven months later when, on 25 November 1957, XA847 achieved a speed of Mach 2 for the first time.

The crucial year for the P1B/Lightning project was 1957, for up until then the English Electric product had been in the ambivalent position of being part research vehicle and part potential operational fighter. Indeed, its operational future as an interceptor depended on the provision in the F23/49 specification of armament; this meant that the type could be turned into an operational aircraft relatively easily, aided by the more fundamental factors that it was available and that it worked as advertised. At the

Previous page: A Lightning F6 with overwing fuel tanks and armed with Red Top missiles. Below: The SB5 aeroplane was used to test wing configurations for the Lightning. Bottom: Two Lightning F1s of No 74 Squadron, the first to use the type.

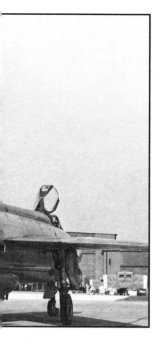

Above: An RAF Lightning F2 of No 19 Squadron. This variant featured Avon 210 afterburning turbojets in place of the F1's Avon 200s. The format of stacked engines was chosen to allow a more streamlined fuselage, thereby reducing drag.

Below: Lightning F6s of the now disbanded No 74 Squadron peel off formation; some of these aeroplanes were taken over by No 5 Squadron after No 74's disbandment.

time, the RAF's main thrust in the fighter field was based around Operational Requirement OR 329 which called for a large interceptor armed with two radar-homing Red Dean AAMs. The Defence White Paper of 1957 put an end to OR 329 on the basis that in future Britain would be threatened by ballistic missiles rather than manned bombers and there was therefore little need for the RAF to acquire a new generation of manned interceptors. Those bombers which might be encountered could be handled by the already existant P1B, an aircraft which the White Paper concluded was advanced enough to deal with any perceivable bomber threat.

Thus, almost by default, the P1B was assured of becoming the RAF's primary interceptor for the 1960s and was accordingly given the service designation Lightning F1 in October 1958. The first of the pre-series P1Bs (XG307) made its maiden flight on 29 October 1959 and service introduction of the type followed rapidly with three of this batch of aircraft being evaluated by the Air Fighting Development Squadron (AFDS) at Coltishall during 1959. The first production Lightning F1 was delivered to the RAF in June of the following year, at the end of which month No 74 Squadron (also based at Coltishall) began to trade its Hawker Hunter aircraft for the new type, becoming the service's first operational Lightning squadron.

The 13 or so operational Lightning F1s were followed by 28 of the F1A model which differed from the earlier aircraft in having provision for a detachable refuelling probe under the port wing, improved windscreen rain dispersal equipment and UHF radio as standard. The first Lightning F1A (XM169) made its maiden flight on 16 August 1960 and the variant was issued to No 56 Squadron (Wattisham) during December 1960 and to No 111 Squadron early in the following year.

The Lightning's potential was further developed in the F2 variant which featured more powerful afterburning Avon 210 turbojets, an improved navigation system, an automatic flight control system, a liquid oxygen supply and a standby DC generator. A total of 55 F2 aircraft were ordered, with the first production example (XN723) making

its maiden flight on 11 July 1961. In the event, only 42 aircraft were completed to this standard and these were issued to No 19 Squadron in December 1962 and No 92 Squadron in March 1963. These units were initially based at Leconfield, but in September 1963 No 19 Squadron transferred to Gütersloh in West Germany, closely followed by No 92 Squadron who moved into Geilenkirchen during December. In Germany, the F2 was used primarily in the ground-attack role carrying the four-cannon armament.

The Lightning F3, the first of which (XP693) took to the air on 16 June 1962, may be regarded as the first 'second generation' model of the basic design. The most noticeable difference between it and the earlier aircraft was the introduction of a larger, more angular tail fin intended to cure the problem of high-speed instability which had troubled all Lightning aircraft to date. Internally, the F3 was fitted with the Avon 301 turbojet – offering 5755kg (12,690lb) of thrust dry and 7420kg (16,360lb) with afterburning – the refined AI-23B radar and two Red Top (originally Blue Jay Mk 4) AAMs. The built-in cannon armament was deleted, although the type could house two such weapons in a ventral pack if required, and the model can be regarded as the RAF's first true Mach 2 interceptor.

A total of 68 Lightning F3s were built, with the first examples going to the AFDS (now at Binbrook) during January 1964. As with the F1, No 74 Squadron (now at Leuchars) became the first operational unit to receive the new model in April 1964. F3 strength increased rapidly thereafter with No 23 Squadron (Leuchars) receiving the type in August 1964 and Nos 111 and 56 Squadrons converting in December 1964 and February 1965 respectively. In April 1967, No 56 Squadron took its F3s to Cyprus and No 29 Squadron (Wattisham) was converted to the Lightning during May 1967 to maintain the UK-based interceptor strength.

As noted earlier, only 68 F3 aircraft were actually completed out of an original order for 92 machines. Airframe number 69 and the next 13 aircraft were completed to the F3A standard which was a hybrid bridging the gap between the F3 and the final major production model, the F6. Essentially, the F3A differed from previous models in employing the F6's wing format and enlarged ventral fuel tank. The first F3A (XR752) was delivered to the AFDS on 16 November 1965 and the bulk of the production run was issued to No 5 Squadron (Binbrook) which had reformed on 8 October 1965 specifically to operate the type.

The last major production version of the Lightning was the already-mentioned F6 which came close to realising the basic design's full potential. Retaining the angular fin introduced on the F3, the F6 introduced a new wing format with cranked and cambered leading edges and extended wing-tip chords, an enlarged ventral tank housing 2773 litres (610 gallons) of fuel, provision for two overwing ferry tanks each housing 1182 litres (260 gallons) and, from 1967, an arrester hook for emergency landings. As with the F1 and F3, No 74 Squadron was the first unit to receive the new type during August 1966. No 5 Squadron was next in line, trading its F3As (which were eventually brought up to full F6 standard) for F6s during January 1967. The F6 force was completed when No 11 Squadron (Leuchars) reformed on the type in May 1967 and No 23 Squadron

Above: The bullet fairing on the air intake of this Lightning F6 conceals the fire-control radar. Above right: A Lightning F2A of No 19 Squadron aligns itself with the fuel nozzle of a Victor tanker.

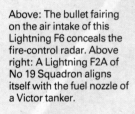

Main picture: Four Lightnings of No 23 Squadron. Left: This Lightning F3 belongs to No 111 Squadron, now disbanded. Top right: Three Lightning variants: from top to bottom, the F53 multi-role export model, the F6 RAF interceptor model, and a T55 export trainer in the colours of the Kuwait Air Force.

received the model in June of the same year.

Following the end of F6 production, approximately 30 F2 aircraft were brought up to the later standard under the designation F2A. The F2A aircraft incorporated the angular fin, revised wing format and ventral tank of the F3 and F6 models together with the built-in cannon armament of the earlier aircraft, not found on the F6. The level of modification incorporated into these aircraft necessitated their virtual rebuilding, creating what many consider the best of the breed.

The introduction of the F6/F2A represented the peak of deployment of the Lightning with the RAF. After its conversion to the F6, No 74 Squadron was posted to Singapore in the late 1960s, where it was disbanded in August 1971 and its aircraft were passed to No 56 Squadron in Cyprus to replace their F3s. The first home-based Lightning unit to be broken up was No 111 Squadron which was disbanded during September 1974, closely followed by No 29 Squadron in December of the same year; No 56 Squadron returned to the UK in January 1975 and began converting to the Phantom early in the following year; No 23 Squadron disappeared in October 1976 and the run-down was completed when Nos 19 and 92 Squadrons gave up their F2A aircraft for Phantoms in 1977. In 1984, the remaining 70-odd Lightnings available to the RAF were concentrated at Binbrook, where Nos 5 and 11 Squadrons operated an assortment of F3, F6 and T5 aircraft, backed up by the Lightning Training Flight and the Lightning Augmentation Flight as a reserve pool. This large surplus of aircraft had been caused by the restriction of operational usage to only two squadrons, and it had been proposed to absorb this in the creation of a third squadron. This plan was later abandoned and Nos 5 and 11 Squadrons will be the sole operators of the Lightning for the remainder of its service life.

At the beginning of the Lightning programme it was realised that there would be a need for a specialised trainer to help convert the RAF's pilots from the subsonic Hunter to the supersonic Lightning. Accordingly, a two-seat, dual-control model was ordered into production as the T4, the first of

which (XL628) made its maiden flight on 1 May 1959. A total of 20 T4s were built, most of which were issued to the Lightning Training Squadron (at Middleton St George). On 1 June 1963, this unit was redesignated as No 226 OCU (Operational Conversion Unit), an identity it retained until it was absorbed into 'C' Flight, No 11 Squadron (now the Lightning Training Flight) during August 1974. In addition to this main training effort, single T4s were issued to each of the F1A and F2 squadrons. The advent of the more powerful F3 led to the creation of the T5 which first flew in March 1962. Twenty-two such aircraft were delivered and were operated in quantity by No 226 OCU and individually by the various F3, F3A, F6 and F2A squadrons.

The Lightning's inflexibility as a weapons platform severely limited its export potential; only two overseas customers, Saudi Arabia and Kuwait, were found for the type. Saudi Arabia was supplied with 34 Lightning F53 single-seaters and six Lightning T55 trainers during the period December 1967 to August 1969. The F53 was based on the F3/F6 series and incorporated a modified ventral tank housing two Aden cannon and 2432 litres (535 gallons) of fuel and two wing pylons capable of carrying a single 455kg (1000lb) bomb. The Saudi Lightnings remained in service until replaced by the F-15 in the early 1980s. Kuwait followed the Saudi example and ordered 12 F53s and two T55s which were delivered between 1968 and 1969, but the Kuwaitis found the Lightning a very complex aircraft to operate and the type remained in service for only eight years before being replaced by the Mirage F1 during 1977.

Above: A Lightning F53 of the Saudi Arabian Air Force comes in to land. The Saudis purchased 34 of these aeroplanes in the late 1960s. In order that they might have a multi-role combat ability, wing pylons for bombs were provided and modifications were made to the ventral tank housing which allowed it to carry two 30mm Aden cannon.

Below: An F6 of the Lightning Training Flight at RAF Alconbury in 1984; its air intake is covered to protect the engine. The Lightning is at the end of its service life and will be replaced during the 1980s by the air defence version of the Tornado.

Lightning F6

Type Single-seat, land-based interceptor aircraft
Dimensions Span 10.61m (34ft 10in); length 16.84m (55ft 3in); height 5.97m (19ft 7in)
Weight Normal take-off 18,144kg (40,000lb); maximum with external loads 18,915kg (41,000lb)
Powerplant Two 5755kg/7420kg (12,690lb/16,360lb) thrust Rolls Royce Avon 301 afterburning turbojets

Performance Maximum speed at sea level Mach 1.06 or 1300km/h (808mph); maximum speed at 10,975m (36,000ft) Mach 2.1 or 2230km/h (1386mph); initial rate of climb 254m/sec (50,000ft/min)
Range Combat radius 972km (604 miles); ferry range 2502km (1554 miles)
Ceiling 17,375m (57,000ft)

Armament Two Red Top AAMs or provision for air-to-air unguided rocket packs or two 30mm Aden cannon in a ventral housing

Bloodbath in Beirut

The Sabra and Chatila massacres

The Israeli invasion of Lebanon on 6 June 1982 inevitably influenced the complex pattern of that country's internal politics. Through a series of victories over his rivals in the period between the end of the Lebanese civil war in 1976 and the Israeli invasion, Bashir Gemayel had established himself as the dominant power in the Christian communities at the head of his Phalangist militia, the Lebanese Forces. His close relationship with the Israelis marked him out as the most likely beneficiary of the invasion.

On the other side, despite differences with the Palestinians in the years since the civil war, the left-wing Muslim militias ranged themselves with the Palestinians and Syrians against the Israelis. The Shi'ite Amal and Sunni Mourabitoun militias played a major part in the defence of West Beirut against the Israelis during the siege which lasted from mid-June to the end of August. The Druze community in the Chouf mountains, lead by Walid Jumblatt (son of the civil war Druze leader Kamal Jumblatt), at first cooperated with the Israeli invaders, who traditionally had a good relationship with the Druze living in Israel itself; however, as the Israelis allowed the Druze's Phalangist Christian enemies to reinfiltrate the Chouf mountains from which they had been driven in the civil war, relations between the Druze and the Israelis soon deteriorated.

Bashir Gemayel saw the Israeli invasion as a heaven-sent opportunity to establish his power over

all of Lebanon. He refused to be a tool of the Israelis – although his militia cooperated with the invaders in maintaining the siege of West Beirut, he turned down Israeli requests for his forces to launch an assault on the beleaguered area. Instead, he wished to exploit the Israeli presence, counting on them to force the Palestinians and Syrians out of Lebanon and fatally weaken his Muslim and Druze enemies.

By coincidence, the six-year term of office of Lebanese President Elias Sarkis was due to end in September 1982. Under normal circumstances, Bashir Gemayel would have stood little chance of being elected as his successor. But with Beirut under siege, the Muslims in disarray and the Christians feeling the need of a strong leader, he had an unrepeatable opportunity. Despite a boycott of the National Assembly by most Muslim deputies, on 23 August Bashir narrowly managed to gather a quorum and win enough votes in the Assembly to be declared president-elect.

The Israelis hoped that Bashir would negotiate a peace treaty with them – in the manner of Sadat in Egypt – which would create a secure Cairo-Tel Aviv-Beirut axis. Whether Bashir would have played this role is questionable (his initial meeting with Israeli Prime Minister Menachem Begin was stormy); in the event, he never got the chance. On 14 September he was killed in a large bomb explosion at his party's headquarters. It has never been established who was behind the assassination, but its

Above: In an alley of a Beirut refugee camp, a shocked and bitter survivor of the Sabra and Chatila massacres stands helplessly by the bodies of two young Palestinian men murdered by Christian militiamen. The massacre occurred under the eyes of Israeli troops, who had entered West Beirut on 15 September 1982 in the wake of the evacuation of the city by the fighters of the PLO. Claiming that up to 2000 Palestinian guerrillas had stayed behind, the Israelis encircled the camps which had been left virtually defenceless.

aftermath was to be bloody.

At the time of Bashir's election, agreement had been reached for the evacuation of Palestine Liberation Organisation (PLO) forces from Beirut. Under this agreement, negotiated with all interested parties by US President Reagan's special envoy Philip Habib, a Multi-National Force (MNF) provided by France, Italy and the United States would supervise the evacuation of the Palestinians and protect the inhabitants of West Beirut from the Israelis and Phalangists after the departure of their fighting men. On 10 September, with all the Palestinian forces and their Syrian allies out of Beirut, the MNF began a withdrawal regarded by many observers as over-hasty.

Preserving order?

The Israelis had agreed not to enter West Beirut, but there was now no effective armed force to stop them should they break their word. Two hours after the public announcement of Bashir Gemayel's death, on 15 September, Israeli forces moved into the city. At the time, Begin and Israeli Defence Minister Ariel Sharon justified the action by claiming the need to preserve order; later, the Israeli cabinet issued a statement alleging that 2000 PLO guerrillas equipped with heavy weapons had remained in West Beirut, in violation of the evacuation agreement. No solid evidence for this was produced, and the Israeli Defence Forces' (IDF) advance encountered little resistance. As targets in the city were bombarded and Israeli planes flew overhead, one IDF column moved into Ras Beirut from the port area while others rolled up from the south. Two columns, one advancing from the direction of the Kuwaiti embassy building and the second along the airport road to the east, surrounded the Sabra and Chatila Palestinian refugee camps.

The Israelis were met by smallarms fire from the Mourabitoun and Amal militias, but the speed of the advance and the firepower they deployed proved to be decisive. By 16 September the IDF was in control of all West Beirut, road-blocks had been established at all major road junctions and the High Command confidently announced that only a few houses in various neighbourhoods remained to be cleared. The operation cost the lives of 30 civilians, with a further 254 wounded. IDF losses were put at eight dead and two tanks destroyed.

Israeli delight at the successful completion of the operation was shortlived, however, as during the following days news filtered out of a massacre in the Sabra and Chatila refugee camps that was to have profound consequences for the immediate future of Beirut. On 15 September senior officers of the IDF in Lebanon, led by Major-General Amir Drori, head of the northern command, and Brigadier Amos Yaron, divisional commander for West Beirut, had met Phalangist officers including Fadi Ephraim and Elias Habeika to discuss the details of an operation to clear the camps of suspected PLO members. At 1500 hours on the following day, a convoy of militiamen accompanied by Israeli paratroopers moved out of Beirut airport and headed for a pre-arranged rendezvous point opposite the Kuwaiti embassy. Three hours later, the militiamen entered Sabra from the southwest and the killings began. The troops involved included members of the Phalangist militia drawn from the Damour battalion, supported by some 50 men of Major Saad Haddad's command and a few score of Camille Chamoun's Tiger Force. In total, an estimated 1200 men were involved in the action, of whom up to half were in the camps at any one time. Israeli cooperation with the militiamen included the firing of flares to facilitate their operations at night and the turning back of civilians attempting to flee the camps. Israeli commanders appear to have been aware that a massacre was under way on 16 September but they failed to intervene until two days later; Israeli soldiers were within 300m (330 yards) of the camps throughout the operation. By 2200 hours on 18 September, when the killings were finally halted, over 1000 people had been massacred, a large number of them women and children. The bodies had been left where they fell or hastily bulldozed into mass graves.

There had been many other massacres in the recent history of Lebanon, but two aspects of the Sabra and Chatila killings caused a worldwide sense of outrage – the involvement of Israel, and the failure of the

Above: Major Saad Haddad, commander of the Israeli-backed South Lebanon Army, some of whose men took part in the Sabra and Chatila massacres. Below: Amin Gemayel, elected president of Lebanon after the murder of his brother Bashir in September 1982.

Left: Israeli Prime Minister Menachem Begin (right) consults with his minister of defence, Ariel Sharon. An Israeli commission of inquiry into the events surrounding the Sabra and Chatila massacres recommended that Sharon be removed from his post. Begin retained him as minister without portfolio, but the shock of the massacres contributed to the prime minister's own collapse and resignation the following year.

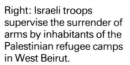

Right: Israeli troops supervise the surrender of arms by inhabitants of the Palestinian refugee camps in West Beirut.

United States' guarantee of the safety of the civilian population implicit in the Habib evacuation agreement. President Reagan immediately ordered the US Marines back into Beirut and the French and Italians returned with them (later to be joined by a small unit of the British Army). Under international pressure, the Israelis agreed to withdraw from West Beirut, the camps and the airport on 1 October and allow UN observers into the city. In Israel itself, the government was pressured into setting up a commission of inquiry to examine the affair; its findings exonerated the Israeli cabinet from direct responsibility for the massacre but called for the resignation of Defence Minister Sharon.

Meanwhile, the internal politics of Lebanon had taken a fresh turn. Immediately following the assassination of Bashir Gemayel, his brother Amin was elected president. Amin Gemayel was known as an opponent of Bashir's militia and as being critical of many of his brother's policies. Although he was a Phalangist leader, his presidency initially enjoyed more support in Muslim West Beirut than in the Christian East, where the Phalangist militia leaders regarded him with deep suspicion. Amin was seriously committed to a policy of at least limited national reconciliation, a path in which he was encouraged by the United States. The Reagan administration in particular backed Amin's plan to reconstruct the Lebanese Army as a means of reasserting central government authority over the warring militias.

US policy in Lebanon was a part of a wider Middle East initiative. On 1 September 1982 the 'Reagan Plan' had been announced, proposing essentially that Israel should withdraw from all territory occupied since 1967, but without the creation of any independent Palestinian state. Although the proposal was rejected both by the Israelis and the frontline Arab states, it remained the basis of an intense diplomatic effort conducted by Secretary of State George Shultz in late 1982 and early 1983. With regard to Lebanon, Shultz sought agreement on a withdrawal of all foreign forces from the country.

At first the Israelis insisted on maintaining bases in southern Lebanon and leaving Haddad's militia in control of the border area, but these conditions were unacceptable to the Lebanese government. After much delay, on 17 May 1983 an agreement was reached between Israel and Lebanon (the 'Shultz agreement') under which Israel would withdraw totally from the country, but combined Lebanese and Israeli forces would patrol the border. The Israeli withdrawal was conditional, however, on a parallel Syrian withdrawal – there were still over 40,000 Syrian and Palestinian forces in the Beqaa Valley and the north. The Syrians immediately denounced the agreement, which consequently proved abortive.

By this time, Amin Gemayel's domestic policy of reconciliation was also in ruins. His revived Lebanese Army completely failed to control the Phalangist militias which, either on their own initiative or at Israel's instigation, carried out a campaign of harassment against Muslims and Druze in West Beirut and the areas to the south. Nor was the Lebanese Army itself, with its American arms and training and its Christian officers, perceived as a neutral force. Shortly after the announcement of the Shultz agreement, groups opposed to the regime, led by Walid Jumblatt, Sulieman Franjieh and Rashid Karami, formed the National Salvation Front to combat the re-emergence of Phalangist dominance in the nation's affairs. By September 1983, a new round of bitter fighting was once again tearing Lebanon apart.

Ian Westwell

Below: Red Cross workers scatter quicklime over the bodies of victims of the Sabra massacre in order to reduce the danger of infection before covering in one of several mass graves in which over 1000 bodies were buried.

Arafat at bay

The PLO and the siege of Tripoli

With the final withdrawal of Palestinian fighters from the besieged ruins of West Beirut on 1 September 1982, the strategy of armed struggle, first adopted by the Palestine Liberation Organisation (PLO) in 1964, seemed to have ended in the total and irrevocable defeat of the Palestinians' military forces at the hands of the Israelis. The Palestinian guerrillas sailed into a new exile, to be dispersed around the whole Arab world, where they were confined to special camps and disarmed. Not even the eternal optimism of PLO Chairman Yassir Arafat could conceal the crisis into which these events threw the Palestinian movement. While Arafat continued to insist that the siege of Beirut had been a glorious Palestinian victory, criticism of his leadership began to grow among members of his own Fatah organisation's military forces.

There had been opposition to Arafat within the PLO before, but his domination of the organisation's largest group, Fatah, had always ensured his ability to preserve his position and with it the basic unity of the PLO. But with the destruction of the extensive administrative and military infrastructure which the Palestinians had created inside southern Lebanon and Beirut by the Israeli invasion of June 1982, Arafat's hold upon his followers was considerably

weakened. His well-known skill in undermining and out-thinking opponents in personal confrontations, both through argument and emotional appeals to the unity of the Palestinian cause, was deprived of the direct contact which it needed in order to be successful. Many Fatah fighters had regrouped in Syria, or else in Syrian-controlled northern Lebanon and the Beqaa Valley, where they were encouraged by Syrian President Hafez al-Assad's regime to blame Arafat for their predicament, and leading figures within the Fatah organisation, particularly its military formations, found support among the rank-and-file for moves to oust him from the leadership.

The massacre of Palestinian refugees in the Sabra and Chatila camps in Beirut was a major factor in the growth of opposition to Arafat's leadership. One of the key roles of the Palestinian military forces inside Lebanon had been the protection of the civilian population of the Palestinian refugee camps there, particularly from attack by that country's Christian militias. This had been one of the main reasons for the heavy PLO involvement in the Lebanese civil war of 1975-76, and for its subsequent build-up of heavy weaponry. In agreeing to the evacuation of Beirut, Arafat had accepted a guarantee from the United States of the safety of the Palestinian civilians

Top left: Chairman of the PLO and leader of Fatah, its largest guerrilla group, Yassir Arafat arrives at a press conference in besieged Tripoli, closely followed by heavily armed bodyguards. Arafat's willingness, after the evacuation of the PLO from Beirut, to explore the possibility of a negotiated settlement to the Palestinian issue led to a split within Fatah. Top: Fatah fighters based in the Beqaa Valley, many of whom joined a revolt led by Colonel Abu Musa (above), a senior Fatah military commander, against Arafat's authority.

on the policy being pursued by Arafat was launched by Colonel Abu Musa, one of Fatah's most senior military commanders. Abu Musa, a graduate of Sandhurst military academy, had been a colonel in the Jordanian Army until 1970, when he had gone over to Fatah during the fighting between King Hussein's troops and the PLO. He subsequently became commander of Fatah's Yarmouk Brigade, made up of former Jordanian troops who like himself were of West Bank origin.

Abu Musa had led the Palestinian defence of West Beirut, and now criticised what he regarded as the abandonment of armed struggle. He called for total rejection of the Reagan Plan, and for an end to contacts with King Hussein, Egypt and opposition groups within Israel who favoured a negotiated settlement with the PLO. His speech was circulated privately after the Aden meeting, but at the 14 February session of the Palestinian National Council (PNC) in Algiers, Arafat was able to rally support around a loose, ambiguous formula which received backing from the more radical Popular Front for the Liberation of Palestine (PFLP) led by George Habash and the Democratic Front for the Liberation of Palestine (DFLP) of Naif Hawatmeh, but effectively allowed Arafat to continue to pursue the contacts which had so angered Abu Musa. The Fatah rebels, including Abu Saleh, who was excluded from the Fatah Central Committee in January, and a group of Fatah military leaders around Abu Musa who were deprived of their commands, now appealed openly for the removal of Arafat.

The rebels forged close links with President Assad of Syria, who ordered the seizure of a shipment of arms from the Soviet Union, destined for Fatah forces stationed in the Beqaa Valley and northern

left behind. The massacre left him open to accusations from his opponents within Fatah of having betrayed his own people.

Both Syria and the Fatah opposition were also angered by the apparent willingness of Arafat to abandon the armed struggle in favour of a strategy of peaceful negotiation. Such a strategy would necessitate establishing links not only with the United States, which announced the Reagan Plan as its contribution to Middle East diplomacy on 1 September 1982, but also Egypt and Jordan, both of which were enemies of the Assad regime in Syria, and both of which were regarded by the Fatah rebels as traitors to the Palestinian cause. The Reagan Plan proposed that Israel withdraw from the territories it had occupied since the Six-Day War of 1967, but did not call for the establishment of a Palestinian state on the West Bank of the Jordan, suggesting instead some form of West Bank self-government in association with King Hussein's Jordan. Though the Reagan Plan was rejected immediately by Israel, Arafat continued to regard it as a basis for possible negotiations, and began a series of discussions with King Hussein who also regarded it as a potential solution.

These developments threatened to isolate Syria, and leave the Fatah fighters still in the territory controlled by Syria without a role. By November 1982, the Fatah rebels were ready to go over to the offensive, but it was only at a meeting of the Fatah Revolutionary Council in Aden, South Yemen, on 27 January 1983, that the first manifestation of open opposition was made. At that meeting, a bitter attack

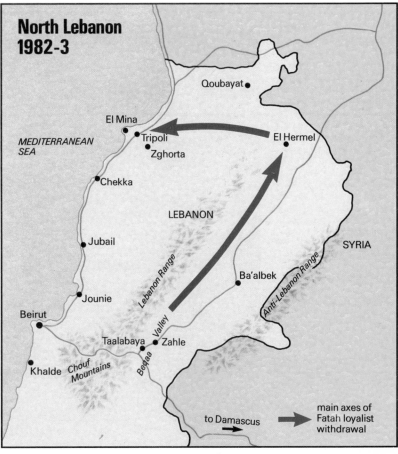

North Lebanon 1982-3

Qoubayat
El Mina
MEDITERRANEAN SEA
Tripoli
El Hermel
Zghorta
Chekka
LEBANON
SYRIA
Jubail
Lebanon Range
Anti-Lebanon Range
Ba'albek
Jounie
Beirut
Taalabaya
Zahle
Beqaa Valley
Khalde Chouf Mountains

to Damascus →

→ main axes of Fatah loyalist withdrawal

Lebanon. The appointment of Abu Hajim and Haj Ismail, two military commanders personally loyal to Arafat, in place of the rebel colonels towards the end of April, brought the crisis to boiling point, and Arafat travelled to Damascus in early May for discussions with Assad in order to avert an open break. Three days later, however, fighting broke out in the Beqaa Valley between Fatah troops loyal to Arafat and Fatah rebel forces backed by local Syrian units. Although the fighting revealed the Fatah loyalists' position to be militarily weak, they received significant political support at first from the Soviet Union, which regarded Arafat as vital to the preservation of Palestinian unity. Pressure from Syria rapidly led Moscow to become less open in its support for Arafat, however. The message was clear – for the Soviet Union, Syria was an indispensable ally in the Middle East, the PLO was not.

The breakdown of unity

Arafat continued to be immensely popular among the Palestinian population in the occupied territories and in the refugee communities scattered throughout the Arab world. He also continued to receive backing from the PFLP and DFLP, who saw the preservation of unity as vitally important to the continued existence of a Palestinian movement. In late June, however, Arafat was humiliatingly expelled from Damascus by Assad, and by early August a temporary ceasefire in the Beqaa Valley had broken down, leading to heavy fighting which continued throughout the next month.

When fighting broke out in the Chouf mountains between the local Druze militia and the Lebanese Army, fighters from both Fatah factions were allegedly involved on the side of the Druze, but the Syrians continued to exert pressure on Arafat's supporters. On 23 September, five days after Arafat

himself had arrived disguised aboard a Cypriot freighter in the north Lebanese port of Tripoli, which was one of his few remaining strongholds in Lebanon, the Syrians ordered his supporters to leave the Ta'alabayah area, near the Beirut-Damascus highway. They were compelled to abandon what had been one of their last bases in the Beqaa Valley and move north by forced marches under Syrian escort to the Hermel area, where they occupied vulnerable positions encircled by Syrian troops for several days, until they were allowed to move on to Tripoli, which they reached on 30 September.

Within Tripoli, the Arafat loyalists were supported by a local Muslim militia group, the Islamic Unity Movement; an attack by this group during October 1983 on the Tripoli offices of the Lebanese Communist Party strained relations between Arafat and the radicals of the DFLP and PFLP, however, and some sections of the PFLP were in favour of joining the rebels. Habash and Hawatmeh were able to control their followers, but the rebels nevertheless were not alone as they began to prepare for an assault on Tripoli. Not only were they backed by one and a half divisions of the Syrian Army, but they were also fighting alongside men of the Syrian-controlled Palestinian Liberation Army and of Ahmad Jibril's Popular Front-General Command.

Skirmishing continued around Tripoli throughout late September and October; Arafat was able to improve his image greatly by reviving his role of the previous year as a beleaguered military commander, prepared to go down fighting against impossible odds. On 12 October, the Fatah offices in Damascus were taken over by followers of Abu Musa, but four days later the Fatah Central Committee meeting in Kuwait voted to back Arafat in his struggle with the rebels. On 3 November, the pro-Syrian rebels began an artillery bombardment of the Badawi and Nahr

Above: Arafat loyalist fighters manning a Soviet-built T54 tank on the defensive perimeter of Badawi refugee camp. In the background, a dense column of smoke rises above the beleaguered port of Tripoli.

Right: Street-fighting men: members of the pro-Arafat Islamic Unity Movement militia move forward to take up positions in the charred shell of a house in the heavily bombarded ruins of Tripoli. The town and the nearby Palestinian refugee camps of Badawi and Nahr el-Barid were ruthlessly shelled by the Fatah rebels and Syrian troops, while Israeli aircraft and naval vessels bombarded the port to prevent any evacuation by forces loyal to Arafat.

el-Barid refugee camps on the outskirts of Tripoli, and later captured the Nahr el-Barid camp.

A ceasefire negotiated by the foreign ministers of the Arab Gulf states held in spite of sporadic fighting until the morning of 15 November, when the rebels launched a renewed offensive. By the following day, most of Badawi camp had fallen to the rebels, and by 17 November it was firmly in their hands. The fighting resulted in particularly severe civilian casualties, many of whom were Palestinian inhabitants of the refugee camps, which helped greatly to swing Palestinian opinion behind Arafat and against Abu Musa's rebels. The Israelis meanwhile, overjoyed to see the Palestinians engaged in a murderous civil war, were blockading and shelling Tripoli harbour in order to prevent any evacuation by either Arafat or his men. They hoped to see Arafat not only humiliated, but finally eliminated by his Fatah opponents. However, Arafat's reputation for being able to survive even the most dangerous situations proved once more to be well founded. International pressure built up on both Syria and Israel to allow an evacuation to take place. Saudi Arabia threatened to cut off financial support from Syria, and the United States sent a special envoy to talk sternly to the Israeli government. Arafat was now regarded as a relatively moderate leader who should be preserved, and Syria as the chief threat to Western and conservative Arab interests. At Christmas 1983 the Greek government sent five ships, flying the United Nations flag and escorted by French warships, to evacuate the hard-pressed Fatah loyalist fighters trapped inside Tripoli. For the second time in 15 months, Arafat and his supporters sailed from Lebanon, this time defeated by their own fellow Palestinians.

Abu Musa was unable to transform his military success into political capital within Fatah or the PLO. The apparent dependence of the Fatah rebels upon Syrian support, and the past record of conflict between Palestinian and Syrian interests, deprived the rebels of the legitimacy and support which they sought, and allowed Arafat to stage a come-back. Freed now of pressure from radical military leaders within Fatah, Arafat continued to pursue a policy which rested more and more upon a recognition that the most important asset left to the PLO was its popularity among the Palestinian population on the Israeli-occupied West Bank. By April 1984, Arafat felt strong enough to establish indirect links with the rebels as a first step towards reconciliation, and in July reached an agreement with the DFLP and PFLP which met some of the criticisms which they had shared with Abu Musa.

All this was in preparation for the meeting of the 17th Palestinian National Council, the highest body of the PLO, which took place in the Jordanian capital, Amman, in November 1984. The choice of meeting-place symbolised the rapprochement which had taken place between the PLO and King Hussein, and marked an end to the bitter and often bloody enmity which had existed between them since the expulsion of the PLO from Jordan in September 1970. The eight-day meeting of the PNC also showed the degree to which Arafat had been able to re-consolidate his leadership of the PLO, but it was clear that limits were being imposed on his style of individualistic diplomacy – which had itself been one of the causes of the Abu Musa revolt.

Inter-Palestinian terrorism

It appeared that the split within Fatah had led to the development of a more collective leadership within that organisation and within the PLO generally, while at the same time, moderates from the West Bank who favoured a negotiated settlement with Jordanian involvement were more prominent and outspoken than ever before. One of these, Fahd Kawasme, a member of the newly-elected PLO executive and a former mayor of Hebron who had been expelled from the West Bank by the Israeli authorities, was assassinated, allegedly by Syrian agents, in Amman on 29 December 1984. His murder was a clear signal that Damascus remained fundamentally opposed to any solution to the Palestinian problem which might be reached without Western recognition of Syria's claim to be the leading Arab power in the region. While the PLO seemed prepared to embark on a new strategy of negotiation, leaving the phase of armed struggle behind in the ruins of Beirut and Tripoli, it was apparent that the road to a peaceful settlement might still be a bloody one, and a new wave of inter-Palestinian terrorism mounted by Syria and its Palestinian supporters seemed almost inevitable. **Robin Corbett**

Below: As Fatah rebels storm Badawi, these pro-Arafat fighters prepare to blow up their recoilless gun to prevent its falling into rebel hands. Below right: Arafat and his supporters sail from Tripoli harbour into a new exile.

MNF

The international peacekeeping force in Beirut

Between 21 August and 10 September 1982 the United States, France and Italy provided troops to supervise the evacuation of Palestinian and Syrian fighters, trapped in West Beirut by the Israeli invasion of the previous June. The task was carried out smoothly, enabling the troops to be withdrawn, but it did little to solve the problems of Lebanon. By 20 September, in the aftermath of the assassination of the president-elect, Bashir Gemayel, an Israeli advance into West Beirut and the massacre of Palestinian refugees at Sabra and Chatila, the foreign contingents had been redeployed, this time as a more permanent Multi-National Force (MNF).

Expressed officially, the task of the MNF was 'to provide a multinational presence as an interpositional force in Beirut which would facilitate the restoration of the sovereignty of the Lebanese government and assure the safety of the persons in that area'; in other words, to impose a barrier between the warring factions and help to create an atmosphere of relative calm in which the new government of Amin Gemayel could reassert its political authority. As such, the force was a 'peacemaking' rather than a 'peacekeeping' body, associated through the terms of its mandate with one particular element of the Lebanese political scene. This inevitably caused a certain amount of strain, made worse by the fact that, as the contingents (including that provided by Britain from February 1983) were deployed according to separate bilateral agreements, negotiated between their home governments and that of Gemayel, each Western power was free to stress the role which it saw as more important – active support for the Lebanese authorities or aid to the local people. Furthermore, there was no MNF headquarters established in Beirut, and although liaison between the contingents was generally good, this lack of central direction produced noticeable differences in operational procedures and attitudes within the four sectors of responsibility. As one British officer put it, 'we have defined our operations according to what each of us does best'.

This was most immediately apparent in the American sector, where a Marine Amphibious Unit (MAU), on detachment from the US Sixth Fleet in the Mediterranean, occupied positions around the International Airport. Comprising a total of 1750 service personnel and including a tank platoon of M60s, an artillery battery of 155mm guns and a helicopter support squadron, the contingent came ashore on 20 September 1982 by means of an assault landing and maintained that sort of combat profile throughout the period of deployment. The troops built elaborate fortified posts, conducted few patrols and made little contact with the local people. To a certain extent this was understandable – the airport was very exposed and, once the Israelis had withdrawn to the Awali Line in September 1983, was flanked by an area of notorious instability – but it also reflected President Reagan's hardline interpretation of the MNF mandate. The Americans made it clear that their primary mission was to ensure Gemayel's survival: a policy manifested in an extensive training programme for the Lebanese Army and, once that army had been attacked in the Chouf mountains in September 1983, in the provision of naval gunfire, air and artillery support.

A similar response was eventually elicited from the French, although initially their tactics were more low-key. They occupied positions in the northwestern suburbs of Beirut itself, deploying a force of 2000 Marines and Foreign Legionnaires in what had been a very prosperous sea-front area. To begin with, they adopted an internal security profile, carrying out frequent patrols, 'showing the flag' and doing all they could to restore a measure of normality to their sector. But this did not last: once the fighting flared up in the Chouf mountains, President Mitterand authorised a gradual escalation of French involvement, culminating in airstrikes on Druze positions on 22 September 1983. Again, this was understandable, particularly as French posts in Beirut had by then been attacked, but it meant that, like the Americans, the French laid the emphasis of their commitment firmly on support for the Gemayel regime.

Above left: A French para cradles his 89mm STRIM anti-tank rocket launcher while out on patrol in the militia battlefield of Beirut. His comrade is armed with the new 5.56mm MAS automatic rifle. Although French troops suffered heavy casualties in terrorist attacks, France was critical of the American decision to withdraw from Lebanon in the spring of 1984. Above: US Marines arrive in Beirut. The close relationship between America and Israel and American support for the Christian Phalangist regime of Lebanese President Amin Gemayel tended to discredit the Marines as impartial peacekeepers. Right: A British MNF soldier stands armed with a Sterling sub-machine gun in the back of a Land Rover.

It was partly as a consequence of their involvement on one side in the Lebanese conflict that, on 23 October 1983, the US and French contingents became the object of Shi'ite terrorist attacks. Just after dawn, a truck packed with explosives was driven through the barrier protecting the US Marine barracks; the driver crashed his vehicle into the building and it exploded, killing 239 Americans, mostly in their beds. An almost identical attack carried out at the same time against the French killed 58 soldiers.

Both the Italian and British contingents were clearly fortunate not to be attacked in such a way, but this was perhaps a consequence of their interpretation of their mandate which precluded direct assistance to the Lebanese Army, concentrating instead on the role of aiding the local population. The Italians fielded the largest contingent in the MNF – 2060 men, drawn from Marine, parachute and mechanised infantry battalions and backed by engineers, a field hospital and a logistics unit – and occupied one of the more difficult sectors, sandwiched between the French to the north and the Americans to the south. Within this area, a range of problems were encountered: in the south, close to the International Airport, the ground was open, necessitating the construction of fortified posts, while further north, in the approaches to Beirut, the refugee camps at Sabra, Chatila and Borj-al-Barajneh needed constant patrolling. At the same time, Italian troops also manned crossing points on the 'Green Line' between Muslim and Christian areas; keeping them open even at the height of intercommunal fighting.

After February 1983 the other side of the 'Green Line' was the responsibility of the British. They contributed a very small force – about 100 men only – drawn initially from the Queen's Dragoon Guards but nine months later relieved by the 16/5th the Queen's Royal Lancers, backed by headquarters personnel, chiefly from the Royal Signals. They reflected the experience of Northern Ireland, mounting constant patrols in Ferret scout cars and concentrating on making contact with the local people. Like the Italians, they proved to be extremely popular.

The difference of policy between the Americans and French on the one hand and the Italians and British on the other eventually made the MNF unworkable. By early 1984, with US and French casualties rising and the level of air and naval support to the embattled Lebanese Army increasing, it began to look as if the MNF would be drawn into the civil war – a policy firmly opposed in both Rome and London. As fighting flared up in the Chouf mountains and in Beirut, first the British and then the Italians pulled their contingents out. On 18 February the Americans followed suit and by the end of the month the MNF had ceased to exist, having collapsed in the face of pressures which it was neither designed nor deployed to resist. **John Pimlott**

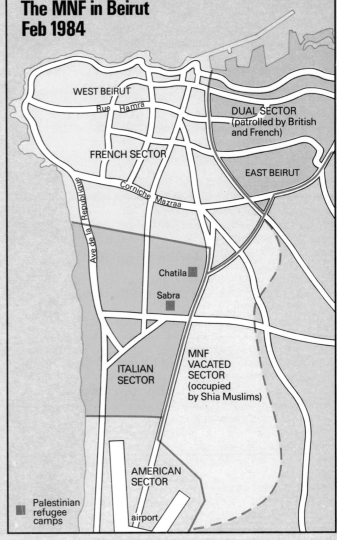

The MNF in Beirut Feb 1984

WEST BEIRUT

Rue Hamra

DUAL SECTOR (patrolled by British and French)

FRENCH SECTOR

EAST BEIRUT

Corniche Mazraa

Ave de la Republique

Chatila

Sabra

MNF VACATED SECTOR (occupied by Shia Muslims)

ITALIAN SECTOR

AMERICAN SECTOR

airport

Palestinian refugee camps

Lebanon in conflict, 1983-84

The Israeli government of Prime Minister Menachem Begin regarded the 17 May 1983 'Shultz agreement' negotiated with Lebanese President Amin Gemayel as a triumph. Arrived at with the close support and involvement of the United States, the agreement in effect formalised the realignment of Lebanon towards Israel and the West. The glaring weakness of the 17 May accord, however, was that it made an Israeli withdrawal from Lebanon conditional upon a simultaneous departure of Syrian troops, while at the same time excluding Syria from the negotiations for a Lebanese settlement. By adamantly refusing to withdraw its troops, Syria was able to re-establish itself in a key role on the Lebanese stage, and totally sabotage the 17 May agreement. The Lebanese Muslim and Druze leaders opposed to President Amin Gemayel's government were equally hostile to the peace accord, joining in a National Salvation Front to counter Christian Phalangist domination of Lebanon.

By this time, the United States was deeply involved in the complexities of the Lebanese conflict. US participation in the Multi-National Force (MNF) was intended to represent an even-handed peacekeeping stance, but its credibility was compromised by the closeness of the relationship between the United States and Israel. President Ronald Reagan's administration saw a strong Israel as being decisively important in preventing the expansion of Soviet influence in the Middle East. The tendency to view every problem and conflict in the world solely in terms of the sharpening confrontation between Moscow and Washington also extended to the Reagan administration's perception of the situation in Lebanon, where it took the form of regarding Syria as the dangerous and aggressive local surrogate of the Soviet Union.

The United States banked on the ability of Amin Gemayel and the Lebanese Army to control Lebanon as foreign forces were induced to withdraw. The Lebanese Army, with a 57 per cent Muslim majority, but largely officered by Christians, had failed totally to prevent the catastrophic civil war during the mid-1970s, itself splitting into several rival factions, including the South Lebanon Army of Major Saad Haddad. Nevertheless, both Amin and the United States believed it possible to rebuild and re-equip the army to enable it to pursue a new and active role. American instructors worked hard to train Lebanese troops in a Christian enclave north of Beirut throughout late 1982 and 1983, but the new strategy depended totally on the continued loyalty of the army's Muslim and Druze troops. As tensions rose in 1983, this loyalty could not be guaranteed.

The focus for a new eruption of Lebanese civil conflict was to be the Chouf mountains, east of Beirut. There, the Israeli Defence Forces (IDF) had initially encouraged the Christian Phalangists to move into what was a mainly Druze area. The Phalangists had long been Israel's closest allies in Lebanon, and their militia, the Lebanese Forces, had been trained and armed by the IDF. In the wake of the Sabra and Chatila massacres, however, Israel was

Militia battl

field

wary of involvement in any further Christian excesses, and sought vainly to control the Christian militiamen in the Chouf. Israel was eager to preserve the Druze as a potential buffer to both the Syrians and to renewed Palestinian infiltration. Despite the alliance which had existed between the Druze and the Palestinians and Muslim leftists during the 1975-76 civil war, the Druze were also determined not to see a return of the Palestinians. In addition, there were close links between the Lebanese Druze and the Druze minority population inside Israel itself, who held the right, unique among non-Jews, to serve as conscripts in the IDF. Israel therefore began to supply arms to the Druze in order to enable them to defend themselves against the Phalangists, and even went so far as to allow the shipment to the Druze of a consignment of weapons from Syria.

Tension mounted in the Chouf during August

Far left: A Druze militiaman fires a burst from his M60 machine gun during the September 1983 fighting in the Chouf mountains above Beirut. Bottom far left: Israeli troops withdraw to the Awali River. Left: Nabih Berri, leader of the Shi'ite Amal movement. His militia became allied to the forces of Druze leader Walid Jumblatt (below left) when fighting spread to West Beirut. Bottom left: Soldiers of the American-trained Lebanese Army which disintegrated during the 1983-84 fighting against Druze and Muslim militias.

1983, as it became increasingly apparent that the Israelis were preparing to stage a withdrawal from the outskirts of Beirut to a more easily defensible line along the Awali River. The danger of a bloody conflict between the Phalangists and Druze for control of the Chouf mountains was real enough, but it also seemed inevitable that there would be a violent clash between the Druze militia and the regular Lebanese Army. The government of Amin Gemayel made clear its intention to reassert central control over the mountains which dominated the Lebanese capital in the wake of any IDF withdrawal, as the first stage of a strategy for reuniting the country.

First, in August 1983, Amin attempted to assert his authority over West Beirut, which was now dominated by the Shi'ite Amal militia. Amal, led by the relatively moderate Nabih Berri, had been founded in 1974 by Shi'ite leader Imam Musa Sadr (who subsequently disappeared while on a visit to Colonel Gaddafi in Libya during 1978). Amal had split during 1982, with a group known as Islamic Amal, led by the former commander of the Amal militia, Hussein Mussavi, breaking away to pursue a much more radical, pro-Iranian fundamentalist line. Amal resisted bitterly the Lebanese Army advance into West Beirut, and prevented it reaching the Shi'ite stronghold in the southern Beirut suburb of Borj al-Barajneh. But the fighting seemed to suggest that the new American-trained Lebanese Army would be able to hold its own in any future internal conflict.

The long-expected withdrawal of the IDF from the Chouf back to the Awali River on 4 September created a totally new situation, which the Phalangist Lebanese Forces sought to exploit. Phalangist efforts to capture key positions in the mountains provoked heavy fighting with the Druze, but within a

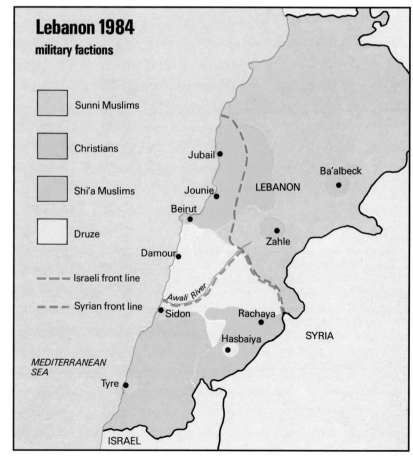

Lebanon 1984
military factions

☐ Sunni Muslims

☐ Christians

☐ Shi'a Muslims

☐ Druze

- - - Israeli front line

- - - Syrian front line

Jubail

Ba'albeck

Jounie

LEBANON

Beirut

Damour

Zahle

Awali River

Sidon

Rachaya

Hasbaiya

SYRIA

MEDITERRANEAN SEA

Tyre

ISRAEL

matter of days the Druze had succeeded in expelling the bulk of the Phalangist militiamen from the Chouf. The Phalangists were thrown out of their previous strongholds of Aley and Bamdoun, and were bottled-up in Deir el-Qamar, appealing to the Lebanese Army for assistance. The intervention of the Lebanese Army on the side of the Phalangists not only failed to redress the balance in the Chouf against the Druze militia, but served to reunite the Druze with their former leftist allies. Soon the Lebanese Army's 8th Brigade was under siege in the mountain town of Souk al-Garb, with US artillery observers in forward positions directing fire from US warships off the Lebanese coast against anti-government forces. US aircraft flew aerial reconnaissance missions from the USS *Eisenhower*, while the World War II-vintage battleship *New Jersey* threw massive shells into the Chouf from its 16in guns.

The involvement of Syrian troops in the Chouf battles on the side of the Druze was an important factor in the American decision to become more directly identified with the defence of the Lebanese government. It also threatened to lead to a direct US-Syrian confrontation, with the added danger of the possible entry of the Soviet Union into the Lebanese crisis, should Syrian security be directly threatened by the United States.

Concessions to avoid confrontation

The dangers of the situation were apparent to everyone, and led both sides to make a number of concessions, allowing the convening of a National Reconciliation Committee in Geneva on 31 October 1983. The meeting was attended by President Amin Gemayel, the leaders of all the most important Lebanese factions and Syrian foreign minister Abdel Halim Khaddam, whose presence reminded everyone of the necessity of Syrian support for any peace formula, and of its continued opposition to the 17 May agreement with Israel. Within a year, Syria had regained much of the ground which it had lost as a result of the Israeli invasion.

The conference concluded in November with the establishment of a constitutional consultative committee. This was charged with the task of finding a new constitutional formula which would allow the formation of a coalition government satisfactory to all interested parties – a daunting task. The conference also set up a security committee which was made up of representatives of the Druze, Amal and Lebanese Forces militias, as well as of the regular Lebanese Army, in order to coordinate ceasefire arrangements and avoid further clashes exploding into all-out civil war.

The violence which had erupted in September 1983 had already escalated dramatically, however, heralding the emergence of a new and potentially even more dangerous factor in Lebanese politics. On 23 October, the US Marine and French barracks in Beirut were both destroyed in suicide attacks by terrorists driving trucks loaded with explosives. 239 US Marines were killed and 58 French troops. Shortly afterwards, on 4 November, 28 Israeli soldiers and 33 civilians were killed when a terrorist bomb blew apart the Israeli military headquarters in Tyre.

The group most widely regarded as being responsible for all three attacks was Al-Jihad al-Islami (Islamic Jihad or Holy War), an extremist Shi'ite

fundamentalist group with close links to the Khomeini regime in Iran. Islamic Jihad had been formed from an alliance of two breakaway groups from Amal – the radical Islamic Amal of Hussein Mussavi and the Herzbollah (God's Party) – and a contingent of some 650 Iranian Revolutionary Guards who had established a base at Baalbek, in the Syrian-occupied Beqaa Valley. Mussavi denied direct responsibility for the Beirut and Tyre bombings, but made no secret of the fact that he approved of them wholeheartedly.

Following the Tyre attack, both Israel and Syria mobilised their troops, and US and French aircraft were fired on from Syrian-occupied territory. On 16 November, Israeli aircraft bombed a suspected terrorist base of Islamic Jihad at Nabi Chit in the Beqaa Valley, and on the following day French Super Etendards operating from the aircraft carrier *Clemenceau* off the Lebanese coast carried out a strike against a base used by Revolutionary Guards and Islamic Amal in the Baalbek area. The United States was also drawn further into the Lebanese quagmire when two of its jets were shot down by the Syrians while carrying out airstrikes in the hills around Beirut. French and American involvement in Lebanon seemed to be the cause of a coordinated series of terrorist bomb attacks on their embassies and other targets in the Gulf state of Kuwait on 12 December 1983, for which Islamic Jihad, backed by Iran, was held to be responsible.

Maintaining tension

The ability of Syria to maintain tension in Lebanon and inflict heavy damage on both the Israelis and the MNF without running the risk of a direct conflict, merely by providing support for or turning a blind eye to the activities of Shi'ite extremists, continued to strengthen its bargaining hand. But it was the events of February 1984 which finally ended the hopes of the Amin government and the United States for a resolution of the Lebanese crisis relying solely upon the dubious potential of the Lebanese Army.

During February 1984, extremely heavy fighting once more broke out in West Beirut, as Amal militiamen fought to expel the Lebanese Army from the positions which it had captured in the autumn of 1983. Backed by fighters of Walid Jumblatt's Druze militia, they broke through to the coast south of Beirut, cutting off large numbers of Phalangist militiamen from the Christian strongholds of the north. After several days of fighting during which American positions around Beirut airport came under regular artillery and sniper fire, Amin Gemayel was left in control of little more than his own presidential palace at Baabda on the outskirts of Beirut. The Lebanese Army collapsed completely, as Muslim and Druze soldiers refused to fight for the government which was seen as now being totally identified with the Christian Maronite minority and the Phalange. Whole units went over to the opposition militias, taking their American-supplied weapons with them. The United States was forced to accept the failure of its policy in Lebanon, and the MNF troops were withdrawn during February 1984 under the humiliating protection of Druze militiamen, armed with US-made M-16s captured from the Lebanese Army.

Amin was forced to travel to Damascus for discussions with Syrian President Hafez al-Assad, during

Above left: A US Marine artillery battery on the edge of Beirut airport trains its guns on the Chouf mountains where fighting raged during September 1983. By early 1984, the Marines were under fire from Muslim and Druze militia forces in West Beirut. Above: The barracks of the French contingent of the MNF after a suicidal Shi'ite bomb attack on 23 October 1983 in which 58 French troops died; 239 US Marines were killed in a simultaneous attack on their barracks.

Left: As the Lebanese parliament met to vote the government extraordinary powers on 11 June 1984, 90 people were killed in a fresh outbreak of shelling in Beirut.

which the Lebanese president pledged to scrap the 17 May agreement with Israel. Dependent now upon Syrian support for his continued survival as president, Gemayel reconvened a second round of National Reconciliation talks in Lausanne, Switzerland during March, and on 26 April, Rashid Karami, a pro-Syrian Sunni, was appointed prime minister. The new Lebanese government contained representatives of the opposition National Salvation Front, as well as Amal leader Nabih Berri, who was made minister for southern Lebanon – an area with a large Shi'ite community which was still under Israeli occupation.

A serious problem still existed in the south, however, where the Israelis were meeting increasingly bitter and violent opposition from the predominantly Shi'ite population. Attacks by members of Islamic Amal cost the IDF a growing number of casualties, and by January 1985, the Israelis had lost some 600 dead since their invasion of Lebanon in June 1982. Tight Israeli security measures, including severe restrictions on movement into and out of their occupation zone, as well as widespread arrests of Shi'ite suspects by members of the Israeli security service, Shin Beth, did little to prevent the growth of terrorist violence, and increased opposition to what the Shi'ites suspected might well turn out to be a long-term occupation such as that of the West Bank of the Jordan.

The inability of the Israeli government to achieve any clear objective in Lebanon after the expulsion of the PLO led to growing dissatisfaction within Israel, and contributed greatly to the emotional collapse of Prime Minister Menachem Begin and to his final resignation and replacement by Yitzhak Shamir on 16 September 1983. The Shamir government continued to pursue a hardline policy in Lebanon, refusing to withdraw until Syrian troops were also pulled out. Economic crisis and the failure in Lebanon undermined the Shamir government, however, and in September 1984, a new coalition government was formed, led by Shimon Peres, head of the Labour Party. In January 1985, the Israeli government announced a three-stage withdrawal plan, under which the IDF would pull back first from the Sidon region, then from the Beqaa Valley, and finally back into Israel itself, leaving the pro-Israeli South Lebanon Army, led since the death of Major Saad Haddad by Major-General Antoine Lehad, a Maronite former officer in the regular Lebanese Army, to occupy a strip of Lebanese territory along the border.

The Israeli decision seemed to leave the resolution of the conflict in Lebanon to its original protagonists – the Christian, Muslim and Druze communities and their militias. The Palestinian fighters had been expelled, the Western powers had burnt their fingers in the MNF and were unwilling to become further involved. Only Syria seemed to have been able to sustain the cost which entanglement in Lebanon demanded, and its claim to a voice in Lebanese affairs had been almost universally accepted as both legitimate from the point of view of Syrian security, and inevitable given the power of Damascus to sabotage any agreement arrived at without its approval. **Robin Corbett**

Below: Lebanese Shi'ites demonstrate their sympathy for the Iranian Khomeini regime. The largest Shi'ite group was Nabih Berri's Amal, but a breakaway extremist Islamic Amal helped found a terrorist group known as Islamic Jihad which was thought to be responsible for a number of the most serious attacks on Israeli and MNF troops. The emergence of the Shi'ites as a powerful radical force in Lebanese politics was one of the side-effects of a decade of civil war and foreign intervention.

The
REPUBLIC F-105
THUNDERCHIEF

Conceived as a successor to the Republic F-84F Thunderstreak with the US Air Force (USAF), the F-105 was a specialised tactical strike fighter, which could carry nuclear weapons in an internal weapons bay and operate at supersonic speed at low level. As such it was a weapon well suited to the 1950s US strategy of massive retaliation, which envisaged a quick recourse to nuclear warfare in response to Soviet aggression. Named the Thunderchief, but more often known by such unflattering nicknames as the 'Thud', 'Lead Sled', or 'Ultra Hog', the F-105 was the world's largest and heaviest single-seat fighter. The first flight of the prototype YF-105A on 22 October 1955 was a success, exceeding Mach 1, but the full flight test programme, involving 15 aircraft, suffered setbacks and delays. The greatest problems arose from the USAFs decision to revise the F-105's avionics completely, substituting the AN/APN-105 system, which used a terrain-avoidance/ground-mapping radar, in place of an inertial navigation set. Consequently, the F-105B initial production version entered USAF service three years behind schedule and production costs soared.

The Thunderchief's massive 10.66m (34ft 11in) long fuselage was constructed in four sections and

Above: One Thunderchief refuels from the 'buddy pack' carried aboard another. Right: An F-105G Wild Weasel electronic counter-measures aeroplane of the 57th Tactical Fighter Weapons Wing. Below right: F-105s of the 388th Tactical Fighter Wing, flying from their base at Korat in Thailand, drop 340kg (750lb) bombs on Viet Cong positions.

Previous page: Two Thunderchiefs of the US Air Force Reserve on a practice flight. Above: F-105s bomb Vietnamese positions during the Rolling Thunder bombing offensive against North Vietnam.

Right: An F-105D of the 355th Tactical Fighter Wing armed with a Bullpup air-to-surface missile. The Thunderchief used such missiles against precision targets (bridges, ammunition dumps) vital to the North Vietnamese war effort.

was mainly circular, with a reduced width in the centre to lower supersonic drag. A 4.5m (15ft) long internal weapons bay was located beneath the mid-mounted swept wing and the rear fuselage could be unbolted and removed to facilitate engine maintenance.

The powerplant of the F-105B was a Pratt & Whitney J75-P-5 turbojet, regarded as a reliable and rugged engine, which delivered 10,660kg (23,500lb) of thrust with afterburning. This thrust value could be further increased on take-off, by means of a water injection system, to a total of 12,000kg (26,500lb). However, the F-105's take-off performance left much to be desired and it was found that a fully-laden aircraft required a run of some 2400m (8000ft) to become airborne in the humid conditions of Southeast Asia. The wing-root mounted engine air intakes incorporated a unique variable-inlet system, which regulated the air flow to the engine throughout the speed range. Fuel was carried in seven fuselage tanks and the total internal load of 4390 litres (1160 gallons) could be increased by fitting a 1475-litre (390-gallon) tank in the weapons bay, as well as by carrying underwing drop tanks. Small ailerons were fitted to the outboard

trailing edges of the wings, but at high speed their function was taken over by spoilers mounted forward of the flaps on the wings' upper surfaces. Another unusual control feature was the four-petal speed brake mounted at the extreme rear of the fuselage, which in the closed position formed the engine exhaust nozzle.

The first F-105Bs were issued to the 4th TFW (Tactical Fighter Wing) at Eglin AFB (air force base) Florida, and this unit was responsible for the type's protracted service flight testing. The programme was not completed until 1960 and even then the F-105B's serviceability rate remained poor. As a result of these problems only 75 F-105Bs were manufactured and in 1964 the type was phased out of the USAF's first-line inventory and passed on to the Air National Guard and Air Force Reserve. In the same year the F-105B was issued to the 'Thunderbirds' formation display team, replacing the F-100C. However, the large and heavy Thunderchief was not suited to the tight formation-flying routines of the team and, when an F-105B crashed in the course of a display in May 1964, the Thunderbirds reverted to flying F-100 Super Sabres.

In 1959 an improved model of the Thunderchief, the F-105D, began its flight test programme. It was a heavier aircraft than the F-105B, the gross weight rising from 18,100kg (40,000lb) up to 23,855kg (52,500lb), and consequently was fitted with a more powerful engine, the 11,125kg (24,500lb) thrust J75-P-19. Its navigation and attack system was much improved by fitting a new attack radar, an autopilot and Doppler navigation radar, which enabled the aircraft to carry out an automatic attack on its target with nuclear weapons. However, for conventional bombing under blind conditions more precise aids were required and these were eventually fitted to a small number of F-105Ds in a modification known as 'T-stick II', with the additional avionics accommodated in a distinctive humped fairing along the top of

the fuselage. The F-105D entered service with the 4th TFW in 1961 and a total of 610 had been accepted by the USAF when production ended in 1964. This model formed the basis of the two-seat F-105F conversion trainer, which had its forward fuselage extended by 99cm (39in) to accommodate a second cockpit and a 12cm (5in) extension to the vertical tail fin to improve directional stability. Otherwise the F-105F was very similar to the F-105D and it retained the single-seat aircraft's combat capability.

By the mid-1960s a total of eight USAF wings had been equipped with the F-105D. In the United States, in addition to the 4th TFW, the 23rd TFW, the 355th TFW and the 388th TFW flew Thunderchiefs. F-105Ds operated with United States Air Forces in Europe with the 36th TFW at Bitburg and the 49th TFW at Spangdahlem, while in the Far East they flew with the 8th TFW based at Itazuke and later Yokota in Japan and with the 18th TFW at Kadena on Okinawa. It was in the latter theatre that the F-105D was to see

combat as the United States became embroiled in the Vietnam War. The earliest missions were flown from Korat airbase in Thailand by aircraft on temporary detachment from wings based in the United States. However, as the air war intensified, two F-105 wings were assigned to the combat theatre: the 355th TFW at Takhli and the 388th TFW at Korat. These aircraft bore the brunt of the USAF's bombing effort over North Vietnam in 1965-68, during the Flaming Dart and Rolling Thunder campaigns. They carried out more bombing strikes than any other aircraft type and they were faster than any other aeroplane in the USAF inventory for bombing duties at low level.

Nevertheless, the war in Southeast Asia imposed many unforeseen demands on an aircraft designed primarily for the very different conditions of a major war against the Soviet Union. Among the modifications required to suit the F-105D to combat in Southeast Asia was the fitting of external bomb racks

Left: A tail-view of an F-105B, the first Thunderchief variant to enter service with the US Air Force. Below far left: The Thunderchief's unusually-shaped wing-root air intakes are unique amongst aeroplanes capable of supersonic speeds. Below left: Two F-105Ds of the US Air Force Reserve perform a steep climb. Below: F-105Fs of the Georgia Air National Guard flying over the Appalachian Mountains. The Thunderchief ended its career with the US armed forces in 1984, replaced by the F-16.

to increase its ordnance load. Ironically, such was the expenditure of aircraft ordnance during the early months of the air war against North Vietnam, that by mid-1966 there was a bomb shortage and F-105s were perforce sent into action with a much reduced bomb load. The internal weapons bay, intended to house a tactical nuclear weapon, was never used for conventional bombs, but was instead fitted with an auxiliary fuel tank. Other necessary modifications included the fitting of armour plate to the aircraft, the provision of electronic counter-measures jamming pods to neutralise surface-to-air missile fire-control radars and the arming of F-105s with AIM-9 Side-winder air-to-air missiles, to give the strike aircraft a greater measure of self-defence capability than already provided by the built-in M61 20mm cannon. F-105s in fact proved to be dangerous opponents for North Vietnamese interceptors and a total of 28 MiG-17s were shot down in combat by 'Thud' pilots.

One of the highlights of the F-105's bombing

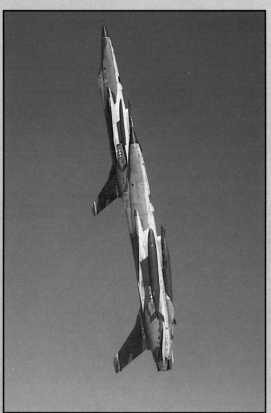

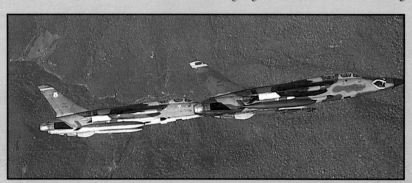

Above: This F-105F is fitted with electronic counter-measure equipment for the suppression of enemy surface-to-air missiles. Left: An F-105D lands, showing the unusual air brake opened petal-fashion around the exhaust.

campaign was a series of attacks on strategically-important – and therefore heavily defended – bridges in North Vietnam. The two most important targets of this type were the Paul Doumer Bridge on the outskirts of Hanoi and the Thanh Hoa Bridge further south. The latter, nicknamed the Dragon's Jaw, was a massive structure which proved to be virtually immune from damage by conventional bombs. The Doumer Bridge was first attacked on 11 August 1967, after restrictions on bombing in the Hanoi area had been lifted. The 355th TFW, followed by the 388th TFW, ran the gauntlet of an intense barrage of AA fire to drop three of the bridge's spans into the Red River. A second strike on 25 October put the repaired bridge out of action again and two final air strikes in November were so successful that the bridge was closed to rail traffic until April 1968. At that time bombing was restricted to the area between the demilitarized zone and the 19th parallel and no further attacks were possible.

When air attacks on North Vietnam resumed in the spring of 1972, the 'Thud' had been replaced by the F-4 Phantom in the fighter-bomber role. However, the two-seat Wild Weasel version, which was specially equipped to locate and attack surface-to-air missile sites, remained in service. The first modified F-105Fs, fitted with radar warning and homing receivers and anti-radiation missiles, reached Thailand in 1966 and by 1972 the F-105G, fully modified for the Wild Weasel mission, was in combat. F-105Gs remained in frontline service with the USAF, equipping the 35th TFW at George AFB California, until July 1980. Their retirement marked the end of the Thunderchief's career with the active duty units, but squadrons of the Air Force Reserve and Air National Guard continued to operate F-105Bs and F-105Ds until 1984, when the Reserve's 466th Tactical Fighter Squadron at Hill AFB, Utah, converted onto the F-16 Fighting Falcon.

Republic F-105D Thunderchief

Type Single-seat tactical strike aircraft
Dimensions Span 10.66m (34ft 11 in); length 20.43m (67ft); height 6.01m (19ft 8in)
Weight Empty 12,710kg (28,000lb); maximum take-off 23,855kg (52,550lb)
Powerplant One 11,125kg (24,500lb) thrust Pratt & Whitney J75-P-19 turbojet with afterburner

Performance Maximum speed at 11,000m (36,000ft) Mach 2.1, or 2235km/h (1390 mph); maximum speed at sea level Mach 1.1, or 1375km/h (855 mph)
Range Tactical radius with warload of sixteen 750lb bombs 370km (230 miles); ferry range 3860km (2400 miles)
Ceiling 15,250m (50,000ft)

Armament One 20mm M61 cannon with 1029 rounds of ammunition, plus up to 5450kg (12,000lb) of ordnance, including iron bombs, rocket pods, AGM-12 Bullpup ASMs and AIM-9 Sidewinder AAMs for self-defence

Above: The Thunderchief was originally intended to serve in the low-level nuclear strike role but its versatile stores-carrying ability, demonstrated here, enabled it to fulfil conventional bombing duties during the Vietnam War.

Below: Two F-105s of the New Jersey Air National Guard, towards the end of their careers. Over 800 Thunderchiefs were produced by Republic Aviation between 1954 and 1964.

Reagan's rebels

Nicaragua's Sandinistas face a US-backed insurgency

In July 1979, the overthrow of the dictator Anastasio Somoza Debayle brought to power the Frente Sandinista de Liberación Nacional (FSLN) in Nicaragua, after a prolonged civil war which left 50,000 dead. The end of the conflict was not to bring peace to Nicaragua for long, however, and the country was soon to be the focus of intense pressure from the United States raising fears of a full-scale invasion.

American hostility to the new Sandinista regime was not simply based on a general rejection of the legitimacy of left-wing governments in Central America, but also specifically on a perception of Nicaragua's role in the troubled military and political scene of the whole region. The United States repeatedly claimed that Nicaragua, along with Cuba and at the prompting of the Soviet Union, was playing a major role in arming and supplying guerrilla groups in neighbouring El Salvador and intended to export its revolution to Honduras and Guatemala. During the Sandinista war against Somoza, the administration of President Jimmy Carter, preoccupied with the human-rights situation in Latin America and fearful of the long-term consequences if narrowly-based and reactionary dictatorships were allowed to proliferate in the region, had adopted a lukewarm attitude to the Somoza regime, while seeking to head off a Sandinista victory and promote an acceptable alternative. Even after the Sandinistas came to

power, the US government continued to make small amounts of aid available to the new regime during 1979 and 1980. As Carter's bid for re-election approached, however, and the Iran hostage crisis directed the spotlight to his alleged weakness over foreign affairs, a harder line began to emerge, to be taken up with greater force by the incoming administration of President Ronald Reagan from January 1981.

Yet the evidence of Nicaraguan arms supplies to Salvadorean guerrillas has generally been speculative or non-existent. As late as September 1980, the Carter administration certified that there was no evidence to suggest that Nicaragua was arming the rebel forces in El Salvador. For the next six months, with both the Nicaraguans and the rebels in El Salvador fearing the possible consequences of a Reagan victory, there were persistent reports that both Cuba and Nicaragua were supplying arms to the rebels as they sought to organise a 'final offensive' that would bring them to power before Reagan could take office. However, no concrete evidence was ever presented, and a White Paper issued by the State Department in February 1981 and claiming to present hard evidence of arms shipments was revealed later the same year to have been largely fabricated by middle-ranking intelligence officers. Whatever the truth regarding flows of arms in that short period, the

Above: A guerrilla patrol of Eden Pastora's wing of ARDE, the Costa Rica-based Contra group, armed with AK assault rifles and US-manufactured M79 grenade launchers, moves carefully through the Nicaraguan jungle. Pastora's men lost US backing in 1984, when they refused to unite with the Honduran-based Contras, the FDN. Neither FDN nor ARDE guerrillas were capable of occupying Nicaraguan territory for any length of time.

United States since 1981 has mounted an extensive and sophisticated arms interdiction programme in El Salvador itself, along the Honduran border between Nicaragua and El Salvador, and in the Gulf of Fonseca, as well as in the Caribbean Sea off Nicaragua's northern coast. US-directed border patrols watch permanently for overland deliveries, the US 224th Military Intelligence Battalion, based at the recently extended Palmerola air base in Honduras, has operated OV-1 Mohawk reconnaissance aircraft over El Salvador 24 hours a day, and further reconnaissance work is undertaken by C-130 planes from the US Southern Command headquarters in Panama. In addition, listening ships and launches patrol the seas, while permanent radar stations operate from Tiger Island, in the Gulf of Fonseca, and from Cerro La Mole in Honduras. Despite this intensive activity, no arms shipments have been traced. A former CIA analyst, David Macmichael, stated in 1984 that all evidence of arms flows disappeared in the spring of 1981.

Nonetheless, US military pressure on Nicaragua mounted after 1980. This was partly through a general increase in the US military presence in the region – chiefly in Honduras. For direct attacks on Nicaragua during this period, however, the United States depended upon Nicaraguan opponents of the Sandinista regime, known as the Contras (*contra-revolucionarios* or counter-revolutionaries), based in camps in Honduras and Costa Rica. Small groups of Contras had begun to assemble in Honduras immediately after the fall of Somoza, consisting in the main of fleeing National Guardsmen, the ex-dictator's chief supporters; others of Somoza's men set up camp in Florida and in Guatemala. As the political situation in Nicaragua deteriorated, however, they

were joined by other groups of exiles, offering the Americans a potential insurgent force with real credibility.

During the 1970s in Nicaragua the struggle against Somoza had come to involve representatives of practically every social and economic group in the country, uniting people of widely differing interests and political attitudes, and victory in the revolutionary war had invested the Sandinista guerrilla leaders with almost unchallenged authority and popularity. Inevitably, however, after the victory differences between the component parts of the anti-Somoza coalition had tended to re-emerge. On taking power, the Sandinista leaders promised elections within five years, but in a country with no tradition of democratic rule, and with the previous administration in a state of total collapse, power was held initially by a nine-member junta (reduced to three in 1981) and a

Stars and Stripes over Honduras

The 1980s have seen a mounting US military presence in Honduras. Strategically located between Nicaragua and war-torn El Salvador, Honduras has a competent air force in regional terms, equipped with reconditioned Israeli Super Mystères and a number of A-37 Dragonfly bombers, but its army has been traditionally regarded as ineffective. Since 1980, though, this situation has been transformed. US Special Forces Mobile Training teams have been active in the country since then, the army has been reorganised, hundreds of US advisers have entered the country, and US military aid has risen steeply. Training has been extended, and a massive programme of infrastructural development has seen substantial work since 1982 on the Palmerola, Golosón and La Mesa airfields, and a string of landing strips down the Nicaraguan border, notably the new base at Durzana, 40km (25 miles) within Honduras, equipped to handle the heaviest of aircraft. These facilities later served to support a series of large-scale semi-permanent US exercises in the area, notably Big Pine I in the spring of 1983 and Big Pine II in the summer of the same year, deploying 1600 and 5500 US troops respectively, and the 1984 Granadero I manoeuvres, which brought Salvadorean and Honduran troops together. However, the hostility that still exists between these two neighbouring states (who fought a brief border war in 1969) was one factor in growing Honduran disenchantment; this was particularly directed at the priority given to training Salvadorean officers and men at the Regional Military Training Centre in Honduras from mid-1983. The replacement of General Gustavo Alvarez as Honduran army commander-in-chief by the more nationalistic General Walter Lopez early in 1984 led to a refusal to accept further Salvadorean troops for training, and threatened the increasingly close relationship between the United States and Honduras. Indeed, it has been suggested that the scale of the US presence could destabilise the Honduran regime, creating new problems for the Americans.

Left: Daniel Ortega (left), coordinator of the ruling Sandinista junta, in discussion with Eden Pastora at a rally in the Nicaraguan capital, Managua, in May 1981. By early 1983, Pastora was leading anti-Sandinista ARDE guerrillas.
Below: Sandinista militiamen check the wreckage of a US-built helicopter, shot down during a Contra operation over Nicaraguan territory.
Bottom: A column of Sandinista troops, equipped with Soviet BTR-60 APCs, on border patrol.

co-opted council of state, drawing primarily on the mass organisations developed by the Sandinistas during the course of the civil war.

The new regime was dominated by 'moderate' Marxist elements led by Daniel Ortega who prevailed over the more radical groups associated with guerrilla veteran and minister of the interior, Tomás Borge. The result was a commitment to a mixed economy, combining private and state ownership, and political pluralism – the acceptance of the existence of parties and newspapers representing a wide range of political viewpoints. At the same time, the leadership was unwavering in its commitment to an eventual socialist society in Nicaragua, and this inevitably alienated businessmen and other middle-class elements who had initially supported or participated in the Sandinista government. By 1982 the regime was in conflict with the country's leading newspaper, *La Prensa*, which was not banned but was subjected to censorship, and arrests of some political opponents had sown distrust. There was also a serious conflict with the Indian population of Nicaragua's Atlantic coast – the Miskito, Sumo and Rama – who resented the regime's efforts towards integration. The regime found itself in a vicious circle, as its efforts to cope with the growing security crisis – in March 1982 a state of emergency was introduced, curtailing political rights – increased opposition. The expansion of the army, the Ejército Sandinista Popular (ESP), and of local militias to meet the Contra threat put a strain on the economy, already damaged by the effects of the civil war and by financial pressure from the United States. Although the Sandinistas still commanded the support of the majority of the population, the threat to their continued rule was serious.

American covert financial aid and military training for the Contras was under way at least by 1981 and the first serious attacks on economic targets in Nicaragua began in March 1982. As the Contras grew in numbers, however, their internal politics became complex and divisive. The original National Guardsmen were joined in exile by a considerable number of Indians (notably Miskito), conservatives representing the Nicaraguan business classes, and former Sandinistas disillusioned with the regime. Even these groups were divided amongst themselves, the Indians for example splitting into outright opponents of the regime led by Steadman Fagoth and a more conciliatory group led by Brooklyn Rivera.

In general, the Sandinistas' hardline right-wing opponents gathered in Honduras, where they formed the Fuerzas Democráticas Nicaraguenses (FDN), still closely associated with Somoza's National Guard and led by a former National Guard officer, Colonel Enrique Bermudez. Those Contras who rejected association with the former dictatorship established themselves in Costa Rica, on Nicaragua's southern border, forming the Alianza Revolucionaria Democrática (ARDE). Prominent among the leaders of ARDE were the famed former Sandinista guerrilla leader Eden Pastora – 'Commandante Zero' – and businessman Alfonso Robelo who had participated in the first Sandinista administration after Somoza's overthrow. Brooklyn Rivera's Indian followers associated themselves with ARDE, while Steadman Fagoth's Miskitos allied themselves with the FDN. The Americans worked hard to unite the FDN and the ARDE, but there was an obvious gap between those who sought a liberalised version of the Sandinista revolution and those inspired by a nostalgia for Somoza's regime.

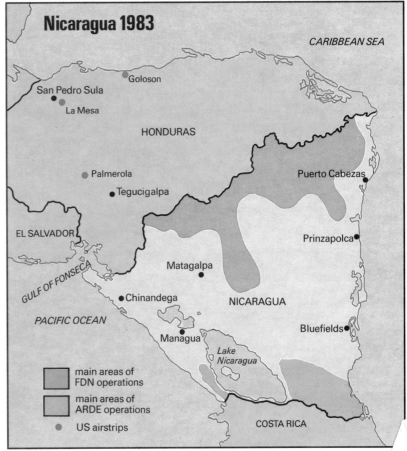

Nicaragua 1983

CARIBBEAN SEA

Goloson

San Pedro Sula

La Mesa

HONDURAS

Palmerola

Tegucigalpa

Puerto Cabezas

EL SALVADOR

Prinzapolca

GULF OF FONSECA

Matagalpa

Chinandega

NICARAGUA

PACIFIC OCEAN

Bluefields

Managua

Lake Nicaragua

COSTA RICA

main areas of FDN operations

main areas of ARDE operations

US airstrips

In 1982 most military activity involved small-scale incursions by FDN forces into northern Nicaragua, inflicting considerable loss of life and economic damage. ARDE began similar operations in the south in April 1983. In most areas the Nicaraguan Army could count on the support of the local population and their militias in opposing these incursions, but on the predominantly Indian Atlantic coast they carried out counter-insurgency operations against the local people, forcibly relocating the Indians away from the border zones.

Through 1983, military pressure on the Sandinista government mounted. US covert aid to the insurgents was running at around $20 million a year and some 150 CIA operatives were reckoned to be involved in support of the Contras. Almost throughout the year US forces carried out military exercises in Honduras within miles of the Nicaraguan border, and the US Navy cruised just off the country's Pacific and Atlantic coasts. US spy-planes and radio-interceptors provided the Contras with detailed intelligence on their enemy, and Honduran-based aircraft dropped supplies and ammunition to insurgents inside Nicaragua.

The Contras and the CIA

One effect of CIA support for the Contras was to reverse the usual balance of insurgency and counter-insurgency, in that it was the insurgents who had access to the higher level of equipment. In September 1983, for example, ARDE sent two light aircraft to carry out a rocket attack on Managua airport and in February 1984 an A-37 and five helicopters attacked northern Nicaragua from Honduras. Air attacks and seaborne commando raids – presumably launched from American vessels offshore – devastated oil storage facilities, forcing the Nicaraguan government to introduce petrol rationing in October 1983.

Despite the Contras' apparent ability to strike at will from the air or the sea, however, they needed a decisive victory on land, and this they could not achieve. Between August 1983 and January 1984 the FDN and ARDE launched a number of major offensives involving up to 10,000 troops, but they were repelled by the Nicaraguan Army – expanded to number almost 50,000 – aided in part by local militias. Neither Contra group proved capable of holding any amount of territory for any length of time, although with US support they could continue to mount attacks and inflict losses almost indefinitely.

In 1984, however, the US programme of support for the Contras suffered severe set-backs. At least from March 1984 – and possibly earlier – the Contras had been mining Nicaraguan ports under the direction of US advisers; vessels damaged by the mines included a Soviet oil tanker. The revelation that the mining had taken place from a CIA 'mother-ship' caused an uproar in the United States and led to a judgement against the US government in the International Court in the Hague. A number of further reverses worsened the US position, including the death on a flying mission over Nicaragua of two members of the elite Special Forces Unit of the Alabama National Guard in September, reviving persistent rumours of direct involvement of US citizens and soldiers in battle alongside the Contras, and the publication in October of a CIA operational manual 'Psychological Operations in Guerrilla War', which among other things advocated selective

Left: A US instructor at a Contra training camp in Florida takes a break during target practice. Backing for the Contras by the Reagan administration was a source of controversy in the United States, and in June 1984, Congress blocked funds for the anti-Sandinista rebels.

Below: FDN Contras, many of whom were former Somoza National Guardsmen, in a remote village on the border between Honduras and Nicaragua in December 1983. By early 1985, the massive Contra and US military presence in Honduras was threatening to destabilise one of Washington's most important allies in the region. Below right: Over 1.5 million gallons of diesel oil, vital to the Nicaraguan economy, goes up in smoke following a CIA-backed Contra sabotage attack on the port of Corinto. The city's 23,000 civilian inhabitants were evacuated in late 1983 on the order of the Sandinista junta.

assassination as a destabilising tactic. In June 1984 Congress voted to cut off funds for Nicaraguan operations, blocking President Reagan's request for a further $21 million.

Meanwhile, the Sandinista government had taken its own measures to defuse the situation. In the wake of the US invasion of Grenada in October 1983, fears of a direct US military intervention were acute. To avoid giving the Americans any pretext to act, most Cuban advisers were asked to leave Nicaragua. In December the Sandinista government announced its acceptance of the Contadora peace proposals advocated by Colombia, Mexico, Panama and Venezuela – and initially welcomed by the United States. The essence of the Contadora plan was the removal of all foreign intervention in Central America, but the peace process also required the Sandinistas to hold democratic elections. They agreed to phase out the state of emergency through 1984, permitting free political activity for opposition parties, in preparation for elections in November.

The United States professed itself totally dissatisfied with the Nicaraguan position, and military pressure was unrelenting. Both ARDE and the FDN launched offensives in April 1984, and US manoeuvres in the region continued. Continuing efforts to unite the Contra groups led to a split in the ARDE, as Pastora remained adamantly opposed to any alliance with the ex-National Guardsmen of the FDN and rejected the control of the Contra operations by US advisers. On 30 May, Pastora narrowly escaped death in a bomb attack during a press conference, presumably motivated by his independent stance. Reportedly US supplies to Pastora's group were cut off, contributing to set-backs for the Contra forces in the south during June and July, when the Nicaraguan Army effectively drove them out of the country. Robelo's ARDE group did agree to unite

with the FDN, however.

On 4 November the elections were held in Nicaragua. Despite a boycott by some opposition parties, they were recognised as free and fair by a wide range of experienced foreign observers – although dismissed as a 'farce' by the United States. The Sandinistas gained some 63 per cent of all votes cast, confirming both their ascendancy in the country and the fundamental pluralism of the political system. Two days later, in the midst of the presidential elections in the United States, rumours inspired by the Pentagon suggested that the Soviet cargo ship *Bakuriani*, nearing Nicaragua, was carrying MiG fighters for the Nicaraguan Air Force. While President Reagan let it be known that such an escalation of armed capability in the region would not be tolerated, the Nicaraguan authorities hastily mobilised the population against the threat of a US invasion. The rumours regarding the MiGs were interpreted by the Sandinistas as attempting to create a pretext for intervention by US troops in Nicaragua in the 'honeymoon' period following Reagan's expected re-election. The Nicaraguan government appealed to the United Nations to denounce a possible US invasion.

Fighters or gunships?

In the event, nothing happened. The supposed cargo of MiGs turned out to be Mil Mi-24 Hind helicopter gunships, appropriate to the Sandinistas' counter-insurgency needs. The US administration nonetheless continued to refer to the regional threat posed by the Nicaraguan armed forces, although expert military analysts argue that Nicaragua's offensive power is extremely limited, with its air force virtually non-existent (a couple of vintage Lockheed T-33s) and its Soviet T-55 tanks ill-equipped to tackle the conditions that any strike into Honduras would entail. The arrival of the Hind helicopters and the planned acquisition of Czechoslovakian L-39 Albatross subsonic jet trainers should redress the balance of airpower against the previously superior Contra air forces, but will not constitute a credible offensive threat to Nicaragua's neighbours.

By the end of 1984, it seemed clear that the Contras could not hope to command enough support in Nicaragua to overthrow the Sandinistas, although with continued backing from such sources as Argentina, Israel, Taiwan and Guatemala, they could continue to operate after the Congressional halt to US funding. Conciliatory gestures and offers of amnesty from the Sandinista government were likely to draw a number of Contras out of armed opposition – Brooklyn Rivera and his Indian supporters were keen on a truce, for example – but the Contras would continue to inflict considerable damage for the foreseeable future.

Despite the activity of the Contras, however, the greatest threat to Nicaragua's security remained a direct US intervention. This would come from a rapid deployment of forces based in the United States itself, drawn from such sources as the 18th Airborne Corps at Fort Bragg and the 28th Marine Amphibious Unit at Camp Lejune, North Carolina (each involved in manoeuvres in Honduras in 1984), and aircraft carriers in the Caribbean. For its defence, Nicaragua would rely on its ability to put the greater part of its adult population under arms, and to wage an interminable war in the countryside after the forced evacuation of Managua. **Paul Cammack**

Crisis in the Caribbean

The United States invades Grenada

On 13 March 1979, some 40 activists of the New Jewel Movement (NJM), armed only with a handful of rifles, shotguns and pistols, took control of the True Blue barracks of the Grenadan Defence Force. There was little concerted resistance by forces loyal to the island's prime minister, Eric Gairy, and soon NJM supporters were taking over police stations throughout Grenada, seizing weapons and arresting members of the security forces and of Gairy's private army, the Mongoose Gang, with which he had harassed and persecuted political opponents. Radio Grenada was captured by Hudson Austin, an NJM leader, armed only with a gas pistol.

Gairy had been the dominant political figure in Grenada for 30 years, and he had enjoyed almost total control of the island since February 1974, when Grenada had achieved total independence after some two centuries as a British colony. Remaining within the British Commonwealth, Grenada retained Queen Elizabeth as its head of state, represented on the island by a British-appointed governor-general, but Gairy's power was in effect nearly absolute. Realising that British influence in the region was being replaced by that of the United States, Gairy sought to establish close relations with Washington, and proclaimed his staunch anti-communism.

By the late 1970s, however, the growing authoritarianism of the Gairy regime was leading many members of the civil service and security forces to question the legitimacy of his rule. The opposition NJM was able to establish useful contacts with some of these disenchanted government employees, and from sympathisers within the security forces it was able to receive a number of weapons and some rudimentary military training. It was also from these

contacts that the NJM learned on 10 March 1979 that Gairy planned to liquidate the NJM leadership in a desperate attempt to hang on to power.

Using the opportunity of a visit by Gairy to the United Nations in New York, the NJM launched the coup of 13 March, and established a new NJM-dominated regime under a People's Revolutionary Government (PRG). Maurice Bishop was the new prime minister and Bernard Coard his deputy and minister of finance, while Hudson Austin became a general in command of a new People's Revolutionary Army (PRA).

Promising a wide-ranging programme of reform, the NJM benefited from the widespread disillusionment with the years of Gairy's rule. Measures were introduced to improve social benefits and education, and stress was laid upon consultation with the people through local assemblies. But there were no plans for free elections, and several opponents of the new regime were arrested and imprisoned. The left-wing character of the NJM and its establishment of diplomatic relations with Cuba on 14 April 1979 immediately provoked the hostility of the United States, which sought to undermine the revolutionary regime in Grenada by a policy of economic blockade. US efforts to block economic assistance to Grenada through the International Monetary Fund (IMF) and World Bank were not entirely successful, since guided by Coard, the PRG was scrupulously careful to honour the provisions of all its loans.

Coard's programme of economic reconstruction was remarkably moderate, concentrating on the key sectors of tourism and agriculture. One of the most important measures taken to boost both of these was a project for the construction of a new civil airport at

Below: Prime Minister Maurice Bishop. Both charismatic and popular, Bishop played a key role in maintaining a close link between the government and the ordinary people.

Point Salines, near the capital, St George's. Intended to replace the existing small civil airport at Pearls, Point Salines was to have a 2750m (9000-foot) runway, capable of taking long and medium-haul jets night and day from Europe and North America. The project was partly financed by the IMF and the EEC, and planning was in the hands of the British company, Plessey Airports Limited, while Cuba provided the construction workers to build the new airport.

An 'unsafe destination'

With the inauguration of Ronald Reagan as US president in January 1981, pressure on Grenada increased dramatically; the country was denounced as a centre of Soviet and Cuban influence in the Caribbean, as well as a base for the export of revolution and terrorism. The US State Department advised American tourists that Grenada was an 'unsafe destination', and tourism dropped by some 10 per cent. More seriously, Washington accused Grenada of building a military airfield at Point Salines, which it claimed would be available to Cuban and Soviet military aircraft. This was denied by the Grenadan government, the EEC and Plessey, which pointed out that the airport would lack many attributes vital to any modern military airbase, including such basics as radar, anti-aircraft defences and engineering repair facilities. Grenada accused the United States of preparing an invasion of the island, and its fears were strengthened by a number of US military exercises in the area, including a mock invasion, during a larger manoeuvre called Ocean

Venture '81 in August 1981, of an island code-named Amber and the Amberines – the official title of Grenada is Grenada and the Grenadines, and Amber is a place near Point Salines. In the face of this apparent threat, the government laid great emphasis upon building up the island's defences, and formed a part-time militia, which was trained by Cuban military advisers.

By 1983, however, the unity of the NJM had already begun to disintegrate from within. While Bishop retained his popularity with the people of Grenada, Coard and his group of Marxist supporters seemed intent upon pushing the revolution towards a dogmatic application of the historical lessons which Coard had deduced from his study of the Soviet and Cuban revolutions. In October 1982, Coard had resigned from the NJM leadership on the grounds of overwork, but he retained and increased his influence within the party.

In June 1983, Bishop undertook a visit to Washington in order to improve relations with the United States and avert the danger of US military intervention. President Reagan refused to meet him, and his discussions were confined to the State Department, but on his return he found that he faced bitter criticism from within the NJM. He had failed to seek authorisation or backing for his attempt at diplomacy, and Coard and his supporters suspected that he was prepared to reach a compromise with Washington which would lead to an abandonment of their radical goals. In July, there was a call for a discussion of the party's leadership – an implicit criticism of Bishop – and at a meeting of the NJM

Bishop and Coard

In 1970, 26-year-old barrister Maurice Bishop arrived back in Grenada after several years of study and work in Great Britain, to find the Gairy regime very much not to his taste. Bishop had been heavily influenced by radical and left-wing ideas, and in particular by the example of the leaders of the American civil rights movement, Martin Luther King and Malcolm X, and the African socialism of Tanzanian leader Julius Nyerere. His return to Grenada came shortly after an unsuccessful Black Power revolt by army rebels on the nearby Caribbean island of Trinidad, and he took a prominent part in a demonstration in their support.

But it was a demonstration organised shortly afterwards by a group of striking nurses, which was broken up with over 30 arrests by Gairy's police, that led to Bishop's name becoming a household word in Grenada. Bishop helped defend the nurses during a long court-case, which received publicity throughout the Caribbean, and ended after seven months with the acquittal of all the accused.

Bishop became involved with a small group of opponents of the Gairy regime, and in 1973 helped found the New Jewel Movement (NJM). The new party began to establish itself by campaigning actively on the issues of unemployment, welfare and civil liberties, but came under growing pressure from the Gairy regime. On 18 November 1973, Gairy's Mongoose Gang beat and seriously injured

six leading members of the NJM, including Bishop. This incident, which became known as Bloody Sunday in Grenada, provoked an outbreak of angry protests and a three-month general strike during which Bishop's father, Rupert Bishop, was shot by police.

Bernard Coard did not come to public attention until 1976, when he was elected to the Grenadan Assembly alongside Bishop. He had recently returned to the country after studying economics in Britain and the United States. Coard was a close friend of Bishop, but the two were in many ways quite different. While Bishop was gregarious, attractive and popular, and a man whose great strength was his intuitive grasp of political realities, Coard was more remote, and moved by ideas rather than passions. He had been deeply affected by his studies of Marxism-Leninism, and on his return to Grenada sought to spread his ideas in the NJM through a study and discussion group which he founded, known as the Organisation for Education and Liberation. This group played an important part in helping to transform the NJM during the late 1970s from little more than a loosely organised campaign into a more formally structured and disciplined party.

During the early years after the NJM's seizure of power in 1979 the contrasting qualities of the two men were a source of strength to the regime, but eventually the division between Bishop's popular appeal and political realism on the one hand and Coard's control of party organisation and ideology on the other was to destroy the regime.

central committee on 14-16 September, Coard's supporters proposed that the party adopt a dual leadership, to be divided between Bishop and Coard. On 25 September, the joint leadership proposal was overwhelmingly endorsed at a meeting of NJM members.

Although Coard commanded a majority within the NJM, however, Bishop was still enormously popular with the people of Grenada. He also enjoyed close relations with the Cuban government of Fidel Castro, whose support he attempted to win during a stop-over in Havana at the end of a two-week tour of Eastern Europe in early October. Though Bishop was received with great warmth in Cuba, there was no formal reception when he arrived home in Grenada, and on 12 October a meeting of the PRA criticised what it described as 'right opportunism', in what was a thinly-disguised attack on Bishop.

Later in the same day, Bishop's security guards were withdrawn from his home by the central committee, and on 13 October he was placed under house arrest and expelled from the NJM. News of his arrest spread quickly, and provoked first disbelief and then hostility towards the new leadership. Increasingly unpopular and isolated, Coard was forced to rely on Austin's PRA, as even the militia was now suspect.

On the morning of 19 October, a large crowd gathered in St George's Market Square to show their support for Bishop, and groups of demonstrators began to move up the hill to the house on Mount Royal where Bishop was under detention. The entrance to the house was guarded by soldiers with armoured cars, but a small group managed to enter from the rear and release Bishop, who emerged confused and in apparently poor physical condition. Moving back into the centre of St George's, Bishop and his supporters made for Fort Rupert (named after Bishop's dead father), where they began to distribute arms and organise resistance. In the midst of this activity, however, three PRA armoured cars and a truck-load of troops roared into the fort's outer courtyard, firing at the crowd which broke up in terror, with many throwing themselves over a high wall to escape.

Bishop was appalled, and quickly ordered his few armed supporters to surrender. The last words he was

heard to say were 'Oh God, Oh God. They have turned their guns against the masses.' Most of Bishop's supporters were allowed to escape, but he and his closest associates were taken under guard into the main courtyard of the fort. Soon afterwards bursts of machine-gun fire were heard from the fort, and it was later established that Bishop and six others had simply been lined up and shot.

These tragic events broke the final link between the NJM and the Grenadan people, and though the formation of a Revolutionary Military Council (RMC) under General Austin was announced, it remained without support. Criticism also came from

Above: Marines regroup after landing from a Chinook helicopter near the Grenadan capital, St George's. Left: A US Marine, armed with an M-16 with grenade-launcher attachment, and with an M72A2 LAW rocket-launcher slung on his back, checks out a street in St George's before moving forward. The US forces encountered unexpectedly heavy resistance during their invasion, both from the Grenadan army and militia, and from Cuban construction workers. Right: American paratroopers raising the flag on Grenada.

abroad, both from friends and enemies. The United States made clear its unease over the latest events, but Bishop's murder was also condemned by Fidel Castro, who only days earlier had welcomed him at Havana airport. The Caribbean Community imposed severe economic sanctions on Grenada, which many thought would lead to the collapse of the new regime, while on 21 October, the Organisation of Eastern Caribbean States, meeting without Grenada, voted to call for US military intervention. The following day, Dominican Prime Minister Eugenia Charles telephoned Grenadan Governor-General Sir Paul Scoon; she informed him of the proposed US military intervention, but later argued that the proposal for such an operation had originated with Scoon himself.

The Reagan administration was eager to eradicate what it saw as a nest of communists and terrorists in its own backyard, while the presence of several hundred US medical students on Grenada at St George's University Medical School provoked fears of a new hostage crisis. The news that 239 US Marines had been killed by a terrorist explosion in Beirut on 23 October undoubtedly strengthened the US resolve to intervene against 'terrorism' in the Caribbean, and ships already underway for Lebanon were diverted to take part in the invasion of Grenada.

The RMC was aware of preparations for an invasion, and appealed to Cuba for military assistance. Cuba, however, was profoundly shocked by the killing of Bishop, and refused to become entangled in an imminent confrontation with the United States on behalf of a regime which it now evidently regarded as being run by criminals. Havana ordered its personnel on Grenada only to become involved in any fighting if they themselves came under attack, but sent a senior army officer, Colonel Pedro Tortolo Comas, to brief them and prepare them for an invasion.

The force which was gathered to invade Grenada contained a small element from the six Caribbean islands – Jamaica, Antigua, St Lucia, Dominica, St Vincent and Barbados – which had called for US intervention. This contingent totalled a mere 300 soldiers and policemen and took no part in any fighting, being given the task of accompanying US

military patrols once order had been restored and of supervising the detention of suspects. By far the most important element of the invasion force was provided by the United States, which assembled a naval task force of 15 vessels, including the aircraft carrier USS *Independence* and amphibious assault ship *Guam*. As well as A-6 Intruder and A-7 Corsair aircraft flying from the *Independence*, the invasion force was able to call on air support from US aircraft operating from nearby Barbados, including the awesome firepower of AC-130 Hercules gunships, each armed with four 20mm guns and four 7.62mm Miniguns.

Operation Urgent Fury

The invasion, code-named Operation Urgent Fury, began at around 0530 hours on 25 October, with 400 men of the 22nd Marine Amphibious Unit (MAU) landing by helicopter from the USS *Guam* at Pearls airport on the eastern side of Grenada. They encountered little resistance, and having secured the airfield for the operation of US aircraft, the *Guam* re-embarked 200 of the Marines and steamed around the northern tip of the island towards the capital, St George's.

Almost simultaneously with the assault on Pearls, a force of some 500 US Army Rangers attempted to drop by parachute on the airfield construction site at Point Salines. Heavy groundfire forced two of the transport aircraft to circle high above the airfield, where an intense firefight had broken out between the advance party of Rangers on one side and troops of the PRA and a large number of Cuban construction workers on the other. The Rangers had to call in fire-support from AC-130s before the remainder of their group could land. The American troops later reported that they had been fired on while parachuting in, and that they had come immediately under heavy attack from the Cubans, who were described by Major James Holt, commander of the 82nd Airborne Division, as 'much tougher than expected: they were professionals.' Cuba later denied this, and it soon became apparent that the vast majority of the Cubans on Grenada were construction workers who had merely received some military training in the Cuban militia, and who had been hastily armed when

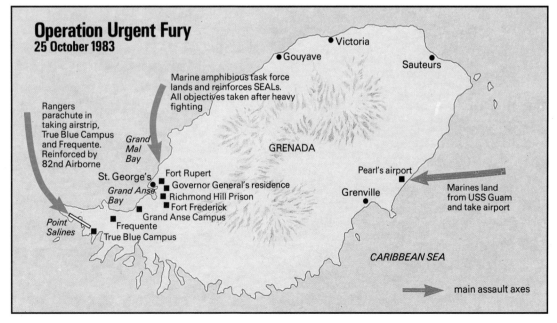

Operation Urgent Fury
25 October 1983

Marine amphibious task force lands and reinforces SEALs. All objectives taken after heavy fighting

Rangers parachute in taking airstrip, True Blue Campus and Frequente. Reinforced by 82nd Airborne

Grand Mal Bay

Victoria

Gouyave

Sauteurs

GRENADA

Pearl's airport

Grenville

Marines land from USS Guam and take airport

Fort Rupert
Governor General's residence
St. George's
Richmond Hill Prison
Grand Anse Bay
Fort Frederick
Grand Anse Campus
Point Salines
Frequente
True Blue Campus

CARIBBEAN SEA

→ main assault axes

a US intervention became certain.

The second wave of US troops to land at Point Salines were 750 paratroopers of the 82nd Airborne Division, flying in direct from their base at Fort Bragg, North Carolina. They too dropped into heavy fire, this time from a number of armoured cars which had arrived at the airport perimeter. The Americans were surprised by the determination of the resistance which they encountered, and called in airstrikes by Intruders and Corsairs to allow them to secure the airstrip which was vital to their plans. Meanwhile, near St George's on the west of the island, an 11-man navy SEAL (Sea, Air and Land) team was pinned down by heavy fire from a PRA armoured car at the governor-general's residence. Their mission had been to land on the coast under cover of darkness and secure Scoon so that he could be lifted out to safety. Scoon's authority was thought to be vital in order to legitimate the US military operation, but it was not until almost 24 hours later that resistance around his home was eliminated and he could be taken by helicopter to the *Guam*.

The SEAL team was relieved by Marines of the 22nd MAU who had landed from the *Guam* just north of St George's at Grand Mal Bay at around 0400 hours on 26 October. Equipped with M60 tanks and Amtrac amphibious armoured personnel carriers, they took up positions around St George's while the Rangers and 82nd Airborne advanced from Point Salines. The troops moving in from the south had to overcome stiff opposition from PRA soldiers and teenage militia fighters, many of whom were women, and fierce fighting took place around Fort Frederick and Richmond Hill prison. As they moved forward, the Americans came across several survivors of the mental hospital, which had been destroyed with

Above: A tense scene during the invasion, as US troops arrest a suspected NJM supporter. Left: Policemen of the small Caribbean element of the invasion force escort Bernard Coard soon after his capture. It had been the conflict between Coard and Bishop, leading to the latter's arrest and death, which opened the way to outside intervention, and undermined the NJM regime's popular support.

some 30 casualties during a US air raid on the afternoon of 25 October.

Late on the afternoon of 26 October, American paratroopers launched an assault on the Grand Anse campus of the medical school, where those few American students who had not flown out by charter flight before the invasion were concentrated. Storming in from the sea, helicopter gunships and AC-130s blasted the surrounding area, destroying two hotels nearby and thoroughly frightening the students. Once the campus was secured, the students were flown out by Chinook helicopter to Point Salines, and from there to Barbados and Charleston in the United States by C-141 transports. The final stage of the invasion was the capture of St George's, which fell late on 26 October after a US airstrike had gutted Fort Rupert and routed its small garrison. The operation had cost the Americans 18 dead and 113 wounded; 24 Cubans and 16 Grenadans were killed in action, and a number of civilians also died.

The Cuban question

The US continued to claim that Cuban combat troops had been involved in the fighting, and that many of these, along with Grenadan troops loyal to the RMC had taken to the hills to continue a guerrilla war. It soon became clear, however, that only some 20 Cuban military personnel had been present on the island, most of whom were army instructors, and that all were accounted for, either dead, wounded or surrendered by 27 October. Cuba was asked to withdraw its diplomatic mission from Grenada, but it refused to do so until all of its nationals had been released and repatriated. This took place on 3 November, and the Cubans received a hero's welcome when they arrived home in Havana.

On Grenada, sporadic resistance was soon mopped up, and Coard and Austin were both arrested, as were many other NJM members and supporters. Scoon authorised the formation of an interim government, and although the bulk of the invasion force – which at its peak numbered 7355 men – was soon withdrawn, some 300 military police remained to maintain order, along with 150 Jamaican troops.

The US military victory, even though won by overwhelming force against slight opposition, was immensely popular in the United States, especially when it became clear that the US forces were largely welcomed by the local population. There was bitter criticism of the American action, however, from some of the Nato allies, concentrating not only on the violation of the sovereignty of an independent country in which the Americans had indulged, but also on the lack of prior consultation within the alliance. The British government was especially annoyed that a Commonwealth state had been invaded without Britain even being informed in advance. The Grenadan operation tended to confirm European fears that the Reagan administration was devoted to 'military adventurism'.

In Grenada, Sir Paul Scoon announced that free elections would be held within a year, and on 3 December 1984, a coalition led by the New National Party of Herbert Blaize won 14 of the 15 seats in the island's assembly, beating Gairy's party, which won only one seat and 36 per cent of the vote, and a group known as the Maurice Bishop Patriotic Movement, led by Kendrick Radix, which won no seats and received a mere five per cent of the votes cast. Ironically, work on the controversial Point Salines airport went ahead, but now under the aegis of the United States.   **J.S.Common**

Right: Fidel Castro (centre) and his brother Raul (left), Cuba's minister of defence, welcome Cuban casualties returning to Havana. Although described as 'professionals' by the Americans, the Cubans were almost all construction workers with basic military training. Below: American medical students, whose safety had been one of the reasons given for the intervention, prepare to fly home from Point Salines.

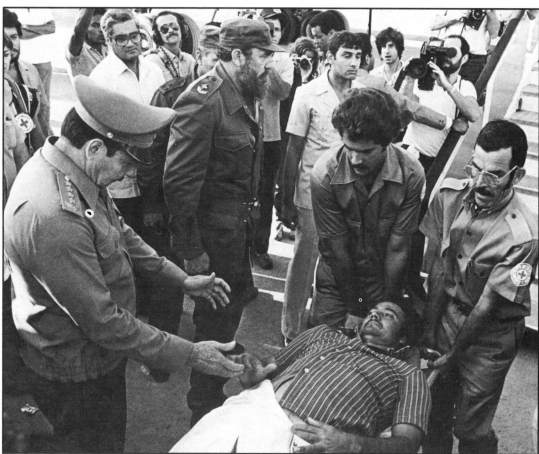

War and the media

The influence of press and television in modern conflicts

There has been little, if any, meeting of minds between war correspondents and the military hierarchy since the Crimean War, when the use by London newspapers of independent reporters to cover the battlefield situation may properly be said to have begun. Correspondents want to report as much as they can, as quickly as they can, about the progress of a war; the military usually seek to restrict such reporting, especially if it is unfavourable to them. During World War I, the British War Office did everything possible to hinder the activities of reporters on the Western Front, while during World War II, Prime Minister Winston Churchill complained frequently about what he regarded as over-zealous and possibly harmful reporting by the BBC and the press about the war and British government policy.

Hence there was little that was new in the often hostile relations between the British media and the Ministry of Defence during the Falklands War of 1982. There has always been – and presumably always will be – an immense gulf between the media's demands for instant and full access to information about the military campaigns they are covering and military insistence that such knowledge should be severely restricted to avoid disclosures to enemy intelligence. In general, control of the media has been much more successful during total wars like World War II than during the more limited wars after 1945. A common assumption about the righteousness of the Allied cause brought agreement between the media and the military and political elites; official censorship was augmented, and indeed often replaced, by self-censorship effected by reporters and news editors themselves. While the censorship imposed on the British media by the 1939 Emergency Powers Act was all-embracing (in Cairo reporters had to clear no less than six military and civilian censorship agencies before transmitting reports of the African campaigns to London), in practice the severe penalties that could be imposed were seldom employed. For the most part press, radio and newsreels in the United Kingdom, and in the United States after 1941, presented a favourable, and often glamourised, version of Allied land, sea and air efforts, minimising Allied losses (such as the heavy death-toll suffered by the Canadian contingent in the ill-fated Dieppe landing in 1942) and magnifying Axis losses (for instance, of aircraft during the Battle of Britain and of tanks during the Western Desert campaigns).

Such restraints – both formal and self-imposed – were much more difficult to enforce after 1945. Wars were confined to relatively small areas of the globe and where the Western powers were involved their existence was not threatened by military reverses. Life in the homeland was scarcely affected and the media felt free to comment on the conduct of the war,

untramelled by official censorship. Of course, for the small power ranged on the other side this did not hold true: North Korea and North Vietnam, for instance, knew that their very survival was at stake and both exercised the most efficient and severe control on the reporting of their side of the battle. In general, communist countries imposed almost total censorship, but such a degree of control could not be exercised in the Western democracies.

The Korean War (1950-53), while it often provided examples of sharp differences between the military and reporters on the spot, is perhaps not a good example of the extreme kind of hostility between media and the military which characterised other post-1945 wars. All the major US newspapers and radio networks gave support to the war effort and tended to refuse to publish material which reflected badly on the United Nations Command or its South Korean allies. At first UN commander General Douglas MacArthur refused to censor news material leaving Korea, preferring to rely on the self-restraint of the correspondents themselves in matters affecting military security. MacArthur did extend special privileges to those reporters who were sympathetic to his cause: as in all wars, correspondents were largely dependant on the military for transport, accommodation and food, and those who were critical of MacArthur tended to be denied such favours. However, in December 1950, after detailed reports of UN troop movements began to appear in the Western press, and when on-the-spot correspondents commented adversely on the behaviour of US troops during the retreat from the Yalu, MacArthur imposed a formal censorship on all press reports, radio broadcasts and film emanating from Korea, with fierce penalties (including deportation)

Above: A television camera-crew films Iraqi troops fresh from battle near the front line in the Gulf War with Iran. Television coverage of war has been an important factor in societies such as the United States, in which public opinion is crucially important.

imposed on transgressors. While this amounted to a general ban on any criticism of the UN conduct of the war, in practice it caused only temporary irritation, since by mid-1951 the war had reached a stalemate and public interest in the issue subsided.

The next major US involvement in armed conflict followed a rather different pattern. Both the media and public opinion became increasingly critical of the performance of US forces in South Vietnam and later began to question the merits of the entire enterprise. Television ownership, both in the United States and elsewhere in the West, had greatly expanded since the 1950s, and there was increasing evidence that people had now begun to rely more on this medium than on the newspaper press for news and information about current events. There was no formal censorship, although both Presidents Kennedy and Johnson pressed editors and proprietors, with mixed success, to be cautious about what they published. Although General Westmoreland, the US army commander in South Vietnam during 1964-68, did issue a set of 15 ground rules to guide war correspondents, the US military preferred to rely on persuasion and exhortation rather than actual control to get its message across. Free transport and comfortable accommodation were offered to journalists in the expectation that, in return, they would faithfully report the reassuring briefings that were handed out to them about the progress of the war against the Viet Cong.

However, the increasing number of correspondents who began to appear in South Vietnam could

Above: British pressmen prepare copy on the Falklands in 1982. Although often regarded as a nuisance by the military, journalists shared many of the dangers and hardships of the campaign.

Left: A US soldier stands idly by as a Viet Cong suspect is tortured. Photos like this had a profound effect in weakening American public support for the Vietnam War. Official briefings (below: President Johnson addresses newsmen on the prospects for peace in Vietnam) lost credibility in the face of aggressive war coverage by newsmen on the spot.

not all be handled in this way and many of them visited the various operational sectors, where they were able to see for themselves that the situation was not quite as rosy as it had been painted by base information officers. Reports about the mismanagement of the war and the incompetence of the South Vietnamese allies soon began to appear in the American press, reinforced by television film of the major engagements which brought the horrors of war directly into the homes of the American people. The Tet offensive of 1968, while a disaster for the Viet Cong, came as a great shock to an American public that had hitherto been given confident reports by American commanders that the Viet Cong were at their last gasp. Subsequently many American commanders and senior officers attempted to blame misrepresentation and biased reporting by the American media for their defeat. In fact the American public were already beginning to have serious doubts about the war in 1967 and it is likely that media coverage merely reinforced these doubts.

Nevertheless, the dangers of unrestrained and unrestricted reporting became a matter of faith to most American and Allied service personnel in the wake of the Vietnam War. The lesson was not lost on the British Ministry of Defence. Britain's experiences of conventional warfare since 1945 had been restricted (apart from a contingent in Korea) to the 1956 Suez expedition, but this was too short in duration and too inconclusive to provide any useful lessons on the control of the media. Most of Britain's campaigns after 1945 consisted of long drawn out counter-insurgency activities in Malaya, Kenya, and other colonial territories across the globe. The very longevity of these struggles, in areas remote from the immediate concerns of the British public, their low-key nature, and the dangers of reporting them, ensured little beyond sporadic media interest.

The Northern Ireland crisis after 1969 produced new problems in the control of sensitive military information. British press and broadcasting eventually imposed on itself a form of self-censorship, after some earlier reporting had aroused protests from the military and members of parliament. This system did not prove wholly satisfactory to the security forces, but the experience gained by the army in handling the press provided useful lessons for any similar future military situation.

The British public was seldom given much in the way of reliable or up-to-date information on the tactical progress of the Falklands War in 1982. Indeed, the Royal Navy, faithful to Winston Churchill's ruling in 1945 that 'a warship in action has no place for journalists', had not wanted to carry any war correspondents with the Task Force. It had relented to the extent of allowing a few British (but no foreign) correspondents, television journalists and radio reporters to be embarked only after vehement media protests. Relations between the correspondents and their naval hosts soon reached rock-bottom during the long and cramped sea voyage. Communications to London were restricted and dependent on naval channels; press reports were restricted in length and transmissions confined to the night time (which meant that they missed the next morning's editions); technical difficulties ensured that television film did not arrive in London until several days after an event had been filmed, which lessened its impact considerably. Once the Task Force had landed, restrictions on reporting and on communicating the reports to London were more onerous, often for justifiable military reasons.

Accurate speculation

The lack of hard news from the front prompted press and television editors to fill news space and air time with speculations about likely military developments, using for this purpose their established defence correspondents and a specially recruited team of retired service experts. This kind of activity enraged the Ministry of Defence, whose own contribution to the debate consisted of a daily and uninformative on-the-record press briefing, supplemented later by informal and non-attributable material that was equally uninformative. The ministry complained that speculation about likely military operations, such as an accurate guess on the BBC World Service on 27 May that the Parachute Regiment was about to attack Goose Green, played into the hands of Argentinian intelligence. Task Force commanders protested that the little information the ministry was providing was still too revealing and they frequently withheld information from London, such as the failure of Argentinian bombs to explode, for fear that leaks would alert the Argentinian military to their own shortcomings. The media in turn accused the Ministry of Defence of concealing information (such as the full extent of British losses) in various sea and land engagements and of misinformation and news manipulation, for instance in denying that any landings were contemplated at the very moment that they were taking place.

Some of these accusations were justified, but much of the hysteria which was generated on both sides – such as virulent attacks on the BBC's alleged lack of partiality for the British cause – was both excessive and unnecessary. The military options available to Task Force commanders were limited by the nature of the terrain, and could be guessed at quite accurately with the aid of a map by Argentinian

intelligence, without the assistance of British television. Many of the weapons systems used by the British forces, and commented on at home by military experts, had been offered for sale to the Argentinian armed forces, complete with specifications, during the previous decade. Very often, the Ministry of Defence itself had only a sketchy knowledge of what was going on in the Falklands and much, but by no means all, of its misinformation can be attributed to this ignorance, together with a fair amount of muddle and confusion. The ensuing fuss by the media prompted the House of Commons Defence Committee to investigate the relations between the Ministry of Defence and the media during the war, but the myth that the British authorities had established tight control over the media had by then gained widespread currency and was difficult to refute entirely.

When the United States invaded Grenada on 25 October 1983, controls imposed on the American media exceeded anything the British had been able to achieve during the Falklands War. Rumours about the prospective invasion were denied by White House Press Secretary Larry Speakes in good faith, as he had not been told by the president of the pending operation. No reporters were allowed on Grenada until 24 hours after the invasion – although a *Time* reporter managed to smuggle himself onto the island shortly before the landings – and it was another 24 hours before they were permitted to file any stories. On 27 October the US Navy was still chasing away private boats suspected of carrying journalists to the island and severe restrictions on those already on Grenada made accurate reporting impossible. Inevitably this led to a storm of media protest, and a subsequent official inquiry concluded that the media should in future be allowed access to similar conflicts 'to the maximum degree possible consistent with the security of the mission and the safety of the troops'. It remains to be seen what practical effect this recommendation will have. **Michael Dockrill**

Above: Rows of human skulls, allegedly belonging to some of the countless victims of Khmer Rouge atrocities in Kampuchea, laid out for the cameras of Western reporters by the Vietnamese after they overthrew the Khmer Rouge in 1979. All governments, including both communist regimes and liberal democracies, were conscious of the power of the media and sought to exploit it to justify their actions.

Key Weapons

AMPHIBIOUS ASSAULT SHIPS

The world's leading practitioner of amphibious warfare is the combined operations' team of the US Navy and the US Marine Corps. The triumphant progress of these two services across the Pacific during World War II has given them a large pool of experience in amphibious operations that has been demonstrated since 1945 at Inchon (1950), Beirut (1958), at various times during the Vietnam War, during the Mayaguez operation (1975) and on Grenada (1983).

US amphibious assault ships used in early postwar operations were World War II designs, and as they were replaced by new designs during the 1960s some were transferred to the navies of allied nations. The heart of this fleet were the LSTs (landing ship, tank) and the LSDs (landing ship, dock). The LST was designed with the capability of crossing the Atlantic, and was nicknamed the 'large slow target' because of its low speed of 12 knots. It had a displacement of 1625 tonnes unloaded and could put ashore a 500-tonne load; an anti-aircraft armament of seven 40mm guns was carried. Over 1000 LSTs were built during World War II.

The LSD was designed to carry pre-loaded landing craft over long distances and its most important feature was the well deck, which would flood to put the landing craft into the water. They could carry up to 14 LCM(3)s (landing craft, medium-Mk 3) or 41 LVTs (landing vehicle, tracked). A 5in gun was carried as well as 40mm and 20mm AA guns.

The first postwar amphibious assault ships were the Thomaston class, the first of which was commissioned during 1954. The class comprises eight ships and, although similar in appearance to the wartime LSDs, includes some improvements on previous designs. Most important was the increase in speed over the wartime LSD (15 knots to 20 knots) which is the standard for all postwar vessels. The docking well is larger and can take nine LCM(8)s but these still must be pre-loaded as there is no connection between the docking well and a deck for vehicle storage amidships, although cranes are provided for manoeuvring the load. A landing platform for helicopters can be placed over the docking well.

Helicopters attracted the attention of the Marine Corps as early as 1948 and experiments led to the conversion of the USS *Thetis Bay*, an escort carrier, in 1955 to an LPH (landing platform, helicopter). The impressive results from this led first to the conversion (as an interim measure) of three Essex-class carriers to LPHs and then to the introduction of the LPHs of the Iwo Jima class, the first of which was commissioned in August 1969. The seven ships of this class carry 25 helicopters each; up to seven CH-46 Sea Knights or four CH-53 Sea Stallion helicopters may be operated simultaneously, landing the Marine battalion that would be transported. The USS *Guam*, the fourth ship of this class, brought the 22nd MAU (Marine Amphibious Unit) of 2000 men to Grenada. The major drawback to the Iwo Jima class is the inability to make beach assaults, which means the MAU can possess only the lightest weapons.

The lack of a heavy-equipment landing capability means that the Iwo Jima class ships always operate in a squadron including an LPD (landing platform, dock), of which there have been two classes built

Previous page: HMS *Intrepid* was to be disposed of during 1982, but the Falklands War intervened and saved it from the breakers. Above: The inside of a US assault ship, with landing craft loaded with trucks in the well deck. Left: A stern view of the USS *Spiegel Grove,* of the Thomaston class, showing an experimental hovercraft being carried in the docking well.

Above right: The USS *Guadalcanal,* third ship of the Iwo Jima class, sails past the coast of Beirut in May 1983. Right: The Austin-class LPD (landing platform, dock) USS *Cleveland* has the variable length hangar, just aft of the superstructure, fully extended. Far right: The ramp and derrick arms of the Newport-class vessel USS *Fresno,* give vehicles carried by the ship direct access to the beach.

since the war: the Raleighs and the Austins. These vessels are intended to combine all the features of a traditional amphibious assault squadron in one ship. The docking well is much shorter than that in the LSDs and in place of cranes uses a monorail to transfer equipment from the forward cargo holds. About half of an MAU can be carried on these ships but the provision of vehicle space in the hull and, in an emergency, on a flight deck over the docking well, makes these ships useful for the heavy equipment of Marine tank units.

The World War II-era LSTs that served on after 1945 began to be replaced in 1969 by the Newport class. They are of an unusual appearance, even for amphibious warfare ships, due to their being given a pointed bow (in order that they might attain the 20 knot speed demanded by the United States for its amphibious squadrons) yet still requiring a ramp so that tanks can be driven directly off the ship onto the beach. The twin derrick arms at the front support a 34m (112ft) ramp made of aluminium and capable of taking a 75 tonne load. There is also a ramp at the stern that permits the unloading of vehicles directly into smaller landing craft, the water or onto a pier. The 20 ships of this class also transport four pontoon causeway sections that are manipulated into position by means of two derrick cranes.

At the same time as the Newport class of LSTs began to be commissioned, a new class of LSDs also entered service. Slightly larger than the Thomaston class (13,700 tonnes to 11,270), the Anchorage class has an enlarged troop-carrying capacity (376 to 340), an additional landing craft (an LCM6) carried on the

deck and the ability to transport helicopters as well as tanks and trucks.

A new type of specialised ship that began to enter service at the start of the 1970s was the LCC (landing, command and control). There are two of these vessels, USS *Blue Ridge* and USS *Mount Whitney*, and they are based on slightly enlarged hulls of the Iwo Jima class. They are lavishly provided with communications equipment, including satellite transmission links and analysis systems such as the NTDS (naval tactical data system – a combination of digital computer displays and transmission links which assess tactical data from various sensors and provide a display of the tactical situation).

The most versatile members of the US amphibious warfare fleet are the five LHAs (general purpose amphibious assault ship) of the Tarawa class. These ships began to be commissioned in 1976 with the USS *Tarawa* and at 39,300 tonnes are comparable in size to a World War II aircraft carrier. Both a helicopter hangar and a docking well are provided in these ships and they are unusual in having vertical sides for two-thirds of their length. The ship has a large and flexible carrying capacity: 30 helicopters, four LCUs (landing craft. utility), some 160 vehicles and nearly 2000 men (in addition to the 900 crew) could be carried at once.

The Royal Navy operates the Fearless-class LPDs, which demonstrated their value during the operations to recapture the Falkland Islands. The *Fearless* and *Intrepid* are slightly smaller than the US Navy's LPDs

Below: The communications ship USS *Blue Ridge*. Bottom left: The USS *Saipan*. Right: The *Ojika,* a Japanese Mirua-class ship. Below right: The French ship *Ouragan,* an LSD (landing ship, dock). Below far right: HMS *Fearless* engaged in a cross-decking operation to transfer stores.

but are comparable ships, carrying four LCUs, 20 main battle tanks, four LCVPs (landing craft, vehicle and personnel), and facilities for operating seven or eight helicopters off the flight deck aft. Normally 350 men would be carried, but up to 670 can be taken aboard in cramped conditions.

Both Japan and France have small amphibious forces: Japan operates the three-ship Atsumi-class and Miura-class LSTs and France the two Ouragan-class LSDs. The Japanese vessels are slow (14 knots) and small ships (Atsumi 2400 tonnes, Miura 3200 tonnes) built to the traditional LST design. The Ouragans are medium-sized (8500 tonnes) vessels, carrying 349 troops, two LCTs or 18 LCMs, plus three LCVPs. A removable helicopter deck can be provided above the well deck and, with the addition

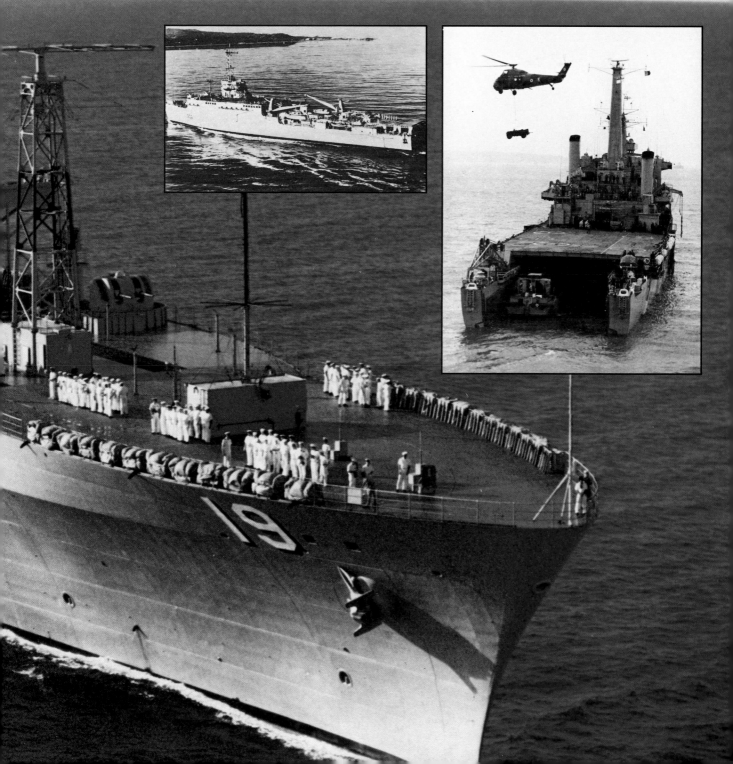

of a temporary deck in the well, helicopters, AMX13s or other cargo can be carried, although the number of landing craft would be reduced.

The Soviet Navy has been developing an amphibious assault force since the mid-1960s. Prior to this, the Soviet Navy had very small seaborne assault forces, but an expansion in this capability began soon after Admiral Sergei Gorshkov became commander-in-chief in 1956. At first smaller landing craft were built but a major class of landing ships, the Alligator LSTs, began to enter service in 1966. Ramps are provided at both bow and stern on these 4500-tonne vessels and they can carry a cargo of about 50 tanks. There are four sub-variants, all lightly armed with anti-aircraft guns, differing primarily in the intended role: transport or beach assault.

The next major amphibious class to enter Soviet service was the Ropucha class of LSTs, still under construction in 1984 at a rate of about two per year. Built at Gdansk, Poland, for the Soviet Navy, these ships, like the Alligators, have bow and stern ramps for roll-off/roll-on operations. Unlike the Alligators, the Ropuchas have a special accommodation for two naval infantry companies, although at the expense of the number of tanks that can be carried, down to 24. One ship of this class has been transferred to the navy of the People's Democratic Republic of Yemen.

The largest amphibious assault ships of the Soviet Navy are the Ivan Rogov class; these LPDs of 13,000 tonnes are of a comparable size to the Royal Navy's Fearless class. A reinforced naval infantry battalion of 550 men, complete with armoured personnel carriers and 10 PT76 light tanks, can be transported in these ships. The stern well deck accommodates air cushion vehicles and a landing craft. A hangar for five helicopters is in the forward part of the superstructure. In 1984, two of these ships were in service and it is anticipated that eventually four vessels will serve, one each with the Northern, Baltic, Black Sea and Pacific Ocean fleets.

Nations whose interests demand the projection of military power beyond their own borders can regard forces delivered by air as sufficient for a quick policing operation. However, in the face of determined opposition or in the absence of a secure airfield, the need for heavy equipment demands amphibious assault ships that can land both tanks and men.

Below left: A Ropucha-class LST (landing ship, tank) of the Soviet Navy. Below: The *Nikolai Vilkov,* one of the Alligator class of Soviet landing ships, under way with a deck of cargo. The Alligators come in four versions, two intended for beach assaults and two for transport duties. Bottom: The *Ivan Rogov,* name-ship of its class, at sea in the Indian Ocean. The deck forward is loaded with trucks and armoured personnel carriers.

Shadow boxing

Possible origins of a superpower conflict

The period since 1945 has been marked by the predominance in world affairs of two superpowers, the United States and the Soviet Union, and the prospect of a potential conflict between them has loomed menacingly on the horizon. Yet despite the accumulation of a fearsome nuclear armoury on both sides, military adventures in various parts of the globe, and the occasional stand-off in an atmosphere heavy with paranoia, no direct encounter between the superpower forces has occurred in 40 years.

Ideologically, there could hardly be a greater contrast between the Marxist-Leninism of the Soviet Union and the capitalism expounded by what Winston Churchill called 'the arsenal of democracy'. Yet, in many respects, the interests of the superpowers are surprisingly similar. Certainly, there is a view, much favoured by the Chinese, for example, that the relationship between the superpowers is a mixture of conflict and cooperation – both aspire to

Below: Soviet Foreign Minister Andrei Gromyko (left) shares a moment's pause from the strains of East-West confrontation with US Secretary of State George Shultz during a meeting in December 1984. Despite the sharp deterioration in relations between the superpowers during the 1980s, a realistic desire to avoid all-out war continued to prevail, and the talking went on.

undisputed mastery and that engenders conflict in so-called 'contested zones'. However, at the same time, both superpowers are concerned to prevent any third party entering the contest for world dominance, as evinced by the Non-Proliferation Treaty of 1968, which the Chinese interpreted as the superpowers preserving their own nuclear monopoly. The superpowers also collaborate to the extent that they do not make direct intrusions into one another's established spheres of control. Thus, the United States did nothing to assist Hungary in 1956 or Czechoslovakia in 1968, while the Soviets did not intervene to save the Allende regime in Chile in 1973. When Nikita Khrushchev broke this rule in the Cuban missile crisis of 1962, it led to perhaps the most dangerous moment in superpower relations since 1945.

Superficially, there is something to be said for the Chinese concept of a 'world condominium conspiracy' by the superpowers. In the case of the Soviet Union, there is little doubt that open confrontation with the West is something that the leadership wishes to avoid, not least in view of the enormous losses suffered in that 'Great Patriotic War' that exercises such a lasting grip on the Soviet mentality. Consequently, there has always been an interest in the promotion of demilitarisation and 'Finlandisation' of their immediate neighbours, nuclear free zones having been offered to Scandinavia and a 'system of collective security' in the Indian Ocean. The Soviet Union also has pressing domestic concerns which counsel caution. The last of the European empires, the Soviet Union embraces many races and languages while its sheer size inevitably brings problems in terms of centralisation. Much of the protein in the Soviet diet derives from fish which can only be caught off other states' coasts. Soviet agriculture has been grossly inefficient and declining industrial productivity has necessitated the importation of substantial quantities of foreign technology at great cost in terms of depleting foreign currency reserves.

Raw materials need to be exported to pay for imports and, to maintain the level of such exports, the Soviets must pursue increasingly inaccessible natural resources which, in turn, requires Western technological expertise.

The United States embarked on the role of the world's 'policeman' after World War II with great reluctance. Traditionally, American foreign policy has swung between extremes of isolationism and interventionism. Prior to 1917, the United States was essentially isolationist, with few interests beyond Latin America. After World War I, the US Senate refused to ratify participation in the League of Nations and isolation was only abandoned as a result of the Japanese attack on Pearl Harbor in December 1941. President F.D. Roosevelt always intended to withdraw US forces from Europe within two years of the end of World War II and, although this was subsequently reversed by President Harry Truman, isolationism has remained a potential force in US political affairs. Indeed, the alarm bells were rung throughout the Far East in May 1977 when President Jimmy Carter announced a phased withdrawal of US ground forces from South Korea by 1982. Carter had not intended to pull out air force personnel and suspended phased withdrawal in April 1978, but it clearly demonstrated that the United States was not necessarily always going to bear the burden of protecting states such as Japan under a 'nuclear umbrella' unless such states did more to defend themselves. Similarly, American politicians periodically express dissatisfaction with the retention of US forces in Europe and raise the spectre of withdrawal. As recently as June 1984 Senate came to the vote for the first time on an amendment to reduce troop levels in Western Europe: it was proposed to reduce forces by 20,000 per annum for five years from 1986. After strong lobbying by President Reagan, however, the amendment was rejected.

In short, there are reasons, other than a common desire to avoid a nuclear holocaust, that contribute to a certain caution in the foreign policies of both superpowers. But there are also grounds for conflict. The very nature of the Soviet Union's internal difficulties, its chronic sense of insecurity and the sheer paranoia deriving from the belief that 'Western imperialism' is inherently hostile to 'socialism' are important factors. So, too, are the absence of internal

Left: American demonstrators accuse Soviet leader Yuri Andropov of responsibility for the death of US Congressman Larry McDonald, who was killed when a Soviet fighter shot down a civilian Korean airliner in September 1983. The pressure from US public opinion, outraged by such events, sometimes drove US administrations to take a tougher line with Moscow than some professional diplomats would have wished. Below left: US Air Force combat controllers during an exercise in Korea. The Reagan administration stressed the importance of a high military preparedness, both in East Asia and in other regions of East-West confrontation.

Below: Young members of the Sandinista militia guard the small town of Jalapa in Nicaragua against US-backed Contra rebels. Both superpowers sought to maintain domination over their own spheres of influence, and while Washington backed the Contras against the left-wing Sandinistas, Soviet troops in Afghanistan fought against Western-backed Mujahidin. Below right: A US warship escorts an oil tanker in the Persian Gulf. The Iran-Iraq Gulf War was a potential source of superpower conflict in a region rich in vital oil deposits.

constraints on the leadership in a totalitarian state and the irresistible urge of the Soviets to seize any opportunities presented to them on the world stage. Opportunism has brought unwelcome long-term commitments – as in Cuba, Ethiopia, Vietnam and Afghanistan – but, equally, the risks taken have often paid off handsomely and served to undermine Western influence at low cost.

Domestic concerns may conceivably compel the Soviet Union to devote more resources to solve internal difficulties. It was argued that Yuri Andropov, who briefly led the Soviet Union from November 1982 to February 1984, was primarily concerned with rooting out inefficiency and corruption at home. It was often suggested that younger members of the ruling Politburo, such as Mikhail Gorbachev, might likewise turn to domestic issues when power came their way with the inevitable disappearance of the entrenched ailing gerontocracy. However, it has also been argued that a younger leadership will be no less bound by the historical obligation to promote the spread of communism and that it might even be more willing to seize opportunities presented by the strength of its armed forces in order to achieve a measurable improvement of the Soviet position as insurance against an uncertain future. Nor should it be forgotten that the so-called 'Brezhnev Doctrine' of September 1968 reserved the right of the Soviet Union to intervene wherever it deemed that socialism or the interests of socialist states were under threat. The precise limits of Brezhnev's 'socialist commonwealth' were never defined and could stretch to include not only Eastern Europe but Albania, Yugoslavia, Afghanistan and, presumably, any state in which communism has achieved power or might do so in the future. 'Fraternal assistance' has, of course, been extended to a number of states and the treaties of friendship and cooperation concluded with states such as Angola, South Yemen and Syria provide for such a contingency; the Soviets have consistently refused to abrogate a 1921 treaty with Iran which allows for their intervention in certain circumstances.

The United States, for its part, is driven by a paranoia which is a mirror image of Soviet ideological fears – a deeply ingrained conviction that the world must be saved from the threat of communism which ultimately menaces the American way of life. There has often been a dichotomy in US foreign policy between realism and idealism, translated in contemporary terms into a tension between the recognition of spheres of influence and 'crisis management' on the one hand, and a crusading zeal against the Soviet Union's 'evil empire' on the other. Although the realist strand is always likely to be uppermost among professional US policymakers, the crusader spirit has a strong following among the American public and therefore among politicians, including presidents, seeking electoral support. Another danger factor is a buoyant confidence in American power widely felt by its people in the 1980s, perhaps making the United States significantly less fearful of war than their Soviet counterparts. A comparison of the losses of the two powers in World War II (the Soviet Union about 20 million, the United States 300,000) also helps explain a difference of attitude.

Policy in the backyard

And yet even the Reagan administration has shown some signs that the United States is not irreducibly committed to a strong reaction to any Soviet initiative. The exception is, perhaps, in its own 'backyard' of Central America where, ironically, the Soviets lack real 'reach' and have only become involved through invitations to do so which have arisen more often than not from US errors of policy. By comparison with Central America and the Caribbean, the Middle East and its oil supplies are no longer as vital to the United States as was once the case. Nor is the United States quite as committed to the support of the Republic of South Africa's hold on southern Africa with its strategic raw materials and dominance of the Cape route.

Nevertheless, the most likely cause of any future conflict between the superpowers might well be a more positive US reaction than has often been the case in the recent past to a Soviet foreign policy gamble. That gamble itself would probably be more likely to occur in an area of the globe where neither of the superpowers has direct interests, perhaps through the agency of clients or allies whose independent regional rivalries could not be contained by Washington or Moscow. Many conflicts have occurred in the past as a result of design; but more still have occurred through error born of mutual distrust.

Ian Beckett

Chronology 1981-84

EUROPE AND NORTH AMERICA
1981

January
20 **United States** Ronald Reagan inaugurated as president.
February
9 **Poland** General Jaruzelski made prime minister.
23 **Spain** Lieutenant-Colonel Molina of the Civil Guard seizes parliament and holds deputies hostage for 18 hours before surrendering.
March
30 **United States** President Reagan wounded in attempted assassination.
April
1-30 **Poland** Nationwide disorders.
12-14 **United States** Reusable space-shuttle *Columbia* makes first flight.
May
5 **Northern Ireland** Bobby Sands dies in hunger strike in the Maze prison.
13 **Italy** Pope John Paul II shot and wounded in St Peter's Square, Rome.
August
7 **Poland** General strike halts Polish industry.
September
4-12 **Soviet Union** holds 'West 81' exercises near Polish border.
October
2 **United States** President Reagan authorises building of 100 MX ICBMS and new B-1 bomber.
19 **Poland** General Jaruzelski takes over as Communist Party leader.
November
30 **Switzerland** Intermediate-range Nuclear Forces (INF) talks begin between the United States and the Soviet Union in Geneva.
December
13 **Poland** General Jaruzelski proclaims martial law.

1982

May
30 **Spain** becomes sixteenth member of Nato.
June
18 **Soviet Union** conducts first successful test of a 'killer' satellite.
25 **United States** Alexander Haig resigns as secretary of state, replaced by George Shultz.
29 **Switzerland** Strategic Arms Reduction Talks (START) convened in Geneva.
October
8-14 **Poland** Parliament dissolves Solidarity union; unrest continues.
November
10 **Soviet Union** Leonid Brezhnev dies after 18 years as Party leader.
12 **Soviet Union** Yuri Andropov, former KGB chief, succeeds Brezhnev.
30 **Belgium** Nato defence ministers agree to begin deployment of cruise and Pershing II missiles by the end of 1983.
December
20 **United States** Congress approves record military budget.
30 **Poland** Martial law suspended.

1983

March
23 **United States** President Reagan announces his Strategic Defense Initiative (SDI) for space-based anti-ballistic missile defences.

June
9 **Northern Ireland** Gerry Adams, Provisional IRA leader, elected MP for West Belfast.
16 **Soviet Union** Yuri Andropov elected president.
17 **United States** Successful test of MX missile.
November
7 **United States** Congress approves deployment of MX missiles in hardened silos.
14 **Britain** First US cruise missile delivered to Greenham Common.
23 **Switzerland** Soviet delegation quits INF talks after arrival of US missiles in Germany. START talks also halted.

1984

February
9 **Soviet Union** Death of President Andropov.
13 **Soviet Union** Konstantin Chernenko elected General Secretary of Communist Party in succession to Andropov.
April
11 **Soviet Union** Chernenko elected president.
October
12 **Britain** IRA bomb attempt to assassinate leaders of Conservative government at Brighton.
November
22 **Soviet Union and United States** agree to hold talks in Geneva on 7-8 January 1985, on reopening strategic arms talks.

SOUTHEAST ASIA
1983

January
5 **Kampuchea** Vietnamese launch offensive in west.
May
2 **Kampuchea** Vietnamese partially withdraw troops.
June
1 **Philippines** agrees to allow US to retain military bases.
August
21 **Philippines** Opposition leader Benigno Aquino assassinated by state security forces.

SOUTH ASIA
1981

April
10-30 **Afghanistan** Fighting reported to have spread to 23 of the 29 provinces; Kandahar captured by Afghan guerrillas but later lost.

1982

March
24 **Bangladesh** Army chief General Ershad seizes power and imposes martial law.
June
3 **Afghanistan** Russians and Afghans both claim victory after three weeks of fighting in Panjshir Valley.
October
29 **Afghanistan** United Nations General Assembly calls for Soviet withdrawal.

1983

July
23-30 **Sri Lanka** Rioting against Tamil minority spreads throughout country.

1984

June
6 **India** Army expells Sikh militants from Golden Temple and Akal Takht in Amritsar.
October
31 **India** Prime Minister Gandhi is assassinated by Sikh militants.

EAST ASIA
1982

October
16 **China** conducts successful test of submarine-launched ballistic missile.
December
16 **Soviet Union** deploys MiG-21 aeroplanes on Etorofu Island, claimed by Japanese but occupied by the Soviets.

1983

September
1 **Soviet Union** Air Defence Force shoots down a South Korean airliner flying in Soviet airspace.

1984

September
26 **China** British and Chinese diplomats reach agreement for transfer of Hong Kong to China in 1997.

MIDDLE EAST
1981

January
5 **Iran and Iraq** Heavy fighting in Khuzestan; Iraq claims Iranian counter-offensive crushed.
April
1-29 **Lebanon** Heavy fighting between Syrian forces and Phalangist militia; Syrians encircle Zahle and deploy SAM missiles in Beqaa valley.
May
25 **Arabian Peninsula** Gulf Cooperation Council formed by Saudi Arabia, Kuwait, Oman, the United Arab Emirates, Bahrain and Qatar.
June
7 **Iraq** Israeli air attack puts Osirak nuclear reactor in Baghdad out of action.
22 **Iran** President Bani-Sadr dismissed from office, confirming dominance of Islamic fundamentalists.
August
19 **Libya** Two Libyan Su-22s attack US F-14s over the Gulf of Sirte; the Libyan aeroplanes are shot down.
6 **Egypt** President Sadat assassinated; he is succeeded by Hosni Mubarak.
November
14 **Egypt** Joint US-Egyptian manoeuvres to test US Rapid Deployment Force.

1982

January
19 **Israel and Egypt** reach agreement on Israel's withdrawal from Sinai.
March
22 **Iran** opens major offensive against Iraq, claiming recapture of Iranian territory.
April
25 **Israel** completes withdrawal from Sinai, which

is returned to Egypt; a multinational peacekeeping force is deployed

May
24 Iran Army reaches Iraqi frontier, recaptures Khorramshahr.
June
3 Israel Ambassador to Britain, Shlomo Argov, shot and seriously wounded in London.
6 Lebanon Israeli Defence Forces invade Lebanon in Operation Peace for Galilee.
9-10 Lebanon Israelis destroy Syrian anti-aircraft missiles in Beqaa Valley and virtually wipe out Syrian Air Force.
13 Lebanon Israeli siege of Beirut begins.
25 Lebanon Syrian operations effectively ended with defeat at hands of Israelis.
July
13 Iraq Iran invades, approaches Basra.
August
4 Lebanon Israeli forces advance into West Beirut, halted by fierce resistance. Palestinian and Syrian forces to withdraw under international supervision.
12 Lebanon Israeli cabinet agrees to ceasefire around Beirut.
18 Iran Iraqi forces bomb Kharg Island, Iran's main oil terminal.
21 Lebanon French paratroopers, the vanguard of the Multi-National Force (MNF) from France, Italy and the United States, arrive in Beirut.
31 Lebanon Palestinian and Syrian forces complete evacuation of West Beirut.
September
1 Israel US President Reagan announces Middle East peace plan which would involve an Israeli withdrawal from the West Bank of the Jordan.
1 Lebanon MNF begins withdrawal from Beirut.
14 Lebanon President-elect Bashir Gemayel assassinated.
16-18 Lebanon Phalangists massacre Palestinian refugees in the camps of Sabra and Chatila.
20 Lebanon redeployment of the MNF to Beirut.
21 Lebanon Amin Gemayel, brother of Bashir, is elected president.

1983

February
7 Iran launches major offensive against Iraq.
10 Lebanon British contingent to the MNF in Beirut begin patrolling the city.
April
18 Lebanon US embassy in Beirut bombed; 47 killed.
June
4 Lebanon Fighting breaks out between pro- and anti-Arafat factions of the PLO.
May
4 Iran Expulsion of 18 Soviet diplomats; communist Tudeh party is banned.
17 Lebanon 'Shultz agreement' between Lebanese government and Israel for withdrawal of Syrian and Israeli forces; agreement denounced by Syria and Lebanese opposition.
September
3-4 Lebanon Israeli troops withdraw to the Awali River; fighting follows between Druze militia in the Chouf and government and Christian militia forces backed by the US MNF contingent.
15 Israel Prime Minister Menachem Begin resigns.
October
23 Lebanon Shi'ia Muslim suicide truck bombs kill 239 US Marines and 58 French paratroopers in Beirut.
31 Lebanon National Reconciliation Committee meets in Geneva.
November
3 Lebanon Renewed fighting between Fatah factions around Tripoli.
December
3 Lebanon United Nations approves plan to evacuate Arafat's Fatah forces from Tripoli to Tunisia and North Yemen.
20 Lebanon Arafat's forces leave Tripoli under the protection of French warships.
12 Kuwait Coordinated Shi'ite terrorist bomb attacks on French and US targets.

1984

February
18 Lebanon US contingent of MNF begins withdrawal from Beirut after collapse of Lebanese Army and renewed intercommunal fighting.
22 Iran begins major offensive near Basra, suffering heavy casualties.
June
5 Saudi Arabia shoots down Iranian Phantom violating its airspace.
September
13 Israel Shimon Peres, leader of the Labour Party, forms government of national unity.

CENTRAL AMERICA
1981

January
10 El Salvador Guerrillas of the Farabundo Martí National Liberation Front launch offensive.
24 El Salvador US delivers $15 million-worth of military aid to government.
March
16 Belize signs agreement with Britain on independence.

1982

January
27 El Salvador Half of Salvadorean Air Force destroyed in guerrilla attack on Ilopango airbase.
February
1 El Salvador US announces further $55 million-worth of military aid.
March
18 Nicaragua First serious clash between US-backed insurgents and Sandinista government forces.

1983

August
8 Guatemala President Montt overthrown in military coup.
October
19 Grenada Prime Minister Maurice Bishop killed by political opponents within his New Jewel Movement.
25 Grenada US troops, supported by Caribbean contingent, invade Grenada and overcome resistance from government forces and Cuban workers.
December
15 Grenada US combat troops leave island; support troops remain.

1984

April
10 Nicaragua US Senate condemns CIA involvement in mining Nicaragua's harbours.
May
6 El Salvador Napoleón Duarte wins election.
September
1 Nicaragua Helicopter attacking Santa Clara is shot down with two US Special Forces men aboard.
October
15 El Salvador Start of peace discussions between rebels and government.
November
4 Nicaragua Election victory for Sandinista government.

SOUTH AMERICA
1981

December
11 Argentina General Leopoldo Galtieri, commander-in-chief of armed forces, is made president.

1982

March
19 Falklands Argentinian scrap merchants land on island of South Georgia.

April
2 Falklands Argentina invades and overcomes British Marine garrison.
3 Falklands South Georgia seized by Argentinian force.
12 Falklands Britain declares 200-mile Maritime Exclusion Zone around islands.
25 Falklands Britain retakes South Georgia.
May
2 Falklands Argentinian cruiser *General Belgrano* sunk by British submarine HMS *Conqueror*.
4 Falklands British destroyer HMS *Sheffield* sunk by Exocet missile.
21-25 Falklands 3 Commando Brigade establishes beachhead at San Carlos; air attacks inflict heavy damage on British fleet but Argentinians suffer unacceptable level of losses of aircraft.
28 Falklands British paratroopers capture Goose Green and Darwin.
June
1 Falklands 5 Infantry Brigade begins disembarking at San Carlos.
8 Falklands *Sir Galahad* severely damaged by Argentinian air attack; 51 killed.
11-12 Falklands British take Mount Harriet, Two Sisters and Mount Longdon.
13-14 Falklands British take Wireless Ridge and Mount Tumbledown. Argentinian forces surrender in Port Stanley.
17 Argentina General Galtieri dismissed.

1983

October
30 Argentina Presidential election won by Raul Alfonsin of Radical Party.

AFRICA
1981

February
9-17 Zimbabwe Clashes between supporters of Prime Minister Mugabe and Joshua Nkomo.
June
27 Uganda Tanzania completes withdrawal of 10,000 man force.
September
1 Central African Republic President Dacko overthrown by General Golingba.
December
31 Ghana Flight-Lieutenant Rawlings seizes power.

1982

February
1 Senegambia created by confederation of Senegal and Gambia.
March
13-19 Angola South African troops attack SWAPO camp inside country.
June
7 Chad Army led by Hissène Habré captures capital Ndjamena; Habré forms government.
August
1 Kenya Attempted coup involving air force officers and students repressed.
November
7 Upper Volta Colonel Zerbo overthrown, replaced by Major Ouedraogo.

1983

March
8 Zimbabwe Joshua Nkomo flees the country.
August
14 Chad French paratroopers block advance of Libyan-backed rebels.
15 Zimbabwe Nkomo returns from self-imposed exile.

1984

March
16 Mozambique signs Nkomati accord with South Africa, a non-aggression pact.

Guessing game

Plans for fighting World War III

Above: Kitted-out for nuclear, biological and chemical (NBC) warfare, two crewmen emerge from the turret of their M1 Abrams tank to man their machine guns during an exercise in a West German forest. Such exercises strive to simulate the conditions of a real modern war in central Europe. Right: Soviet Naval Infantry mounted on T55 tanks land from an amphibious assault ship. Although in no way matching the capability of the United States, Soviet naval power expanded during the 1970s and 1980s, creating a new interventionary potential.

Although the serious deterioration of relations on all levels between the Soviet Union and the West during the late 1970s and early 1980s, often described as a new Cold War, provoked much anxious discussion of the possibility of rising tensions leading to a military confrontation between the superpowers, few experts appeared to have any very plausible conception of just how such a war might break out, although there was much speculation on how it might be fought and what its consequences might be.

The cockpit of the first Cold War had been central Europe, and the generation which had experienced World War II tended to imagine a new world war breaking out there. By the early 1960s, however, spheres of influence in Europe had become extremely sharply defined and conflicts outside of Europe seemed far more likely to provide the fuse which might spark off a global war. Both superpowers maintained extensive forces outside Europe which might quite credibly fight the first engagements between the two sides – in the Persian Gulf, for example, or the Indian Ocean. The large concentra-

tions of Nato and Warsaw Pact forces facing one another in Europe, however, made it almost inevitable that the major trial of strength in a conventional war would happen there.

Both the armed forces of Nato and of the Warsaw Pact have had to adapt their military thinking to new developments in technology, such as the changing balance between armour and infantry brought about by the introduction of effective infantry anti-tank missiles, or the increasing importance of helicopters as a source of mobility and firepower. Although always struggling to keep up in the race for new technology, the Soviet Union was not slow to adapt tactics appropriate to the contemporary battlefield.

Soviet military thinking has always laid great stress on the importance of maximum firepower and mobility, which had also been a traditional characteristic of the pre-revolutionary Russian Army. This attitude was a consequence of the need to defend the country's long and vulnerable borders, but it was often overlooked by Western observers, who concentrated upon the enormous mass of Russian armies rather than their tactics. By the late 1970s, the Soviet Army had begun to introduce the concept of the Operational Manoeuvre Group (OMG) amongst its forces stationed in Eastern Europe. The task of the OMG in wartime would be to exploit any breakthrough of the enemy's lines by the first echelon of the Soviet forces, and strike deep into his rear against specific targets, including nuclear weapons, airfields, bridges and strategic road junctions, as well as vital command, control and communications (C^3) systems.

Of varying sizes (anything from a reinforced regiment to a corps or army), the OMG would probably be formed *ad hoc* by Soviet commanders to exploit any opportunity which might present itself, and would operate independently of the main Soviet advance. Although containing motorised infantry, self-propelled artillery, engineer and chemical warfare units, the OMG would probably be a predominantly armoured formation which would probe for the enemy's point of weakness and attempt to bypass any resistance, leaving it to be mopped-up as the main front advanced. The increased capability of Nato troops to inflict heavy losses on Warsaw Pact

armour with anti-tank missiles, however, and the growing threat posed by Western attack helicopters would seem to suggest that the OMG would need to be accompanied by strong infantry elements, and that it would be supported by the large numbers of Mil Mi-24 Hind helicopter gunships now stationed in Eastern Europe, including at least five regiments, each of 80 Hinds, with the Group of Soviet Forces in Germany (GSFG).

The weakness of an echeloned configuration is that it would be vulnerable to tactical nuclear or high technology conventional weapons. It has been argued, therefore, that the Soviet Army would attack on a broad front in order to avoid decimation by such Nato strikes, while relying upon the OMGs to provide the element of depth and speed needed to ensure success. Nevertheless, it seems certain that any Soviet advance would be preceded by an overwhelming concentration of firepower against the enemy front, with anything up to 100 artillery pieces

Above: Soviet Mil Mi-24 Hind-D helicopter crewmen plan a mission. Heavily armed and armoured helicopters are key weapons on the modern battlefield, and pose a serious threat to both tanks and infantry.

Below: Soviet T55 tanks advancing at speed across the snow. Taken seriously as a major threat since 1945 by the West, it is doubtful how effective the Soviet Union's massive tank armies would be today against combat helicopters and anti-tank missiles.

per kilometre of front providing a massive punch which would be followed up by the Soviet tanks.

Strategically, the Soviet aim would be to move into Nato territory so swiftly and deeply that forward-based Nato nuclear systems would be overrun before a request for their use by unit commanders could have gone through the Allied nuclear chain of command. A deep advance, for example to the Rhine, would also have the effect of placing millions of Allied civilians, including most of the population of West Germany, behind Soviet lines – a potentially inhibiting factor to any Nato use of nuclear weapons against first echelon Soviet forces.

AirLand Battle

The uninviting prospect of becoming either a conventional or nuclear battlefield has made West Germany one of the main proponents of the Nato policy of Forward Defence, committing forces to holding a line near the border between the two Germanies. In the 1980s, however, new concepts were emerging in Nato which, while not abandoning Forward Defence, developed the West's conventional strategy in the direction of greater mobility and aggression. In particular, the adoption of a new basic field manual (FM 100-5) by the US Army in August 1982 reflected a major rethink in American attitudes to conventional warfare. The doctrine contained in the 1982 FM 100-5 was known as AirLand Battle, and was in many ways comparable to the OMG concept which had been adopted by the Soviet Army. Whereas the previous US Army doctrine, as contained in the 1976 field manual, had been known as 'active defence', it had been criticised as leaving the initiative with the enemy, and for being essentially reactive. AirLand Battle, on the other hand, was imbued with an aggressive spirit and the idea of taking the battle to the enemy. Instead of a linear defence, without significant reserves or depth, AirLand Battle called for a deeply echeloned defence operating on an 'extended battlefield', which meant on enemy territory.

While AirLand Battle was a US Army doctrine only, it was applicable to any theatre of war in which US troops might be engaged, including Europe. It was complemented, however, by the evolution of a new doctrine, known as Follow-On Forces Attack (FOFA) by Nato's Supreme Headquarters Allied

Powers Europe (SHAPE), and enunciated most clearly by the Nato supreme commander in Europe, General Bernard W. Rogers in 1982. Rogers proposed that Nato exploit its technological superiority over the Warsaw Pact by employing high-technology conventional weapons such as terminally-guided sub-munitions (TGSM), remotely-laid minefields and conventional missiles. Massed Soviet tank units in second echelon formations, it was argued, would be the target of Nato conventional strikes deep inside Warsaw Pact territory, as would airfields, C^3 systems and strategic points in the East European transport system. All this would deprive the Warsaw Pact advance of depth and momentum, while Nato troops, supported by modern attack helicopters and large numbers of anti-tank missiles, would be able to deal with the Warsaw Pact spearhead.

The proponents of AirLand Battle and FOFA argued that this would help raise the nuclear threshold which was widely perceived as having

sunk so dangerously low that Nato conventional forces on the central front had become little more than a tripwire in case of Soviet attack, with a rapid escalation to nuclear warfare being inevitable. Critics countered that these new doctrines were dangerous in that by raising the nuclear threshold and creating the impression that 'war-fighting' and 'war-winning' in a superpower conflict were even conceivable, they were in effect lowering the threshold of war itself, and subverting the doctrine of deterrence upon which Nato had been based.

Nor was it certain that any Soviet advance would rely upon the close support of a second echelon, as after reorganisations of Soviet forces in Poland, East Germany and Czechoslovakia during the early 1970s, it appeared more likely that any attack would be over a broad front, and mounted by the forces already in position, with powerful hammer blows being delivered by OMGs, which would only be concentrated for specific operations. It was arguable that instead of the 'deep strike' of FOFA, Nato should develop a 'shallow strike' capacity which would give forward Nato troops the ability to counter strong Warsaw Pact formations without resort to tactical nuclear weapons.

However it was to be conducted, any conventional defence of Western Europe would be dependent upon the mobilisation of the vast military and industrial resources of the United States, and Nato strategy laid great emphasis upon the rapid transportation of troops and equipment across the Atlantic in time of war. This lifeline across the Atlantic would be a vulnerable Achilles heel, liable to disruptive attack by Warsaw Pact forces, and the seaports, such as Antwerp and Rotterdam, through which men and supplies would have to pass would be inviting targets for Soviet conventional or nuclear missiles.

There was a close relationship between logistical planning and Nato maritime strategy. The development of a Soviet capability to deploy large groups of naval vessels on the high seas provided Moscow with the means to extend its political influence in peacetime, but in wartime would represent a threat to Nato supply lines across the North Atlantic. To meet this challenge, and the much more serious threat posed by the Soviet Union's large submarine fleet, Nato would deploy a formidable naval force, whose backbone would consist of US Navy carrier battle

The Nato central front

Nato forces in Europe	
Belgium	27,794 troops
Great Britain	56,761 troops
Canada	6700 troops
France	48,500 troops
W. Germany	495,000 troops
Netherlands	5500 troops
US	216,700 troops

Rostock
Hamburg
2nd Guard's Tank Army
tank div
EAST GERMANY
POLAND
3rd Shock Army
Berlin
Magdeburg
20th Guards Army
tank div
8th Guards Army
1st Guards Tank Army
Dresden
31st Tank Army
Frankfurt
18th Guards MR Div
Prague
CZECHOSLOVAKIA
48th MR Div
WEST GERMANY
Nato
Warsaw Pact
unaligned
Munich
AUSTRIA
SWITZERLAND
ITALY

Left: A nuclear-capable US 155mm M198 howitzer firing a Copperhead round. Nato reliance upon tactical nuclear weapons threatened to lead to a rapid escalation of any East-West conflict to an all-out nuclear exchange. Below, far left: British troops armed with a MILAN anti-tank missile. Below left: A French Aerospatiale Gazelle anti-tank helicopter launching a HOT missile. Tank-busting helicopters might give Nato a new edge in conventional warfare against the Warsaw Pact. Right: US Navy nuclear-powered attack submarine USS *San Francisco* cruising on the surface while on patrol. Submarine and anti-submarine warfare would play a crucial part in any future war at sea.

groups operating through the Iceland Gap against the Soviet Northern Fleet based at Murmansk and Archangelsk, and in support of Nato's northern flank in Scandinavia. The protection of sea lanes and allied convoys would also be a priority task of Nato naval forces in the Atlantic, although there is some debate over whether or not close escort of convoys or the maintenance of 'defended lanes' would be the most economical and successful way to employ scarce naval assets.

In the Nato view, the progress of the conventional war would determine whether or not it was necessary to escalate to a nuclear level, proceeding from the use of battlefield and tactical nuclear weapons up to strategic nuclear exchange. The Soviet Union has never made any secret of its rejection of this view, asserting that any war between Nato and the Warsaw Pact would necessarily be a nuclear war. Even if the Soviets could be persuaded to play ball, the Nato idea of a graduated response relies on the maintenance of a very high standard of control and communications, which would allow central commanders to make the essential decisions and see them fully implemented in all sectors. However, the vulnerability of command and information networks to technical defects and breakdowns, or to enemy action, such as electronic counter-measures or simple destruction, makes it open to question whether or not commanders will be able to exert the degree of control which is necessary to prevent unchecked escalation. This vulnerability is a particular problem in any scenario involving the use of nuclear weapons.

Fighting blind

Since the late 1950s, scientists have been aware of the existence of a phenomenon known as electromagnetic pulses (EMP), which are unleashed by nuclear explosions and constitute a blast of radio energy which is attracted to metal structures such as aerials, destroying transistors and integrated circuits. Even a relatively small nuclear explosion high in the atmosphere over Western Europe could have the effect of knocking out large amounts of Nato communications equipment, effectively blinding Nato forces and making any coordinated military response impossible.

Although the chain of command for the control of nuclear weapons is one of the most closely guarded secrets of all, some details of the US system are known. At the head of a worldwide command and control network stands the National Command Authority, which resides in the president in normal times, but should he be eliminated or placed out of communication with the rest of the system in wartime, would pass down the chain of command, from the secretary of defense through the commanders of the six US unified military commands (Strategic Air Command, North American Aerospace Command, and the Atlantic, Pacific, European and Central Commands). Should all of these levels of command be eliminated or cut off, the authority to release nuclear weapons then moves to the commanders of nuclear-capable units, and in the last resort to individual bomber, missile, submarine or nuclear-capable artillery unit commanders.

If it was the Soviet Union which launched the nuclear first strike, the US National Command Authority would be alerted to the incoming enemy nuclear attack by an early warning radar system

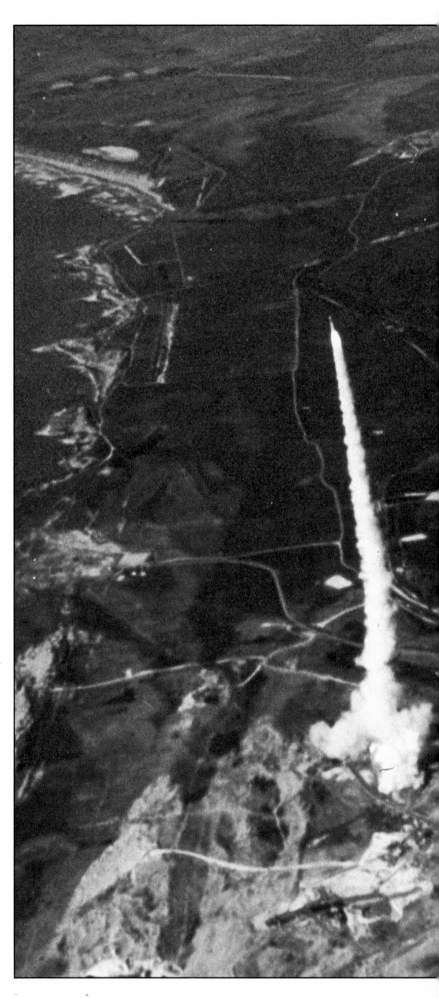

which stretches from Alaska and Greenland to the United Kingdom. Should this system detect enemy missiles, the president would be immediately warned, and would be transported, along with the nuclear codes necessary to release US nuclear weapons (which always accompany him, carried by an air force officer in a briefcase known as the 'golfball') to an airborne command post from which he could direct operations even if military command centres on the ground had been destroyed. These airborne command posts – E-4Bs (converted Boeing 747s) – are in direct communication with US-based ICBM wings and with the permanently airborne navy command posts which relay instructions to US nuclear missile submarines. Through satellites, the airborne command post would also be in touch with US strategic and tactical nuclear forces based throughout the world, including those in Britain and

Western Europe.

Whether this complex and sophisticated system would function in a wartime emergency is open to question, and it has been suggested that the very sophistication of the technology employed to provide maximum control of military forces could lead to a failure that would realise the nightmare which plagues all strategists of nuclear war – the possibility of finding oneself in a situation where rational responses are not possible. Without a sophisticated system of communications and control, the nuclear weapons of both sides would be launched almost at random by local commanders.

This scenario is in stark contrast to the optimistic theories of those who speculate on the rational use of nuclear weapons to achieve some political aim, with the possibility of controlled escalation and a limited nuclear war which would end by negotiation. In such

Left: A US Minuteman III ICBM being test-launched from a Strategic Air Command silo. Right: The US president's airborne command post – a converted Boeing 747 – lifts off on a practice mission. In case of war, the president would control the US nuclear forces from such an aircraft. Below: In the depths of a US missile silo, the crew test launching systems. In order to launch, both officers must turn their firing keys simultaneously.

theories, the concepts of 'first strike' and 'second strike' figure very largely – a first strike capability being the capacity to launch an opening attack in a nuclear war which would be powerful and accurate enough to destroy the bulk of the enemy's nuclear forces before they could be used; while a second strike capability is the capacity to absorb such a first strike by the enemy and yet still be able to launch a retaliatory blow, either at his remaining nuclear systems or his population centres. Although experts have cast grave doubt upon the possibility of either side ever being able to achieve a 'useable' first strike capability, it continues to be the Holy Grail after which many strategists seek.

But the key question of the nature of the circumstances in which such a war might be unleashed remains unanswered. The most diverse alternatives have been offered, from a surprise attack by the Soviet Union (a persistent American nightmare, prompted largely by a folk-memory of the Japanese attack on Pearl Harbor in 1941), to an opportunist grab by the Soviet Army for some West German city such as Hamburg, in the hope that the limited nature of its loss would prevent the West from resorting to a full-scale conventional or nuclear response. All of these scenarios are improbable, but fears remain that the very sophistication of modern military technology could accidently provoke a war if the electronic, rather than the political, system blows a fuse.

Robin Corbett

Chances of survival

The probable effect of nuclear war on civilians

Under the nuclear war doctrines which prevailed until the 1970s, the main point of nuclear weapons was their ability to inflict appalling casualties on an enemy's civilian population. Yet, paradoxically, the high level of civilian casualties expected in a nuclear war is also a major inhibiting factor preventing their use against military or economic targets. If the 'winning' of a nuclear war is to be considered a feasible objective for military planners, they must believe that damage to their own population, economy and social structure would be 'tolerable'.

The effects of a nuclear war on civilians are to some extent matter for speculation, the only real example after 40 years of nuclear capability remaining the two bombs dropped on Japan in 1945. Compared to the weapons available to modern nuclear powers, the Hiroshima and Nagasaki bombs were quite small: 12.5 kilotons and 22 kilotons respectively. Both of these bombs were airburst over their target, obliterating 10 square km (4 square miles) of Hiroshima and 5 square km (2 square miles) of Nagasaki. Exposed flesh was burned at a distance of 3km (2 miles) from the epicentre. Most of the few survivors within 0.8km (0.5 miles) of the explosion died from exposure to radiation within a week. Deaths from radiation sickness continued for a month, and in the longer term cancers, eye-cataracts and leukaemia have occurred at a higher level than normally expected amongst the survivors. Figures for deaths in the two explosions have varied widely, but an estimate of 70,000 in Hiroshima and 35,000 in Nagasaki has often been quoted.

It has been pointed out that 83,000 people were killed in a conventional firebomb attack on Tokyo in the same year, and also that during the 1930s the probable civilian casualties from future conventional bombing raids were greatly exaggerated – it was widely supposed that the social order would collapse under sustained aerial bombardment, whereas in fact Germany and Japan continued to function even in 1945. There are good reasons to believe, however, that apocalyptic visions of the effects of a future nuclear war are not similarly exaggerated.

The effects of nuclear explosions have been exhaustively observed in tests. The first impact is from a flash of heat. Immediately after a nuclear explosion, X-rays are emitted in large quantities, producing a fireball which rapidly expands and rises to form the mushroom cloud. The heat of the fireball would cause burns over a wide area, particularly affecting people caught in the open, and would start fires, even initiating firestorms under the appropriate climatic conditions (as seen in Hamburg, for example, during

Right: An H-bomb detonates. A one-megaton airburst will probably kill all persons within a radius of 8km (5 miles) either through blast, heat or radiation. Below right: Destroyed fire engines at Hiroshima. Damage to rescue services would make help for the victims of a nuclear attack very scarce. Inset: A casualty at Hiroshima.

conventional bombing in World War II). After heat comes the effect of blast, potentially fatal to a distance of 5km (3 miles) from a one-megaton airburst. The shock-wave, followed by violent winds, would cause heavy casualties through falling masonry and flying broken glass over a wide area. With the heat and blast comes a release of radiation, although the initial burst of rays would largely affect people already killed in any case by the explosion. The debris sucked up in the explosion also becomes radioactive, however, and its return to earth – either floating down quite quickly or falling later in rain and snow – spreads radiation over a much larger area, varying according to wind speed and terrain. With the wind blowing in that direction, a one-megaton groundburst on Manchester, for example, could transfer potentially lethal radiation as far as London. The level of radioactivity would fall to a tolerable level in a few days even in quite heavily affected areas, so that people who remained well sheltered for that length of time could then emerge unscathed. However, in the long term radiation absorbed through eating affected foodstuffs would damage health in a variety of ways, leading to cancer, genetic defects, and so on.

Translating these effects into figures for possible casualties in a future war is obviously speculative. Much would depend on the nature and extent of a nuclear exchange. Even if military, economic and political targets were carefully chosen, many would be in or near major population centres. To take the example of Britain, it is possible to identify some of the most likely targets and the probable form of attack upon them: the UK and Nato command centre for naval forces at Northwood, in west London,

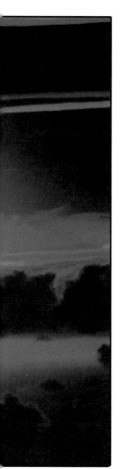

Medical effects of a one-megaton nuclear airburst over London

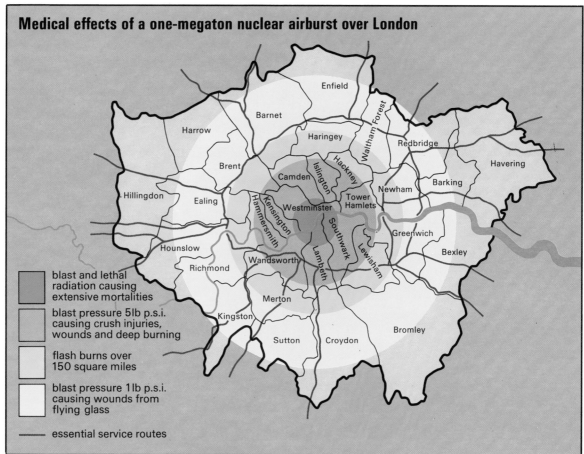

- blast and lethal radiation causing extensive mortalities
- blast pressure 5lb p.s.i. causing crush injuries, wounds and deep burning
- flash burns over 150 square miles
- blast pressure 1lb p.s.i. causing wounds from flying glass
- —— essential service routes

might be subjected to groundburst high-yield warheads; Martlesham Heath in Suffolk is a switching centre for the US armed services telephone network and thus the likely target of a low-yield groundburst; Liverpool and Birkenhead are major port facilities used by the US Navy; nuclear power stations would probably be the targets of groundburst warheads; Teeside, with its valuable oil refineries and chemical plants, might be targeted with an airburst; Birmingham would be a prime target because of its industry and its importance as a road and rail junction; the US Navy's sound surveillance system for anti-submarine warfare at Brawdy in Wales would be attacked with a groundburst; the CIA's satellite communication centre at Morwenstow in Cornwall might be targeted with a low-yield airburst. These and many other targets, situated in a densely-populated country, would ensure that for Britain a nuclear war would be an unprecedented catastrophe. Quite conservative estimates have set the initial level of deaths or serious injuries in a nuclear strike on Britain at between 40 and 70 per cent of the population. The destruction of most medical facilities would lead to the eventual death of all serious casualties.

The probable death rate in large, relatively sparsely populated countries, would be much lower, however. Although the United States and the Soviet Union would be the main targets for one another's nuclear forces, their sheer size offers their populations much better chances of survival – large areas of their land mass would probably escape destruction or contamination. The chances of a successful exercise in civil defence by both superpowers can be taken seriously – whereas in Britain, even the most optimistic scenarios see civil defence offering little mitigation to the effects of an attack. The Soviet Union takes civil defence especially seriously, with well developed plans for the mass evacuation of cities – expected to take about five days to complete – the protection of machinery needed for economic recovery, and the maintenance in shelters of enough essential personnel to guarantee the continued existence of the state structure. In 1978, some US experts calculated that the Soviet Union might reduce its losses to 5 per cent of the population, whereas 50 per cent of American citizens would die in a full exchange. This calculation lacked credibility in either direction, the US figure being far too high and the Soviet one far too low in the opinion of most observers, but it is true that the United States has not pursued civil defence planning on the same scale. A realistic figure for fatalities in the Soviet Union and the United States might be 20-30 per cent dead in the aftermath of a nuclear war.

A diseased world

The longer term effects of a full-scale nuclear exchange are even harder to calculate, but would certainly involve more heavy losses. With power stations and oil refineries destroyed, transport cut off and food supplies disrupted, even initially unaffected parts of the population would have to cope with potentially fatal conditions. In severely damaged areas, unsanitary and overcrowded living conditions, poor nutrition and inadequate medical supplies might cause outbreaks of infectious diseases such as dysentry, cholera, diphtheria, polio and meningitis, taking a further toll of survivors. Much would depend on whether large areas of the globe remained sufficiently unaffected by the war to react with aid and supplies to devastated countries.

In the 1980s, the emergence of the hypothesis of the 'nuclear winter' cast doubts on all prospects for recovery after a nuclear attack. The atmosphere might become clogged with smoke from the many fires caused, producing a 'nuclear winter' when sunlight could be reduced to a hundredth of its normal level, which would prove insufficient for agricultural growth. The ozone layer might be stripped away from the earth by increased amounts of nitric oxides in the atmosphere; this would increase the amount of ultraviolet radiation reaching the earth, disrupting the food chain to the point where all life might be threatened.

Although all such calculations are speculative, they still cast doubt on the rationality of plans for fighting and winning a nuclear war. Whichever side claimed eventual victory, its own population would inevitably be among the losers.   **Graham Brewer**

Right: Shelters and protective clothing would reduce the immediate casualties, at the cost of more pressure on limited post-attack resources.

Effects of radiation

After a nuclear attack those that have survived the heat and blast of the explosion itself may still fall victim to the deadly radioactive fall-out that follows. The human body can safely absorb a daily dose of only half a rad per hour and not more than 10 rads per day. The following table illustrates the effects of likely radiation levels in the open at various distances from a single megaton explosion in windless conditions.

Dose (rads)	Symptoms	Deaths
over 5000 (up to 3km – 2 miles)	Nausea and vomiting. Convulsions, lethargy, brain damage and respiratory failure	100% in 48 hours
1000-5000 (up to 8km – 5 miles)	Temporary nausea and vomiting. Then recurrence with also diarrhoea, fever and disturbed blood/salt levels. Death from collapse of circulation	100% within 14 days
600-1000 (up to 10km – 6.5 miles)	Nausea and vomiting for 2 days. Lapse and then recurrence after 5-10 days. Symptoms as above for up to 4 weeks. Death from internal bleeding or infection	98-100%
200-600 (up to 19km – 12 miles)	Nausea and vomiting for 2 days. Lapse for 4 weeks. Recurrence for up to 8 weeks. Diarrhoea, low white blood cell count, blood blisters, bleeding and infection. Loss of hair above 300 rads. Death within 2-12 weeks from infection or internal bleeding	0-98%
100-200 (over 19km – 12 miles)	Nausea and vomiting for less than 1 day. Lapse for 2 weeks. Recurrence for 4 weeks. Low white blood cell count	0%

G.K PROTECTION

Key Weapons

THE HAWKER HUNTER

The Hunter was the Hawker Company's first jet fighter to serve with the RAF and it became that service's standard interceptor fighter during the late 1950s. Its introduction into service from 1954 onwards plugged a serious gap in the air defences of the United Kingdom, as the Gloster Meteor F8 which it replaced was inferior in performance to the latest Soviet aircraft. Indeed, so serious was the performance gap between British fighter aircraft and their potential opponents that the North American F-86 Sabre was pressed into RAF service in Germany during 1953 to make good this deficiency. The swept-wing Hunter was a slight improvement over the Sabre in terms of performance, but because it had been conceived as a high altitude interceptor, rather than as an air superiority fighter, it lacked the Sabre's range. Its armament of four 30mm Aden cannon was one of its most advanced features, although ironically it was to be the cause of many of the Hunter's early development problems.

The Hunter prototype first flew on 20 July 1951 with Hawker's chief test pilot, Squadron Leader Neville Duke, at the controls. This aircraft was later fitted with an afterburning Avon engine and in 1953 Duke used it to establish two new world speed records. Standard production Hunters were fitted with non-afterburning Rolls Royce Avon 113 turbojets – the Hunter F1 – or with Armstrong Siddeley Sapphire 101s – the Hunter F2. No 43 Squadron RAF, based at Leuchars in Scotland, was the first frontline unit to be equipped with the Hunter F1 and by 1955 five squadrons were flying the early marks of Hunter. Experience with the initial service variants revealed two serious problems with the design. The first was its inadequate range: the Hunter F1 carried only 1473 litres (324 gallons) of internal fuel, giving it an endurance of some 40 minutes. The second problem affected only the Avon-powered F1: it was found that when the guns were fired at high altitude, hot gases were ingested by the engine causing it to surge and then flame out. These problems were rectified in the next variant.

The Hunter F4 and its Sapphire-powered equivalent the F5 were fitted with additional fuel in wing

Page 2303: A Hunter FGA6 of 229 OCU (operational conversion unit) performs a loop. Above: An FGA9 of 45 Squadron; the bulges under the cockpit are to collect ammunition links from the guns. Left: A Hunter fires a salvo of rockets during target practice. Below left: Hunter prototype WB188 set two World Absolute speed Records in 1963. Below centre: This particular T8 trainer, the prototype, was supplied in reconditioned form to the Singapore Air Force in 1969. Below right: One of the Hunters used in the RAF's original handling trials.

leading-edge tanks and could carry 455 litre (100 gallon) drop tanks on two underwing hardpoints. This went some way to alleviate the Hunter's range problems and the F4's Avon 115 was less prone to surging than its predecessor. Consequently the Hunter F4 was built in substantial numbers and eventually equipped a total of 22 RAF fighter squadrons based in the UK and Germany. Once its early development problems had been overcome, the Hunter proved to be a very popular fighter in RAF service. Its handling qualities were considered by its pilots to be outstanding and its prowess as an aerobatic aircraft was legendary. In 1958 Hunters of the RAF's Black Arrows team (provided by No 111 Squadron) performed a spectacular 22-aircraft formation loop at the Farnborough Air Show. The Hunter F6, powered by the surge-free Avon 200 series turbojet, began to reach the RAF fighter squadrons in 1956. Its four underwing hardpoints gave this mark a useful secondary ground-attack capability. The inner pylons usually carried 1055 litre (230 gallon) drop tanks, leaving the outer pylons free for bombs or air-to-ground rockets.

In 1958 a two-seat operational training version of the Hunter, the T7, entered service with the RAF. This mark served with No 229 Operational Conversion Unit at Chivenor in Devon, and most operational Hunter squadrons had a few on strength. During the 1970s the Hunter T7 served alongside the Gnat T1 as advanced training aircraft with No 4 Flying Training School and in the mid-1980s the type is still used to train Buccaneer pilots at RAF Lossiemouth. The last versions of the Hunter to enter RAF service were conversions of the F6 intended for the ground-attack and fighter reconnaissance roles. The Hunter

FGA9, fitted with a braking parachute and improved air-conditioning, served in the ground-attack role with squadrons in the Middle East and Far East between 1960 and 1968, and saw limited action in Aden and during the Confrontation in Borneo. The Hunter FR10 carried three reconnaissance cameras in the nose, but was otherwise similar to the FGA9. It principally served with Nos 2 and 4 Squadrons in RAF Germany. Single- and two-seat versions of the Hunter also served as training aircraft with the Fleet Air Arm as GA11s, PR11s and T8s. The latest variant of the two-seat T8, the T8M, currently serves with No 899 Squadron at Royal Naval Air Station Yeovilton. It is fitted with a Blue Fox radar and head-up display and is used for Sea Harrier pilot conversion training.

In terms of numbers exported, the Hunter is undoubtedly the most successful postwar British fighter aircraft. The first foreign sales came in the mid-1950s, with the Belgian and Netherlands air forces adopting the type. A total of 460 F4s and F6s were built under licence by Avions Fairey and SABCA in Belgium and Fokker in the Netherlands. They were withdrawn from service in the early 1960s and replaced by the F-104G Starfighter, but substantial numbers of them were bought by Hawkers for refurbishment and re-sale. In all some 400 'remanufactured' Hunters were sold to foreign air forces during the 1960s. In Europe Hunters served with the Royal Swedish Air Force, the Royal Danish Air Force and the Swiss Flugwaffe. Switzerland acquired a total of 152 single-seat Hunters and eight two-seaters and most of these remain in service in the mid-1980s. One Hunter squadron is assigned to air-defence duties, but the majority of the Swiss

Hunters serve with nine ground-attack squadrons. In order to enhance their efficiency in this role, they are to be fitted with Maverick air-to-surface missiles and electronic-countermeasures equipment.

The Hunter found a good market in the air forces of the Middle East and Gulf regions during the 1960s and 1970s, and was supplied to Abu Dhabi, Iraq, Jordan, Kuwait, Lebanon, Oman, Qatar and Saudi Arabia. However, the fighter's combat record in the region has been generally disappointing. Jordan lost her entire force of 21 Hunters during the 1967 war with Israel before they had a chance to show their worth in combat. In 1983 the Lebanese Air Force's single squadron of Hunters attempted to intervene in the civil war, but several aircraft were destroyed for negligible results. Iraq operates some 30 Hunters, organised into three squadrons, but their impact on the ground fighting in the Gulf War with neighbouring Iran has been minimal. Only in Oman, where a single squadron of Hunters flies with the Sultan's air force, did the type enjoy some success, flying counter-insurgency missions against rebels in the Dhofar Province.

Peru and Chile were the only South American states to purchase Hunters. The former received 16 single-seat F52s and a single T62 two-seater, which

Above: Rhodesian Air Force Hunters saw much action against black nationalist guerrillas during 1966-79. Left: Iraqi Hunters are reported to have flown in support of the army during the 1980 invasion of Iran.

Below left: A Chilean Hunter. Hunters bombed the Moneda Palace, the Chilean president's residence, during the coup of 11 September 1973. Below: Lebanese Hunters have seen action against Druze and Muslim militiamen south of Beirut. Right: Swiss Air Force Hunters flying over the Alps.

was delivered in 1956 and remained in service until 1980. Chile purchased a total of 39 Hunters and these were supplemented in 1982-83 by a further 12 aircraft withdrawn from RAF stocks. The Chilean Air Force plans to maintain two Hunter-equipped squadrons in service until the 1990s.

Six Hunters were delivered to Kenya in 1974, allowing that country to form a single fighter-bomber squadron on the type. They were withdrawn from use in 1980, following the delivery of F-5Es, and four were passed on to the air force of newly-independent Zimbabwe. They joined the nine survivors of 12 Hunter FGA9s originally supplied to Rhodesia in 1963 before its unilateral declaration of independence. During the guerrilla war the Hunters had flown with No 1 Squadron Rhodesian Air Force on counter-insurgency operations. In 1983 three Zimbabwean Hunters (plus a BAe Hawk and a Cessna 337) were destroyed in a much publicised sabotage operation at Thornhill airbase.

In the Far East, Hunters equipped the first combat squadrons of the newly-formed Republic of Singapore Air Force in 1968. A total of 47 Hunters was acquired for air defence, attack and tactical reconnaissance duties, serving with No 140 (Osprey) Squadron and No 141 (Merlin) Squadron at the former RAF base of Tengah; 35 of these remained in service in 1984. The Indian Air Force (IAF), which was one of the most important foreign operators of the Hunter with a total of 230 in service, is currently phasing out the type in favour of the Jaguar and MiG-23. The Hunter first entered IAF service in 1957 and saw combat in the September 1965 conflict with Pakistan, flying defensive patrols and carrying out close support and interdiction missions. The Hunters proved to be excellent ground-attack aircraft, but fared less well in air combat. One Pakistan Air Force F-86 Sabre pilot, Wing Commander Mohammed Alam, claimed the destruction of five IAF Hunters in a single mission and it is thought that at least 12 Hunters were lost in air battles. Consequently, the type was restricted to ground-attack missions during the 1971 Indo-Pakistan War, when it played an important part in the IAF interdiction campaign.

After nearly three decades of service, the Hunter is now nearing the end of its flying career. A total of some 1970 were built and Hunters have served with more than 20 air forces. It is a measure of the aircraft's fine flying qualities that it remained in RAF service as a weapons and tactics trainer until the mid-1980s. Although it never saw action in its originally intended role as an interceptor, it proved to be a versatile and reliable tactical fighter and is generally acknowledged to have been one of the classic fighter aircraft of the postwar era.

Below left: A Swiss Air Force Hunter takes off from a motorway during an exercise. Bottom: Hunters of the RAF's Tactical Weapons Units, where RAF Strike Command pilots gain experience of flying high-performance jets. The Hunter is now being phased out of service and replaced in this role by the BAC Hawk trainer.

Hawker Hunter FGA9

Type Single-seat ground-attack fighter
Dimensions Span 10.26m (33ft 8in); length 13.98m (45ft 10in); height 4.01m (13ft 2in)
Weight Empty 6540kg (14,400lb); maximum take-off 11,170kg (24,600lb)
Powerplant One 4608kg (10,150lb) thrust Rolls-Royce Avon 207 turbojet

Performance Maximum speed at 11,000m (36,000ft): Mach 0.95, or 1008km/h (627mph)
Range Combat radius 560km (350 miles); ferry range 2975km (1850 miles)
Ceiling 16,290m (53,400ft)

Armament Four 30mm Aden cannon with 150 rounds per gun, plus 910kg (2000lb) of bombs or air-to-ground rockets on underwing hardpoints

Danger zones

The world's most contentious areas

At the present time, almost a quarter of the world's states are actively involved in armed conflicts of one kind or another. Many of these concern internal security, but many others result from local rivalries and the clash of regional ambitions. Such conflicts have alway existed, and will doubtless continue to occur in the future. The danger now, however, is that with the world far more interdependent than previously, such conflicts can escalate and spread beyond their initial regional limitations.

Few of these conflicts are a direct result of the East-West confrontation which many persist in regarding as the fundamental cause of almost every major and minor international crisis. On the contrary, the region in which this confrontation does exert a dominant influence – Europe – has enjoyed a period of relative stability since World War II, largely thanks to the solidity of the opposing alliance systems and the sharp definition of spheres of influence. In fact, the one persistent conflict in the region which contains the seeds of a potential military clash – that between Greece and Turkey – occurs between states which are both members of the Nato alliance.

If the peace and stability in Europe since 1945 are largely a result of the solidity of the Nato and Warsaw Pact alliances, then the potential effects of the hostility which divides Greece and Turkey are clearly considerable. The situation has understandably been exploited by the Soviet Union, which has made great efforts to establish a warm relationship with the Greek government of socialist Prime Minister Andreas Papandreou, while the United States has opted for continued emphasis upon maintaining close links with Turkey. The significance of this American policy lies in the importance of maintaining Nato control over the vital Bosphorous Straits, through which the Soviet Black Sea Fleet must pass in order to operate in the Mediterranean or beyond.

In the nearby Middle East and Gulf areas, both the United States and the Soviet Union have a close interest in a number of confrontations and conflicts which are largely of local origin, but whose significance again transcends the immediate region. In particular, the Gulf War between Iran and Iraq, although stalemated and with no end in sight after four years of fighting and an enormous toll of casualties, offers inflammable material from which a superpower conflagration might erupt.

Following the fall of the pro-Western Shah in Iran in 1979, and the emergence of fundamentalist Islam

Below: On one of the world's most sensitive borders, a Nicaraguan soldier maintains a careful watch for Contra rebels infiltrating from Honduras. As in many parts of the world, rebels operating from safe bases in neighbouring countries and backed by enemy governments (in this case the United States), pose a serious threat to internal security, while the danger of border clashes leads to regional instability.

as a radical new force in the region, the Soviet Union intervened in neighbouring Afghanistan to prevent a victory there by fundamentalist Mujahidin rebels and to prop up the pro-Moscow regime. Growing instability in the region, coinciding with an overall deterioration in East-West relations, profoundly disturbed the United States, which reacted by creating a Rapid Deployment Force whose task was to protect American interests in the area. The proximity of this region to the Soviet Union, and the threat posed to Western oil supplies by the Gulf War, created the possibility of mutual suspicion and misunderstanding leading through over-reaction and escalation to a direct military clash. Though neither superpower had any interest in such a development, neither exercised a great deal of influence over the main protagonists in the Gulf War, particularly Iran, and this lack of control over events rendered the situation unpredictable and volatile.

Iranian ambitions

The apparent dependence of the Iranian fundamentalist regime upon the continuation of the Gulf War in order to ensure its own popularity and survival was one of the most serious barriers to a negotiated peace settlement, but also suggested a much deeper problem which might pose a long-term threat to regional stability. Although militarily the Khomeini regime has been unable to overcome the increasingly effective Iraqi defences, the existence of large Shi'ite minorities throughout the Gulf creates fears that they might become a Fifth Column for Iranian influence and expansionist ambitions. The narrow social base of many of the regimes in the Arabian peninsula, coupled with falling oil revenues and the delayed reverberations of the world economic crisis, contributed a further source of instability in the area during the mid-1980s.

In the Middle East, the Arab-Israeli conflict creates the constant danger of renewed warfare, and even though Israel announced a withdrawal from southern Lebanon in January 1985, the underlying issue of the future of the Palestinians and of the occupied territories continues to sustain hatreds and tensions. One result of the Israeli intervention in Lebanon has been the emergence for the first time of the previously powerless Shi'ite community there as a new, militant force in Lebanese politics, and one which will be of decisive importance for the future of Lebanon. Whether the Shi'ites will be opposed by Lebanon's other communities is still uncertain as the Israelis prepare to pull back, and there remains a possibility that the departure of the Israelis will be followed by a trial of strength leading to a renewed civil war.

In spite of the conviction of a large number of Israelis that their problems on their northern border can be solved by withdrawal, no such option has been suggested for the occupied West Bank, the Gaza Strip or the Golan Heights. In spite of the Camp David agreement, which called for the creation of some form of Palestinian autonomy on the West Bank and in the Gaza Strip, and numerous international peace initiatives (including the 1982 Reagan Plan which called for an autonomous 'Palestinian entity' on the West Bank), Israel continues to promote the settlement of these predominantly Palestinian areas with Jewish communities – between 1982 and 1984, the number of Jewish settlers on the West Bank grew from 20,700 in 71 settlements to 42,600 in 114.

Regardless of the damage inflicted on the PLO's military potential as a result of the Israeli invasion of the Lebanon in 1982, its continued prestige amongst West Bank Palestinians makes it a vital factor which must be reckoned with in any calculation of the possibility of a negotiated settlement to the Arab-

Bottom left: Anti-communist Mujahidin perch on the rusting hull of a knocked-out Soviet BTR-60P APC. Soviet efforts to bind Afghanistan firmly to the communist camp have been challenged by US covert aid to the Mujahidin, and helped convince the US of the need for a Rapid Joint Deployment Force (RJDF), capable of intervening both in the Gulf region and nearer to home. Below: Men of the 82nd Airborne Division (part of the RJDF), which took part in the invasion of Grenada in October 1983.

Right: Vietnamese troops enjoy a meal in a Kampuchean pavement cafe. Hanoi's regional ambitions have led to the invasion and occupation of Kampuchea, a large Vietnamese military presence in Laos, conflict with Thailand and fighting with China. Bottom: Although Europe has been more stable since World War II, these Soviet troops in Czechoslovakia during the 1968 invasion show the willingness of Moscow to use whatever force necessary to retain control of Eastern Europe.

Israeli conflict. So far, that conflict has resulted in five major wars and innumerable incursions into the territory of neighbouring Arab states by Israeli military forces. In the absence of a negotiated settlement, there seems little reason to believe that this pattern will not be repeated in the future, and the intimate involvement of the superpowers (the US with Israel and the Soviet Union with Syria) leaves the Middle East one of the most sensitive points of East-West confrontation, and one where escalation is a constant danger.

Since the end of World War II, conflict has been almost endemic to Southeast Asia, and many countries there have experienced wars or insurgencies. In Indonesia, a non-communist nationalist movement gained independence from the Dutch in 1949, and thereafter concentrated upon developing and maintaining the unity of a nation composed of countless islands, scattered in an arc around the southern tip of the Malay peninsula. This island chain straddles the route through which much of the seaborne trade must pass upon which the rapidly growing economies of the Pacific Basin depend. In addition, the limited number of channels through the Indonesian archipelago capable of allowing the passage of nuclear submarines from the Pacific to the Indian Ocean, free of detection by enemy satellites, makes the islands of great strategic significance to the military planners of both the United States and the Soviet Union. Indonesia is relatively stable under President Suharto, but the massive size and influence of the Indonesian Communist Party (PKI) until its decimation in 1965, and the recurrence of separatist tendencies and rebellions within Indonesia, suggest a latent potential for unrest and revolt which may in the future threaten stability and security in the area.

Ethnic rivalries

Elsewhere in Southeast Asia, the internal roots of major conflicts have often been obscured by the involvement of external forces. In Indochina, the solid foundation of first the Viet Minh and then the Viet Cong movements in the tradition of Vietnamese nationalism was obscured by what the West regarded as the threat of communist expansionism. After the communist victories of 1975, however, local factors emerged as dominant in the development of conflicts. The centuries-old ethnic rivalry between the Vietnamese and the Khmers of Kampuchea (as Cambodia is now called) resurfaced first as ideological differences, and then as border clashes and full-scale war, which led to the Vietnamese invasion of Kampuchea in December 1978. The subsequent occupation of Kampuchea by the Vietnamese Army and the war which it has fought against the Khmer Rouge and Khmer Serei guerrillas have proven to be a major source of tension in the region, and contain the seeds of an expansion of the conflict to include other states, both within Southeast Asia and beyond, which regard their interests as threatened by the extension of Vietnamese influence into Kampuchea.

The Khmer Rouge's main backer, China, has already invaded the northern border provinces of Vietnam on one occasion in February 1979 as a punishment for the occupation of Kampuchea, and has on several subsequent occasions threatened to repeat the lesson which was apparently ignored by Hanoi. Vietnam, on the other hand, has sought to dissuade Thailand from persisting in its support for the Khmer Rouge and Khmer Serei by staging a number of assaults across the Thai-Kampuchean border against guerrilla bases and refugee camps, as well as repeatedly shelling Thai territory.

In the Philippines, Muslim and communist guerrillas have been fighting for over a decade against the regime of President Ferdinand Marcos, and their grip upon the countryside, particularly on the southern island of Mindanao, continues to grow. The development of a strong urban opposition movement, especially following the murder of opposition leader Benigno Aquino in August 1983, has posed a new and more serious challenge to Marcos, however, and since his health apparently began to deteriorate during 1984, the role of the armed forces has become increasingly important.

Although the Philippines faces no serious external security threats, it occupies a key role in the regional balance of power by virtue of the presence of important US military bases at Subic Bay and Clark air force base. The question-mark which hangs over the future of the Marcos regime, and the possibility of any successor regime facing mounting internal instability, therefore poses a threat to regional security and stability which has broader implications.

Indian influence

In South Asia, a single power – India – has established a large measure of regional dominance. Since the 1971 war which led to the creation of Bangladesh as an independent state, Pakistan has not been strong enough to challenge India over their contested border. To the south, Sri Lanka's severe internal conflict with the Tamil guerrillas may increase India's influence, either through the creation of an Indian-backed Tamil state on the island or through an arrangement for India to cut off support for the guerrillas in return for concessions from the Sri Lankan government. Indian regional predominance reduces the chances of international conflict, but India has its own internal difficulties that could threaten the unity of the country and, consequently, regional stability. In 1984, conflict between the government and the Sikhs was especially acute, leading to the assassination of Prime Minister Indira Gandhi.

Since the end of the Korean War in 1953, the situation in Northeast Asia has been relatively stable, and both North and South Korea, while retaining the proclaimed aim of achieving an eventual reunification, have largely concentrated upon their own internal consolidation and economic development. Again, it is essentially the danger of internal instability in North and South Korea which poses a possible threat to security on the Korean peninsula, and with it the danger of an extension of any conflict to include the major powers with interests in the region – China, Japan, the Soviet Union and the United States. The uncertainty of the eventual succession to ageing communist leader Kim Il Sung in the North, and the recurrence of social and political unrest in the South, are dangerous in that they offer both sides the possible temptation of exploiting the other's problems by making a bid at a military solution to reunification.

Whether ethnic, social or economic, the conflicts which may develop in the coming years in East and Southeast Asia possess a common factor which has marked the history of both regions for the last four

Left: A victim of a Palestinian grenade attack lies wounded in a Jerusalem street. The Israeli occupation of the West Bank, and a mounting rate of Jewish settlement there – against which 'Peace Now' Israeli demonstrators protested in July 1983 (below left) – is a serious obstacle to a Middle East peace settlement.

Below: A US military adviser (left) trains Nicaraguan Contra rebels in riverborne assault tactics at a base in Honduras. Insurgency and the threat of US military intervention make Central America an area of extreme tension during the mid-1980s. Bottom: Nicaraguan Sandinista troops mount a truck under the gaze of 1930s rebel leader General Sandino.

a left-wing, pro-Soviet military regime came to power in 1974 largely as a consequence of a previous drought, famine in areas such as Eritrea and Tigre has been added to civil war as a crisis facing a government forced to rely upon Soviet arms supplies and Western food aid in order to survive. The continued insistence of the government in Addis Ababa on maintaining a unified, centralised state in the face of the demands of the Eritrean and Tigrean guerrilla movements for independence would seem to suggest a persistence of the internal wars which have contributed to the tragic crisis which faces Ethiopia.

In southern Africa, the continued military and economic dominance of South Africa over its black African neighbours remains the single most important strategic factor, and seems to suggest that the balance of power in the region will remain strongly weighted in the West's favour. By 1985, through a policy of economic pressure, support for rebel guerrillas and outright military intervention, South Africa had forced each of its neighbours to accept agreements limiting the activities of guerrillas belonging to South Africa's own banned African National Congress (ANC), and had brought them more closely into Pretoria's economic sphere of influence. This local dominance necessarily transformed the internal South African political situation into a factor of prime importance to the stability of the

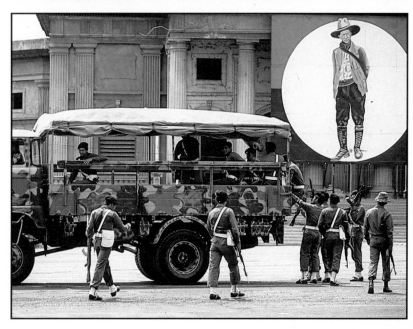

decades – a potential for external involvement and intervention. Nevertheless, the dominant superpower in the region remains the United States, whose position has been strengthened by a close relationship with Peking. The Soviet Union, although now enjoying military and naval facilities in Vietnam, has as yet only a limited potential for intervention, and has made little headway in efforts to increase its political influence in an area otherwise largely dominated by strongly anti-communist regimes.

In Africa, on the other hand, the situation is far more fluid, although of relatively marginal strategic significance. The swift rise in Soviet influence during the 1970s has not continued in the 1980s, leaving the West still in a strong position. In northern and central Africa, the willingness of France to resort to military intervention in order to protect its interests and those of its local allies remains an important factor in the security of a number of countries, and has been encouraged by the United States as a barrier to the ambitions of Libyan leader Colonel Muammar Gaddafi, who is regarded in Washington as a local proxy for the Soviet Union. While French intervention has indeed been successful in propping up pro-Western regimes in Chad, Zaire and the Central African Republic, however, a number of vital local factors indicate a growing potential for regional instability and conflict.

In the Sahel region of northern Africa, for example, the catastrophic effects of a long-term drought and desertification, leading to large-scale famine and migrations, may have unpredictable consequences for the future of a number of states. In Ethiopia, where

Left: Excess gas burning off in the oilfields of Abu Dhabi. Falling oil revenues and large Shi'ite minorities make several Gulf states vulnerable to internal subversion by pro-Iranian fundamentalists. Iran also maintains extensive territorial claims in the Gulf, and remains locked in a bitter war with neighbouring Iraq. Right: A young Iranian fighter – his assault rifle decorated with the portrait of Khomeini – ready for a new offensive against Iraq.

Far right: Iranian Revolutionary Guards lie dead in their fox-holes following a failed offensive. Below: The Iranian oil terminal on Kharg island, target for a number of unsuccessful Iraqi missile attacks. Oil remains the currency which pays for the Gulf War, and a possible motive for superpower intervention.

whole region, but it emerged during a period when political opposition from within the country's black majority was growing in intensity and violence. Regardless of whether or not ANC guerrillas would in future be able to conduct a military campaign across South Africa's northern borders, the country's internal conflict will inevitably have repercussions for the security and stability of the whole of southern Africa during the coming decade.

Meanwhile, in Latin America and the Caribbean, a region traditionally regarded as the secure 'backyard' of the United States, and one which has enjoyed relative peace since the end of World War II, the Americans saw their influence threatened as a consequence of left-wing insurgencies, notably in Central America. The Sandinista victory in Nicaragua in 1979 was a revolutionary success that Washington remained determined to reverse, and the Reagan administration was equally committed to defeating the guerrilla forces fighting in El Salvador. Elsewhere in Central and South America, insurgency may be latent, but can always break out when conditions are right. In Peru, for example, the Maoist Sendero Luminoso (Shining Path) guerrilla movement has exploited economic discontent among the Quechua-speaking Indians inhabiting remote mountain areas to create a deep-rooted insurgency which poses a mounting security threat. The campaign of violence began on 18 May 1980, on the day of the first elections in Peru for 12 years, and by 1984 the Sendero Luminoso was able to field large units for attacks upon prisons and government-held villages.

These revolts, which are essentially the product of centuries of economic exploitation and political repression of largely peasant populations, threaten the entrenched power of oligarchies and military dictatorships which receive support from the United States because of a mutual hostility to communism and the spread of Soviet and Cuban influence in the region. But the narrow social base and extreme unpopularity of these regimes are major factors in the creation of an almost endemic instability which is a continual threat to the security of all states in the area. The problem of spiralling external debts afflicts almost every country in Latin America, sharpening existing social and economic discontent, and seems certain in the future to increase pressures for fundamental change, which in turn may provoke a new cycle of military intervention and violence.

But while many countries face serious internal security threats, there has not been a major war fought between the countries of Latin America since the 1930s – yet still, large and expensive military establishments are maintained. Brazil, for example, has 274,000 men under arms; Argentina and Cuba both have establishments of 153,000 men; and Peru's armed forces number 135,000. (By way of comparison, Canada, with a population similar to Argentina's, keeps a military establishment of 82,858). Although to some extent these large forces are seen as 'schools of the nation', their main role remains the maintenance of political order – often through direct armed intervention.

What emerges most clearly from such a short overall review of some of the potential areas of conflict in the world over the coming decade is the overwhelming importance of local factors, and the peripheral significance of the competition between the capitalist West and the communist East as a cause of regional wars and internal insurgencies. Nevertheless, such conflicts do not occur in a strategic vacuum, totally isolated from the security interests of the great powers – the potential for external intervention always exists, and with it the danger of escalation and superpower confrontation.

J. S. Common

Drawing the line

Border disputes as a source of conflict

Territorial disputes have been a staple source of human conflict since the earliest days of civilisation. In the contemporary world, mutually agreed and recognised borders have been achieved by a large number of countries, often after bitter wars fought in previous centuries. Western Europe and South America are two areas in which much bloodshed has resulted in an eventual accord between most neighbouring states on their frontier lines (although Chile, for example, still has a significant territorial dispute with Bolivia). In other parts of the world, however, especially where boundaries are newer, peace is frequently threatened by trials of strength to decide the geographical limits of a state's authority. These are obviously most likely to occur if serious economic or strategic interests are at stake, although as the 1982 Falklands conflict amply demonstrated, states could also go to war for territory of no immediate material or military value.

The Falklands was an example of a kind of territorial dispute in which Britain has been widely involved, where an existing independent state wishes to take over neighbouring territory still under colonial rule or being decolonised. In Central America, Britain is still defending newly-independent Belize against the claims of Guatemala; in Europe, Britain refused to allow Cyprus to become part of Greece at independence, and British possession of Gibraltar has long been a bone of contention with Spain; in Asia, Britain fought to prevent Indonesia taking over the northern half of the island of Borneo when that area became independent, and the future of Hong Kong was disputed with China until an agreement was reached in 1984. The major current territorial conflict to arise in this way, however, is being fought in the wastes of the Western Sahara, formerly

the Spanish Sahara, in northwest Africa. As in most of Africa, the borders in this region were laid down by colonial powers, cutting across ethnic divisions and traditional domains. The rulers of Morocco had a claim, based on their golden era in the late Middle Ages, to territory extending far to the south of their existing realm, including part of Algeria, the Spanish Sahara and Mauritania. When Spain decided to withdraw from its African colony in the mid-1970s, it was pressured into handing the territory over to Morocco and Mauritania, who divided it between them, but ever since the local population, backed by Algeria, have fought a guerrilla war against Morocco (Mauritania having soon withdrawn from the fray). Algeria and Morocco have in the past engaged in border skirmishes, and this, plus the continuing 'Greater Morocco' claim to Mauritania, makes the whole region extremely unstable.

Further to the east in the same vast desert zone, Libya under Colonel Muammar Gaddafi lays claim to the north of its neighbour Chad – the so-called Aozou Strip. Just as Morocco's interest in the Western Sahara is increased by the presence there of phosphate deposits, Libya's desire to control northern Chad is not unconnected with the known existence of uranium in the area. Libya has been effectively in occupation of the Aozou Strip since the early 1970s, but its interest in who rules Chad led to further direct involvement in 1983, the advance of Libyan troops on the Chadean capital, Ndjamena, only being stopped by a French interventionary force.

Perhaps surprisingly, these Saharan territorial disputes have been the exception rather than the rule in post-independence Africa. The frontiers inherited from the former colonial powers in the early 1960s were totally artificial, cutting across tribal bound-

Above: A Moroccan GPMG-crew guarding a sector of the Western Sahara, control of which is disputed with the Polisario guerrilla movement, supported by Libya and Algeria. Below: Israeli troops fire on Arab demonstrators in the town of Nablus on the occupied West Bank. Israel keeps a firm grip on the West Bank and the Gaza Strip, and has annexed the Golan Heights, captured from Syria in 1967.

aries, splitting ethnic, religious and linguistic groupings, and dividing economically closely-related regions. This, along with the weakness of independent African regimes, could easily have led to an orgy of territorial conflicts as states readjusted to more natural boundaries. That this did not happen can largely be attributed to African states' intense awareness of the problem. The Organization of African Unity (OAU) holds the defence of existing borders as one of its main articles of faith, precisely because virtually every frontier in Africa would have to be redrawn were the principle abandoned. There have been attempts at secession which led to major conflicts – the Biafra War in Nigeria and the Katanga conflict in the ex-Belgian Congo (Zaire) – but only Somalia has broken ranks in sub-Saharan Africa and seriously sought to upset the colonial settlement.

Since 1960, when the former British and Italian Somalilands united to form a Somali Republic, successive governments in Somalia have claimed the right of self-determination for all ethnic Somalis, a large number of whom live in neighbouring Kenya and Ethiopia. It is assumed that 'self-determination' would mean agreement to join Somalia, thus annexing large areas of both neighbours for the Somali state. Between 1963 and 1968, Somali tribesmen in Kenya, encouraged by the government in Mogadishu, harassed first British colonial forces and then, after independence, Kenyan government forces. The conflict subsided after OAU pressure on Somalia to accept the existing frontiers, but the Somali claim to the Ogaden region of Ethiopia, which had already led to fighting in 1964, was then pursued with mounting vigour, leading up to a full-scale Somali invasion of Ethiopia in 1977. After the defeat of this invasion in 1978, the conflict rebounded on Somalia, which from 1982 found itself fighting off an Ethiopian-backed insurgency.

In East Asia, a major potential source of border conflicts since 1945 has been, and remains, the effort of the Chinese communist government to re-establish the borders of China that had been eroded during the long decline of the Manchu Empire. Great concern was caused to all China's neighbours after the establishment of the communist regime in 1949 by the publication of an official map including within China all the former Celestial Empire's tributary

Above: Soviet Border Guards, a military formation responsible to the KGB, patrol a section of the Far Eastern Sino-Soviet frontier. Armed clashes here during 1969 led to heavy casualties, and territorial disputes still sour relations between Peking and Moscow.

Below: A guerrilla fighter of the West Somali Liberation Front, which continues to operate in the Ogaden region of Ethiopia. Somali territorial claims also extend to Djibouti and areas of Kenya, and represent a major source of instability in East Africa.

states up to and including Malaysia; but in fact China has shown great restraint, apart from its invasion of Tibet, a traditional tributary, in 1955 and its crushing of the Dalai Lama's revolt four years later. Between January 1960 and November 1963 China signed border treaties with no less than five of her adjoining neighbours – Burma, Nepal, Pakistan, Mongolia and Afghanistan.

Twice, however, the People's Liberation Army (PLA) has invaded the territory of troublesome neighbours with whom the frontier line was a matter of contention. In 1962 five divisions of the PLA broke through into northeastern India, only to withdraw a month after the fighting began, and in February 1979 some 200,000 Chinese troops crossed into Vietnam, again withdrawing a month later. In both cases China was in fact resisting territorial claims by its neighbours – although also in both cases, the Chinese military action was essentially punitive in intention, with wider political goals than the question of small strips of border territory. It is possible that the unresolved dispute with Vietnam – which includes the contentious question of possession of the Spratly and Paracel Islands – might still lead to further fighting, largely because of the intense ideological rivalry between the two communist states.

The greatest danger of conflict lies, however, along the 6600km (4150-mile) border between China and the Soviet Union, where perhaps 1.5 million Chinese troops face some 700,000 Soviet soldiers. During the 19th century, Tsarist Russia seized over a million square km (380,000 square miles) of the Chinese Empire, and it is quite possible that one day the Chinese will demand the return of all these territories – acquired, the Soviet Union itself agreed in 1920, by a 'predatory policy'. The highest point of tension to date occurred in 1969, when fighting flared up on islands in the disputed Amur/Ussuri Rivers, and a Soviet nuclear strike against China seemed a distinct possibility. At present, China is militarily in no position to assert any wider claims against the Soviet Union.

China satisfied its desire for sovereignty over Hong Kong in late 1984, when Britain agreed that control would pass to Peking once the lease on the colony expired. Another Western colonial remnant, Macao, remains in Portuguese hands only since it suits the Chinese to keep it that way. The major dispute off China's coast concerns Taiwan, last refuge of the Nationalists defeated by the communists in 1949. Peking seemed in mid-1980 to be seeking some compromise arrangement which would bring the island under China's sovereignty while permitting a large measure of autonomy.

Before leaving East Asia, mention must be made of the Kuril Islands occupied by the Soviet Union at the end of World War II, but claimed by Japan. A re-militarised Japan might well press this dispute vigorously – and dangerously – before the end of the present century.

The division of the Indian sub-continent between Muslims and Hindus in 1947, creating India and Pakistan, left a border problem in Punjab and Kashmir that has been a source of conflict on three occasions – in the immediate aftermath of independence, in 1965 and in 1971. Since the creation of Bangladesh as a result of the 1971 war and the consequent weakening of Pakistan, tension on the Punjab/Kashmir border has tended to decline, but with both Pakistan and India possibly seeking to develop a credible nuclear capacity, the unresolved border question retains a worrying potential for major future conflict.

Borders in question

It is perhaps in the Middle East that borders are at their most fragile, with the existence of states widely questioned by their neighbours. The British and French colonial powers imposed frontiers on the remnants of the Turkish Empire after World War I, and the situation was further complicated by Israel's successive wars against the Arab states. While all the Arab countries except Egypt refuse to recognise Israel within any borders, Jordan has a specific claim to the occupied West Bank and Syria regards the Golan area annexed by Israel in 1982 as its own. But the existence of Jordan in its present form – a hybrid product of British policy yoking together very different desert Arab and settled Palestinian populations – is put in question by the demand for a Palestinian homeland. Further north, Syria has never fully accepted the creation of Lebanon as a separate state, a consequence of French imperial policy, although it appears that Syria will settle for influence over Beirut rather than dreaming of annexation. Only on the frontier between Israel and Egypt does an acceptable border appear to have been established, except for a few minor points of contention.

In the Arabian peninsula, frontiers still have to be established in parts of the vast Empty Quarter, but the main point of dispute is the border between North and South Yemen, regarded by both sides as an artificial division, although they cannot agree on a plan for unification and came to armed conflict over the issue in the early 1970s.

The most costly border war since 1945 is being fought between Iran and Iraq, whose Gulf War overtly concerns a dispute over a small strip of border and the Shatt al Arab waterway. Evidently, ideological differences centring on the confrontation between Sunni and Shi'ia Islam are more important than the actual territory involved. Iran's regional territorial claims – to Bahrain and Kuwait, for example – are only comprehensible in terms of Shi'ite against Sunni Muslim, and of Iran's aspirations to regional dominance, although historical justification is advanced for the Iranian position.

An interesting point about the Middle Eastern

Above: West German Border Guards survey the frontier with the East. One of the most dangerous borders in the world, both for its minefields and its importance for East-West relations, the inter-German frontier is nevertheless a stable line which divides Nato and the Warsaw Pact.

Right: A French Foreign Legion patrol in the Chad desert, armed with the new 5.56mm MAS automatic rifle. Libyan claims to the northern Aozou Strip of Chad have complicated the resolution of the Chad civil war. Far right: Vietnamese Border Guards engage in a stone-throwing confrontation with their Chinese opposite numbers. Border clashes have continued since the Chinese invasion of 1979.

Changing borders in central Europe

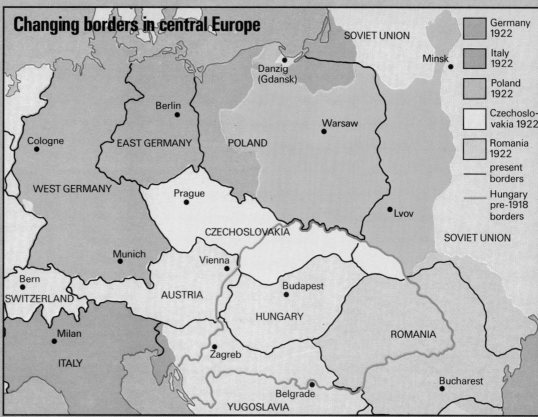

Germany 1922
Italy 1922
Poland 1922
Czechoslovakia 1922
Romania 1922
present borders
Hungary pre-1918 borders

SOVIET UNION
Minsk
Danzig (Gdansk)
Berlin
Warsaw
Cologne
EAST GERMANY
POLAND
WEST GERMANY
Prague
Lvov
CZECHOSLOVAKIA
SOVIET UNION
Munich
Vienna
Bern
SWITZERLAND
AUSTRIA
Budapest
HUNGARY
Milan
ROMANIA
ITALY
Zagreb
Belgrade
Bucharest
YUGOSLAVIA

conflicts is that 'nationalism', in the sense understood in the West, plays little part. In Europe, the aspiration to include all members of one nation within one state has long been the basis for territorial disputes. This could still be a potent source of conflict in central and eastern Europe. World War I and World War II both produced radical changes to borders in the area, finally creating the frontiers we see today. But these are far from satisfactory to the national consciousness of many countries involved. Germans, in particular, often express a deep dissatisfaction not only with the division of their nation in two, but also with the handing of large areas of Prussia to Poland and the Soviet Union at the end of World War II. If the prospect ever arose, the Poles would hardly accept the return of territory to the Germans, however, although they themselves might claim territory to the east taken by the Soviet Union. Some Hungarians, to take another example, still look back to the Greater Hungary which formed part of the Austrian Empire before World War I, with particular claims to areas of Romania and Czechoslovakia which have a large population of Hungarian speakers. Such potential disputes are kept totally dormant by the dominance of the Soviet Union over the whole area, but they would constitute an extremely dangerous complicating factor if any 'liberation' of communist Eastern Europe were to take place.

A final border dispute to be mentioned is that concerning Northern Ireland. The division of Ireland in two has never been accepted by the Dublin government, except as a temporary *fait accompli*. The constitution of the Republic refers to all of Ireland as one territory. Yet it is not to be expected that any government in the south will commit itself to an armed struggle to evict the British; force will be employed only by the IRA.
Graham Brewer

Who rules the waves?

On 10 December 1982 a treaty dealing with nearly every aspect of sea law, the Convention on the Law of the Sea, was signed by 117 states. This convention, the end product of nearly 10 years of arduous negotiations, represented an international effort to establish a comprehensive regime to govern the three-fifths of the planet's surface covered by water. Such an effort had certainly become necessary, for during the four decades since World War II the oceans had become a focus of growing confusion, discord and disorder. Indeed, the oceans, for centuries an *arena* of conflict, had developed into an important *source* of conflict.

This turbulence can be attributed largely to a dramatic increase in competition to exploit the sea's food and mineral resources. Rising demand for such resources, stimulated by an explosive population growth and pressures for higher living standards, led mankind to look increasingly to the seas to supplement or replace land resources. At the same time, technological advances made it easier to exploit the sea's reserves, both protein and mineral. As a result of these two trends competition for the actual or potential riches of the seas became more and more intense. The upshot was a scramble for oceanic jurisdiction not seen since the 17th century, reflected in attempts to stake out maritime claims in the form of exclusive economic zones (EEZs) and to extend territorial seas beyond the traditional 5km (3-mile) limit. Inevitably, claims and counter-claims have led to a growing number of disputes and conflicts.

Many of these disputes have been concerned with the sea's foodstocks, notably fish. Of course, mankind has been taking fish from the seas since time immemorial, but in recent years the 'take' has risen

Below: The USS *New Jersey* (centre), a World War II US battleship, brought out of mothballs and refitted with cruise missiles by the Reagan administration, under escort from a Wichita-class replenishment oiler, a Knox-class frigate, and a Charles F. Adams-class destroyer. While the superpowers compete for control of the oceans, most states are increasingly concerned to assert their hold over their own territorial waters.

markedly. Between 1950 and 1970 the total world fish catch rose from 20 million tonnes to nearly 70 million tonnes, an increase accounted for mainly by the development of high-technology distant-water fishing fleets by the Soviet Union, Japan and other states. This massive increase in the world catch has had serious effects. Some stocks of fish have been threatened to the point of extinction by over-fishing (a problem exacerbated by pollution), stimulating efforts by the fishing communities affected to protect stocks and livelihoods. Consequently, disputes over fishing rights have been both frequent and widespread.

One such dispute, that between the Soviet Union and Japan, involved numerous incidents in the Sea of Japan and the Sea of Okhotsk. The Soviet Union, though keen to retain the right to fish off the shores of other states, took a strong line against Japanese fishing activities off the Soviet Pacific coastline, impounding over 3000 Japanese fishing boats and imprisoning over 9000 Japanese fishermen, some for as long as seven years, between the late 1940s and the mid-1970s. Another long-running dispute, the so-called 'tuna wars' of the 1950s, 1960s and 1970s, saw Peru and Ecuador seizing and imposing fines on US fishing vessels operating in waters claimed by these two Latin American states. Argentina proved itself to be equally, if not more, sensitive to foreign 'encroachment', opening fire on two Soviet and two Bulgarian fishing vessels operating off her coastline in October 1977.

However, perhaps the most notable of the numerous fishing disputes to have occurred since 1945 are the so-called 'cod wars' between Britain and Iceland. Iceland, an island state heavily dependent on

The race for control of the sea

off-shore fishing for its economic survival, has extended its fishing limits (that is, an off-shore area in which the coastal state claims exclusive jurisdiction) four times since World War II – from 5km to 7km (3 miles to 4 miles) in 1952, to 20km (12 miles) in 1958, to 50km (30 miles) in 1972, and eventually, in 1975, to 320km (200 miles). On each occasion Iceland acted unilaterally, leading to protests from countries affected that the Icelanders had flouted international law. Nevertheless, on each occasion Iceland eventually got more or less what it wanted, though not without a struggle. The waters in question were traditional, and important, fishing grounds for British trawlermen, and on each occasion the British contested Iceland's decision, initially through international law and political negotiation, and afterwards by maritime deployment. In three of these cases – 1958, 1972 and 1975 – violence ensued, albeit at a low level.

During the first cod war (September 1958-February 1961), Icelandic gunboats attempted to put grapples on British trawlers and to send boarding parties on them, fired blank shots so as to force British skippers to a halt and engaged in dangerous manoeuvres such as cutting across the bows of British ships; Britain, for its part, sent Royal Navy Fishery Protection vessels into the disputed waters to support its trawlermen. In the second cod war (September 1972-November 1973) Icelandic harassment of British trawlers became so serious, despite the presence of civilian support ships, that the British government felt compelled to send in Royal Navy frigates. The navy's intervention led to a decline in harassment of the trawlers, but there were incidents between British vessels – frigates and support tugs – and Icelandic gunboats, including several collisions. The third cod war (October 1975-June 1976) followed a similar course. Once again British trawlers were harassed by Iceland's small force of gunboats, and once again Britain despatched

Above: Merchant vessels moored off the Jordanian port of Aqaba. An Egyptian threat to blockade the Gulf of Aqaba to Israeli shipping in 1967 led directly to the Six-Day War, and control of vital shipping lanes remains a major source of contention in many areas of the world.

civilian support ships and naval frigates to protect its trawlermen. There were numerous incidents. Icelandic gunboats cut the warps of 45 British trawlers, there were collisions between the gunboats and British frigates and one gunboat, the *Thor*, actually fired at British vessels. By the time the 'war' had ended 15 British frigates out of 20 deployed (there were between four and six on station at any one time) had been damaged, at a cost of over £1 million.

If competition for the sea's food resources has given rise to disputes and conflict, so too has competition for the sea's energy and mineral resources, notably oil and gas. Perceptions of declining reserves on land, together with advances in technology, have encouraged a rush to explore and exploit the resources on and under the seabed; indeed, by the mid-1970s some 20 per cent of the world's oil and gas production was coming from off-shore fields. Not surprisingly, the discovery or even the promise of seabed riches has led to conflicting claims for jurisdiction over oceanic island groups and associated continental shelves, and sometimes to confrontations and military clashes.

Allies divided

One such confrontation took place early in 1974 between fellow members of Nato, Greece and Turkey. Divided by historic enmities, the Cyprus question and mutually exclusive territorial claims to the Aegean Sea, the Greeks and Turks found their differences exacerbated by the discovery of oil and gas in that sea. Greece, which had already claimed virtually the entire Aegean, announced in February 1974 that significant oil and gas deposits had been found in the northern Aegean and claimed exclusive rights to all mineral resources on the continental shelf. Turkey, which had already claimed sovereignty over roughly half the Aegean Sea, now had an economic as well as a strategic reason for opposing the Greek claim. The dispute led both sides to place their armed forces on alert and to engage in naval demonstrations. By June 1974 the oil issue had become overshadowed by the more pressing Cyprus question, but it remained a serious factor in Graeco-Turkish relations, reinforcing rival claims to the Aegean and compounding the differences between two Nato members.

Left: HMS *Yarmouth*, a Type 12 British frigate, displays serious bow damage after a collision with the Icelandic gunboat *Baldur* during the 1975-76 cod war. The importance of the sea as a source of food and minerals provides a further stimulus to competition and conflict.

In the same year, anxiety to stake out claims to potentially oil-rich areas of the South China Sea led to conflict between the Chinese People's Republic and South Vietnam. At stake were the seas around two island groups – the Paracels and the Spratleys – the latter occupied by South Vietnam, Taiwan and the Philippines, and the former by South Vietnam and China. In August 1973, South Vietnam declared its intention to survey for oil in the seas off her coastline adjacent to the Spratleys, and in the following month declared the Spratley Islands part of South Vietnam. China responded by reaffirming its claim to both island groups and, in January 1974, drove the South Vietnamese off the Paracels, occupying the entire archipelago after a brief but fierce clash that involved land, sea and air forces. This did not end the dispute, however, because after the collapse of South Vietnam in April 1975, the successor regime in the unified state of Vietnam placed its troops on the Spratleys and laid claim to both island groups. The

future of the archipelagos and their surrounding seas has remained a significant issue in Sino-Vietnamese relations.

Another conflict for possession of a group of islands – Argentina's invasion of the Falkland Islands in April 1982 – can also be attributed, in part at least, to the prospect of seabed riches. True, Argentina's claim to what it calls the Islas Malvinas was long-standing, but that claim was given greater impetus by the alluring prospect of oil and protein – krill – riches in the seas around the islands. Indeed, the prize was not so much the islands themselves as the massive extension of the South American mainland on which they sit. Acquisition of the Falklands and its dependencies would have given Argentina a stronger case for claiming jurisdiction over the continental shelf and its extension into the Antarctic, another area of potential mineral wealth.

While competition for the sea's protein and mineral resources has given rise to a number of confrontations and conflicts, it should not be assumed that the oceans have degenerated into a kind of politico-legal jungle. Most parties to disputes of the sea have been reluctant to use force as a means of gaining their

Above: On board an Argentinian patrol boat, the crew of an anti-aircraft gun search the sky for enemy aircraft. Following the 1982 war with Britain, the re-equipment and modernisation of the Argentinian Navy poses an increasing threat to Fortress Falklands. Top: A Nicaraguan patrol boat circles a Swedish merchant ship, damaged in a sabotage attack by US-backed Contra rebels in the port of Corinto. The ability of the US to impose blockades on left-wing countries, such as Nicaragua and Cuba, added to its dominance of Central and South America.

objectives, either because they have lacked sufficient military strength, or because they have had moral, political or legal reservations about using force. Indeed, the majority of maritime disputes since 1945 have been settled without recourse to violence, by political negotiation and legal arbitration. Moreover, there has been a growing international recognition of the need for at least a minimum level of order in maritime affairs, as illustrated by near universal participation in the third UN Conference on the Law of the Sea (UNCLOSIII). This conference, convened in 1974 to resolve the problems that had arisen since the 1958 and 1960 sea-law conferences, eventually devised a comprehensive treaty dealing with most aspects of sea law, including the extent of territorial waters (20km – 12 miles) and EEZs (320km – 200 miles), jurisdiction over continental shelves, measures to prevent marine pollution, transit rights through international straits and a system for settling maritime disputes. The treaty was adopted by the UN General Assembly in April 1982 and was signed by 117 states in December 1982; another 39 states added their signatures over the next two years. The final document, the Convention on the Law of the Sea, promised to make disorder at sea much less likely.

Nevertheless, the possibility that further confrontations and conflicts will take place over the sea's resources – and over other maritime issues like transit through territorial straits – cannot be dismissed. The Convention may have raised great hopes, but few states have ratified it and the United States, objecting to clauses relating to the 'internationalisation' of deep-sea mining activities (most of this mining has so far been carried out by US-dominated multinationals), has been reluctant to sign at all; in any case the Convention, like the UN Charter, will be subject to varying interpretation and to varying degrees of commitment by individual sovereign states. Some maritime disputes are likely to lead to conflict regardless of legal ruling or conventions, particularly in cases where the economic stakes are extremely attractive and where relations between the parties concerned are already strained or hostile because of other issues. It may well be, therefore, that conflict over the sea's resources will continue to be a characteristic feature of international relations for some time to come. **Francis Toase**

Key Weapons

TACTICAL NUCLEAR WEAPONS

Tactical nuclear weapons have been important to Nato's war plans since 1953. At present the doctrine of flexible response, involving the possible use of tactical nuclear weapons in the face of a successful Soviet conventional offensive, continues to be Nato's policy to fight its next war, and in line with this strategy around 7000 tactical nuclear warheads are thought to be deployed with Nato forces in Europe today.

A tactical nuclear weapon can be defined as a nuclear device used to influence the course of fighting in a specific combat zone. Intermediate-range missiles, like cruise and Pershing II, and medium-range bombers stand on an uncertain borderline between tactical and strategic use; this article will restrict itself to exclusively tactical weapons, comprising short-range missiles, bombs carried on attack aircraft, nuclear-capable artillery and atomic demolition mines.

Tactical nuclear bombs in the US stockpile comprise the B28, B43, B57 and B61 types, which are compatible with a variety of tactical and strategic aircraft, including the F-111, the A-4 Skyhawk, the A-6 Intruder, the A-7 Corsair II and the F/A-18 Hornet attack aircraft. The B28 has a yield of 70-1450 kilotons, the B43 1000 kilotons, the B57 depth bomb 20 kilotons, and the B61 from 100-500 kilotons.

The last US nuclear-armed air-to-surface missiles, the Bullpup and Walleye, were withdrawn from service in 1978-79, leaving the nuclear capability of tactical aircraft entirely to gravity bombs. However, missiles with stand-off capabilities and improved accuracies are currently under development. These projects include the Tactical Air-to-Surface Munition/Extended Range Bomb and the Terminal Guided Extended Range Missile.

The smallest nuclear weapons are nuclear land mines, more frequently referred to as ADMs (atomic demolition munitions). Two types are employed with the US Army and Marine Corps: the MADM (medium atomic demolition munition), a one to 15 kiloton device weighing about 180kg (400lb), and the SADM (special atomic demolition munition), a sub-kiloton landmine weighing about 70kg (150lb). The MADM is designed for employment by engineer units while the SADM, being man-portable, is intended for use by special forces and commando units. It is thought that about 600 ADMs are deployed in Europe, South Korea, Guam in the Pacific and the continental United States. A number of British, Dutch, and West German engineer units have been trained to emplace ADMs.

Page 2323: A French Pluton missile is test-launched. The launch vehicle's chassis is based on that of the AMX30 tank. Bottom left: A Pershing IA missile being prepared for launch and (inset) being launched. This missile was first deployed in 1969 and is now being replaced by the Pershing II. Left: The Honest John is a rocket system first deployed by the US Army in 1953.

ADMs are intended primarily to disrupt the movement of enemy forces, making obstructions obliging the enemy to concentrate these forces in a mass, thereby creating more targets for other nuclear weapons. MADMs used in this way would mostly be detonated on friendly territory; SADMs would be used behind enemy lines. ADMs with a remote delivery capability have been under study but the projects under development – the Tactical Earth Penetrator Warhead, the Shallow Burst Munition and the Nuclear Cratering Explosive – were cancelled in January 1981. There have been no further plans to replace the ADMs with new nuclear systems; rather, it is intended to replace them gradually with non-nuclear mines as conventional capabilities are improved.

Nuclear-capable artillery weapons are the most widely dispersed and numerous of battlefield nuclear weapons, with over 3500 guns and two warhead types deployed. These are the 0.1 kiloton W48 155mm fission warhead and the one to 12 kiloton W33 8in fission warhead. Approximately 5000 nuclear artillery shells are deployed. This category of weapons once included the Davy Crockett portable recoilless gun, which was capable of firing the smallest nuclear projectile ever devised; however, since the blast radius exceeded the range, the system proved unpopular and was withdrawn from service before 1970. US Army nuclear-capable artillery currently deployed comprises the M114 155mm gun, the M109 155mm gun and the M110 8in gun. Other Nato countries employ: in 155mm the M59 gun, the M44 self-propelled howitzer, the M198 howitzer and the FH-70/SP-70 howitzers; in 8in the M55 self-propelled howitzer. The newest guns – the M198 howitzer of the US Army and the FH-70 and SP-70 – have ranges of 30km (18 miles), and the older guns are being converted using longer gun barrel tubes and muzzle brakes. A number of artillery projects are currently under development for deployment in the next few years.

Surface-to-surface missiles form another important part of Nato's tactical nuclear weapons inventory. The Pershing IA is the longest-ranged and highest-yield US Army tactical nuclear weapon, and was first deployed in 1969, replacing an earlier model of the same system. It is carried by wheeled vehicles based on the M656 truck comprising an erector-launcher, a programming and power station transporter, a firing-control truck and a radio vehi-

The simplest forms of tactical nuclear weapons are gravity bombs that might be carried on an F/A-18 (below) or artillery shells such as might be fired by this M109 155mm self-propelled howitzer (bottom).

cle. The missile itself uses an inertial guidance system that operates until the second stage cuts out; the warhead ranges from 60 to 400 kilotons. More than 300 Pershings, with 180 launchers, are deployed with the US Army and West German Air Force in Europe (although the Americans control the nuclear warheads for the West German missiles). Deployment of the replacement for the Pershing I, the longer-range Pershing II, began in 1984.

The Pershing I was designed to strike at targets some distance behind the battlefront. Shorter-ranged missiles such as the Corporal and Sergeant were intended to attack targets just behind the enemy's troops at the front line. The Corporal was first deployed in the 1950s and served with the US and British Armies. It was steered by means of radio commands, the course being followed by radar, and used a liquid-propulsion rocket motor. The Corporal suffered from a slow rate of fire (only one missile could be fired every six to seven hours) and required careful maintenance, so a replacement was soon sought. The Sergeant missile incorporated many improvements: solid-fuel propulsion, inertial guidance and a reduction in the number of support vehicles. The Sergeant first entered service in 1962 and was withdrawn during the mid-1970s.

The short-range Lance missile is more widely deployed than Pershing, with 100 launchers operational in the Belgian, British, Dutch, Italian, US and West German Armies, although the 945 nuclear warheads are all in US hands. The Lance is propelled by liquid fuel and uses inertial guidance, having

previously been aligned with the target. The Lance is carried to its launch position by an M688 loader/transporter carrying two missiles which it transfers by means of a crane to an M752 launch vehicle. There is also a towed launcher that can be pulled by a 2.5-tonne truck or slung beneath a helicopter. It is planned to replace Lance with the Corps Support Weapon in the late 1980s.

The United States also had tactical nuclear missiles with extremely short ranges of around 32km (20 miles). The famous Honest John was an unguided artillery rocket that first entered service in 1953. It was fired from a rail mounted on a truck and atmospheric conditions had to be taken into account for targeting purposes. Nuclear warheads could also be mounted on the Lacrosse surface-to-surface missile which, like the Corporal, was guided to the target by means of radio control, in this case in the hands of a forward observation officer. The missile was fired from a launcher mounted on the back of a 2.5-tonne truck. Short-range missiles like these are now obsolescent with the arrival of rocket-assisted shells in the late 1970s, which can travel 30km (18 miles).

Nike Hercules is the only land-based nuclear surface-to-air missile in the US inventory, with about 500 deployed in Europe; it can also be used in the surface-to-surface mode. Belgium, Greece, Italy, the Netherlands and West Germany are supplied with the system, and nuclear warheads may also be

Right: Frog-7 rockets of the Soviet Army advance through a forest during a training exercise in winter. Below right: An SS-12 Scaleboard missile of the Soviet Army on its transporter. Bottom right: The Soviet Scud-1B missile is also in service with the Warsaw Pact nations, Egypt and Libya.

Below: A Lance missile of the US Army is fired from its M752 launcher-erector vehicle. The Lance is in service with other Nato nations, but the nuclear warheads are under US control.

supplied to systems deployed in South Korea. However, some nuclear warheads for this missile have been withdrawn from Europe, and it is planned to replace the Nike Hercules with the conventional Patriot missile.

There are a number of US sea-based tactical nuclear ASW (anti-submarine warfare) weapons as well as surface-to-air missiles. However, none of these would be employed against a tactical land objective and many are being withdrawn from service. US Navy tactical weapons are some of the oldest in service; they include the W44 warhead for the Asroc (anti-submarine rocket) system, the W45 warhead on the Terrier surface-to-air missile, the W55 for the Subroc (submarine rocket) nuclear depth charge, the B57 nuclear depth bomb, as well as the previously mentioned B43 and B61 bombs. Under development is a nuclear warhead for the Standard surface-to-air missile and a new bomb.

The French Army introduced its own tactical nuclear missile in 1974 with the Aérospatiale Pluton, a two-stage solid propellant rocket roughly equivalent to the US Lance system. The warhead can be either a 15 kiloton or a 25 kiloton yield device. This weapon is deployed with five specially formed regiments on French soil.

It can only be assumed that the Soviet Union has tactical nuclear bombs, but it is certain that they have air-to-surface missiles with nuclear warheads. The AS-3 Kangaroo, AS-4 Kitchen and AS-6 Kingfish missiles could all be used in the tactical role against enemy forces to the rear of the front line, but the fact that they are carried by medium- and strategic-range bombers suggests that this would be unlikely.

The main strength of Soviet tactical nuclear capability lies in the missile forces attached to the army. Three types of weapon are used: the Frog (free rocket over ground), the SS-1 Scud and the SS-12 Scaleboard. The Frog is a series of rockets, similar in concept to the Honest John. It is unguided and speed brakes are used to adjust the course. The Frog-9 is the latest in the series, entering service in the late 1970s. The SS-1 Scud has appeared in three variants, the A, B and C, and was first displayed in 1957. It is carried on a tracked vehicle and consists of a single-stage liquid propellant missile that uses inertial guidance. Capable of hitting targets 280km (174 miles) away, it has a longer range than the Lance system. The Frog and Scuds are the only missiles capable of carrying nuclear warheads that have been used in anger: Scud Bs, Frog-2s, Frog-3s and Frog-7s, all with conventional warheads, were fired at Israeli forces in 1973 but nothing vital was hit.

The SS-12 Scaleboard is the longest-ranged tactical missile in the Soviet arsenal, capable of reaching targets up to 800km (500 miles) away. It is carried on an eight-wheeled vehicle and uses solid fuel propulsion. Little is known of this missile and it may not have been a success as a replacement is already entering service, even though the Scaleboard only began deployment in 1969.

The Soviet tactical nuclear weapons now being introduced represent a new generation of which little is known. Three new systems have been deployed since 1976, the SS-21 in the Frog series, the SS-22 in place of the SS-12 and the SS-23 for the Scud. Deployment of all these weapons has been limited, suggesting that there are either production problems or that they are considered of limited combat value.

Soviet artillery makes less use of nuclear shells than those in the Western nations, but since the 1970s more attention has been paid to this. The 180mm S-23 gun can fire a 0.2 kiloton nuclear round and a similar projectile can be fired by the SAU-152 self-propelled howitzer.

Finally, we come to the Enhanced Radiation (ER) weapon, referred to more popularly as the neutron bomb. This is a thermonuclear device designed to maximise the lethal effects of high energy neutrons produced by the fusion of deuterium and tritium and to reduce the blast from the explosion. The special characteristics of the device allow high velocity neutrons to penetrate tank armour, and react with it to produce deadly gamma radiation, thus disabling the crews. Modern tanks are relatively impervious to blast and heat, so the advantages of the ER weapon to Nato in stopping a Soviet attack are clear. Deployment of ER artillery shells to Europe has been blocked, however, by a hostile reaction from both public and politicians, which concentrated on the supposedly sinister implications of the weapon's ability to kill people while leaving property intact. More realistic criticisms focussed on a possible lowering of the nuclear threshold and the fact that the shells would be fired at targets inside West Germany in the event of a Soviet advance.

Nato's theory of the use of tactical nuclear weapons in general is open to similar objections: they are too likely to be employed in circumstances where collateral damage to friendly civilians would be extensive, and they involve an immense risk of escalation. The Soviet Union, for its part, has made it clear that the use of tactical nuclear weapons would be part of a war without limits.

Right: A Soviet SS-1 Scud-B in its firing position. During 1982-83, the Soviet Army began deployment in Eastern Europe of the successor to this missile, the SS-23, as part of a new generation of tactical nuclear weapons.

Below: US soldiers prepare a towed version of the Lance for firing. This is a very versatile system, capable of being delivered to its launch area by CH-47 Chinook helicopter, or parachuted from a C-130 transport plane.

Weapons systems 1945-85

The air war

In many ways the year 1945 marked a watershed in the history of combat aircraft design and development. The advent of nuclear weapons clearly opened a new era in the history of warfare, and during the first postwar decade the strategic bomber and its principal counter-measure, the interceptor fighter, were given high priority in design and production resources.

The Soviet Union was faced with a massive US lead in strategic bombers in the late 1940s and during the 1950s produced the medium-range Tupolev Tu-16 Badger and two long-range bombers, the turboprop-powered Tu-20 Bear and the turbojet-powered Myasishchev M-4 Bison, as a nuclear-delivery force. In the United States, the Strategic Air Command operated several new bombers, including the B-36 Peacemaker, the jet-powered B-47 Strato-jet and, in 1955, the eight-jet B-52 Stratofortress which remains in service in 1985. The US Navy, not wishing to concede the important nuclear deterrent mission to the sole control of the USAF (United States Air Force), was active in developing a range of shipboard nuclear bombers for service aboard its aircraft carriers. This programme culminated with the A-5A Vigilante of 1958 (capable of a Mach 2 speed), which ironically served only in the reconnaissance role for most of its career. It was not only in the sphere of strategic bombing that nuclear weapons made an immense impact on aircraft development, since with the miniaturisation of nuclear devices, a new class of tactical nuclear attack aircraft emerged.

The USAF's F-84G of 1951 was the first single-seat fighter-bomber to be armed with nuclear weapons and this tactical nuclear role was originally the *raison d'être* of the US Navy's A-4 Skyhawk.

The threat of strategic bombers encouraged a great sense of urgency in the development of interceptor fighters. The Soviet Union's first postwar jet aircraft, the MiG-15, was designed to attack formations of massed bombers, as were its successors, the MiG-17 and the supersonic MiG-19. The United States at first based its air defence on a mixture of single-seat day interceptors, exemplified by the F-80 Shooting Star and the F-86 Sabre, and two-seat night fighters, such as the F-89 Scorpion and the F-94 Starfire. By the mid-1950s the USAF had succeeded in combining these two parallel streams of development into a single design. This was the F-102 Delta Dagger, a single-seat, supersonic all-weather interceptor, which for 20 years formed the backbone of Air Defense Command's interceptor force and was succeeded by its descendant, the F-106 Delta Dart.

While this development of high-performance interceptors and strategic bombers went ahead in preparation for a war that was never fought, the United States became involved in conflicts which demanded other forms of airpower delivering conventional munitions. The Korean War (1950-53) was fought by a mixture of piston-engined aircraft, many of them veterans of World War II, and the newer jets. The latter were often found unsuited to

Above: Egyptian Air Force and US Navy aeroplanes fly over the Nile Valley during an exercise. The aircraft in this flight comprise a snapshot of aeroplane development since 1945. At the rear of the formation is the MiG-17, which entered service in 1955 as an interceptor with a limited all-weather capability; at the formation's centre is the F-14, which entered service in 1972 and incorporates computers, all-weather radar and variable-geometry wings. Leading the formation is an F-4E Phantom, followed by an F-16 (second row top), a Mirage V (second row bottom), a MiG-21 (third row top), a Shenyang F-6 (third row bottom), an A-7 (fourth row top) and an A-6 (fourth row bottom).

the conditions of a limited war fought far from the American homeland. Yet when the United States again became engaged in a limited war a decade later over the jungles of Southeast Asia, the same problem recurred. High-speed jet fighter-bombers such as the F-100 Super Sabre and F-4 Phantom II were unsuited to dealing with the fleeting and indistinct targets offered by a guerrilla enemy. However, since more appropriate close air support aircraft, such as the piston-engined A-1 Skyraider, were in comparatively short supply, the faster jets had perforce to adapt to local conditions. Similarly, the F-105 Thunderchief, which had been designed to undertake the low-level tactical nuclear strike mission against Soviet forces, was pressed into service in the conventional role to attack targets in North Vietnam. Soviet forces in Afghanistan are faced with an identical dilemma, as only their Sukhoi Su-25 Frogfoot close air support aircraft are suited to counter-insurgency operations. In general the major air forces can only afford to procure small numbers of specialised counter-insurgency aircraft – such as the USAF's OV-10 Bronco and AC-130 Spectre gunship – and so have to rely on their standard fighter and attack aircraft during limited wars and guerrilla conflicts.

If the lessons of Korea and Vietnam have proved to be hard to implement, then the need for tactical mobility of air forces first highlighted by the Berlin crisis of 1948-49 has been better met. Not only have both the United States and Soviet Union developed large tactical and strategic air transport forces, but the former has greatly increased the mobility of virtually all its tactical and strategic aircraft by equipping them for in-flight refuelling. Since 1950

the USAF has operated a fleet of in-flight refuelling tanker aircraft (most notably the KB-29, KB-50, KC-97 and KC-135), primarily to extend the range of its strategic bombers but also to an increasing degree able to support long-range deployments of tactical aircraft.

The role of in-flight refuelling is but one of a range of new air force missions which have been introduced since 1945. Others include the fast-developing specialisation of electronic warfare (EW), carried out by the EF-111A Raven, EA-6B Prowler and a host of modified bomber and transport types. Airborne early warning (AEW), pioneered by the US Navy in the late 1940s, is today an important mission for all advanced air forces, with the US Navy's combat-proven E-2 Hawkeye in service with a number of other air arms, the E-3 Sentry in USAF and Nato service and the Nimrod AEW Mk 3 being developed for the RAF. The USAF has pioneered the defence suppression mission, with F-105G and F-4G Wild Weasel aircraft specially equipped to hunt and destroy enemy surface-to-air missile sites. On the other hand, with the great improvements in payload, range and capabilities of the modern attack and strike aircraft, the medium and light bomber has virtually disappeared from the ranks of the world's air forces.

Advances in many areas of science and technology have been applied to the design and construction of combat aircraft over the past four decades, resulting in machines of unprecedented complexity and cost. The most important innovations have been made in propulsion systems, aerodynamics, electronic systems (usually known as avionics) and aircraft armaments, but there is virtually no aspect of aircraft manufacture that has been unaffected by technological progress.

Left: An F-14 fires a Sparrow air-to-air missile. The development of such missiles dramatically lengthened the ranges at which aerial combat could take place, as well as providing a highly accurate munition for shooting down enemy aeroplanes. Right: A Victor aerial tanker refuels a Phantom. Support aeroplanes such as the Victor greatly increased the mobility of fighter squadrons and made possible round-the-world transfer flights.

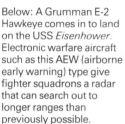

Below: A Grumman E-2 Hawkeye comes in to land on the USS *Eisenhower*. Electronic warfare aircraft such as this AEW (airborne early warning) type give fighter squadrons a radar that can search out to longer ranges than previously possible.

The introduction of the jet engine towards the end of World War II was a technical landmark of tremendous significance, as it enabled aircraft to fly at speeds and altitudes impossible to achieve with a piston-engined powerplant. Yet the early turbojets were in many respects unsatisfactory and it was not until 1954, when the F-100 Super Sabre entered service with the USAF, that a military aircraft in squadron service could exceed the speed of sound in level flight. Rocket and ramjet powerplants were experimented with – and indeed the first aircraft to fly faster than Mach 1 was the rocket-powered Bell XS-1 in 1947 – but the practical application of such engines has generally been confined to unmanned missiles. The introduction of afterburning, whereby a jet engine's thrust was augmented for short periods by igniting fuel in the exhaust pipe, contributed to increased powerplant performance but consumed fuel at a prodigious rate. It was first employed by interceptor fighters of the 1950s, such as the American F-86D, F-89 and F-94 and Soviet MiG-17 and MiG-19. The afterburning turbofan, such as the Pratt & Whitney F100 fitted to the F-15 and F-16 and the RB199 fitted to the Tornado, has a much lower fuel consumption than the turbojet and consequently has been adopted by most current high-performance military aircraft. Modern powerplants combine high thrust output with a low installed weight, so that the F-15 Eagle, for example, has a thrust-to-weight ratio of 1.4 to 1, giving it a phenomenal vertical climb performance.

By the early 1980s combat aircraft speed and altitude performance had reached a plateau. The F-15 with its maximum speed of Mach 2.5 and combat ceiling of 19,800m (65,000 feet) represented the optimum performance attainable with current

technology. If these limits are to be exceeded, then much new and expensive technology needs to be employed. This is shown by the futuristic Mach 3 Lockheed SR-71 strategic reconnaissance aircraft, which is constructed largely of titanium alloy in order to resist the temperatures encountered at high speed and is powered by a unique turbojet/ramjet hybrid powerplant. However, within the constraints of current manufacturing capabilities much new ground can be broken. For example, vertical take-off and landing (VTOL) techniques are in their infancy. The British Harrier and Sea Harrier fighters which pioneered VTOL operations with the Royal Air Force, Fleet Air Arm and US Marine Corps are subsonic aircraft, but clearly the vectored-thrust powerplant that they employ could be further developed to enable supersonic VTOL performance to be achieved. Another potential area of development is dual-role capability, whereby the same aircraft can perform both fighter and attack roles. The F-18 Hornet, which is currently re-equipping fighter and attack squadrons of the US Navy and Marine Corps, is a good example of such an aircraft.

The science of aerodynamics has made an important contribution to the development of the modern military aeroplane. The swept-back wing, originally developed in Germany during World War II, was the key to achieving successful trans-sonic performance and was first applied to the F-86 Sabre and MiG-15 of the Korean War period. Later in the 1950s, aerodynamicists made a further important discovery with the 'Area Rule' principle, a form of wasted streamlining which improved air flow at supersonic speed. It was first applied to the F-102 interceptor of 1955, which was also the first delta-wing combat aircraft. To improve the manoeuvrability of delta-winged fighters, canard foreplanes were fitted to the Swedish Viggen, and the idea has been taken up by the Israelis for the Kfir and by France for the Mirage IIING. The great innovation of the 1960s was the variable-geometry or 'swing' wing, pioneered in service by the USAF's F-111 interdiction/strike aircraft. This device enabled the wing's angle of sweepback to be varied either to suit it to low-speed cruising flight, take-off and landing with the wings fully forward, or, at the other extreme, to supersonic flight with the wings fully swept. The technique is expensive, its machinery heavy and complex, and so it has not been universally adopted, but has found favour in the Soviet Union with the MiG-23/27 and Tu-22M designs and in Europe with the Tornado.

Electronic revolution

Perhaps the least publicised revolution in postwar aircraft development has been the proliferation of electronic systems – computers, radars and numerous other systems for flight management, navigation and weapons' aiming. Avionics systems generally account for about one-third of a modern warplane's cost and, of course, in the case of specialised missions such as AEW and EW the proportion is even higher. Two examples of the impact of electronics must suffice to illustrate their tremendous importance. The first is in anti-submarine warfare

(ASW), where high-speed computer processing of raw data obtained from radar, sonar and other sources is performed aboard the P-3 Orion and Nimrod ASW patrol aircraft to give these machines a fully-autonomous submarine-hunting capability. Interdiction is a second area of operations which has greatly benefitted from the application of advanced avionics systems. Aircraft like the F-111, Tornado and Soviet Su-24 Fencer depend upon radar for terrain-following and avoidance at low level, for navigation and target acquisition, while self-contained inertial navigation systems can provide very accurate information on an aircraft's position without the need for radar or radio transmissions which would betray its presence to an enemy.

Weapons development also has had its impact on the shape of postwar military aircraft, most notably with the development of air-to-air and air-to-surface missiles (AAMs and ASMs). By the early 1960s the United States was so confident in the capabilities of its AAMs that the F-4 Phantom was produced for the USAF and US Navy with an all-missile armament. The USAF later reversed this decision and fitted a rapid-fire cannon to its F-4E model; thereafter fighter aircraft have generally carried a mixed armament of cannon and AAMs. Long-range stand-off missiles have much improved the survivability of strategic bombers, with the USAF progressively introducing

Right: A Kfir C2 of the Israeli Air Force. This aeroplane incorporates delta configuration wings and canard foreplanes. Below right: The British Harrier and its Sea Harrier relative have demonstrated the viability of the vertical take-off concept in warplanes.

Below: The Soviet Air Force enthusiastically adopted the variable-geometry wing for its fighter aircraft, as shown by these MiG-23s. The 'swing wing' has not been an entirely successful development, as its weight increases fuel consumption.

the AGM-28 Hound Dog in 1961, followed by the AGM-69 SRAM (1972) and AGM-86B Air Launched Cruise Missile (1982). An even wider range of specialised weaponry has been produced for attack aircraft, including laser-guided bombs, cluster bombs and munitions dispensers, as well as ASMs such as the AGM-65 Maverick and Soviet AS-7 Kerry.

Perhaps what is most striking about the stage that combat aircraft development has reached in the mid-1980s is that to an increasing degree development is constrained not by what it is possible to design and build, but rather by what can realistically be afforded. A good indication of this process is a comparison of the $178,408 unit cost of an F-86A Sabre in 1949 with the $12 million cost of an F-16 Fighting Falcon 30 years later. The inevitable consequence of the increase in complexity and cost of military aircraft has been a drastic cutback in the numbers procured. In 1945 the US Army Air Force had a total of over 33,000 aircraft, whereas the total for the USAF in 1984 is under 10,000, including reserves. While no doubt the increased individual effectiveness of modern aircraft goes some way to compensate for their lack of numbers, the problems of maintaining an effective fighting force of costly warplanes is one which affects all air forces in the 1980s. **Anthony Robinson**

Weapons systems 1945-85

The land battlefield

In the 40 years since 1945 the rapid advances in all aspects of technology have been reflected in some remarkable developments in land weapons. While the most revolutionary innovations were not to occur until the 1960s, the early postwar period still brought new weapon designs, despite the depressed nature of postwar economies.

In fact, in the field of infantry weapons, the first new rifle to appear in the postwar world, the now legendary Soviet AK-47, had been conceived before the end of the war. Designed as a short-barrelled assault rifle and calibred at 7.62mm, it has earned a high reputation as a simple and reliable weapon. Its popularity is demonstrated by the 30 million that have been manufactured everywhere from Finland to the China Sea.

While the Soviets were successfully introducing the AK-47, new rifles were also being developed in Western countries. Most of these also chose the 7.62mm calibre, which became the Nato standard calibre in 1953, although there were some designs, like the British EM2 at 7.11mm, using smaller calibres. In 1961 the United States, despite having argued against the EM2 during the early 1950s, decided to reduce the calibre of its service rifle to 5.56mm, by adopting the M16 (Armalite), a lighter, shorter-ranged weapon than any other in military service.

This move to a smaller calibre is now a confirmed trend, as the ability of a rifle to be lethal at ranges in excess of 3km (2 miles) is considered unnecessary. The Soviet Army now has in service a 5.45mm rifle – the AK-74 – which owes much to the AK-47. France has also adopted a new smaller-calibre rifle, the 5.56mm MAS, which was used by some French troops in the Lebanon in 1983-84. The 5.56mm MAS is of the 'bullpup' design, which effectively lacks a butt and so assumes a more compact form than more conventional types like the British SLR.

While most countries in the postwar period saw parallel development of infantry rifles, the situation with regard to MBTs (main battle tanks) was quite different. During the war, the Soviet Union had introduced the T34, an impressive vehicle that did not need to be replaced until the beginning of the 1950s. In Britain, development of the Centurion started during the war but it was not completed in time to see active service. However, during the 40 years since 1945 the Centurion has done yeoman service for many countries and it is still in service with some armies today, its longevity being due to a design which has lent itself to progressive modification and upgrading. In the early 1960s the British briefly introduced the Conqueror. Its design favoured protection and armament at the expense of mobility. In 1963 the Chieftain, intended to be the successor to the Centurion, began to replace both the Conqueror and Centurion in British Army service. The Chieftain maintained the British tradition of concentrating on protection, and at the time of its introduction it was the best-protected tank in the world.

Meanwhile, in the Soviet Union a new MBT, the T54, was introduced in 1949, replacing the T34; it

Left: Warsaw Pact T55 tanks during the Friendship 84 exercises in Poland. Despite advances in anti-tank missile technology, and the emergence of the combat helicopter as a new factor on the battlefield, the main battle tank remains the prime weapon, both of offence and defence.

Below: An Irish Guardsman, armed with a 5.56mm M16 and equipped for NBC warfare, stands guard over his section's MCV-80 mechanised infantry combat vehicle. Below right: The AK-47 is a popular weapon because of its robustness and reliability, especially with irregular forces: these are Nicaraguan Contra insurgents.

had better armour and a 100mm gun in place of an 85mm gun. The T54 itself began to be replaced in 1963 by the up-gunned (to a 115mm smoothbore) and larger T62. The next generation of Soviet tanks, the T64/72 models, introduced more radical changes in Soviet tank engineering, which had hitherto followed a step-by-step progression. Besides improvements in automotive design, their protection was enhanced by the addition of a form of laminated armour. The addition of an automatic loader allowed the crew to be reduced from four to three. A further increase in gun calibre took place, a 125mm smoothbore now forming the main armament. While Soviet technology on some of their earlier tank models may have lagged behind that of the West, the T72 seems to equal its Nato contemporaries.

Tank technology

New breakthroughs in Western tank design occurred in the 1970s. British concern with armour protection produced the Challenger tank incorporating both standard steel alloy armour and a laminated structure usually referred to as Chobham armour. This provided a significant increase in protection for a moderate weight penalty representing a major leap forward in tank technology. In the United States a radical change came with the selection of a gas-turbine engine for the M1 Abrams. This gives the M1 extremely good mobility, but at the cost of high fuel consumption and great expense. Indeed, it may not be insignificant that the British chose a diesel engine for the Challenger in the light of the Americans' experience with the gas-turbine.

As the MBT developed, so did the APC (armoured personnel carrier) and the MICV (mechanised infantry combat vehicle). During the 1950s, the US

Army used the M59 and M75 APCs before replacing them by the air-portable M113 in 1960, a machine which has seen worldwide service. It was to set a trend in the use of aluminium armour.

The Soviet Union has a mixture of tracked and wheeled armoured vehicles including the BTR series of APCs and the BRDM wheeled reconnaissance vehicles. The BMP, the world's first MICV, was introduced in 1967 and aroused considerable interest. It showed how Soviet tactics were concentrated on the mobile battle, with the BMP's role as 'battle taxi' augmented by its ability to enter combat with a 73mm gun.

Although the tank remains pre-eminent on the battlefield, many weapons have challenged its supremacy with varying degrees of success. The one that has come closest is the ATGW (anti-tank guided weapon). Continuous development of this began in the 1950s, with the introduction of the SS 10 and Entac in France. These were guided by the transmission of course corrections down a trailing wire and proved to be very successful weapons. More ATGWs were introduced during the 1960s, such as the British Vigilant and Swingfire systems and the Soviet AT-3 Sagger, perhaps the best-known anti-tank missile in the world, due to its good performance against Israeli armour when used by the Egyptians in the 1973 Yom Kippur War. These first-generation missiles had one major drawback: the operator not only had to track the target, but also to steer the missile onto it. The introduction of a second generation during the 1970s, including missiles like the US TOW (tube-launched optically-sighted wire-guided) and the European Milan, brought an improvement in accuracy. Now it was only necessary for the operator to track the target, the missile's

course being corrected automatically.

Currently, the anti-tank missile designer is searching for a true 'fire-and-forget' system, where once fired the missile will be capable of finding the target on its own. A further step along this path was taken with the introduction of the Hellfire by the United States in 1984. This third-generation missile contains a laser sensor in its nose which homes onto a target illuminated by a forward observer's laser-designator. The operator simply fires the missile.

The main limitation of the ATGW is its poor performance at short range, because of the time needed after launch for the operator to gain full control of the missile (in the case of a TOW 500m – 1640 feet); high accuracy is only achieved at longer ranges. This gap at short ranges is filled by a variety of man-portable anti-tank weapons. Some, like the US M72 LAW (light anti-tank weapon) and the Soviet RPG-7, are based on rocket designs while others, like the Swedish 84mm Carl Gustav, are recoilless systems. Both types have their supporters and will continue to be employed; the successor to the Carl Gustav – the AT4 – has been accepted for US service, while France and Britain have chosen disposable rocket systems.

The concept of the vertical deployment of weapons emerged in Vietnam; the helicopter served as a platform for heavy machine guns and rockets,

and consequently the step to fit an ATGW as well was only a small one. This combination seriously threatens the dominance of the tank on the battlefield. With the reappearance of low-speed ground-attack aeroplanes such as the A-10 Thunderbolt II, plus the threat from strike aircraft, the need for ground troops to be able to defend themselves against aerial attack has never been greater.

Bloodhound and HAWK

Just as missiles have been used to defeat armour, so too they have been pressed into service against aeroplanes. The first SAMs (surface-to-air-missiles) were deployed in 1953, the Nike-Ajax system in the United States. By 1960, there were many systems in service, including the Soviet SA-2 Guideline, the British Bloodhound and the US HAWK (homing-all-the-way-killer). The potential of these missiles to bring down aeroplanes was great enough for strike aircraft to change completely their attack profiles. For them to survive, it became necessary for a mission to be flown at the lowest possible altitude. This then led to the production of low-altitude SAMs.

The first generation of these was introduced in the late 1960s, when the US M48 Chaparral and the Soviet SA-6 Gainful low-level SAM systems came into service. Most of these systems are mounted onto

Choppers

A major development in land warfare since World War II has been the increasing use of helicopters in a wide variety of roles. The first helicopter to see military service was the Sikorsky R-4, which was used by the US Army Air Force as an observation aircraft in Burma in 1945. However, it was in the Korean War (1950-53) that helicopters first made their mark on the conduct of battle. They were used in two very important roles, the rescue of downed pilots and the evacuation of the wounded (medevac or casevac). The major problem with the early helicopters used in Korea was the poor power-to-weight ratio of the engines, which left little room for anything beyond the weight of the machine itself.

The development of turboshaft propulsion by the French Sud-Aviation and Turbomeca companies in 1955 enabled this problem to be overcome, and the usefulness of the helicopter for military operations was soon established. In 1956, during the Suez crisis, British Royal Marine Commandos were airlifted by helicopters onto their assault beach, the first use of vertical envelopment in war. At this time, the French were also using helicopters to carry troops into battle against Algerian nationalist guerrillas. To provide these men with mobile fire-support, machine guns and rockets were also put on helicopters, the birth of the helicopter gunship.

These rudimentary beginnings were followed by the widespread use of helicopters during the Vietnam War. A whole division – the 1st Cavalry Division (Airmobile) – of 16,000 men and 400 helicopters (mainly UH-1Ds carrying 14 men or six stretcher cases) and fixed-wing aircraft, was brought into service to carry out assaults by air. The concept of the gunship was refined still further, as UH-1C helicopters were armed with 2.75in rockets and a

Minigun. The UH-1C was merely a modification of an existing utility design; the first purpose-built helicopter gunship was introduced to Vietnam in autumn 1966: the AH-1 Huey Cobra.

Also in the 1960s, the helicopter's potential as a heavy-duty logistic transport was realised. The Boeing Company's Vertol division developed a large twin-rotor helicopter, the CH-47 Chinook, capable of lifting a 7258kg (16,000lb) payload. Helicopters proved their value in this role during resupply operations in Vietnam.

With the development of wire-guided anti-tank missiles, the helicopter was provided with an effective weapon enabling it to serve in the front line of a battle involving main battle tanks. Tank-killer helicopter units were formed by most major armies during the 1970s, and the helicopter is considered to have a major role to play in any future war by both the Warsaw Pact and Nato forces. But it is interesting to note that the helicopter has not yet been tested under adverse battlefield conditions. They suffered a high loss rate in Vietnam when they faced any substantial return fire from the ground. It may be that operating very close to the ground – flying up above the treetops only to fire their munitions at an enemy already spotted by troops further forward – they will be battle-winners in a full-scale modern war on land, but this remains to be proven.

They have certainly already demonstrated their worth in logistical missions. From the evidence, it seems that a British victory in the Falklands War of 1982 would have been an improbable outcome if the helicopter had not been available for supply transport, as the terrain ruled out the heavy trucks normally used in this role. In this sense, although the question of the helicopters' capabilities in battle remains open, they can be considered campaign-winners.

vehicles for greater mobility. To produce comprehensive coverage and greater numbers, simpler man-portable systems such as the US FIM-43A Redeye and the Soviet SA-7 were brought into service. The 1980s have seen the improvement of these systems for low-level defence by the introduction of all-angle heat-seekers, such as are found on the FIM-92A Stinger man-portable SAM which entered service with the US Army in 1981.

An alternative means of low-level air defence is the anti-aircraft gun. An aeroplane is a difficult thing to hit but a relatively soft target; if a high volume of fire is directed to a predicted intercept point, there is a fair chance of bringing an aeroplane down. The North Vietnamese shot down as many as a thousand US aeroplanes using highly concentrated gun emplacements, a significant number even if it only represents about one per cent of the number of sorties flown. The problem with guns is their high ammunition expenditure, which makes considerable demands on logistic support.

The accuracy of anti-aircraft guns has been improved by the incorporation of radar-tracking into the individual gun's fire-control system. The first mobile system so equipped was the Soviet ZSU-23. First seen in 1965, this weapon is now nearing obsolescence as aeroplanes are being armoured to withstand 30mm cannon fire, and are therefore proof against the 23mm guns of the ZSU-23. New mobile anti-aircraft gun systems will probably follow the lead of the 1971 West German Gepard, armed with 35mm guns. Indeed, the United States' controversial Sergeant York DIVADS (divisional air-defense system) is armed with twin 40mm Bofors L/70 guns to replace the M163 Vulcan system armed with 20mm guns. Radar-directed and computer-controlled systems like these are very expensive and, to provide defence of area targets, must be deployed in large numbers. Consequently, the British decision to employ an all-missile system for aerial defence is easily justified.

While missiles show cost-savings in most roles, their weakness lies in dealing with large formations of helicopters, when the rate of fire is likely to be inadequate. The optimum solution probably lies in a gun-missile mix. In 1973, the Egyptians had considerable success operating the ZSU-23 with the SA-6 missile in such a way that the guns forced attacking aeroplanes up into the missile's engagement envelope. However, while the advantage of such tactics is clear, the expense for most nations would be prohibitive.

As artillery weapons, rockets and missiles now complement the role of guns in an environment where the tactics of modern armour put an increasing emphasis on mobility. Almost all missiles are now mounted on mobile carriers and in the US and British armies self-propelled guns now outnumber towed ones. Towed fieldpieces are now confined mainly to motorised divisions relying on trucks for transport, rather than the mechanised divisions where infantry are carried in APCs. Some towed gun developments have taken place: for example, the British have replaced the Italian 105mm pack howitzer with their own Light Gun, also in 105mm. The 155mm FH70, although a towed gun, was designed to enable it to be developed into the self-propelled SP70. In fact, most towed guns of today are partially self-propelled, as they incorporate an auxiliary power unit that allows the gun to be manoeuvred about the battery position.

Air-transportable artillery

The establishment of the trend to self-propelled artillery goes back to World War II when they were already in use with the armies of all the major combatants. During the 1950s the United States introduced a number of new self-propelled artillery designs, but since these were very heavy and impossible to transport by air, design work began on a new series of guns which emphasised transportability. The M107 175mm and the M110 8in self-propelled guns incorporated an aluminium hull that gave the necessary lightness for air transport and were provided with power-actuated gun elevation, gun traverse, ammunition-handling and ramming so that they could come into action quickly. The M107 has had an unsatisfactory service life, however, and is being replaced by the M110A1, an improved model of the M110. This trend towards self-propelled artillery is confirmed by the concentration of the Soviet Army on 152mm M1973 and 122mm M1974 self-propelled howitzer development.

The major technical advances in artillery since World War II have gone on in the realm of shells, range and rate of fire. Better use of metals has enabled more effective fragmentation shells to be brought into service. Anti-tank projectiles have been refined since 1945: fin-stabilised shot and high-explosive squash-head shells have greatly increased the destructive effects of tank guns. The range of guns has been increased by the use of longer barrels to increase muzzle velocity, more propellant in the shells to produce greater gas pressure, and muzzle brakes to reduce both the effects of the firing on the recoil system and the weight of the barrel necessary for higher muzzle velocity. Range can also be increased by a rocket booster on the shell, an arrangement known as the rocket-assisted projectile;

Top left: A Canadian Army Centurion tank on exercise during the early 1970s. The Centurion was essentially a World War II design, but nevertheless gave excellent service with the British, Israeli and Indian armies, amongst many others. It was gradually replaced in the British Army during the 1960s by the Chieftain. Centre left: A British 17-pounder anti-tank gun in action in the Western Desert during World War II. By the mid-1980s, anti-tank missiles had largely superseded artillery in this role, and were particularly potent when mounted on helicopters. Left: A British Army Westland Lynx, firing a TOW anti-tank missile.

the disadvantage of this is that the booster takes up room normally filled with high-explosive, reducing the kill factor of the shell. The rate of fire has been improved by the use of mechanical rammers.

These improvements and the greater use of self-propelled guns have one very important drawback: cost. Consequently, to maintain weight of fire, there still remains a role for simpler area weapons like the mortar. Many countries still complement their arsenal with large-calibre mortars capable of ranges up to 10km (6 miles), although Britain has limited its mortar calibres to a maximum of 81mm.

The accuracy of indirect-fire weapons such as artillery and mortars has been greatly improved by technical advances. Solving ballistic equations has always been a major problem for gunners. The invention of the laser range-finder, equipment for acquiring meteoreological data and computers for solving ballistic equations have been combined to produce extremely accurate shooting, as exemplified by the performance of British artillery during the Falklands War.

Rapid advances in technology since 1945 have made offensive weapons more deadly and defensive weapons more difficult to penetrate. The speed at which actions are fought has also been increased, as have the ranges possible. However, a law of diminishing returns may be setting in, as the increased sophistication of modern weapons is forcing their costs upwards; it remains to be seen whether this will have any long-term effect on the scale of equipment that is made available to modern armies.

Ed Trowbridge

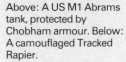

Above: A US M1 Abrams tank, protected by Chobham armour. Below: A camouflaged Tracked Rapier.

Above left: Soviet D-1
152mm towed howitzers.
Above: The Blowpipe is
the British man-portable
anti-aircraft missile system.

Weapons systems 1945-85

At the end of World War II, the US Navy had emerged as the most powerful fleet in the world. At its core lay carrier battle groups, known as task forces, which consisted of one or more aircraft carriers – with a complement of around 100 aeroplanes – together with an escort made up of cruisers and destroyers. In battles across the Pacific and Atlantic Oceans, aircraft carriers had demonstrated the ability to destroy enemy shipping at distances far beyond the range of even the biggest guns; any nation concerned with its maritime power was now required to maintain aircraft carriers in place of the traditional large, heavily-armed battleships. The only type of ship that approached the aircraft carrier's ability to determine the outcome of war at sea was the submarine; it had demonstrated this in the war waged by Germany on the merchant shipping of Britain in the Atlantic, and the US destruction of Japanese merchant and military shipping in the Pacific.

However, World War II had also produced a weapon which it was thought might have made conventional naval forces obsolete – the atomic bomb. Some experts believed that a nuclear device would be capable of destroying groups of ships concentrated into task forces, thus rendering them too vulnerable for use in a major war. In any case, their relevance in the context of the new strategy of nuclear deterrence was questionable. Despite efforts by the US Navy to push the idea of carrier-borne aircraft as a major element of US strategic nuclear forces, they were accorded low priority compared with the land-based strategic bombers. The cancellation in 1949 of the US Navy's proposed United States-class aircraft carriers was an early victory for the proponents of the case against conventional seapower. However, events were soon to alter the terms of the debate.

The limited war fought in Korea in 1950-53 gave those who supported the maintenance of a force for fighting conventional war a powerful argument against those who sought to prepare only for nuclear war. The importance of aircraft carriers to the aerial offensive that gave the UN forces air superiority on the peninsula reinforced appreciation of the carrier's ability to place an airfield in the vicinity of any battlefield. The main obstacle in the way of further developments of the aircraft carrier lay in fears that high-performance jet aeroplanes could too easily penetrate the defensive screen provided by the anti-aircraft guns of the escort ships in the task force.

Development of missiles for use against jet aeroplanes, to give the carrier task forces more complete air defence, went on throughout the 1950s. The Terrier SAM (surface-to-air missile) entered service on the USS *Boston* in 1955, the first warship whose primary armament consisted of missiles. This type of weapon removed the last objection to the construction of new classes of aircraft carriers for the US Navy, and the mid-1950s saw the laying down of the Forrestal class, the first of a series of conventionally-powered ships whose displacements were around 80,000 tonnes. These ships were effectively floating aerodromes, with all the equipment and facilities to maintain their carrier air wings of 70 aeroplanes. The large size of these ships was due to the demands of the jets that now made up their aeroplane complement; these big planes required larger decks. Steam catapults and angled flight decks were introduced by the Royal Navy and later adopted by the US Navy to cope with these new demands.

Another important development that was to enhance the capability of the aircraft carrier was the application of nuclear power to surface-ship propulsion. The USS *Long Beach* was the first ship so driven, and was completed in 1961, shortly before the USS *Enterprise*, the first carrier with a nuclear reactor. The advantages of this form of propulsion over more conventional forms lay largely in the

Main picture: Ships of the US Seventh Fleet perform an anti-submarine warfare exercise. Carrier battle groups like this are at the heart of the US Navy's plans for fighting future wars; they provide the ability to project airpower throughout the world.

Naval armaments

Right: A Victor III-class nuclear submarine of the Soviet Navy. The projection from the rudder is a low-frequency towed-array sonar. The introduction of nuclear propulsion to submarines greatly increased their operational flexibility.
Below: A Mk 10 launcher with two Terrier surface-to-air missiles. Shipboard anti-aircraft missiles enable vessels to cope with the high performance jets of postwar air forces.

greater operational flexibility achieved through a capacity for sustained high speed and the reduction in the requirements for replenishment. Both Soviet and US ships now operate using nuclear power, including the Virginia-class cruisers, the Nimitz-class aircraft carriers and the Kirov-class cruisers.

Faced with the threat posed by the US Navy's carrier battle groups, in the immediate postwar years the Soviet Navy opted to build a fleet of surface ships that would combine with submarines to challenge any enemy forces approaching Soviet territory and defeat them at sea in a traditional ship-to-ship engagement. After Stalin's death in 1953, a cheaper coastal-defence option involving the use of shore-based airpower, fast attack craft and submarines was chosen, and in line with this a series of radar-guided missiles launched from aeroplanes were designed and put into service. It was soon realised that to mount similar missiles on the fast attack craft would present a considerable improvement over the torpedo, which was their traditional armament.

The first Soviet SSM (surface-to-surface missile) was the SS-N-1 Scrubber, installed on the Krupny-class destroyers that first entered service in 1959. Design of this missile probably began at the same time that the Forrestal-class aircraft carriers of the US Navy were laid down, in 1952-53. The second Soviet SSM, the SS-N-2, was first seen mounted on the hull of a P6 torpedo boat in place of the normal torpedo armament, a modification that was designated the Komar class. They were followed by the Osa class, a successful fast attack craft purpose-built to carry four SS-N-2 missiles.

The threat posed by these missiles was highlighted by the sinking of the Israeli destroyer *Eilat* on 21 October 1967 by an Egyptian Komar-class missile boat. The fact that there had not been enough time for the out-dated defence systems aboard the Israeli ship to react to the incoming missiles had a great impact on the subsequent design of ships' defensive systems. The growth of high-speed computer technologies and more efficient radar systems enabled ship designers to provide the means to detect the incoming missiles and to process the information rapidly enough for evasive or defensive measures to be taken. However, these systems absorbed space

Left: Helicopters, like this Kaman H-2 Seasprite, have proved a valuable addition to the anti-submarine warfare capabilities of the world's navies. Below left: HMS *Trafalgar* in drydock reveals its teardrop hull form for higher underwater speeds. Below: The Soviet Whiskey-class submarine U-137 aground in Swedish territorial waters. This class was based on the German Type XXI design, which set the standard of postwar diesel-electric submarines.

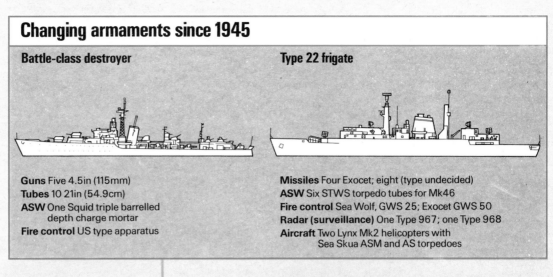

Changing armaments since 1945

Battle-class destroyer

Guns Five 4.5in (115mm)
Tubes 10 21in (54.9cm)
ASW One Squid triple barrelled depth charge mortar
Fire control US type apparatus

Type 22 frigate

Missiles Four Exocet; eight (type undecided)
ASW Six STWS torpedo tubes for Mk46
Fire control Sea Wolf, GWS 25; Exocet GWS 50
Radar (surveillance) One Type 967; one Type 968
Aircraft Two Lynx Mk2 helicopters with Sea Skua ASM and AS torpedoes

previously used for armament; the armament also required more space as it too became more sophisticated, employing accurate but bulky missile systems in place of the traditional gun armament.

This problem produced a new solution: in the mid-1970s the United States and the Soviet Union began considering the construction of large cruisers using nuclear propulsion and heavily armed with SSMs and SAMs. But the eventual course followed by the two nations diverged: the United States abandoned the project in favour of renovating its World War II Iowa-class battleships, up-dating their electronics and equipping them with SSMs; the Soviet Union constructed its own version of the US Navy's abandoned 'strike cruiser', the Kirov class (perhaps because they lacked any World War II-era battleships to recondition). So at the end of 40 years of naval developments the battleship, thought to have been killed off by airpower, received a new lease of life, partly because it might be able to take several hits from the SSMs that could easily sink a smaller ship like HMS *Sheffield*.

Both 'big missile' ships like the *New Jersey* and aircraft carriers still faced an old threat that called into question their usefulness in modern warfare. The submarine of 1984 was probably the most potent class of ship in service in the world's navies. The

rapid advances in the technology of their construction since the end of World War II have greatly reduced the weaknesses under which the submarine operated in that war.

Some of these advances were already in hand at the end of the war, embodied in the German Type XXI-class U-boat. The Allied countries adopted these into their postwar designs, utilising the improved hull streamlining and large-capacity batteries to produce the high speeds that would enable the submarine to outrun any escort vessels pursuing it and remain underwater. The production of more sensitive sonars compensated for these advantages somewhat and, on the principle of setting a thief to catch a thief, the US Navy mounted sonars into remodelled World War II-vintage submarines (known as guppies – greater underwater propulsive power – because of their improved complement of batteries) so that they would be capable of hunting down their opposite numbers in enemy fleets.

These developments made the submarine even more vital to warfare, but it was still forced to return to a port in order to replenish its fuel and supplies, limiting its operational radius; neither could it travel at high speeds on electric batteries for an extended period of time. The big breakthrough in submarine endurance came in 1954 with the commissioning of the USS *Nautilus* which showed that a nuclear reactor could be put to sea to propel a submersible. When combined with the 'teardrop' hull form first applied in the USS *Albacore* in the previous year, these developments enabled the submarine to manoeuvre more effectively underwater at speeds in excess of 30 knots. The offensive power of these vessels was further enhanced by developments in the field of torpedo armament: the introduction of passive acoustic homing devices on torpedoes in the late 1950s made them a much more accurate weapon.

However, new weapons were now being introduced to counter the increasingly effective submarine. In 1960 a new anti-submarine weapons system was introduced by the US Navy that provided an improvement over the old depth charge. The Asroc (anti-submarine rocket) is a ballistic rocket carrying either a homing torpedo or a nuclear depth charge. Its most important feature is the Mark 114 Underwater Battery Fire Control System which computes the future position of the target from its current course, and makes adjustments to the angle at which the missile is fired. The high speed of response and long range of this weapon have made it a dangerous opponent for the submarine and very popular with the navies of the Nato alliance.

Listening for submarines

Developments in sonar and helicopters have also come to the aid of the submarine hunters. Sonars come in two varieties, the passive which listens for noise produced by the target, and the active which sends out soundwaves to bounce off the target (calculations are made from the time taken by the wave to return). Most sonars in service today are highly sensitive and part of a complex electronic system involving the use of computers to speed calculations and reaction times. An interesting variant of the traditional fixed sonar is the variable depth sonar, popular with the Canadian Armed Forces' Maritime Command, and also in use with the navies of other nations. In this system the sonar is on the end of cables, the length of which can be adjusted if necessary. Similar to it are the dipping sonars on helicopters.

The helicopter has proved to be a valuable aid in the submarine chase. Aeroplanes performed well in the task of sinking submarines in World War II, but the helicopter provided the opportunity to give every reasonably-sized escort vessel in a convoy its own aerial support. The exceptional manoeuvrability of the helicopter means that a submarine, once located, will find it difficult to outrun or out-turn its pursuer, its only hope being that fuel restrictions will force the hunter to break off the chase. The submarine's constructors have sought to make their creations less easy to track, and have begun to incorporate anti-magnetic or non-magnetic materials in their construction, to defeat such devices as the magnetic anomaly detector which can locate a submarine by the disturbance its metal hull creates in the earth's magnetic field.

If naval warfare by the mid-1980s was largely concerned with ways of tracking down submarines, through aircraft carriers and their helicopter-equipped escorts and through hunter-killer submarines, the main reason was the development of the ballistic-missile submarine as a vital part of the modern nuclear arsenal. Whereas the attempt to turn aircraft

carriers into a part of the strategic nuclear strike force petered out in the 1960s, the missile-launching submarine has gone from strength to strength, ever since the USS *George Washington*, the first of the type, was launched in 1959. The difficulty of locating submarines means that submarine-launched missiles offer an essential retaliatory reserve, impervious to any surprise first strike which might eliminate a country's land-based nuclear forces.

So the years since 1945 have seen the submarine, as strategic missile launcher, usurp the position once held by the aircraft carrier as the fleet's capital ship. Yet for the purposes of power projection – asserting the influence of a superpower in distant corners of the globe – aircraft carriers and the new versions of the old-style battleship remain of prime importance.

Paul Szuscikiewicz

Despite the powerful armament that can be packed aboard a small ship – such as the 770 tonne Nanuchka class and their SS-N-9 missiles (below) – the navies of the superpowers still want large fighting ships such as the 28,000 tonne Kirov class (bottom) of the Soviet Fleet or the US Navy's reconditioned Iowa-class battleships of 57,000 tonnes.

Weapons systems 1945-85

The nuclear age

Between the first successful explosion of a nuclear device in July 1945 and the end of 1984, five nations acquired an established nuclear weapons capability. The United States was the first to explode a nuclear weapon, in 1945; the USSR did so in 1949, Britain in 1952, France in 1960 and China in 1964. In addition, India exploded a nuclear device in 1974, but apparently has not built any nuclear weapons since then. Most people believe that both South Africa and Israel have nuclear weapons but neither country is known for certain to have tested a nuclear device, nor have the political leaders of either country admitted to having nuclear arms.

The basic atom-bomb developed in 1945 used a fission chain reaction to produce a very large amount of energy in a very short time – a very powerful explosion. This fission occurs in uranium or plutonium material, the isotopes uranium-235 and plutonium-239. Fission occurs when a neutron enters the nucleus of an atom of one of these materials, which then breaks up, releasing a large amount of energy. The original nucleus is split into two radioactive nuclei, and two or three neutrons are released; these neutrons can be used to produce a self-sustaining chain-reaction, provided at least one of the neutrons released in each fission produces the fission of another nucleus.

To achieve a self-sustaining chain reaction, it is necessary for the radioactive material to be concentrated at its critical mass. A critical mass of a bare sphere of plutonium-239 metal would be about 10 kg (22lb), the size of a small grapefruit. Using a technique called implosion, in which a plutonium sphere is surrounded with conventional high-explosive lenses to compress a mass slightly less than

Above: A Minuteman missile in its silo. The delivery of nuclear warheads by intercontinental ballistic missiles has been, until the present, a method of strategic attack against which there has been no viable defence.

Left: A V-2, the world's first operational ballistic missile, is launched. The captured research from the German rocket programme provided a major part of the basis for Soviet and US postwar missile developments.

critical to a mass which is slightly greater than critical, a nuclear explosion can be achieved with about 2kg (4lb) of plutonium-239. A 2kg (4lb) sphere of plutonium-239 has a radius of about 2.8cm (1in), smaller than a tennis ball.

In the atomic bomb which destroyed Nagasaki, on 9 August 1945, about 8kg (17.5lb) of plutonium metal were used. The plutonium core was surrounded by chemical explosives arranged as explosive lenses focussed on the centre of the plutonium sphere. When the lenses were detonated the sphere was compressed uniformly by the implosion. The compression increased the density of the plutonium so that the slightly less than critical mass was made slightly more than critical; it then exploded.

In the Hiroshima atomic bomb a different design was used. A sub-critical mass of uranium-235 was fired down a gun barrel (from an old naval gun) into another sub-critical mass of uranium-235 placed in front of the muzzle of the gun. When the two masses came together they formed a greater than critical mass and a nuclear explosion took place. About 60kg (132lb) of uranium-235 were used to produce a nuclear explosion with a destructive power equivalent to that of the explosion of about 13,000 tonnes of TNT (13 kilotons).

The gun design is cruder than the implosion method and is rarely, if ever, used in modern nuclear weapons. Nuclear weapon design has advanced considerably since 1945, as shown by a comparison of the physical characteristics of old and new designs. The Nagasaki bomb, for example, weighed about 4500kg (9920lb) and its explosive power was equivalent to that of 22 kilotons of TNT; a modern Mk12A US thermonuclear warhead weighing about 100kg (220lb) yields an explosive power of about 350 kilotons.

To get these more powerful nuclear explosions – rising in many cases to one megaton or more – nuclear fusion, rather than fission, is used. The fusion process is the opposite of fission. Instead of splitting heavy nuclei, as is done in fission, the fusion process consists of forming (or fusing) light nuclei into heavier ones; isotopes of hydrogen are fused together to form helium. The reaction, like fission, produces energy and is accompanied by the emission of neutrons. There is no critical mass for the fusion process and therefore no theoretical limit to the explosive yield of fusion weapons – hydrogen bombs (H-bombs) as they are usually called.

Whereas the fission process is relatively easy to start – one neutron will initiate a chain reaction in a critical mass of uranium or plutonium – fusion can only be started if the light nuclei are raised to a very high temperature. In a typical H-bomb the hydrogen isotopes used are deuterium and tritium. In order to make these materials fuse together, a temperature of around 100 million degrees Centigrade (180 million degrees Fahrenheit) is required. This is provided by exploding a fission device – an atomic bomb – which achieves such a temperature at the moment of the fission explosion. An H-bomb, therefore, consists of a fission stage, which is an atomic bomb acting as a trigger, and a fusion stage, in which hydrogen is fused by the heat produced by the trigger.

The first use of fusion in a nuclear weapon was in a so-called 'boosted' weapon, in which some hydrogen was placed at the centre of the plutonium sphere in an ordinary atomic bomb. The fusion

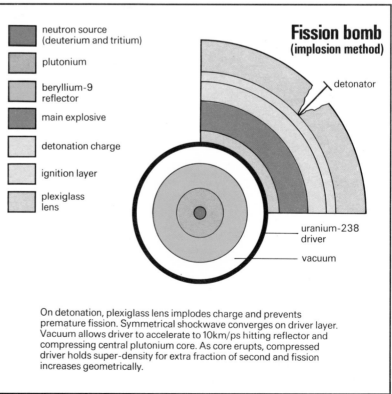

neutron source (deuterium and tritium)	
plutonium	
beryllium-9 reflector	
main explosive	
detonation charge	
ignition layer	
plexiglass lens	

Fission bomb
(implosion method)

detonator

uranium-238 driver

vacuum

On detonation, plexiglass lens implodes charge and prevents premature fission. Symmetrical shockwave converges on driver layer. Vacuum allows driver to accelerate to 10km/ps hitting reflector and compressing central plutonium core. As core erupts, compressed driver holds super-density for extra fraction of second and fission increases geometrically.

Left: A Titan II missile of the US Strategic Air Command is launched from its underground silo. The missile carries a nine megaton nuclear warhead. Below: A Soviet Delta III-class nuclear submarine capable of firing ballistic missiles, a mode of missile deployment introduced by the US Navy in 1959. The submarine is difficult to detect, and so provides an excellent strategic reserve; it is unlikely to be located and destroyed as part of a pre-emptive attack. The disadvantage is that the missiles carried are not as accurate as land-based ones.

energy produced by the explosion of the atom-bomb increased the explosive yield of the weapon several times. In fact, yields of about 500 kilotons can be produced by a boosted weapon; an ordinary fission bomb is limited to yields of about 30 kilotons. But in a proper H-bomb in which, by an appropriate design, a large amount of hydrogen is made to undergo fusion, very large yields have been obtained. For example, the USSR exploded an H-bomb in 1962 with a yield of 58 megatons, equivalent to the yield of about 3000 Nagasaki bombs. Even higher yields could be obtained, but there is little point in such large explosions; even the largest city would be completely devastated by a nuclear warhead of 10 megatons.

The history of American nuclear weapon developments can conveniently be divided into four main periods: an early research period, from 1945 to 1955; a peak production and growth period, from 1955 to 1967; a period when numbers remained constant but during which important operational improvements were made, from 1967 to 1980; and a second growth period in which a new generation of nuclear weapons

is being produced and deployed and new technologies are being widely adapted, from 1980 onwards. By and large, Soviet nuclear-weapon developments have followed American ones with a time gap of three to five years.

The United States had expended its first three atomic bombs by the end of August 1945. A shortage of plutonium-239 and uranium-235 limited the numbers of nuclear weapons added to the American arsenal in the early years. Nevertheless, by the end of 1946, the United States possessed the components for nine atomic bombs; by 1948, they had 50; by 1950, 450; and by 1952, the number of nuclear weapons in the American stockpile was 1000. Until 1952, all the nuclear weapons produced in the United States were bombs to be dropped by aeroplanes. It was in that year the first non-aircraft-delivered tactical nuclear devices were deployed; these were nuclear artillery shells for a 280mm gun. Between 1953 and 1955, the United States deployed three new types of tactical nuclear weapons: Corporal and Honest John surface-to-surface missiles, and nuclear landmines (known as atomic demolition munitions).

Nuclear delivery

In 1953, US military scientists developed a deliverable H-bomb. This development made possible the production of nuclear warheads with very high explosive yields but with relatively low physical weights. Although at this time the delivery of US nuclear devices was still almost solely the province of the manned bomber, preliminary work was already underway to produce a missile capable of delivering a nuclear warhead onto another continent.

Between 1955 and 1967, there was a massive increase in the number of nuclear devices deployed by the United States: in 1955 they numbered 2250 and by 1967 they had grown to 32,000, an all-time record. The first intercontinental ballistic missile (ICBM), the Atlas-D, was deployed in April 1958 equipped with a warhead of several megatons yield. To introduce an element of uncertainty into the exact placement of a nuclear missile, the US Navy began to deploy submarine-launched Polaris ballistic missiles carried on nuclear submarines.

Between 1967 and 1980, the numbers of nuclear devices in the US stockpile decreased, so that by 1980 the number was 25,000. The decrease was due to the withdrawal from the arsenal of a large number of aircraft bombs and the retirement of nuclear-tipped air-defence missiles. Also, fewer warheads were deployed because new designs were more efficient and reliable. The capabilities of missiles to deliver an effective attack were improved by the introduction of multiple independently-targetable re-entry vehicles (MIRVs) into service on US strategic missiles in 1970; a single missile could carry a number of warheads, each of which could be aimed at targets hundreds of kilometres apart.

During the 1980s, the Americans plan another big increase in the size of their nuclear arsenal. They intend to deploy 23,000 new warheads and withdraw 16,000, for a net increase of 7000. This will bring the total number of nuclear warheads in the stockpile to 32,000 in 1990, a number equal to the previous record in 1967. The new warheads will be very much more accurate than the ones withdrawn from the arsenal. The deployment of these very accurate

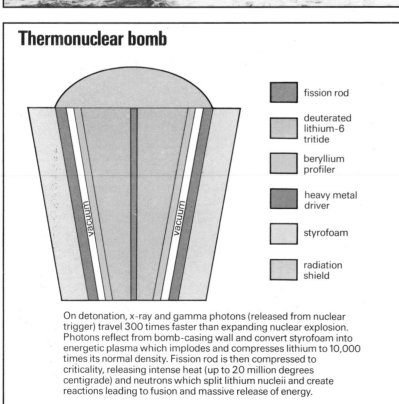

Thermonuclear bomb

- fission rod
- deuterated lithium-6 tritide
- beryllium profiler
- heavy metal driver
- styrofoam
- radiation shield

vacuum

vacuum

On detonation, x-ray and gamma photons (released from nuclear trigger) travel 300 times faster than expanding nuclear explosion. Photons reflect from bomb-casing wall and convert styrofoam into energetic plasma which implodes and compresses lithium to 10,000 times its normal density. Fission rod is then compressed to criticality, releasing intense heat (up to 20 million degrees centigrade) and neutrons which split lithium nucleii and create reactions leading to fusion and massive release of energy.

warheads could be causing nuclear policies to be changed from nuclear deterrence based on mutual assured destruction to nuclear warfighting.

The most important new strategic nuclear weapons scheduled for introduction during the 1980s are the MGM-118A Peacekeeper ICBM, the Trident II submarine-launched ballistic missile, and the air-launched cruise missile to be carried on B-52 and B-1B strategic bombers. The most important tactical nuclear weapons to be deployed in the 1980s are the Pershing II surface-to-surface missile, the ground-launched cruise missile, and the sea-launched cruise missile. All of these new weapons could be seen as nuclear warfighting weapons.

The Soviet arsenal of nuclear weapons has developed along lines similar to that of the United States. The Soviet Union began working on an atomic bomb in 1943, after reports had been received of similar work proceeding in foreign countries. Development was accelerated after the United States used their bombs in 1945, and the first test of a plutonium bomb was made on 29 August 1949. At this time the Soviet Union, like the United States, was forced to use long-range bombers (copies of the B-29 Superfortress) to deliver their nuclear weapons; but high priority was given to their rocket programme, using captured German technology as a basis (as to a large extent did the Americans). The SS-3 Shyster, introduced in about 1955, was the first long-range nuclear missile capable of carrying a nuclear warhead.

The Soviet Union has deployed a greater number of models of missiles, indicating that their designs may not be great successes. Certainly, the use of unstable liquid propellants in the great majority of their strategic missiles shows that technological backwardness has been a continuing problem for the Soviets since World War II. However, they have used their advantages to overcome their weaknesses: the higher failure rate of liquid-propelled missiles over solid-fuelled ones has led to the development of cold-launch techniques that permit missile silos to be reusable, an advantage in nuclear warfighting if the silo escapes destruction. Despite early handicaps, the Soviet Strategic Rocket Force has developed to the point where it can be regarded as the equal of the nuclear forces available to the United States.

Developments in the technology of nuclear weapons have largely been confined to the two superpowers. The other nations with nuclear forces have made use of existing systems acquired from the United States and the Soviet Union and applied to their own nuclear arsenals. The Chinese have used Soviet models as the basis for their bomber and missile programmes, although their weapons are produced indigenously. At the other extreme, the British deterrent force is based on a missile – the Polaris – supplied complete by the United States (although the submarines to carry the missiles and the warheads are of British design). France's missiles use US technology for their guidance systems.

The superpower nuclear arsenals contain nuclear versions of virtually all types of military munitions bigger than a hand-grenade. Their total explosive power is equivalent to about 15,000 megatons. Some idea of the enormity of this figure can be realised from the fact that it is equal to about 1·25 million Hiroshima bombs. The total amount of explosives used by man in wars throughout history is equal to about 20 megatons; the nuclear arsenals are, therefore, about 750 times more powerful than all of the explosives used in wars so far. **Frank Barnaby**

Above: A B-52 testing a CF-6 turbofan engine. The Stratofortress has been the mainstay of the US bomber force since 1955, and during its time of service it has seen its mission change from high- to low-altitude penetration in the face of defensive surface-to-air missiles. Above inset: A ground-launched cruise missile flies a test flight. Cruise missiles provide a versatile means of delivery for nuclear warheads.

Weapons development

Change and continuity

It is a widely held assumption that modern warfare is being transformed by the development of technology, and it is certainly true that weapons are now more accurate than ever, highly automated, and in some cases extremely destructive. But the developments of the last 40 years and those projected for the future, pose a number of important questions, both about the direction of the changes that are taking place – involving an escalation of complexity and cost – and about their relation to the tactical and strategic conduct of warfare.

In many ways, it could be argued that the remarkable thing about warfare since 1945 has been its failure to change. The scenes in San Carlos Water during the 1982 Falklands War, for example, with attack aircraft running the gauntlet of anti-aircraft fire to bomb warships while infantry came ashore in landing craft, would have been basically familiar to a World War II soldier – despite the increased speed of air action and the generalised use of missiles. This was not, of course, the most sophisticated possible

Above: The cockpit of an F-15. Managing the information provided by this large number of dials is very difficult, even for an experienced pilot, and distracts him from the actual flying of the aeroplane in a combat situation. The provision of head-up diplays has gone some way towards alleviating this, but a contemporary pilot still has a much greater workload than his World War II counterpart.

modern battlefield, but most of the equipment deployed was the same as that in service with the superpowers. Existing plans for superpower warfare follow the same concepts that ruled in 1945 – strategic and tactical bombing (even if the missile now fulfils much of the role of the World War II bomber), armoured thrusts depending on the tank's firepower and mobility, submarines and aircraft carriers as the key vessels in the sea war, and so on.

Of course, important changes have taken place in the design and performance of even those weapons systems directly descended from World War II equivalents. As examples, in land, sea and air warfare respectively, we can take the tank, the destroyer and the fighter aircraft, following through their postwar development.

The tank has remained the primary offensive weapon of the world's armies throughout the postwar era. Comparison of the Soviet World War II vintage T34 and the contemporary T72 yields useful information about developments in tank design since 1945. The calibre of the main armament has increased from 85mm to 125mm, and the T72's gun is a smoothbore, unlike the rifled one on the T34. The armour of the T34 was 75mm at the thickest point, proof against most anti-tank guns firing tungsten shot at 1000m (1095 yards); the armour of the T72 is a composite type, capable of stopping all but the most powerful HEAT (high explosive anti-tank) warheads. The accuracy of the tank's armament has been increased through the introduction of several technical improvements: a laser rangefinder, analogue ballistic computers and a stabilised gun. Finally, in the T72 an automatic loader for the gun is in use, allowing the crew to be reduced from four to three.

Since World War II, the destroyer has evolved from a multi-purpose escort for valuable groups of ships to a warship with a specialised role to counter submarine and aeroplane attacks. An important feature of the contemporary destroyer is its missile armament, replacing the light guns in the anti-aircraft warfare role and the torpedo in the anti-ship role. Anti-submarine capabilities have been augmented by the embarkation of a helicopter, and surveillance systems have been expanded from a fire-control radar to a suite of search and fire-control radars with electronic warfare equipment.

The introduction of jet propulsion during World War II enabled fighter aeroplanes to travel at higher speeds than hitherto possible, and developments in aerodynamics were at hand to prevent any severe loss in manoeuvrability. The higher speeds made fighters harder targets to hit and, to increase the offensive power of jets in air combat, fire-control radars and air-to-air missiles were introduced during the 1950s. This has led to a reduction in the number of guns carried and an increase in the ranges at which combat takes place. New materials have also been introduced into the construction of modern warplanes: first titanium was used for a more heat-resistant structure at supersonic speeds; now, in the latest generation of aeroplanes, composite materials that have the strength of metals but weigh less are used.

These newest fighters are designed to maintain their stability solely by means of a computer system manipulating their control surfaces; effectively, an inherent instability is built into the aircraft to improve manoeuvrability. However, increasing sophistication has involved the use of expensive electronic equipment, forcing up the cost and size of the modern fighter, and making the cost of maintaining an adequate air force very high indeed.

As well as developments to existing systems, there have been a few new systems, little used in World War II, that have had a major impact on warfare; the most important of these are probably helicopters and missiles. Helicopters have provided a great increase in mobility for armed forces. Men can be rushed to a critical point at high speed using transport helicopters. Gunships can bring firepower to bear from above, giving forces on the ground heavy weapons' support even in the most rugged terrain. The major disadvantage of helicopters is their vulnerability to defensive fire; this may possibly be overcome by flying low to the ground and behind treelines, as favoured by the US Army. The helicopter has proved most useful in counter-insurgency campaigns, precisely because of its high mobility in all types of terrain.

Dead on target

Missiles have probably had the greatest impact on all forms of warfare in the postwar era. Their most important feature is a high degree of accuracy, vital to the fast environment of the modern battlefield. This accuracy has meant that the rate of attrition in combat is much greater, as a higher proportion of projectiles strike home to deadly effect. The primary aim of the missile designer is to produce a weapon that can be targeted and fired, after which the operator can turn his attention to acquiring a new target, leaving the missile to do its work. This 'fire-and-forget' capability has been achieved in air and sea combat, but on land, missiles still have to be guided to their targets by means of steering instructions sent down a trailing wire or by laser designation. One of the effects these weapons have had on warfare is to make concealment and surprise essential to the prospects of success in an operation; once seen, a target is likely to be hit by almost every missile operator in the vicinity.

Examining these weapons' developments, certain trends prevalent in their design become evident. There is a requirement that every shot be made to count, and this is reflected in the quests for accuracy by incorporating sophisticated rangefinders, surveillance systems and homing devices in modern weapons. The introduction of computers responds to the need for rapid fire-control calculations. Automated equipment is increasingly used to reduce expensive manpower requirements and time spent on support, rather than fighting, tasks, and also to speed response. New types of materials are being researched to provide greater protection or strength, preferably with a reduction in weight.

The most important developments have all been characterised by the increasing use of electronic equipment. The world's first electronic war was World War II. Electronics, in the shape of radar and jamming measures, were extensively used during the bombing campaigns by both the offence and the defence. Radio beams were used to guide bombers

towards their target; radar was employed to detect incoming enemy bombers. Naturally, moves were made to counter these uses of electronic technology, thereby introducing the battlefield of the airwaves to warfare.

Despite a hiatus in the first 10 years after the war, electronic warfare soon received widespread attention from the postwar military establishments, and a particular spur was provided by the Vietnam War. To locate the enemy on the ground, air-dropped sensors were emplaced at strategic points along the borders of South Vietnam; the Igloo White programme used such devices to detect movements along the Ho Chi Minh Trail. The use of surface-to-air missiles in the defence of Hanoi and Haiphong against US bombing attacks led to the use of specialised jamming pods (such as the ALQ-71) or aeroplanes (such as the EB-66) in combination with anti-radiation missiles (the AGM-45 Shrike, for example) by the US Air Force and Navy to defeat a radar-based system of air defence.

Below: The helicopter (these are Sikorsky CH-53Gs) has made vertical envelopment tactics much easier by eliminating the need for parachute drops, giving a new dimension to modern land warfare.
Bottom: Air-to-air missiles – like the Sparrows and Sidewinders on this F-15 – have had a great impact on aerial combat in the postwar era through their great accuracy, although, contrary to some expectations, the aerial gun has maintained its place in close-quarters dog fights.

Below: The American TOW (tube-launched optically-controlled wire-guided) is an example of the sort of anti-tank guided weapon which has given infantry the ability to engage and defeat the modern tank, despite its improved armour. Bottom right: Naval warfare of today is largely concerned with the defeat of enemy submarines. The nuclear-propelled submarine has become a vital component of the modern battle fleet because of its long-range cruising capability.

The future developments in this field are likely to set the tempo of battle in coming wars. To give just one example, the EXJAM (expendable jammer) system is currently being tested by the US Army. This comprises a number of transmitters in a 155mm artillery shell. After firing, the transmitters are ejected at pre-set intervals, falling to earth along the flight path. They then transmit a jamming signal, confusing the enemy's communications.

The electronic dimension will clearly be important to future weapons, but the fragility of such devices raises the question of reliability. The US Navy's F-14 incorporates an impressive electronics array, but breaks down every 20 minutes of flight and requires nearly 98 man-hours of maintenance per sortie. The US Army's M1 Abrams tank averages one breakdown per 70 kilometres (43 miles) of driving.

The sophisticated electronic and automation systems now incorporated into modern weapons systems, apart from contributing to the reduction in reliability of modern weapons, are also sometimes of dubious effectiveness. A-6 attack aeroplanes of the US Navy were used against truck convoys on the Ho Chi Minh Trail; their complex all-weather attack system supposedly makes them more accurate, but they could only account for 0.6 enemy trucks per mission. The A-26 Invader, a World War II vintage attack bomber, carried out the same mission using a night telescope to spot targets, and achieved a kill-rate average of two trucks per mission.

The increased use of complex machinery, whether electronic or automated (and often both), has forced the cost of weapons up. In 1971, some interesting figures were given by a Pentagon defence analyst to the Senate Armed Services Committee: the cost of the avionics of a modern fighter aeroplane amounted to $2.5 million, while the engine cost $2 million. This should be compared to the World War II-era costs of $3000 and $40,000 respectively. Of course, these simple figures take no account of the technical advances that have made jet fighters superior to their

piston-engined counterparts in speed, but do we really get $2.5 million worth from an F-15's avionics? A useful fact to keep in mind when considering this question is that the smaller (because it has less avionics equipment and less powerful engines) F-5 fighter performed well in mass dogfights against the F-15 during an experimental programme carried out by the US Air Force.

Despite their demands for this lavish standard of high-technology equipment on every weapon procured, until quite recently the command staffs of the world's major armies have given little consideration to whether computers and electronics have substantially altered the nature of combat: the tactics prescribed in manuals have been better suited to fighting World War II again. This situation took insufficient notice of evidence which was emerging from the wars in the Middle East that these tactics were outdated; it also produced a mentality incapable of handling the special features of counter-insurgency warfare. The adoption (in the early 1980s) of the concept of AirLand Battle by the US Army and the Follow On Forces Attack by Nato are signs that the effects of improved facilities for command and control and the increased accuracy of modern munitions are beginning to be

assimilated into the theories of the conduct of battle. In future, perhaps, high-technology add-ons to modern weapons will be applied less indiscriminately, and more attention will be paid to precisely where they will be most efficiently disposed.

Finally, and perhaps most importantly, what kind of war do armies want to fight with their weapons? Scenarios of limited conflict between the Warsaw Pact and Nato seem to lack plausibility, especially in the light of Soviet statements in their army manuals that a nuclear environment is the norm for operations. The use of high-technology weaponry against a guerrilla foe did not win the Vietnam War for the United States, and shows no sign of doing so for the Soviet Union in Afghanistan. It is clear that in a limited war – such as the Falklands campaign or the Arab-Israeli conflict – high-technology weapons have only proved useful in conjunction with the factors that have been important to all wars: determination to win, high morale and skilful tactics. If victory in war rests on these intangibles, what advantage will be gained by equipment above the level of technology of such weapons as the Centurion tank, the Kfir fighter and the Saar 5 fast attack craft?

Chester Loomis

Above: A Sea Eagle anti-ship missile, on its trials, is launched by a Sea Harrier. The anti-ship missile provides a cheap method of destroying an expensive ship.

Below: This F-15 is armed with an ASAT (anti-satellite) missile. The ASAT is carried into the upper atmosphere by a jet, where it is fired and uses infra-red homing to reach its target. It relies on kinetic energy to disable the satellite.

Future weapons

Naval developments

Sea combat today is conducted at a much faster pace than it was 40 years ago; the remainder of the century is likely to see this pace accelerate even further as developments in computer technology produce quicker data-processing. Weapons systems will in effect become capable of thinking for themselves in combat situations. Sensors will collect information and process it more rapidly, presenting ship commanders with a list of alternative responses to be followed in the course of the battle. Manning levels on ships will decline as more automation is introduced. The technology that will make all this possible is either already in existence or under development in 1985.

Currently, many weapons systems either under development or just entering service employ microprocessors and computers as information managers. For example, the Bofors SAK 57mm/L70 Mk 2 gun, to be mounted on the new Halifax-class Canadian frigates, employs two microprocessors. These are linked to the ship's combat information centre, and a continuous exchange of information proceeds between them. The computer in the combat information centre transmits instructions to the gun, telling it where to aim. The microprocessors are programmed with data about prohibited firing and aiming arcs (such as the ship's superstructure). If the gun moves toward a prohibited area, the microprocessor guides it around any obstacles that may be in the path to be followed (such as an antenna). The gunlaying is adjusted by the microprocessors to take into account the pitch and roll of the vessel. Two microprocessors are employed so that one may check the other continuously to avoid any errors. The gun also uses computer-control in its automatic loading system, to choose the type of ammunition to be fired (either high explosive or pre-fragmented proximity shells).

Another valuable role for information technology is in the field of fire-control systems. The Kanaris system, developed by the Sperry Corporation, uses computer graphics and displays for target-motion analysis, the control of weapons and their settings, the coordination of attacks and for the command decision process. In effect, the use of a computer speeds the calculations that are necessary in aiming weapons. Computers can also serve as part of the radar and radio direction-finding systems on board the warship. Here they would be part of the ship's combat information centre, converting signals from analogue to digital format or calculating directions, speeds and distances of targets from the information provided by the sensory apparatus.

Above: The combat information centre aboard the USS *Ticonderoga* makes great use of computers and video displays to provide the ship commander with the means of achieving better control of the battle situation. Such stations are now the nerve-centre of the modern naval vessel.

As can be seen, computers are already playing a very important role in the latest naval equipment and this role will increase as computers become more sophisticated. Currently under development is the so-called fifth-generation computer. These machines will be able to employ artificial intelligence to think out answers to relatively simple problems. As an example of what could be possible for a fifth-generation computer, it might have prevented the sinking of HMS *Sheffield*. The computer aboard the *Sheffield* that dealt with information from the electronic support measures sensors was programmed to regard the AM 39 Exocet as a friendly missile; therefore it did not react to the presence of one in the area. A fifth-generation computer would recognise the Exocet as friendly, but the fact that it was attacking the ship would override this preprogrammed information and the anti-missile systems would be brought into effect.

The computer was made necessary to modern naval warfare by the increasing speed of modern armaments. There is nowadays less time available for the computations necessary for evasive action or defensive measures. The problem is increased by the high accuracy of these weapons, an accuracy that is certain to increase as we near the end of the century.

One method of improving the accuracy of weapons is to make their guidance systems more versatile or sensitive. The Japanese ASM-1 anti-ship missile uses semi-active radar homing, but since the system employed is susceptible to jamming by electronic warfare systems, an infra-red passive homing head is under development for the same missile. Since an enemy will not know which of the two homing devices is being employed by the ASM-1 attacking it, defence against the missile will become far more difficult. Another development in guidance is simply the extension of guidance systems to at present unguided munitions. The same project that is to produce the new guidance head for

the ASM-1 is also examining the possibility of placing a similar infra-red homer onto a conventional 220kg (500lb) bomb. French naval gun manufacturer Thomson-Brandt is also applying guidance technology to conventional munitions; in this case, a shell for a 100mm gun is to be provided with infra-red terminal guidance.

Another old weapon being given the ability to perform new tricks is the mine. By the end of World War II, advances in minesweeper technology had reduced considerably the effectiveness of mines, but it seems that today the balance is once more swinging back in their favour. Mines placed in coastal seas can now be fitted with a ship counter, allowing the device to wait until the second or third indication of a ship in the area before detonating, thus defeating the tactic

Above: A PAP 104 submersible minehunting device is lowered into the water from a French Circe-class mine counter-measures vessel. Below left: A model of a broad-beam S-90 type frigate undergoes comparison trials with a model of the Type 12 class. Some naval constructors believe that a broad-beam design will prove superior to the traditional 'long and thin' style.

of sending in minesweepers and minehunters to clear a path for shipping. Mines also now have much-improved sensors which allow them to distinguish types of vessel with precision and ignore the signals with which minehunters seek to detonate them.

Where mines may well prove exceptionally valuable in the future is in deep water. The nuclear-powered submarine, whether carrying ballistic missiles or not, is difficult to track and, once found, difficult to sink. Deepwater mines will threaten these vessels where at present they are safest. Using acoustic sensors to detect a passing submarine, the mine will either fire a torpedo at it, or will be thrust up from the seabed by rockets to detonate near the vessel. Naturally, the deployment of deepwater mines will create a demand for deepwater mine-sweepers, and several designs for these are either under consideration or actually being built by the major navies of the world.

Material changes

These new minesweepers, whether ocean-going or inshore, will probably employ new types of materials in their construction, a trend that is not just confined to these craft that demand unconventional approaches in the face of a versatile opponent. The nature of the duties of a minesweeper demands that its hull be constructed of a material capable of withstanding explosions, while offering a low acoustic and magnetic signature. At one time wood was the alternative used in construction of mine-warfare vessels, but in the last 15 years, a glassfibre reinforced plastic has become the choice of most of the world's navies. The Bofors 57mm/L70 Mk2 is similarly made of glassfibre reinforced plastic to reduce its radar signature. New materials are also being applied to make weapons more durable. A new French torpedo is to be made of a filament-wound carbon fibre that is resistant to pressure and corrosion; it also has the advantage of a lower acoustic

signature than the steel and other metals normally used in the construction of torpedoes. In the same vein, consideration of new materials for the outer skin of a submarine is underway, also to reduce its acoustic signature.

As well as studying the new materials that might be used in warship construction, naval architects are examining the design of the structure. The primary field of interest is in the hull and its length-to-beam ratio. Most vessels of today's navies are built with the traditional hull form, the round bilge; but experiments are now being made with the deep-vee form, where the keel comes to a sharp point. Deep-vee hulls have better sea-keeping qualities than the round bilge hull, and require no more power to propel if designed correctly. They are proving to be a viable alternative for light vessels such as corvettes and fast attack craft.

The length-to-beam ratio is also undergoing new examination, in the light of preliminary studies being carried out into the use of a shorter but wider hull in the design of a new generation of frigates. This is a controversial subject, but proponents of the 'short and fat' alternative believe that more space will be available for weapons and sea-keeping will be improved. Opponents claim that the speed will be insufficient to keep pace with nuclear submarines and that the vessels may pitch more in the water, making a less stable platform. It is interesting to note, though, that ships have been getting beamier in the latest designs.

The trends in naval weapons' technology show that the next 15 years will be marked with the experimentation of new ideas across the board. It is difficult to predict exactly what designs will be taken up and which ones will be put aside, but it is clear that any navy hoping for command of the seas will need to keep abreast of all developments or be forced to surrender the initiative to any potential enemy.

Paul Szuscikiewicz

Below: The HMS *Cottesmore*, a mine counter-measures vessel, has been built with a glass-fibre reinforced plastic hull to defeat mines that detonate when they detect the magnetic signature of a metal hull.

Future weapons

The remaining 15 years of the 20th century are likely to see many radical improvements in the capabilities of military aircraft. New technology will not only enable the aircraft of the next generation to fly higher, faster and further than currently-available aircraft, but it may also endow them with characteristics quite unlike those of any previous warplane. The US Stealth programme, for example, is aimed at producing aeroplanes that will be virtually invisible to radar and will also have low visual and infra-red signatures. Another way of penetrating enemy air defences will be for an aeroplane to cruise at supersonic speed (current aircraft can only fly supersonically for relatively short periods because of the need to conserve fuel), such aeroplanes relying on speed and altitude to outperform enemy interceptors and surface-to-air missiles. Both of these new technologies are likely to stimulate advances in the techniques of air defence, just as the low-flying bomber and strike aircraft have led to the counter-measures of airborne early warning aeroplanes and lookdown/shootdown radar and missile systems. The combat pilot's workload will be considerably eased by the computer management of virtually all aspects of his mission; he will be able to designate any target he sees, simply by looking at it through a helmet-mounted sight; he will be able to control many of his aircraft's systems by using voice commands, rather than having to fumble with knobs and switches as is now the case.

The concept of 'fly-by-wire' (electronically-signalled) controls and the development of carbon-fibre composite materials have greatly influenced the design of a new range of lightweight, highly-agile combat aircraft intended for service in the 1990s. They include the British ACA (agile combat aircraft), which is to be built as a technology demonstrator under the experimental aircraft programme, and the French ACE (avion de combat expérimental). Both of these national designs may serve as the basis for the broadly-similar FEFA (future European fighter aircraft), sponsored by five Nato nations. These aeroplanes are primarily intended for the air-to-air role, but have a secondary ground-attack capability. The characteristics desired from the FEFA include twin-engines for increased reliability and safety in comparison with that given by a single powerplant, an armament of at least six short- and medium-range air-to-air missiles, good patrol endurance and a short take-off run of some 500 m (1640 feet) so that bomb damage to runways need not ground the fighter. The substitution of carbon-fibre composites for more conventional metal alloys permits a considerable saving in airframe weight, without compromising structural integrity. Fly-by-wire controls allow an unstable aircraft, which is uncontrollable by conventional means, to be flown by making use of a computer-directed system rather

Below: Forward-swept wings – such as those on this Grumman X-29 – have been considered for warplanes since 1944, but have not been feasible previously because stress severely damaged the wings' skins. Studies by USAF Colonel Norris Krone demonstrated it was possible to build such wings out of composite materials.

The air battle

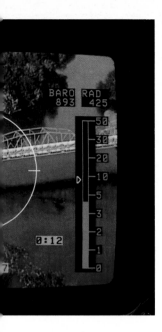

Above: Video displays such as this have become increasingly common on modern combat aircraft. The information shown on the screen greatly aids the calculations necessary to deliver munitions onto the target. Below: This Sikorsky XH-59A uses an unusual dual rotor configuration to improve its speed.

than directly-linked flight controls. Fly-by-wire therefore enables a far more manoeuvrable aeroplane to be built than would be possible with conventional technology. A broadly similar design philosophy to that of the FEFA has been followed by Sweden with its JA39 Gripen, which will replace the multi-role Viggen, and by Israel with its Lavi. All these fighters will accelerate, climb and manoeuvre better than current types.

Little is known about the Soviet Union's advanced combat designs before they appear as prototypes. However, the latest fighter aeroplanes off the drawing boards, the Su-27 Fitter and MiG-29 Fulcrum, provide evidence of an increasing sophistication in Soviet design practice which is likely to be maintained into the 1990s. By contrast, the US Air Force's (USAF) work on an ATF (advanced technology fighter), which is intended to replace the F-15 Eagle in the middle of the next decade, has been widely publicised. Many aspects of new technology are being explored and the most promising of them are likely to be incorporated into the ATF design. The Grumman X-29 test aeroplane will investigate a thin-section, forward-swept wing coupled with canard surfaces, which is intended to offer good manoeuvrability at transonic speeds. Boeing are testing the 'mission adaptive wing' on an F-111. This is a variable-camber surface, the aerofoil of which can be varied in flight to suit it to subsonic cruise, manoeuvring, or supersonic dash. However, even if tests are successful, the mission adaptive wing will have to be much refined to suit it to a thin-wing fighter design. A less complex innovation is the vectored-thrust nozzle, which will be tested on an F-15 Eagle. It can be deflected to angles of up to 20 degrees for

short take-off or to improve manoeuvrability in flight and can be used with full afterburner engaged.

Perhaps the most promising areas of research, however, are those relating to 'decoupled' flight modes and integrated flight and fire-control systems. The AFTI (advanced fighter technology integration) F-16 test aeroplane has demonstrated the capability of decoupling the direction of flight from the attitude of the aircraft. This means that, within small but significant limits, the aeroplane's nose can be slewed upwards, downwards or to one side without altering the flight path. Such a capability will greatly assist with the problems of target designation and weapons aiming in both air-to-air and air-to-ground combat. A related improvement in weapons aiming can be obtained by integrating the aeroplane's fire-control system with the flight controls. This allows a pilot to point his aeroplane approximately in the direction of his intended target, leaving a computer to eliminate his aiming errors and position the aircraft accurately for weapons release.

Other improvements in fighter aeroplane performance are likely to come from advances in the weapons carried. For example, the USAF's ATF will be armed with the AIM-120 AMRAAM (advanced medium-range air-to-air missile) which is fitted with an active radar-guidance system, making it a 'fire and forget' weapon. By contrast, the AIM-7 Sparrow which currently arms the F-15 Eagle makes use of semi-active radar-homing requiring the launch aeroplane's radar to illuminate its target throughout the missile's flight. Future ground-attack weapons may include containers for sub-munitions, which are constructed as lifting bodies so that they can be released at stand-off ranges and fly towards their

targets before releasing the munitions. They are also likely to be shaped as conformed stores to blend in with the contours of the carrier aeroplane in order to reduce drag. There is, however, some controversy over the wisdom of putting advanced technology into weapons which must be expended, rather than into the attack aeroplane which at least has a chance of survival. An even more fiercely-debated question is whether to use manned aeroplanes or remotely-piloted vehicles and missiles in attacks on enemy rear-echelon targets. The United States at present favours a cruise missile for this role, whereas its European Nato partners prefer manned aeroplanes. Target information for these attacks is likely to come from the JSTARS (joint surveillance and target attack radar system) stand-off airborne radar, which will be mounted on the C-18 adaptation of the Boeing 707, and from the PLSS (precision location strike system) carried by the TR-1 surveillance aircraft. Such advanced reconnaissance systems and related command, control and communications equipment form a key area in the emerging technology which could considerably enhance Nato's conventional defences during the 1990s.

Stealth technology will be employed in the ATB (advanced technology bomber), to evade the more sophisticated Soviet air defence system currently being introduced. Stealth involves the reduction of the aeroplane's radar, infra-red and visual signatures to the point where it becomes difficult for early-warning systems to detect the bomber in time for the defences to react effectively. Complete invisibility to radar or other target-acquisition sensors is probably impossible to achieve, but highly-placed USAF sources claim that the present level of Stealth tech-

Above: The development of bomblets has clearly improved the destructive power of modern ground attack aeroplanes. If precision guidance is employed in these weapons they will become even more deadly. Left: The Bell XV-15 tests the tilt-rotor concept, which may produce a rotorcraft superior to the conventional helicopter.

nology is sufficient to render current Soviet air defence systems completely obsolete. Northrop's ATB design, which is at present shrouded in tight security, is probably a relatively small flying-wing design with a blended shape that eliminates sharp angles which would be good radar reflectors. The engines will be well-shielded so that their turbine blades do not reflect radar beams, and any other potential reflecting surfaces will be coated with radar-absorbent materials.

If the Stealth bomber is to remain undetected, it cannot rely on radio or radar navigation bombing aids, whose emissions would betray its presence, but must rather use such passive systems as inertial navigation bombing aids and forward-looking infrared sensors. Stealth techniques have already been demonstrated by the secret Lockheed XF-19.

Significant advances in the design of rotary-winged aircraft are likely to be made within the next 15 years. The tilt-rotor JVX is scheduled to replace the UH-46 assault transport helicopter with the US Marine Corps by the early 1990s and will also serve with the USAF in the combat rescue role. The great advantage of a tilt-rotor design is that it combines the vertical flight performance of the helicopter with the appreciably better payload and range characteristics of a conventional aircraft. For this reason, a tilt-rotor may also be chosen to fulfil the US Army's LHX requirement for a new utility, scout and attack rotorcraft in the late 1990s. Similarly, studies have been made in the United States and Britain to establish the feasibility of procuring a single aircraft type to undertake the roles of transport, in-flight refuelling, maritime patrol, anti-submarine warfare and similar duties. Looking beyond the end of the present century, the USAF's studies of a Trans-Atmospheric Vehicle, which combines the characteristics of a conventional aircraft with those of a low-orbit spacecraft, provide a tantalising glimpse of the shape of military aircraft to come.

Anthony Robinson

Left: The B-1 bomber represents the leading edge of the Stealth technology; rounded edges and radar-absorbent materials reduce this aeroplane's radar signature. Inset left: The F-16 incorporates a limited 'fly-by-wire' system, using electrical signalling in its flight-control system.

Future weapons

War on land

Above: The Infantryman 2000 concept unveiled by Scicon at the British Army Equipment Exhibition in 1984. The helmet is equipped with an image-intensifier, a thermal-imager, a laser target-designator and sound sensors. A head-up display is linked to the man's computer and provides information from his sensory apparatus. The bullpup-type individual weapon may fire either small-calibre caseless rounds for short-range combat, or larger calibre high-explosive, illuminating or smoke rounds.

In the past, the lifespan of a land weapons system has been of the order of 25 years – 10 years in development and 15 years in service. While the operational life will vary, development times in future will tend to be longer, if only because design problems are becoming more difficult to overcome. In Britain, both the new Individual Weapon rifle and the LAW 80 will not now enter service until after 1985, while in the United States the slowdown in progress on the Wasp mini-missile programme has resulted in a cutback in funding and brought a halt to development. With few exceptions, therefore, the systems that will be in service in 1995 are already in development.

Many of the forthcoming advances in battlefield systems will be closely related to those recently achieved in micro-electronics generally and micro-computers in particular. Not only will the weapons be improved, but so also will the systems controlling their employment. Both the processing of data by computer and the transmission of data by communication links will become standard.

Information technology in the British Army is synonymous with Project Wavell. In this system, information will be communicated by Clansman radios linked into the Nato satellite and Ptarmigan communication networks. The high flow of data will be processed automatically by computer, which will also provide the means of storing, updating and transferring the information. Typically, details of such items as reserve demolitions and location states will be available together with reports of enemy contacts and strengths. With the immediate visual display of information, the commander's decision-making time will be maximised.

The 24-hour battle

The acquisition of information on the enemy will depend very much on the use of surveillance equipment both in the air and on the ground. In the air, remotely-piloted vehicles are likely to continue in use in addition to aircraft; they will use sideways-looking airborne radar while flying parallel to the front. On the ground all the well-known systems, such as radar and image-intensifiers, will remain in service and work in conjunction with the new thermal-imagers that can operate in total darkness. These thermal-imagers can be used in conjunction with a wide variety of weapons – MIRA 2, for example, will be fitted to Milan – making the all-weather 24-hour battle a reality.

That the battle will now be fought at night as well as in daylight is unlikely to affect the dominance of the tank on the battlefield. Although weapons will be developed to challenge this dominance, tanks also will be improved to maintain it. As designers have moved to incorporate the 'emerging technology' in their latest models, so costs have risen to the point where a main battle tank such as Challenger is valued at around £1.75 million. The prospect of even more expensive tanks has prompted new thoughts on design, with the aim not only of saving on manufacturing costs but also, by improving the tank's survivability and restorability, of obtaining indirect savings as well. To achieve this aim a number of countries are examining the concept of a single-tier tank – that is, one without a conventional turret but which has the gun mounted on a rotating pedestal. This would result in the breech of the gun being outside the hull of the vehicle, making automatic loading a necessity. While the additional cost of an automatic loader must be set against the savings of a simpler turret, the advantages of reducing the number of crew from four to three should not be forgotten. However, it is not cost which will weigh against the automatic loader, but rather the question of its reliability.

For the British, there will be a decision to make concerning the change to a smoothbore tank gun. Successful development of slipping driving band technology gives the rifled gun an edge at the present time, but inevitably muzzle velocities will increase and at 2000 mps (6500 fps) the theoretical limit of the

technology will be reached. The British could well decide to anticipate this and choose a smoothbore gun for their next tank which is due in the 1990s.

Whichever gun is used, there is unlikely to be a replacement for the fin-stabilised armour-piercing round of ammunition presently employed. It is much more likely that the existing ammunition will be developed further. One possible line of approach is to replace the tungsten carbide core by one of depleted uranium; this would prove beneficial in terms of cost and additional target effects. An improvement in lethality could also be achieved by the addition of a propellant charge in the rear of the penetrator, giving it a rocket effect.

In addition to improvements in tank-gun ammunition, the threat to tanks will be increased by the deployment of new weapons which attack the tank at the top, where the armour is thinner. Much research work has been carried out in the United States into Sadarm (search-and-destroy armour) weapons which are designed for overhead attack. There are several variations on this theme, but the main group consists of sub-munitions delivered to a point above the battlefield by a missile. Once there, the sub-munitions are ejected to float towards the ground by parachute while slowly rotating and searching for a target. Target identification can be achieved by fitting either an infra-red detector or a millimetric wavelength radar in each sub-munition. Once the target is located, a self-forging fragment warhead will be detonated.

A similar approach is envisaged for anti-tank mines, but after parachuting to the ground they would position themselves by means of ground sensor spikes. They would remain in position until the sensor detected vehicle vibrations, when the

warhead would be fired, spinning into the air. As an alternative to detecting vehicle vibrations, the sensor could be one that detects Doppler shift, which would enable the noise from helicopter rotor blades to be recognised.

As far as anti-tank guided weapons are concerned, the next decade is most likely to be a period of consolidation, as the widespread adoption of a new generation of missiles takes place, following the start made recently in the United States with the Hellfire. Already in Europe, formulation of the Trigat family of missiles is underway to produce replacements for missiles such as Swingfire and Milan. The long-range missile will be capable of reaching out to 4.5km (3 miles). The options here for guidance are either laser beam-riding as used on the Hellfire, or a more advanced system requiring the operator only to designate the target, after which an automatic tracker

Top: Laser rangefinders are already in use with the world's armies, and studies are being made to improve their performance in the adverse conditions of dust and fog. Inset top left: The view through an NDS-2 driver's night viewer. The image intensifier and the laser rangefinder will make the 24-hour battlefield a reality. Above: The 105mm FL-12 gun/turret on this Mowag Shark uses an automatic gun-loader.

in the missile would fly it there, culminating in a diving attack. Also included in Trigat will be a shorter range infantry-portable missile for ranges up to 2km (1.2 miles). This is likely to be still based on the principles of infra-red beam-riding as used in the Milan. It will incorporate an overflying attack with a shaped charge jet firing down onto the top of the tank. However, while all these developments are in progress the older missiles will not disappear. There is every chance that the British Swingfire will remain in service for at least another 10 years, while in the United States the Dragon will continue, awaiting a delayed decision on its replacement.

Guided missiles are a well established item in every army's inventory, but free-flight rockets have, until recently, been largely neglected by Nato countries. It has become increasingly necessary, however, for Nato armies to attack large formations before they arrive in the combat zone, and this means attacking at ranges of up to 40km (24 miles) to interdict large area targets such as armoured formations and artillery batteries. Artillery guns lack accuracy at long ranges and, with the limited numbers available, would be unable to fulfil this role. It is essential to be able to attack quickly with a high volume of fire in order to obtain maximum effect before the enemy has gone for cover. The multiple launch rocket system provides a solution to the problem and over the next few years the version manufactured by the Vought Company in the United States will be introduced; not that multiple rocket launchers are a new idea, for the Soviet BM21 had been in service for 20 years before being superseded by the BM27 in 1978.

Rockets can carry a variety of high-explosive warheads, but the Vought system will concentrate on interdiction using mines. In the first phase of development the rockets will contain 644 anti-tank and anti-personnel bomblets, but in the second phase these will be replaced by 28 anti-tank mines. Even-

Above: The 4.85mm Individual Weapon (right) adopts the bullpup design, achieving considerable savings in weight and length over its predecessors like the 7.62mm SLR (left).

Left: An MLRS (multiple launch rocket system) is test-fired at White Sands missile range in New Mexico. Although similar systems are in use with the Warsaw Pact's armies, this MLRS will be unusual in its use of rocket-delivered anti-tank mines against armoured formations.

tually Sadarm projectiles may be carried, but this is far into the future.

For surface-to-air missiles, the next decade will be a time for taking stock, one for using technology to improve the existing systems rather than for introducing entirely new systems. It is a period that the British Rapier could well dominate. The Blindfire system, enabling Rapier to operate at night, is already in service; the Tracked Rapier will be deployed in greater numbers; and, not least, the Americans will be purchasing it. Rapier will be improved by replacing the present high-explosive warhead by a fragmentation warhead. In addition, the system will be made more resistant to the electronic countermeasures employed by aircraft; this is an essential step since Rapier is based on 1960s technology.

Blowpipe into Javelin

Blowpipe has been redeveloped into the Javelin. Originally Blowpipe was designed to be generally available, but its employment changed as budgetary controls necessitated a move to specialised fire teams. To meet the needs of this different scenario, Blowpipe has been modified and enhanced to give it a greater range, enabling it to engage Soviet anti-tank helicopters at their maximum stand-off distance. As Javelin, it includes a semi-automatic command system requiring the operator to track only the aircraft, together with a night vision device giving it a full 24-hour capability.

The electronic counter-measures operated by aircraft against missiles and the counter-counter-measures with which missiles respond are all part of the shadowy world of electronic warfare. Even in a simple aircraft versus missile scenario, the importance of electronic warfare is clear, for whoever has the upper hand will have a significant advantage. But electronic warfare will also be of critical significance in all aspects of the land war. Work will certainly continue on such areas as the interception or jamming of communications, as well as on counter-counter-measures to overcome these. Frequency-hopping radars and radios, which evade enemy search and intercept operations by jumping rapidly from frequency to frequency, will see further development. Also showing considerable promise is the use of 'burst transmission' which involves recording a message and then transmitting it at very high speed, greatly reducing transmission time and making interception much more difficult.

Finally, in the field of smallarms, a radical change in rifle design may soon take place. Heckler and Koch have the G11 under development. The novel design of this rifle allows it to fire caseless ammunition, a round of which comprises a bullet with a rectangular block of propellant at the base, so all that constitutes a round leaves the rifle via the barrel. Also, imaginative engineering has resulted in a weapon of short overall length which at 750mm (30in) is very similar to the British Individual Weapon. In any event, a trend is emerging towards shorter rifles, whether in the form of the shorter barrelled assault rifles or based on the 'bullpup' concept of a buttless rifle.

The next 10 to 15 years will see sweeping advances in land weapons, and their effects on the conduct of battle will be great. The fighting men of the future will clearly be more influenced by technology than their predecessors. **Ben Hill**

Right: A computer displays terrain and troop positions during an exercise of command processes.
Below: New technologies will be applied to communications systems: this is an Israeli field telephone powered by a solar cell.

Future weapons

Development of a new generation of US nuclear weapons began in the early and middle 1970s, and these will provide a significant part of the US strategic forces into the next century. They represent a considerable advance on those weapons already in service, in particular incorporating superior guidance technology. These weapons were not part of any new strategic plan developed in the face of a growing Soviet strategic strength, but were born of the gradual updating of the US nuclear arsenal, with its own internal momentum.

Bound up in the piecemeal authorisations of these various developmental programmes was a serious debate about the continued viability of the three parts of the 'strategic triad' – bombers, submarines and land-based missiles. Particular attention was focussed on the manned bomber and the missile underground in its silo. The introduction of the surface-to-air missile in the 1950s had heralded the end of the traditional strategic bombing tactic of flying very fast at a high altitude. The United States began to work on another option for manned bombers: low-level penetration missions. However, with the cruise missile capable of performing this mission at a cheaper cost, the viability of the manned bomber option was called into question. Pressure from bomber enthusiasts in the US Air Force has led to the retention of the B-1 programme, but the doubts remain unstilled.

Similarly, a question mark hangs over the future of the ICBM (intercontinental ballistic missile) in its

Nuclear delivery systems

silo. Modern missiles are considerably more accurate than their predecessors of 20 years ago. For example, the CEP (circular error probable – the radius around the target into which 50 per cent of the warheads are predicted to fall) of the Soviet SS-13, first seen in 1965, is estimated at 2000m (6555 feet); the CEP of the SS-18, in its most accurate model, is 350m (1140 feet). The silos containing the Minuteman III missiles are hardened to withstand blast pressures of up to $70\mathrm{kgcm}^2$ (500lb psi), which means that a 550 kiloton warhead would have to land within 970m (3180 feet) to be likely to destroy it. The evidence of improved CEPs shows that either silos must be better hardened, or else they will be vulnerable to a counterforce attack.

As two parts of the strategic triad are less viable than they were in the past, greater emphasis is likely to be placed on submarine-launched missiles. Certainly, they are also gaining improved CEPs: the Trident I is estimated to possess a CEP of 400m (1750 feet), enough to be of use as a counterforce weapon. Submarines also, of course, have the advantage of being more difficult to pinpoint than the missile silo. It is possible that the future will see the strategic missile forces of nuclear powers pushed out to sea.

A useful alternative to the rickety parts of the triad may be provided by cruise missiles. At present, though, they are vulnerable to interceptors and surface-to-air missiles, but the technology to get around this may soon be available. The B-1 bomber and its possible successor, the ATB (advanced technology bomber), incorporate the Stealth technology, which consists of radar absorbent materials and the use of a more rounded shape that is a poor reflector of radar beams. The use of such technology on cruise missiles would make them more difficult to detect, and more likely to reach their target.

The system of guidance currently employed in cruise missiles combines inertial guidance – as used in ICBMs – with the matching of the terrain surrounding the target to a map stored in the missile's computer; terminal guidance uses infra-red homing technology. The effect of this is to give the cruise missile a CEP of about 18m (60 feet). Measures are already in hand to improve on this, through the use of magnetic fields and satellites. The magnetic field system probably lies further into the future than the satellite system. The latter would involve satellites placed in orbit – possibly geosynchronous – around the earth. There they would send out a timed signal

Above: An MX missile during a test launch. The MX uses a beryllium globe to hold its inertial guidance system in conditions allowing precision targeting. Top right: The guidance system in the Pershing II may be applied to a new generation of small and mobile intercontinental ballistic missiles. Top right inset: The cruise missile could employ radar-defeating Stealth technology in its next generation. Right: An E-4 command and control aeroplane. The Reagan administration has placed more emphasis on the command structure of US nuclear forces in an attempt to improve nuclear warfighting capabilities.

that would be compared by the receiving cruise missile to a precision clock and Doppler effects, and in this way the missile would locate its geographical position with great accuracy. This would enable the missiles to find their way even across snow-covered terrain or water, which pose problems for the terrain-matching system.

The growing research into ballistic missile defence systems has encouraged study into methods for re-entry vehicles to avoid destruction by anti-ballistic missile systems. One of the most promising lines of development is the MARV (manoeuvrable re-entry vehicle). Missiles equipped with these could be launched on a different trajectory than required to reach the target ballistically. The guidance system of the MARVs would home onto the target, initiating course changes to avoid any defensive systems and to bring the warhead to its impact point.

The miniaturisation of this guidance technology will make possible the construction of a new category of small ICBMs that can be transported to their launch site by truck. These would probably employ a system of terminal guidance such as is found in the Pershing II missile. This is known as radar area guidance and compares sensory data from an active radar in the nose of the missile with a stored image of the area in the computer. The computer makes any final course corrections required.

Perhaps the most important developments in a nuclear warfare capability are improvements to the command and control system. High-speed computers will be employed to speed the decision-making process. Communications satellites whose messages are more difficult to jam – possibly through the use of frequency-hopping radio messages – may be put into space. Satellites may be used to retarget the missiles or warheads after launch, perhaps making use of the abilities of manoeuvrable re-entry vehicles which can be steered to the targets while travelling through space. The amount of systems duplication may be increased to ensure the survivability of commanders, possibly involving more use of aerial command posts such as the Boeing E-4 used by the US Strategic Air Command.

These improvements to the US strategic forces will no doubt have their counterparts in the Soviet Strategic Rocket Force. Their effect will be to make nuclear war more precise in its destructiveness as CEPs shrink, but also more plausible as a military option. Future developments may make the time of mutually assured destruction seem a golden age of security to later generations.   **Chester Loomis**

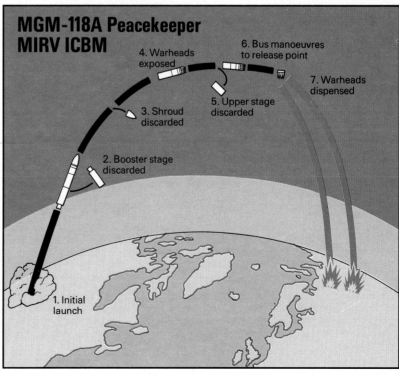

MGM-118A Peacekeeper MIRV ICBM

1. Initial launch
2. Booster stage discarded
3. Shroud discarded
4. Warheads exposed
5. Upper stage discarded
6. Bus manoeuvres to release point
7. Warheads dispensed

Future weapons

Star wars

Since 1957, when the space age began with the launch of the Soviet Sputnik 1 satellite, more than 2000 military satellites have been put into space. At present, three out of every four satellites launched are for military purposes. Satellites are used by the military for many things – reconnaissance, weather forecasting, navigation and communications. Photographic reconnaissance satellites enable the military planners to see what the other side is doing; electronic surveillance satellites allow the military to eavesdrop on what the other side is saying.

The militarisation of space had passed largely unnoticed by the general public, however, until 23 March 1983, when US President Ronald Reagan made a speech on television proposing a new, and very extensive, space defence programme. He asked American military scientists 'to give us the means of rendering . . . nuclear weapons impotent and obsolete.' The president predicted a technological revolution that would enable the United States to 'intercept and destroy strategic ballistic missiles before they reached our soil or that of our allies.' This achievement would let 'free people live secure in the knowledge that their security did not rest upon the threat of instant US retaliation.'

Anti-ballistic missile systems are not new. In the 1960s both the United States and the Soviet Union developed such systems using interceptor missiles of very high acceleration armed with nuclear warheads. The Soviet Galosh system is still operational around Moscow, but the US dismantled its own – based in North Dakota to protect an ICBM (intercontinental

ballistic missile) site – shortly after it became operational in 1975.

To protect the United States against a Soviet attack, an anti-ballistic missile system would have to intercept and destroy almost all of the 10,000 or so nuclear warheads the Soviets are capable of firing at the United States. Several layers of defence would have to be deployed. The first would have to destroy most of the attacking warheads soon after they were fired, whether from land-based silos or submerged submarines, and this means destroying their booster rockets as they are launched. A second layer would attack the warheads as they manoeuvred in space on their MIRV (multiple independently-targeted re-entry vehicle) bus. As the warheads re-entered the atmosphere, close-in missile defences around the warheads' targets would try to destroy survivors of the first two layers.

The weapons in the first layer would probably include high-energy lasers on space battle-stations. Electromagnetic rail-guns and kinetic-energy homing warheads might be used to attack the ballistic warheads as they travelled through space. For point defence, kinetic-energy projectiles might be used, or possibly charged particle beam weapons.

Laser beams are beams of light stimulated to a higher level of energy, and capable of cutting or drilling through hard materials such as steel. Theoretically, if such a high-energy laser could hit a booster rocket or its warhead, it would damage it enough to make it ineffective. Travelling at the speed of light – 300,000 km (186,000 miles) per second – such a

Above: The space shuttle *Challenger* deploys a satellite into orbit round the earth. Satellites are becoming increasingly vital to the worldwide communications network of the superpowers' armed forces. They are already one of the most important sources of intelligence, a role that will become even more valuable as weapons incorporate the Stealth technologies that make radar surveillance more difficult.

Below right: The space shuttle *Discovery* blasts off from the Kennedy Space Centre on 30 August 1984. The use of the shuttle for secret military missions provoked some controversy in the United States.

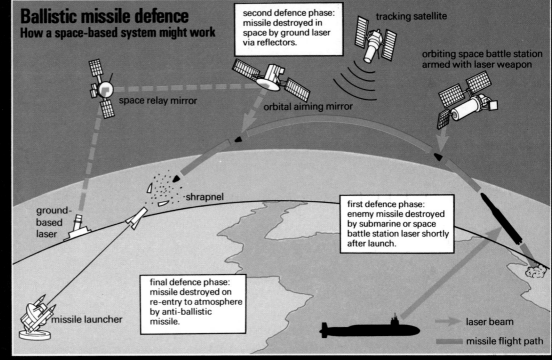

Ballistic missile defence
How a space-based system might work

second defence phase: missile destroyed in space by ground laser via reflectors.

tracking satellite

orbiting space battle station armed with laser weapon

space relay mirror

orbital aiming mirror

shrapnel

ground-based laser

first defence phase: enemy missile destroyed by submarine or space battle station laser shortly after launch.

final defence phase: missile destroyed on re-entry to atmosphere by anti-ballistic missile.

missile launcher

laser beam

missile flight path

beam would be fast enough to attack the missiles before they began to deploy their warheads.

Kinetic-energy projectiles such as the missile used to down a Minuteman warhead over Kwajalein on 10 June 1984, or such as might be fired from an electromagnetic rail-gun, would be used to attack warheads in space as they began to deploy onto their ballistic trajectories. The missile used over Kwajalein was an oversized example for experimentation. It consisted of a two-stage booster, and used a long-wavelength infra-red sensor to detect the target warhead. Prior to impact, a 4.5m (15 feet) diameter circle of steel spines deployed around the projectile, and these destroyed the dummy warhead. Devices like these could possibly be stationed on a battle satellite or delivered from aeroplanes flying high in the atmosphere.

Rail-gun technology is still in its infancy, but a weapon based on this could perhaps be deployed in space on a battle-station. A rail-gun is made up of two copper rails placed parallel to one another, with a projectile in between. A film fuze at the base of the projectile will vaporise into plasma when an electro-magnetic current is passed through one of the rails, and the current then passes through to the other rail to produce a circuit. The plasma's electromagnetic field reacts to the one in the rails and propels the projectile out of the gun at high speed. Major problems faced by scientists trying to design an effective rail-gun are durability and reloading.

The final protective layer of a ballistic missile defence system would consist of ground-based systems such as kinetic-energy projectiles, surface-to-air missiles and charged particle beam weapons. The US Army believes that a kinetic-energy system could be deployable by the end of the 1980s, and could be used to protect ICBM fields. Charged particle beams are made up of electrons accelerated to near-light speed so that they will vaporise their target. The Soviet Union is thought to be working on such a weapon, but the feasibility of it is disputed.

Any space battle-stations would be very vulner-

to attack. This, according to some experts, could make the domination of space a prerequisite for a reliable large-scale ballistic missile defence. Any such plan would require the development of effective anti-satellite weapons so that enemy satellites could be destroyed and space domination achieved.

The USA and the USSR are, in fact, both trying to develop weapons to shoot down the other side's satellites in space. One type of anti-satellite weapon is another satellite, called a hunter-killer or interceptor satellite. The hunter-killer is launched into an orbit that will take it close to its target, the enemy satellite. Signals from the command centre on Earth then manoeuvre the satellite towards its target and the interceptor uses its own radar to make the final approach. When the hunter-killer is at its closest point to its target it explodes and destroys it. Soviet tests with targets and interceptor satellites began in earnest as long ago as 1967. Apparently, the last Soviet test of an anti-satellite weapon took place in mid-June 1982.

Satellite destruction

A different type of anti-satellite weapon consists of a small missile launched into space from a converted fighter aircraft flying at a very high altitude, more than 21,000m (70,000 feet). The missile, which may carry a warhead filled with a conventional explosive or of the kinetic-energy type, is guided close to the enemy satellite. The warhead is then released and guides itself onto the target using a sensor in its nose. The sensor is able to pick up and home in on the infra-red radiation given off by the enemy satellite. The warhead either explodes when it is close to the target satellite or makes a direct hit on it. The US Air Force first tested its anti-satellite missile with an F-15 Eagle in January 1984.

One direct hit on a satellite from a relatively small warhead travelling fast would disable the satellite. The warhead does not, therefore, need to explode if it is accurate. The United States is developing a non-explosive manoeuvring warhead for its anti-satellite weapons, called the miniature homing intercept vehicle. A number of such vehicles could be launched into orbit by a rocket and released near a Soviet satellite. Alternatively, the vehicles could be launched by missiles carried by the F-15 aircraft. Each manoeuvrable vehicle carries an infra-red sensor that guides it to the enemy satellite. The vehicle then rams the target satellite and disables it.

Because a satellite can be so easily damaged by small objects hitting it, another type of anti-satellite weapon under active consideration simply discharges a cloud of ball-bearings, or small pellets, in the path of an enemy satellite. The target satellite is disabled when it flies through the cloud.

Although both the United States and the Soviet Union have developed anti-satellite weapons that are effective against enemy satellites in low orbits, neither have yet managed to knock out satellites in the highest orbits. Both sides would very much like to do this. In particular, they would like to be able to attack the other side's communications and early-warning satellites in their geostationary orbits, about 35,000km (21,500 miles) above the Earth. These satellites move so as to remain always above the same point on the Earth's surface. To attack them would require high-energy laser weapons, of the type envisaged for ballistic missile defence.

Supporters of ballistic missile defence believe that an effective system can be put into operation by early next century; other scientists doubt that the technology can be developed to provide security at a reasonable cost. Trying to find out who is right will trigger off a major new arms race in space. But the greatest danger of such plans is that the opposition will see them as part of a grand design to achieve strategic superiority and domination. They may fear that it would provide enough protection to destroy their own ability to retaliate after a first strike. They may see a pre-emptive strike before the defence system is complete as the only way to counter future strategic inferiority. **Frank Barnaby**

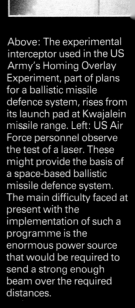

Above: The experimental interceptor used in the US Army's Homing Overlay Experiment, part of plans for a ballistic missile defence system, rises from its launch pad at Kwajalein missile range. Left: US Air Force personnel observe the test of a laser. These might provide the basis of a space-based ballistic missile defence system. The main difficulty faced at present with the implementation of such a programme is the enormous power source that would be required to send a strong enough beam over the required distances.

The wars in peace

A summary of the major conflicts since 1945

Europe

Greek Civil War 1944-49

Civil war broke out in Greece in December 1944 between the Greek Communist Party (KKE – Kommounisitikon Komma Ellados) and royalist government forces, with the most serious of the first round of fighting taking place in Athens, during which British troops defeated the communist National Liberation Army (ELAS – Ellinikos Laikos Apeleftherotikon) in its attempt to seize power. A ceasefire agreed in February 1945 failed to hold, and a second round of fighting broke out during 1946.

The communist forces, now known as the Democratic Army of Greece (DSE – Dimokratikos Stratos Ellados) operated from bases in Yugoslavia, Albania and Bulgaria, and controlled many areas of the mountainous countryside where they had operated successfully against the Germans during World War II. After the enunciation of the Truman Doctrine in March 1947, the Greek government was increasingly able to rely on large amounts of military and economic support from the United States, and by 1948 the tide had begun to turn against the guerrillas.

The balance of forces shifted further against the KKE after the Tito-Stalin rift in 1948, following which first Yugoslavia and then Albania and Bulgaria withdrew their support from the guerrillas. During heavy fighting in 1949, the DSE was decisively defeated by the Greek National Army, and the war ended on 16 October 1949 when the KKE declared a ceasefire on Stalin's orders. The war cost an estimated 12,777 dead and 37,737 wounded amongst the government forces, with approximately 38,000 communist dead and 40,000 captured or surrendered. The bitter legacy of the fighting was to affect Greek politics for decades to come.

Soviet intervention in Hungary 1956

Following the removal of Hungarian Communist Party leader Mátyás Rákosi in July 1956, pressure for reform and an end to Stalinist repression increased dramatically. On 23 October 1956, thousands of demonstrators in Budapest called for fundamental change and the return of Imry Nagy, a reformist leader who had been expelled from the Communist Party in 1953. Clashes between demonstrators and the security police (Államvédelmi Osztaly –

AVO), backed by Soviet troops, led to many civilian deaths, and Nagy, who was appointed prime minister as a gesture of reconciliation, sided openly with the rebels, who were joined by a number of Hungarian Army units.

Announcing the formation of a coalition government, Nagy seemed to have persuaded the Soviet leadership to accept the changes, but on 1 November new Soviet Army units began to move into Hungary. Nagy reacted by withdrawing Hungary from the Warsaw Pact and declaring neutrality, but the Hungarian rebellion remained isolated, and on 4 November Soviet tanks moved into Budapest. In spite of determined Hungarian opposition and ruthless street-fighting which went on for several days, the Soviet troops were soon able to establish control.

Nagy sought refuge in the Yugoslavian embassy, but was lured out by the Soviet promise of a safe-conduct, arrested, and two years later executed for treason. The fighting had cost an estimated 25,000 Hungarian and 7000 Soviet dead, while some 200,000 Hungarians fled to the West. A new pro-Soviet regime under János Kádár embarked on a programme of social and economic reform but continued to demonstrate the strictest loyalty to the Soviet Union and the Warsaw Pact.

Soviet intervention in Czechoslovakia 1968

On 5 January 1968, Alexander Dubček was elected leader of the Communist Party of Czechoslovakia. He advocated an Action Programme of political and economic democratisation but stressed the loyalty of his regime to the Warsaw Pact. Nevertheless, he came under harsh criticism from his Soviet and East European neighbours, and in early August was forced to make a number of concessions which appeared to end the danger of a Soviet military intervention.

At 2300 hours on 20 August 1968, however, Soviet troops, backed by contingents from Poland, Hungary, the German Democratic Republic and Bulgaria, began an invasion of Czechoslovakia which rapidly brought the 'Prague Spring' to an end. Dubček was arrested and flown to Moscow, where he was denounced as a traitor. Unable to find any respected figure to head a new government, however, the Soviet leadership was forced to negotiate with Dubček, and finally allowed him to return to Prague once he had agreed to abandon the Action Programme. In April 1969, Dubček was replaced as Party leader by Gustáv Husák, who promised to continue the Dubček reforms, but in fact maintained a policy of strict control and repression.

There was no military resistance to the Warsaw Pact invasion, but some 70 lives were lost as angry demonstrators clashed with Warsaw Pact troops.

IRA border campaign 1956-62

In 1956, the Irish Republican Army (IRA), based in the Irish Republic, announced the beginning of a border campaign against the North. During the next six years, they managed to carry out a small number of raids across the border, mostly choosing as targets barracks and police stations of the Royal Ulster Constabulary (RUC) and the B-Specials auxiliary police force.

There was little support for the IRA brand of republicanism either north or south of the border, however, and in February 1962 the campaign, such as it was, was called off. Six policemen had been killed and 32 wounded, while the IRA had lost nine volunteers killed. Many IRA activists were interned in the Irish Republic, and its organisation was severely weakened by the failure of the campaign.

Sectarian violence and insurgency in Northern Ireland 1969-

Following a Catholic civil rights campaign which threatened the entrenched power of the Protestant Unionist majority in Northern Ireland, violence erupted during August 1969 and the British Army was sent onto the streets of Belfast and Londonderry to restore order. Although at first welcomed by the Catholic minority, the British forces soon became identified with the Unionist authorities as they attempted to establish control over the Catholic areas, where Republican paramilitaries became increasingly active.

Through 1971, the Provisional IRA mounted an extensive campaign of bombings and shootings which led to the introduction of internment without trial in August 1971. The consequent widespread arrests provoked a hostile response in the Catholic community, and the level of terrorist activity mounted still further. After the 'Bloody Sunday' shooting of 13 civilians by British paratroopers in Londonderry on 30 January 1972, a nadir was reached in relations between the authorities and the Catholic population. In March 1972, the British government took over direct rule of Northern Ireland, and in June an attempt was made at negotiation with the Provisional IRA. Catholic support for the Provisionals was waning, however, and on 31 July the British Army mounted Operation Motorman, seizing control of the 'No-Go' areas in the province, which had provided safe bases for the terrorists.

After Operation Motorman, the level of IRA activity declined and was increasingly concentrated in the rural border areas, although their bombing campaign was extended to the British mainland. As the level of attacks on the security forces fell, however, a wave of sectarian killings arose, many carried out by Protestant paramilitary groups such as the Ulster Volunteer Force (UVF) and the Ulster Defence Association (UDA). The sectarian murders reached their peak in the mid-1970s, falling away after 1977.

A political solution to the crisis remained remote, but by the 1980s violence had been reduced to a relatively acceptable level. The death-toll since the beginning of the Troubles had reached a total of 1686 civilians and 762 members of the security forces by October 1984.

EOKA insurgency in Cyprus 1955-58

In 1955, the population of the British colony of Cyprus was 78 per cent Greek and 18 per cent Turkish in origin. The Greek majority was violently opposed to British control, and favoured *enosis*, or total union with Greece. The leader of the Greek nationalist movement was Archbishop Makarios, but the military wing of the movement, Ethniki Organosis Kyprion Agoniston (EOKA), was commanded by Colonel George Grivas. The first bomb attacks took place in April 1955, and there were frequent murders, often of policemen. On 26 November 1955, a state of emergency was declared, under which EOKA suspects were interned or deported, but by 1956 a few hundred EOKA fighters were holding down a British garrison of some 25,000 men.

In March 1956, Makarios was deported to the Seychelles, but this merely provoked a new wave of killings, although in June of that year the British forces conducted a successful sweep against EOKA guerrillas in the Troödos Mountains. In March 1957, Makarios was released and flew to Athens, but intercommunal violence became increasingly serious, leading both Turkey and Greece to accept the need for a compromise negotiated solution in late 1958.

Greece had supported the call for *enosis*, but Turkey had feared for the future of the island's Turkish minority in a Greek-controlled union. Nevertheless, both sides, together with Makarios, agreed to a compromise of full independence for Cyprus, and on 31 December Grivas ordered his men to halt all operations. In February 1959, Britain signed an agreement on independence, and on 14 December Makarios became the first president of Cyprus. Over 90 EOKA fighters had been killed, together with 104 servicemen. 50 policemen and 238 civilians.

Turkish invasion of Cyprus 1974

Intercommunal violence between Greeks and Turks survived the achievement of independence by Cyprus in 1959, and climaxed in vicious fighting between December 1963 and April 1964, when the intervention of UN troops led to virtual partition, with Turkish enclaves scattered throughout the island.

During early 1974, right-wing Greek extremist supporters of *enosis*, encouraged by the military government in Athens, began to mount violent attacks upon the moderate policies of President Makarios, who retaliated by calling for the withdrawal of the regular Greek Army officers who were serving with the 18,000-man Cyprus National Guard. On 15 July 1974, however, a National Guard coup overthrew Makarios, and installed Nicos Sampson, a former EOKA terrorist, as the new head of government.

Turkey regarded these events as a direct threat to the safety of the Turkish Cypriot minority, and on 20 July began an invasion of the island. Turkish aircraft attacked National Guard barracks in Nicosia, while Turkish paratroopers dropped into the Turkish Nicosia-Kyrenia enclave, and heliborne forces landed just south of the Kyrenia mountains. The main Turkish invasion force came ashore at Five Mile Beach, to the west of Kyrenia, and had little difficulty in establishing a bridgehead against ineffectual National Guard opposition.

Heavy resistance was encountered around Nicosia airport, however, from a contingent of 990 Greek Army troops stationed there under the 1959 treaty. The fighting at the airport continued for two days, until a local UN-negotiated ceasefire came into operation. This was followed on 22 July by a general ceasefire agreement, which left the Turks in control of some 1000 square km (400 square miles) of the island. On the following day, Sampson was replaced by Glafkos Clerides, and the Greek military government fell, discredited by its role in the Cyprus events.

Certain now that Greece would not intervene, Turkey resumed operations on 14 August with an armoured advance on the port of Famagusta, which had a large Turkish community. The Greeks evacuated the city, which was entered by the Turkish Army on 15 August. With the end of this operation, Cyprus experienced a *de facto* partition along the so-called Attila Line, and a separate Turkish-Cypriot administration was established in the north of the island.

ETA terrorism, Spain 1967-

Euskadi Ta Askatasun (ETA), an organisation pledged to the

achievement of an autonomous homeland for the Basques who inhabit the northwestern provinces of Spain and parts of southwestern France, was formed in 1959, and its armed wing, ETA-Militar, began a major terrorist campaign during 1967. The most spectacular ETA operation was the enormous dynamite explosion which killed Spanish Prime Minister Admiral Carrero Blanco in December 1973.

Even after the death of dictator General Franco in December 1975, ETA continued to be active. Its aim was to prevent the transition to liberal democracy under King Juan Carlos, and to provoke a right-wing military coup which it hoped would in turn lead to a nationwide revolution. Even when the Spanish government granted the Basque region a large degree of autonomy in 1979, and later transferred the tasks of the hated Guardia Civil to a Basque security force, ETA-Militar maintained its campaign of assassinations and bombings, although cooperation between the Spanish and French security forces proved increasingly effective in combating the terrorists.

Left-wing terrorism mid-1960s-
One result of the rise of left-wing protest movements during the 1960s, was the development of an underground terrorist fringe. Some of these terrorist groups were totally ineffectual, and were easily broken up by the police. Among these was the Angry Brigade in Britain, which planted a number of bombs between May 1970 and August 1971. Much more serious, however, were movements such as the West German Baader-Meinhof Red Army Fraction (RAF) and the Italian Red Brigades, both of which formed sophisticated networks of well-trained and equipped terrorists with international links – particularly with the Palestinians.

The RAF began as a small group which was responsible for a number of fire-bombings during the late 1960s, but graduated during the 1970s to bombings, kidnapping, hijacking and assassination. By 1972, most of the original leaders were already under arrest, but the most serious RAF operations were still to come. RAF members were involved in the PFLP hijacking of a passenger jet to Entebbe airport in July 1976, and two of them died when Israeli paratroopers mounted a successful rescue mission. The imprisoned RAF leaders were found dead in their cells in October 1977, just after a PFLP attempt to secure their release by hijacking a Lufthansa jet to Mogadishu was brought to a violent end by the intervention of the West German GSG9 anti-terrorist squad. Nevertheless, RAF activity continued into the mid-1980s, supplemented by groups known as the Revolutionary Cells.

Terrorism in Italy was the work of both right and left-wing groups, but the most serious threat during the 1970s came from the Red Brigades, which became active during 1974. They chose police and magistrates as the main targets of their assassination campaign, but their most famous operation was the kidnapping of leading Christian Democrat politician Aldo Moro on 16 March 1978. His dead body was found on 10 May, and subsequently determined government action led to a rapid fall in Red Brigade activity.

Middle East

Jewish independence struggle 1944-48
In pursuit of their aim of establishing an independent Jewish state on the territory of Palestine, which was at the time administered under a League of Nations mandate by Britain, Zionist extremists of the Irgun and Lehi movements began a campaign of terrorism against British forces during World War II. In November 1944, Lehi assassins killed Lord Moyne, the British Minister Resident in the Middle East, and following the refusal of the British government in August 1945 to increase Jewish immigration quotas to Palestine, the Irgun and Lehi began to cooperate with the more moderate Haganah – a Jewish self-defence force – in a mounting wave of anti-British violence.

Attacks on British targets climaxed with the bombing of the King David Hotel, the British administrative headquarters in Jerusalem, on 22 July 1946. The terrorist campaign undermined the British will to remain in Palestine, and in November 1947 the United Nations voted to partition the country between the Arabs and the Jews. Hostility between the two communities had been growing for many years, and as the date for partition in May 1948 drew nearer, a fierce war of assassination and massacre broke out which deepened the division.

As the British began to withdraw in early 1948, open warfare broke out for control of Palestine, and Arabs fled Jewish-controlled areas, which were extended by the Irgun capture of Jaffa and the Haganah seizure of Acre. On 14 May 1948, the independent Jewish state of Israel was proclaimed. A total of 223 British military personnel had been killed in Palestine and 478 wounded.

Arab-Israeli War 1948-49
On the very day of its foundation, Israel faced an invasion by a combined force of some 37,000 men of the Egyptian, Syrian, Iraqi, Lebanese and Transjordanian armies, and an Arab Liberation Army which had been formed by the Arab League. Aiming to prevent the partition of Palestine, the Arabs launched an offensive which began on 14 May 1948 with Syrian and Lebanese troops advancing down the Upper Jordan Valley, while the Egyptian Army mounted a two-pronged assault from the south and, on the following day, Iraqi forces crossed the River Jordan.

Although the Arabs initially achieved a number of successes against the Israelis, who were numerically inferior and weaker in heavy weapons, the Israelis enjoyed the advantage of greater mobility and interior lines of communication, which allowed them to transfer units between the three war fronts as the situation demanded. The Israelis offered fierce resistance, and by 23 May had won the battle for the Jordan Valley; after mid-May, when they began to receive a number of fighter aircraft, they were able to mount air attacks which halted the advancing Arab columns.

From 11 June, a UN-negotiated truce was in effect, but it was broken on 8 July by the Egyptians, who launched a pre-emptive strike against the Israeli Defence Forces (IDF) in the south, where heavy but indecisive fighting continued over the next five days. On 9 July, fighting also recommenced in the north with an IDF attack against the Syrians in eastern Galilee, but after nine days of fighting, both sides' positions remained virtually unchanged. Heavy fighting also took place around Jerusalem, which was held by the Transjordanian Arab Legion, and by 10 July, the IDF had won control of Lod and Ramle.

A second truce came into operation on 18 July. During this pause, the Israelis increased their stocks of heavy weapons and reorganised their forces with such effect that, on 28 October, they were able to mount a large-scale offensive to clear all Arab forces from Galilee, which the Israelis controlled by 31 October. In the south, the IDF successfully outflanked the Egyptians in the Negev, and as dissension began to appear between the Arab states, concentrated its full power to sweep the Egyptians back across the border. The Israelis crossed into Egypt at Abu Aweigila on 27 December, but following a British ultimatum, they withdrew and concentrated their operations around the Gaza area.

On 7 January, a general ceasefire came into effect, and one by one, the Arab states signed armistice agreements with Israel. The war had cost Israel an approximate 21,000 dead and the Arabs 40,000. It left Israel with a strong army, but encircled by bitter and resentful Arab neighbours.

Suez crisis 1956
On 26 July 1956, Egyptian President Gamal Abdel Nasser announced the nationalisation of the Anglo-French Suez Canal Company – a measure taken in retaliation for a Western withdrawal of finance for the Aswan High Dam project. Britain and France decided upon a joint military intervention to retake the Canal; in October Israel agreed to cooperate by invading Egypt, and thus

provide a pretext for the Anglo-French operation.

On 29 October, the IDF invaded Sinai on four fronts, while Israeli paratroopers landed at the eastern end of the strategic Mitla Pass. On 30 October, IDF tanks broke through to the paratroopers' position, and on the following day the Pass was taken after a costly battle. On 31 October, Egyptian airfields began to come under repeated Anglo-French air attacks, and in anticipation of an Anglo-French invasion, Nasser withdrew his air force from Sinai. Left without air cover, pockets of Egyptian resistance in Sinai were mopped up by the IDF, which captured the port of Sharm el Sheikh at the mouth of the Gulf of Aqaba on 5 November. The Sinai campaign had cost 181 Israeli lives, while Egypt had lost some 1500 dead and 6000 captured.

While attempting to block international efforts at the United Nations to bring peace, Britain and France went ahead with their own invasion plans, claiming that they intended to bring an end to the fighting. The real aim, however, was the seizure of Port Said and the Suez Canal, and on 5 November British and French paratroopers carried out an airborne assault on the Port Said area, followed on 6 November by a large-scale amphibious landing. Having occupied Port Said and Port Fuad, the Anglo-French force began to advance upon El Qantara and Ismailiya, but international pressure in the UN General Assembly, and particularly from the United States, forced Britain and France to accept a ceasefire on 7 November, which was monitored by a 5000-man UN international peacekeeping force. Under UN supervision, British, French and Israeli forces withdrew from Egypt. British and French dead were 22 and 10 respectively.

Anglo-American intervention in the Middle East 1958

The rise of radical Arab nationalism in the Middle East was the background for a crisis in Lebanon in 1958. An attempt by Lebanese President Camille Chamoun to retain power by altering the delicately balanced constitution led to conflict between Lebanon's dominant Maronite Christian community, to which Chamoun belonged, and the Muslim opposition. Chamoun appealed for US assistance and US Marines began to land near Beirut from vessels of the Sixth Fleet on 15 July 1958. The intervention succeeded in bolstering the position of Chamoun, but underlying conflicts persisted.

In Jordan, meanwhile, King Hussein was threatened by an internal rebellion backed by the United Arab Republic (a federation of Egypt and Syria) and Iraq, where a branch of his own family had recently been overthrown by a nationalist coup. Hussein turned to Britain and the United States for aid, and on 17 July British troops began to arrive in the Jordanian capital, Amman. The situation was rapidly stabilised.

Six-Day War 1967

During May 1967, tension between Israel and its Arab neighbours mounted swiftly, and both sides prepared for renewed war. On 20 May, Israel began to recall its reservists, and during the early hours of 5 June, Israeli aircraft knocked out the bulk of the Egyptian Air Force while it was still on the ground. At the same time, Israeli tanks crossed the border into the Gaza Strip and Sinai, and made rapid progress in spite of determined Egyptian resistance.

In a series of desert tank battles, the IDF, thanks to its overwhelming air superiority and thorough application of the lessons of the 1956 Sinai campaign, smashed the Egyptian Army, which had made the mistake of distributing its large tank forces piecemeal amongst infantry units. Within four days, seven Egyptian divisions were totally destroyed, and the IDF stood on the eastern bank of the Suez Canal.

On the Jordanian front, the initiative was taken by King Hussein's forces, which attacked shortly before midday on 5 June. The Israelis soon eliminated the Jordanian Air Force, however, and turned their attention to air attacks on the Jordanian artillery which was shelling targets within Israel. The vigour of the Israeli response soon ruled out any question of a Jordanian offensive, and the Israelis exploited their success with an assault on Jordanian Arab Legion positions on the West Bank of the River Jordan. Heavy fighting occurred in and around Jerusalem, and the Jordanian-held eastern half of the city fell to the IDF on 7 June. Fierce tank battles took place around Qabatiya, but despite energetic resistance by the Jordanian Army, the Israelis were in command of the whole of the West Bank by 7 June, when a ceasefire brought the fighting with Jordan to an end.

As on the other two fronts, the Israeli Air Force (IAF) rapidly destroyed the Syrian Air Force at the outbreak of war on 5 June, and thereafter the Syrians confined themselves to small-scale raids across the border and artillery bombardments of Israeli settlements in Galilee from heavily fortified positions on the Golan Heights. As the danger from Egypt and Jordan receded, Israel decided to seize these Heights which dominated northern Israel. An IDF offensive opened on the morning of 9 June with coordinated IAF air strikes against Syrian positions, followed by an infantry assault supported by Sherman tanks. Hand-to-hand fighting was necessary to eject the Syrian defenders from their intricate system of trenches and bunkers, but by 10 June they had abandoned the town of Quneitra and conceded the battle for the Golan Heights.

The war had been a crushing defeat, both militarily and in terms of prestige, for the Arabs, and left the Israelis in occupation of large areas of Arab territory – in the Golan Heights, the West Bank, the Gaza Strip and Sinai. It had cost the Arab states an estimated 13,500 dead and 27,000 wounded, while Israel had lost 689 dead and 2563 wounded.

Palestinian guerrilla and terrorist activity 1964-

The failure of the Arab states to destroy the state of Israel led to the rise of Palestinian groups dedicated to the creation of a Palestinian homeland on all or part of the territory of the Israeli state. The first and most important of these, Al-Fatah, was founded by Yassir Arafat during the late 1950s, but did not mount its first raid into Israel until 31 December 1964. During the next few years, commando attacks multiplied rapidly, but it was the humiliating defeat suffered by the Arabs during the 1967 Six-Day War and the consequent Israeli occupation of the Palestinian-populated West Bank of the Jordan which led to the greatest upsurge in Palestinian military operations.

The defeat of conventional forces, including the Palestine Liberation Army (PLA) units attached to the Arab armies, gave guerrilla tactics a fresh prestige, and Fatah became the dominant group within the Palestine Liberation Organisation (PLO), the umbrella organisation for all Palestinian groups. In March 1968 Fatah won an important propaganda victory when Israeli troops attacking one of their bases at Karameh in Jordan were met with determined resistance, and in February 1969 Arafat was elected chairman of the PLO. However, attempts to create an insurgent movement among the West Bank population were a failure, and cross-border commando raids into Israel had limited impact. Guerrilla attacks were further restricted after the expulsion of armed Palestinians from Jordan in 1970-71, although occasional raids continued from bases in Lebanon.

Beginning in 1968, some Palestinian groups, most notably the Popular Front for the Liberation of Palestine led by George Habash, adopted the tactics of hijacking and international terrorism to highlight the Palestinian case. Two of the most famous PFLP operations were the hijacking of three airliners to Dawson's Field in Jordan in September 1970, and an attack on passengers at Lod Airport in Israel by a group of Japanese Red Army terrorists in May 1972. The Black September group, linked to Fatah, was also responsible for a wave of attacks, including the massacre of Israeli athletes during the 1972 Munich Olympic Games. Israel mounted its own terror operations against the Palestinian terrorists through the 'Wrath of God' hit squads.

Black September, which emerged in November 1971, had ceased operations by the October War of 1973, but terrorist actions continued to be organised by the Libyan-backed National Arab Youth Organisation for the Liberation of Palestine (NAYLP), the Iraqi-supported Abu Nidal break-away group from Fatah, and the PFLP External Operations organisation headed by Wadi Haddad. which began to function autonomously when the PFLP abandoned international terrorism after 1973.

Haddad was responsible for the activities of Carlos (Ilich Ramirez Sanchez), whose most famous exploit was the taking hostage of OPEC oil ministers in Vienna in December 1975; Haddad also masterminded the June 1976 Entebbe hijacking as well as the October 1977 Mogadishu operation. By 1978, his group was in decline, and Haddad himself died of cancer in April. Abu Nidal's Black June group remained active into the mid-1980s, however, although his main targets were PLO moderates associated with Yassir Arafat.

War of Attrition 1967-70

Following the Six-Day War, Egypt embarked on a protracted War of Attrition against the Israeli forces which now occupied the east bank of the Suez Canal and the Sinai peninsula. The first stage of this campaign opened in September 1967, with a phase of 'defensive rehabilitation' during which the Egyptian armed forces were re-equipped by the Soviet Union and heavy artillery duels took place across the Canal. In September 1968, Egypt went over to a phase of 'offensive defence', which entailed not only heavier bombardments of Israeli positions, but also raids by both sides across the Canal. This led Israel to construct a defensive system known as the Bar-Lev Line along the Canal – a lightly held system of fortifications, with the main Israeli reserves kept well back within Sinai.

On 1 May 1969, President Nasser renounced the 1967 ceasefire and the third phase of the Egyptian campaign opened, that of 'liberation'. Lasting some 16 months, this phase saw a serious escalation in the fighting with raids, counter-raids and aerial dog-fights, but by mid-1969 the IAF had established a decisive air superiority over the Canal, which allowed Israel in January 1970 to launch a series of long-range bombing raids deep into central Egypt.

This provoked Egypt to turn to the Soviet Union for greater assistance and in the following month a complete Soviet air-defence division arrived, equipped with batteries of SA-3 missiles. Soviet pilots began to fly defensive combat missions over central Egypt, and the Israelis swiftly suspended their bombing raids. Soviet pilots became increasingly active, and on 30 July 1970 they were involved in a major air battle over the Canal which prompted both the United States and the Soviet Union to exert pressure on Israel and Egypt to de-escalate the confrontation. The July air battle was virtually the last engagement of the War of Attrition, which had cost both sides heavy losses.

Expulsion of Palestinians from Jordan 1970-71

In the wake of the 1967 Six-Day War, during which Israel seized control of the West Bank, Jordan became the main base for Palestine Liberation Organisation (PLO) guerrilla activities, and Palestinian military power began to rival that of King Hussein, many of whose subjects were themselves Palestinian. In November 1968, clashes with the Jordanian Army led to the shelling of Palestinian camps, and there was serious fighting in February 1970.

The seizure of 80 hostages in an Amman hotel by guerrillas of the Popular Front for the Liberation of Palestine (PFLP) in June 1970, two attempts on the life of King Hussein, and the hijacking of three airliners to a remote Jordanian desert airfield by the PFLP on 6 September brought the crisis to a head, and Hussein was pressed by his army to act against the Palestinians. On 15 September, a military government was appointed, and two days later the Jordanian Army began to move against the PLO in Amman, where desperate house-to-house fighting continued for several days.

By 20 September, however, the Jordanian Army was begin-

ning to gain the upper hand, and the most crucial fighting took place in the north, where a regular Palestine Liberation Army (PLA) brigade attached to the Iraqi Army had joined a battle raging around Zerqa. On the morning of the 20th, a Syrian force, comprising some 200 T55 tanks, many of which were crewed by Palestinians, crossed the border into Jordan, forcing the Jordanian Army to withdraw southwards. The Syrian leadership had been divided about the intervention, however, and the column was without air cover. When Jordanian jets attacked, the Syrians suffered heavy casualties and were compelled to retreat back across the border.

On 25 September, PLO Chairman Yassir Arafat agreed to the withdrawal of Palestinian forces from Jordanian cities, and two days later met King Hussein at an Egyptian-sponsored summit in Cairo. Recalcitrant Palestinian groups were meanwhile mopped up by the Jordanian Army. In 1971, the King broke the last vestiges of PLO power in Jordan, when in April he forced the Palestinians to leave Amman completely, and on 13 July launched a final offensive against PLO mountain camps.

October War 1973

On 6 October 1973, Egypt launched an offensive across the Suez Canal that quickly breached the Israeli Bar-Lev Line at several points, allowing the Egyptian troops to set up pontoon bridges across which columns of tanks and infantry began to flow into the Israeli-occupied Sinai. Taken by surprise, the Israelis made the mistake of repeatedly committing unsupported tank units to a hopeless attempt to relieve the Bar-Lev Line, which merely led to heavy losses without any noticeable effect in halting the Egyptian offensive. Their usual dominance in the air and superiority in armoured warfare were largely negated by the Egyptian use of Soviet-supplied mobile SA-6 missiles, anti-aircraft artillery and portable Sagger anti-tank missiles. On 8 October, however, the IDF launched a concerted counter-attack against the Egyptian bridgehead along the east bank of the Canal, but unsupported by air cover or infantry, the Israeli tanks suffered further heavy losses. By the end of that day, the Egyptians had established themselves in a sector some 8km (5 miles) deep within Sinai, protected by an umbrella of air-defence missiles.

The Israelis hurriedly adjusted their tactics away from virtually all-tank units, which were now vulnerable to Egyptian anti-tank weapons, to balanced formations including mechanised infantry and supporting artillery. Israeli reinforcements poured into Sinai, and the IDF High Command began to plan a renewed counter-offensive. This was anticipated on 14 October, however, by fresh Egyptian attacks aimed at diverting Israeli pressure from the Golan Heights front where Syrian troops were heavily engaged. The Egyptians now attempted to capture the Gidi and Mitla Passes as stepping-stones to an assault upon Bir Gifgafa, the major Israeli base in Sinai. This was an ambitious departure from the original Egyptian plan, and played into the hands of the Israelis, who still possessed a great advantage in mobile armoured warfare. This advantage rapidly became evident as the Egyptian armoured advance shattered against strong, well prepared Israeli positions, and after incurring severe losses, the Egyptians were forced to withdraw.

The Israelis now seized the initiative, and smashed their way through to the Suez Canal, which they began to cross north of the Great Bitter Lake on 15 October. The Israeli bridgehead on the west bank of the Canal was rapidly reinforced, cutting off the Egyptian Third Army on the Canal's east bank and threatening the Second Army with the same fate. Egypt was now desperate to achieve a ceasefire, which was supported by the United States and the Soviet Union, both of which were eager to avoid a direct confrontation which might result from an escalation of the Arab-Israeli War. A ceasefire was agreed on 22 October, but fighting in fact continued for another two days until American pressure forced the Israelis to halt.

While the fighting raged along the Suez Canal, Israeli and Syrian troops clashed on the Golan front. The Syrians had unleashed a fierce artillery bombardment to coincide with the Egyptian assault across the Canal on 6 October, followed by waves of Syrian armour which engaged Israeli tanks in a desperate battle for control of the Golan Heights. By the following morning, the Syrians had broken through the Israeli defences on the southern sector of the Heights, but by that evening Israeli reinforcements had begun to arrive in force, stemming the tide of the Syrian advance. The Syrians were also losing a mounting number of men and tanks to IAF ground attacks, and over the following three days were pushed back by a determined Israeli counter-offensive to the positions which they had occupied at the beginning of the war.

On 11 October, the Israelis launched a new offensive into Syrian-held territory, with the aim of bringing Damascus, the Syrian capital, within range of IDF artillery. The Syrians, reinforced by Moroccan, Iraqi and later Jordanian troops, held a strong defensive line of great depth, through which the Israelis attempted to break. The IDF emphasis upon tanks, to the neglect of close infantry support, now resulted in similar heavy losses to those which were being suffered in Sinai against the Egyptians. Nevertheless, the Israelis were able to advance as far as Tel Shams and Tel Antar before both sides agreed to a ceasefire on 22 October.

Israeli losses on the two fronts were 1854 dead, 1850 wounded and 450 taken prisoner; Arab losses are unknown, but were certainly far higher. Nevertheless, the October War delivered a profound shock to the Israelis, who had previously won a succession of crushing victories over their Arab enemies, and was regarded by the Arabs as a great moral victory.

Lebanese Civil War 1975-76
The presence of large numbers of Palestinian refugees and PLO guerrilla fighters in Lebanon, particularly after their expulsion from Jordan in September 1970, threatened to destroy the delicate communal balance upon which the Lebanese constitution was based. Israeli attacks upon Palestinian camps heightened tensions, and fighting broke out in Beirut in April 1975 between Christian militiamen and left-wing Muslim and Druze fighters, who were increasingly backed by the military power of the PLO. Government attempts to employ the Lebanese Army in support of the Christians merely led to the army's disintegration, and as the fighting continued into 1976, a Christian defeat appeared probable.

The prospect of a Muslim-Druze-Palestinian victory provoked Syrian fears of an Israeli intervention, and on 1 June 1976 Syrian troops entered Lebanon and advanced towards Beirut and Sidon. Syrian backing for the Christian-dominated Lebanese government led to heavy fighting with the Palestinians and their Lebanese allies, but a Saudi Arabian peace initiative led to a ceasefire in October 1976, which was monitored by a predominantly Syrian Arab peacekeeping force. Casualties in the civil war have been estimated at around 50,000 dead and over 100,000 wounded.

Operation Litani 1978
On 11 March 1978, a group of Lebanon-based Fatah guerrillas landed on the Israeli coast and hijacked a bus. The raid ended in a gun-battle with Israeli security forces which left 35 civilians and all but two of the Palestinians dead. The incident persuaded the Israeli government to strike against the PLO in Lebanon, and on the night of 14/15 March Israeli troops crossed the Lebanese border in an invasion of southern Lebanon. The invasion was code-named Operation Litani, after the river which was to be the northernmost limit of the Israeli advance.

Over 20,000 Israeli troops took part in the operation, which was accompanied by heavy bombing of Palestinian refugee camps further north. However, the PLO fighters withdrew across the Litani without engaging the IDF, and without suffering any significant losses. On 19 March, the United Nations called for an Israeli withdrawal, and on 22 March the first units of a United Nations Interim Force in Lebanon (UNIFIL) began to take up positions between Israeli and Lebanese forces. The last Israeli troops left Lebanon in mid-April, but a buffer-zone along the Lebanese side of the border remained in the hands of the pro-Israeli militia of Major Saad Haddad.

Israeli invasion of Lebanon and its aftermath 1982-
The Israeli desire to deal a crushing blow to the PLO led to planning for a renewed invasion of Lebanon from the summer of 1981, but it was only on 6 June 1982, following the attempted assassination of the Israeli ambassador to London by Palestinian terrorists, that IDF forces once more rolled northwards across the Lebanese border. Code-named Peace for Galilee, the operation was preceded by a heavy aerial bombardment of targets in Lebanon, including the Litani bridges across which the PLO had been able to retreat unharmed in 1978.

The Israelis advanced on three fronts – the coastal, central and eastern. PLO forces were unable to resist the power and speed of the Israeli attack. The advance on the eastern front brought the Israelis into contact with Syrian forces, and in a series of engagements from 9-11 June the IAF destroyed both Syria's SAM systems in the Beqaa Valley and most of the Syrian Air Force. Over the following weeks, the Syrians were defeated in a number of tank engagements, until a ceasefire was agreed on 25 June.

Meanwhile, on 13 June, the Israelis had put West Beirut under siege. Some 9000 Palestinian fighters, 1500 Syrian troops and 2000-3000 Muslim militiamen held out against a devastating Israeli bombardment for over two months before an agreement was reached for the withdrawal of the Palestinian forces under international supervision. The PLO evacuation was completed by the end of August and the Multi-National Force (MNF) supervising the operation also left on 10 September. Four days later, Lebanese President Bashir Gemayel was assassinated, prompting the IDF to enter West Beirut. The subsequent massacre of Palestinian civilians in the Sabra and Chatila refugee camps led to the redeployment of the MNF on 20 September.

A year later, following an Israeli withdrawal from the Chouf mountains to the Awali River in September 1983, heavy fighting broke out in this area between local Druze and Christian Phalangist militiamen backed by the Lebanese Army. The involvement of the US and French MNF contingents in support of the government of Phalangist leader President Amin Gemayel brought the MNF into increasing conflict with the Druze and Shi'ites, and on 23 October terrorist bomb attacks on US and French barracks in Beirut led to 239 US and 58 French deaths.

Meanwhile, fighting had broken out between two factions of the Palestinian Fatah guerrillas in northern Lebanon. In October 1983, Syrian-backed guerrillas encircled pro-Arafat forces in Tripoli. After international pressure, the besieged guerrillas were evacuated from Tripoli at the end of December.

During February 1984, fierce fighting in West Beirut led to the break-up of the Lebanese Army into its Christian, Muslim and Druze elements, and the successes of the anti-government forces contributed to the decision to withdraw the MNF. The Israelis remained in occupation of the territory south of the Awali River, however, but suffered growing casualties, mainly as a result of attacks by local Shi'ite forces. By early 1985, the Israelis had lost over 600 dead since the invasion began, and on 16 February began to pull back from the Awali as part of a planned three-stage withdrawal from Lebanon.

Civil War in North Yemen 1962-67
Overthrown by a Nasserite military coup in September 1962, the Yemen ruler, the Imam Mohammed al-Badr, withdrew to the mountains where he organised an army of Zeidi tribesmen which received backing from neighbouring Saudi Arabia. The republican government was supported by Egypt, which had 30,000 men stationed in the country by April 1963.

The republican/Egyptian forces controlled the main towns and roads, and enjoyed total command of the air, but even though they employed chemical weapons and napalm against the royalist rebels, they were unable to prise them out of their mountain strongholds. By late 1964, the Egyptian garrison had increased to some 60,000 troops, but the royalist forces were growing in strength, thanks largely to Saudi arms and foreign mercenaries. In August 1965, a ceasefire was negotiated, but the announcement in February 1966 of the British intention to withdraw from its colony in neighbouring Aden provoked a new round of fighting for control of North Yemen.

Following its defeat by Israel in the 1967 Six-Day War, Egypt decided on withdrawal from North Yemen, and the last of its troops left the country in October 1967. Fighting continued, however, and the capital, Sana, was besieged by the royalist army. The republicans turned for aid to the Soviet Union, and received assistance from the left-wing government in South Yemen following British withdrawal and independence in November 1967. The siege of Sana was lifted and royalist forces routed, and in December 1967 their stronghold at Hajjah was captured by republican troops. The Imam was forced into exile and the war ended in an unexpected compromise with the creation of a coalition government.

Radfan insurgency 1964

In January 1964, the South Arabian Federation's British-officered Federal Regular Army (FRA), backed by units of British troops and the RAF, launched a punitive campaign in the mountainous Radfan area along the border with North Yemen, against tribesmen for whom banditry was almost the sole available source of income. By March, the government troops had been withdrawn, but the tribesmen, armed by North Yemen and backed by Egyptian-sponsored National Liberation Front (NLF) guerrillas, continued to be active, forcing the British Army based in Aden to intervene directly.

A British force, including Paras, Commandos and SAS, faced fierce resistance as it moved into the Radfan in an operation which began on 30 April, but the tribesmen were subject to intensive air attack by RAF Hunters and forced to withdraw deeper into the mountains. Tanks and helicopters were deployed to strengthen the British force, which now launched a successful offensive into the Radfan heartland and an assault upon the tribesmen's stronghold in the Wadi Misrah. A battle there on 7 June proved to be the last serious engagement of the Radfan episode, although the area remained a security problem for the British until their withdrawal in 1967.

Aden insurgency 1963-67

In January 1964, Aden Colony joined the Federation of South Arabia, which had been established by Britain in 1958. Aden was the key British military base in the region, but the British presence was opposed by the nationalist Front for the Liberation of Occupied South Yemen (FLOSY) and the Marxist National Liberation Front (NLF), which both embarked upon a campaign of terrorism to force a British withdrawal.

The first serious attack took place in December 1963, and although it was a year before the next incident, during 1965 286 terrorist attacks took place, in 1966 there were 510, and in 1967 no fewer than 2900. The rapid rise in the intensity of the attacks was partly due to the British announcement in February 1966 of an intention to withdraw from Aden by 1968.

Under terrorist and international pressure, Britain advanced the date for withdrawal to November 1967, and during the summer of 1967 some districts of Aden were in open rebellion, which was only quelled after heavy fighting. Mutinies by locally recruited police in June showed how far British control had disintegrated, and during the last few months before independence the main fighting was between FLOSY and the NLF for post-independence power. The struggle was won by the left-wing NLF, which established an independent republic on 30 November 1967. The insurgency had cost some 57 British and several hundred Arab dead.

Dhofari insurgency 1962-75

In 1962, the Dhofar Liberation Front (DLF) initiated a low-level guerrilla campaign in Oman's western province of Dhofar, opposing the repressive and unpopular regime of Oman's Sultan, Said bin Taimur. Despite the weakness of the Sultan's Armed Forces (SAF), the insurgents made little progress. In late 1967, however, following the establishment of a left-wing government in neighbouring South Yemen, Marxist influence within the DLF began to increase, and in June 1968 it was transformed into the Popular Front for the Liberation of the Occupied Arabian Gulf (PFLOAG), which by 1970 had successfully forced the SAF to withdraw from the Dhofari mountains.

The overthrow of Sultan Said by his son, Qaboos bin Said, in July 1970 opened a new stage in the war. Although during the early 1970s PFLOAG reached the peak of its fighting strength with approximately 2000 well-armed guerrillas, Qaboos embarked on a programme of reforms aimed at winning the support of the Dhofaris, backed by a successful counter-insurgency campaign, in which units of the British SAS, and Jordanian, Pakistani and Iranian troops played an important role. By 1975 the largely British-piloted Omani Air Force was bombing rebel artillery positions along the South Yemen border, and at the end of that year PFLOAG activities virtually came to an end.

Kurdish insurgency 1961-

In September 1961, Kurdish demands for autonomy within Iraq led to the outbreak of a civil war which continued for almost 14 years, interrupted by a number of ceasefires and an armistice negotiated in January 1970, under which the Iraqi government agreed to implement the Kurds' demands. The Kurdish rebels, whose armed forces were known as Peshmarga, controlled the mountains of northeastern Iraq, where regular government offensives achieved little, although many Kurdish villages were destroyed by Iraqi bombing raids.

The heaviest fighting occurred after the collapse of the armistice in April 1973, with the Kurds adopting a conventional static defence of the area which they controlled. Nevertheless, the Iraqis advanced to within 32km (20 miles) of the Kurds' headquarters at Chouman, which led to the Kurds' ally, the Shah of Iran, despatching a contingent of Iranian troops to man the Kurds' air defences. Iranian backing was suddenly withdrawn in March 1975, however, when the Shah reached an agreement with the Iraqi government over a long-standing territorial dispute. The Iranian border was closed to the Kurds and, as the Iraqi Army moved in, the revolt collapsed.

The Iranians provided fresh support to Iraqi Kurdish guerrillas following the opening of the Gulf War with Iraq in September 1980. The Iraqi Kurds formed an alliance with anti-government Shi'ite fundamentalists and communists, and by early 1985 controlled a 32km (20-mile) deep strip of territory along the Turkish border.

The Iranians experienced their own conflict with Kurdish insurgents, however. Having fought against the Shah, the Iranian Kurds demanded autonomy after his overthrow in 1979. The Khomeini regime sent Revolutionary Guards into the Kurdish region to suppress opposition, and serious fighting broke out, which continued into 1985, with the Kurds forming an alliance with left-wing Mujahidin guerrillas.

Gulf War 1980-

A dispute over control of the Shatt al Arab waterway, and a bitter enmity between the Shi'ite fundamentalist regime of Ayatollah Khomeini in Iran and the secular Ba'ath nationalist President Saddam Hussein of Iraq, led to increasingly serious border clashes following the Iranian revolution in 1979, and escalated to a full-scale war when Iraqi forces invaded Iran on 22 September 1980.

The Iraqi offensive coincided with artillery and bombing attacks on a number of Iranian towns and military installations. The heaviest fighting occurred in the predominantly Arab Iranian province of Khuzistan, where Iraqi tanks advanced swiftly through the desert. Street-fighting in Khorramshar continued until 13 October, when the city fell to the Iraqis, but by then the initial mobile stage of the war was already over, and the tenacious defence of Abadan by Iranian Revolutionary Guards halted any further Iraqi advance.

Air raids inflicted great damage upon the oil industries of both countries, and as the Iraqis' original lightning campaign was transformed into a protracted war of attrition, casualties mounted dramatically. The Iranians enjoyed the advantage of numbers, which they employed in costly human-wave attacks on Iraqi positions, and by May 1982 they had retaken Khorramshar. In early November 1982, the Iranians succeeded in pushing the Iraqis back across the border. The Iraqis' advantage in military equipment and supplies now began to be felt, however, and their strong defensive positions withstood the increasingly futile Iranian assaults.

From late 1983, Iraqi air attacks on vessels in the Gulf posed a mounting threat to oil supplies from the region, and reduced Iranian oil revenues, but the war nevertheless continued, with both sides apparently regarding the overthrow of their opponent's regime as a prerequisite for peace. By the end of 1984 losses in the war were estimated at from 150,000 to 300,000 Iranians and between 75,000 and 150,000 Iraqis.

South Asia

Kashmir 1947-49

Following the end of the British Empire in India and its partition into the independent states of India and Pakistan, many areas remained under the control of traditional local rulers. One of these was Kashmir, with an 80 per cent Muslim majority but a Hindu ruler. Communal violence grew during 1947, and on 7 November Indian troops intervened against Muslim rebels and invading Pathan tribesmen. Pakistan backed a 'Free Kashmir' movement, but India poured in strong reinforcements, and by November 1948 Indian troops were nearing the Pakistan border. War was averted, however, and a UN ceasefire negotiated. India, which had lost some 6000 men, was determined to retain control of Kashmir and, despite an agreement to hold a plebiscite, annexed the state in January 1957.

Annexation of Goa 1961

Portugal retained a number of tiny colonies along the coast of India after independence in 1947. India attempted to take over these colonies with an influx of non-violent demonstrators during 1955, but Portugal resisted. On 16 December 1961, the Indian government resolved the dispute by sending units of the Indian Army into Goa and the enclaves of Diu and Damao. There was some resistance from the small Portuguese garrison, which lost 51 men and one frigate during 26 hours of fighting; Indian losses were an estimated 24 men killed.

Sino-Indian War 1962

Britain and Tibet negotiated a border in 1914, known as the McMahon Line, which was inherited by India but never accepted by Peking. The dispute over the Sino-Indian border remained purely diplomatic until Indian troops based in the Northeast Frontier Agency began to patrol territory claimed by Delhi on the Chinese side of the McMahon Line in December 1961.

China responded by moving up troops to face the Indian positions, and on 9 October 1962 full-scale fighting broke out as Indian forces attempted to push back the Chinese People's Liberation Army (PLA). The PLA was stronger and better equipped, and in late October moved over to the offensive. Smashing through the Indian lines, the Chinese outflanked Se La and destroyed the Indian garrison at Tembang, while two brigades of the Indian Army were forced into hasty withdrawals and virtually annihilated.

In the western sector, China had built up strong positions along the frontier, and overwhelmed many Indian outposts after heavy bombardments. Having proven its determination and capacity to enforce its claims, China declared a unilateral ceasefire in late November 1962, remaining in occupation of the disputed territory. Chinese losses were unknown, but India had lost some 1400 killed and 4013 captured by the PLA.

Indo-Pakistan War 1965

Following clashes in the Rann of Kutch during January 1965, Pakistan recruited and trained a guerrilla force of some 5000-6000 men which began to infiltrate into Kashmir on 6 August 1965. On 15 August, Pakistani artillery began a bombardment of Indian positions, to which Indian troops replied by crossing the 1949 ceasefire-line in order to block guerrilla infiltration routes.

A Pakistani armoured thrust into Kashmir on 1 September initially overwhelmed Indian defences, but came up against determined resistance around Akhnur. On 5 September, Indian forces launched a diversionary offensive against Lahore, involving several armoured divisions supported by infantry, but the attack was broken off under heavy Pakistani artillery fire, while an assault on Kasur ended in an Indian rout. A Pakistani counter-thrust against Khem Karan broke down in the face of Indian artillery and armour, but India was unable to exploit this limited success.

An Indian offensive in the Chawinda Salient, launched on 7 September, was confused and indecisive, and international pressure combined with the heavy losses which both sides had sustained (both India and Pakistan suffered an estimated 1000 dead and 5000 wounded, while India lost 375 tanks and 35 aircraft to Pakistan's 350 tanks and 19 aircraft) led to a ceasefire on 23 September. Minor clashes continued for several months, but a peace conference during January 1966 resulted in a disengagement agreement on the basis of a return to pre-war positions.

Indo-Pakistan War 1971

The partition of Britain's Indian Empire in 1947 left East and West Pakistan divided by 2000km (1250 miles) of Indian territory. In the December 1970 Pakistani general elections, the Awami League won a sweeping victory in the East which gave it a majority in the national parliament. The military government, based in the West, refused to accept this result, provoking a general strike in East Pakistan; the military government responded by reinforcing the garrison in the East and arresting the leaders of the Awami League, including Sheikh Mujibur Rahman.

By the summer of 1971, resistance to the army in East Pakistan had grown into a guerrilla war, which was increasingly backed by India, where over 10 million refugees had fled. During November 1971, Indian and Pakistani forces clashed on several occasions, and on 3 December Pakistan launched a pre-emptive air strike in the West which led to full-scale war.

India was able to contain the Pakistani offensive in the West, while its own troops, supported by East Pakistani Mukhti Bahini guerrillas, swept into East Pakistan along four main lines of advance over difficult terrain which was broken by numerous broad, unbridged rivers. Having outflanked and defeated the isolated Pakistani garrisons, Indian troops began to shell Dacca on 14 December. On 16 December Pakistani forces in the East, numbering some 57,000 regular troops and 18,000 paramilitary personnel, surrendered.

A ceasefire in the West on the following day brought the war to an end, and Pakistan was forced to accept both the independence of East Pakistan as Bangladesh, and the emergence of India as the dominant military power in the region. Pakistan had lost some 8000 troops killed against India's 3283, while hundreds of thousands of civilians had been killed in the East as a result of Pakistani repression before the Indian invasion.

Tamil insurgency in Sri Lanka 1978

During early 1978, Tamil Tiger guerrillas began to attack police patrols and outposts in the predominantly Tamil areas of north and east Sri Lanka. Fighting against the Sinhalese-dominated central government of Junius Jayawardene, the Tamil Tigers aimed at an independent state – Tamil Eelam.

Repeated anti-Tamil riots and massacres further divided the island state into two hostile communities, and by early 1985, following an attempted Tiger invasion from the Indian mainland, partition seemed a possibility.

Soviet occupation of Afghanistan 1979-

A coup in the Afghan capital, Kabul, on 27 April 1978 brought to power a Marxist government, which sought to introduce rapid change to the country's backward social and economic system. These policies provoked a hostile response from much of the population, and there was soon a full-scale revolt in progress, pitting Islamic fundamentalist Mujahidin guerrillas against government forces.

The Soviet Union, which had long enjoyed a degree of influence in Afghanistan, was heavily committed to support for the Marxist regime – a number of Soviet advisers were killed by the Mujahidin and Soviet military personnel participated in attempts to combat the revolt – but disagreed with the extremist policies of Hafizullah Amin, who took over as president in September 1979.

On 24 December 1979, a massive airlift of Soviet troops to air bases in Afghanistan began, accompanied by the movement of armoured forces across the border from the north. Amin was killed after he refused to resign, and was replaced by the more moderate Babrak Karmal. Although the new government attempted some conciliatory gestures, there was an intense nationalist reaction against the Soviet intervention, depleting the ranks of the Afghan Army and swelling the numbers of the Mujahidin. The 100,000-120,000 Soviet troops became engaged in a long and costly counter-insurgency campaign; even their hold on the main towns and military bases was at times insecure. The failure of the Mujahidin, largely operating from bases in Pakistan, to achieve a unified front helped the Soviets, and the Soviet forces gradually improved their counter-insurgency techniques, so that by 1985 the situation seemed a stalemate. Soviet casualties since the fighting began have been variously estimated at between 5000 and 10,000 dead, while casualties among the Mujahidin and Afghan civilians were certainly much heavier.

Southeast Asia

French Indochina 1945-54

Following the Japanese collapse in August 1945, communist-led Viet Minh guerrillas seized control of much of what is now Vietnam, and the country was proclaimed independent by Ho Chi Minh on 2 September 1945. The French, however, were determined to reimpose their rule over Indochina. The return of the colonial authorities provoked clashes in Saigon in late September 1945, and by November 1946 serious fighting between French and Viet Minh forces in Haiphong marked the beginning of a long war of independence involving guerrilla warfare throughout Vietnam.

Between 1947 and 1949, fighting was concentrated in the Viet Bac region along the Chinese border, but after the Chinese communist victory in 1949, the French withdrew the bulk of their forces for the defence of the heavily populated Red River and Mekong Deltas. Isolated French garrisons began to fall to the Viet Minh who now took the offensive, having been supplied with large amounts of arms and equipment by China.

In January 1951, the Viet Minh began an assault on the Red River Delta, but by June the Viet Minh commander, General Giap, was forced to accept defeat and withdraw his men. Fighting now shifted to northwest Vietnam, between the Red and Black Rivers, and again the Viet Minh laid siege to and captured a number of

isolated French garrisons, whose only means of supply was from the air. By late 1952, the Viet Minh were operating along the Laotian border, and the French attempted to prevent them infiltrating into Laos by stationing a large garrison at Dien Bien Phu. By March 1954, Dien Bien Phu was surrounded by the Viet Minh and under heavy artillery bombardment; the garrison fell to the communists on 8 May.

The loss of Dien Bien Phu signalled the end of French hopes of retaining Indochina. A peace conference already sitting in Geneva agreed to the creation of independent states in Laos and Cambodia, while Vietnam was to be provisionally divided at the 17th parallel – with the Viet Minh controlling the North – until free elections could be held. They never took place, thus sowing the seeds for the Vietnam War.

Vietnam War 1961-75

In December 1961, US advisers were committed in support of the South Vietnamese Army (ARVN) against guerrillas of the communist-led National Liberation Front (NLF), known as the Viet Cong, who were backed by North Vietnam. The US role increased dramatically after alleged attacks on US destroyers by North Vietnamese patrol boats in the Gulf of Tonkin in August 1964, to which America reacted by bombing targets in North Vietnam.

By the start of 1965, a communist victory in the South seemed imminent. US President Lyndon Johnson ordered regular bombing raids against the North (Operation Rolling Thunder, March 1965-November 1968) and the large-scale commitment of US combat troops, rising from 45,000 in May 1965 to 536,100 three years later. By the deployment of their immense firepower, the Americans successfully checked the progress of the guerrillas (increasingly supported by elements of the North Vietnamese Army – NVA), but although official 'body counts' of communist dead were high, the United States failed to win the 'hearts and minds' of the Vietnamese people.

In an effort to reduce US casualties, and thus defuse opposition to the war at home, in the second half of 1967 the Americans adopted the policy of 'Vietnamization', under which the ARVN was to take over the bulk of combat duties. Before this process really got under way, however, in February 1968 the communists launched the Tet offensive, seizing a large number of South Vietnamese towns and cities, while simultaneously besieging the Marine base at Khe Sanh. Although the Tet offensive was repulsed with heavy communist losses and Khe Sanh was relieved, these events undermined American confidence in eventual victory.

US President Richard Nixon, who took office in January 1969, had a dual commitment to the withdrawal of US troops and a hard line towards North Vietnam. Peace negotiations opened in Paris and the first US troop withdrawals were announced in June 1969, but the war continued. As the ARVN increasingly took over from US forces in combat, on the communist side North Vietnamese troops predominated over NLF guerrilla forces decimated by years of fighting and by the 'Phoenix' counter-insurgency programme. The number of US personnel in Vietnam had fallen to 156,800 by 1971, but efforts to cut communist supply routes from the North along the Ho Chi Minh Trail led to an extension of the war when ARVN and US troops crossed into Cambodia in April 1970 and into Laos in February 1971.

Convinced that the United States was determined to withdraw, North Vietnam attempted a conventional invasion of the South which began on 30 March 1972. The NVA was soon in control of most of the northern province of Quang Tri, while NVA units advanced across the Laotian border against Kontum, and in the south across the Cambodian border against Loc Ninh, which was overrun on 5 April. By late May, the North Vietnamese offensive was losing momentum, however, partly as a result of enormous US air support for the ARVN, which recaptured Quang Tri City in mid-September. The invasion also provoked a resumption of US bombing raids against the North on 17 April 1972 (Operation Linebacker I), and the mining of North Vietnamese ports.

Although North Vietnam had suffered a military set-back, its fundamental assumption about US intentions had been correct, and by late 1972 the Paris peace talks seemed on the verge of success. A stalemate in the negotiations during December led to intensive American bombing attacks against Hanoi and Haiphong (Linebacker II), but on 23 January 1973 a peace agreement was signed which led to a ceasefire on 27 January, and to a total withdrawal of US troops by 29 March.

Large areas of the South remained under communist control, and by the autumn of 1973 attempts to negotiate a peaceful internal settlement had collapsed. The ARVN was able to retain the military initiative throughout 1973, but while the North continued to build up its forces, American support for the South began to crumble. The communists began to move over to the offensive, and during mid-1974 made many important gains. The apparent weakness of the ARVN encouraged Hanoi to gamble on an all-out military victory, and on 10 March 1975 the NVA opened its final offensive in the South.

The ARVN disintegrated as the NVA advanced in the Central Highlands and from the north. Within three weeks, the NVA had overrun half of South Vietnam, and was advancing rapidly down the coast on the capital, Saigon. As South Vietnam collapsed, the United States withdrew military aid, and on 30 April, shortly after the last Americans had been evacuated by helicopter from the roof of the US embassy, NVA tanks crashed through the gates of the presidential palace in Saigon, ending a war which had cost North Vietnam an estimated one million dead, South Vietnam some 400,000, and the United States 47,000.

Laos 1958-75

The French withdrawal of 1954 effectively left control of Laos divided between two brothers, Souvanna Phouma at the head of the Royal Lao Forces, and Souphanouvong leading the communist Pathet Lao. The United States, determined to avoid a communist takeover, was split between official support for Souvanna Phouma and unofficial CIA backing for right-wing elements who opposed Souvanna Phouma's search for conciliation with the Pathet Lao. In 1958, after a right-wing coup, civil war broke out between rightist and communist forces.

In July 1962, the civil war was temporarily ended by the establishment of a neutralist coalition government. The following year, however, the communist Pathet Lao withdrew from the coalition and fighting recommenced. The Pathet Lao soon controlled much of eastern and northeastern Laos along the border with North Vietnam, which provided it with a great deal of support with the aim of maintaining the security of the vital Ho Chi Minh Trail which ran through eastern Laos to the battlefields of South Vietnam.

The conflict in neighbouring Vietnam led to a growth in the secret involvement of the United States, which not only backed the Royalist forces and an army composed of CIA-organised Meo tribesmen, but also launched a bombing campaign which continued even when Washington called a halt to the bombing of North Vietnam in 1968. North Vietnamese involvement in Laos also led to an attempt by the South Vietnamese Army (ARVN) to cut the Ho Chi Minh Trail in Operation Lam Son 719 in February 1971, but the North Vietnamese Army (NVA) hit back strongly, and forced the ARVN to withdraw from Laos in late March. The Pathet Lao/NVA forces now began to capture a growing number of their enemy's positions, including the Meo base at Long Cheng in December 1971, a defeat which marked the end of the Meo as an effective military force.

As part of the Paris peace negotiations with the United States, North Vietnam agreed to press the Pathet Lao to accept a negotiated settlement, and in February 1973, the Royalist government concluded a ceasefire agreement with the Pathet Lao which brought American involvement in Laos to an end. Sporadic fighting continued, however, and the Pathet Lao strengthened its position, until, in the spring of 1975, with the final NVA offensive in Vietnam under way, it seized the remaining Royalist strongholds, and in June entered the capital, Vientiane.

Khmer Rouge insurgency in Cambodia 1963-75

Cambodia's ruler, Prince Norodom Sihanouk, faced a small-scale insurgency by communist Khmer Rouge guerrillas during the 1960s. This was easily contained, however, and Sihanouk also kept his country out of the Vietnam conflict – although the border areas were used by Vietnamese communists as supply routes and bases.

In March 1970, Sihanouk was overthrown in a military coup led by Lieutenant-General Lon Nol, who appealed for US military assistance, and from April to June 1970, US and ARVN troops operated in eastern Cambodia. However, the Khmer Rouge, now backed by the NVA, formed a National United Front with Sihanouk, and their insurgency suddenly achieved a new scale, threatening Lon Nol's US-backed regime. The 1973 Vietnam ceasefire agreement led to a reduction in North Vietnamese assistance, but the Khmer Rouge maintained their pressure, and by February 1974 were close enough to shell the capital, Phnom Penh. The siege of Phnom Penh lasted until 17 April 1975, when the Khmer Rouge entered the city, in which all resistance had disintegrated.

Vietnamese occupation of Kampuchea 1978-

After the Khmer Rouge victory in 1975, Cambodia was renamed Kampuchea. Relations with Vietnam, now united after the victory of Hanoi, were never close, and border clashes had reached a serious scale by 1977. By late 1978, Khmer Rouge troops were operating deep inside Vietnamese territory, and Hanoi reacted on 25 December by mounting an invasion of Kampuchea which led to the the fall of the Khmer Rouge and the installation of a pro-Vietnamese government in Phnom Penh under Heng Samrin.

The Khmer Rouge continued to resist the Vietnamese occupation from bases along the Thai border, and, backed by China and Thailand, fielded some 30,000 guerrilla fighters by early 1985, far outnumbering the military strength of the anti-communist Khmer Serei movement, which also opposed the Vietnamese presence.

Chinese invasion of Vietnam 1979

On 17 February 1979, the Chinese People's Liberation Army (PLA) crossed the border into the northern provinces of Vietnam in retaliation for Hanoi's December 1978 invasion of Kampuchea. Relations between Vietnam and China had also been soured by a long-standing territorial dispute, and by Vietnam's treatment of its large Chinese minority, many of whom had fled to China.

The main Chinese objectives appeared to be the provincial capitals of Lao Cai, Cao Bang and Lang Son, but by 20 February the initial PLA advance had bogged down against determined resistance by Vietnamese forces, which were largely composed of regional militia. Concentrating now on the capture of Lang Son in order to secure at least a symbolic victory over the Vietnamese, the Chinese were able to take the hills surrounding the town, which was evacuated by the Vietnamese on 5 March.

Satisfied that they had inflicted suitable punishment for the overthrow of their Khmer Rouge allies in Kampuchea, the Chinese began a withdrawal that was completed during mid-March, largely unhindered by the regular Vietnamese units which had now been moved up by Hanoi. The estimated casualties of this short campaign were 20,000 Vietnamese killed and between two and three times as many Chinese.

The Malayan Emergency 1948-60

During World War II, the main resistance to the Japanese occupation of Malaya came from the Malayan People's Anti-Japanese Army (MPAJA), which was organised and led by the Malayan Communist Party (MCP). Following the end of the war and the return of the British, the MCP concentrated for several years upon legal political and trade union activities, but in June

1948 opened a campaign of guerrilla struggle against the British colonial authorities. The MPAJA was re-formed under the new title of the Malayan Races Liberation Army (MRLA), and began to operate in groups of between 50 and 200 men, but these soon proved to be vulnerable to the security forces and difficult to supply, and early efforts to establish liberated areas failed.

Finding its strongest support amongst the Chinese squatters who lived along the edges of the jungle in which its guerrillas operated, the MCP, itself largely composed of ethnic Chinese, conducted a campaign of terrorism against the security forces, government supporters and the European managers of tin mines and rubber estates, but the British responded with a sophisticated and successful counter-insurgency strategy which included the relocation of the Chinese squatter communities in protected 'new villages', and the coordination of military and police tactics under civil control, with great emphasis being laid upon the collection of intelligence on MCP activities.

The MRLA suffered increasingly heavy casualties as the British strategy began to show results, and by July 1960 when the Emergency was lifted, had lost almost 7000 dead. Nevertheless, communist guerrillas, commanded by the veteran leader Chin Peng, continued to operate in remote jungle areas along the Malay-Thai border even in early 1985.

Indonesian War of Independence 1945-49

On 17 August 1945, only two days after the surrender of Japan, Indonesian independence was proclaimed by nationalists who opposed a return of the pre-war Dutch colonial regime. Fighting broke out in October 1945, when British troops arrived in Indonesia to evacuate Europeans who had been wartime prisoners of the Japanese. Heavily outnumbered by the nationalist forces, the British brought in reinforcements during a ceasefire and established control of Surabaya after three weeks of heavy fighting.

During 1946, the Dutch took control of Indonesia from British and Australian forces, but recognised the authority of the Indonesian republic on the islands of Java, Madura and Sumatra. Talks between the two sides led to the creation of a Federal United States of Indonesia, which recognised the sovereignty of the Dutch crown, but the Netherlands remained committed to regaining control by military means, and mounted pacification operations from bases in the main cities. The nationalist People's Army was well armed, numerous and popular, however, and the Dutch were forced, under pressure from international opinion, to accept a ceasefire in late 1947.

Fighting amongst the Indonesians themselves, between Nationalist forces led by Sukarno and those of the Indonesian Communist Party (PKI), ended in a defeat of the communists, but encouraged the Dutch to attempt once more to gain a military victory. In December 1948 they launched a new offensive, and they were successful in capturing the republican capital of Yogyakarta. The Indonesians maintained a relentless guerrilla war, however, which forced the Dutch to accept Indonesian independence in December 1949, although they retained control of West Irian until 1962.

Indonesia's Confrontation with Malaysia 1963-66

In May 1961, Britain and Malaya agreed to a plan to create a federation between Malaya and a number of smaller British colonies in the area, including Singapore, Sarawak, North Borneo (later renamed Sabah) and Brunei. This was strongly opposed by neighbouring Indonesia and left-wing nationalist groups in Sarawak and Brunei. An Indonesian-backed revolt in Brunei, launched in December 1962, was suppressed by British troops, but Indonesian President Sukarno began training volunteers for guerrilla operations in Sarawak and Sabah.

The volunteers, largely composed of members of the Indonesian Communist Party (PKI) and the left wing of the Sarawak United People's Party, began mounting raids into Sarawak in April 1963 and, following the formation of Malaysia in September 1963

(which was greeted with violent anti-British riots in the Indonesian capatal Djakarta), Indonesian infiltration became a growing threat. Operating from bases along the Indonesian side of the 1560km (970-mile) border, the guerrilla volunteers were faced by a small British Defence Force, backed by Australian, New Zealand and Malaysian contingents, which relied upon helicopter-borne mobility to respond to incursions.

During 1964, units of the regular Indonesian Army were deployed along the border with Sarawak. When Indonesia launched a number of unsuccessful raids against the Malayan mainland, British forces were sanctioned to cross into Indonesian territory, but only to a depth of between 9000 and 18,000m (10,000-20,000 yards). These raids allowed the British gradually to establish domination of the border area, greatly reducing the ability of the Indonesians to mount operations against Sarawak.

An unsuccessful communist coup in Indonesia during September 1965 led to a military counter-coup, and the policy of confrontation with Malaysia was brought to an end in the following year. Indonesian losses during the Confrontation had been 590 dead, an estimated 222 wounded and 771 captured, while Commonwealth military and civilian casualties were 150 dead and 234 wounded.

Karen revolt in Burma 1948-55

When Burma achieved independence from Britain in January 1948, it faced several insurgencies, mounted both by the Burmese Communist Party and a number of minority hill tribes. The most serious hill-tribe insurgency was that of the 2 million-strong Karens, who claimed an independent state which would have included much of southern Burma. Units of the Karen National Defence Organisation (KNDO) occupied Moumein and several other towns in the south, and the government of Prime Minister U Nu formed local volunteer units to combat the rebels.

By 1949, the government faced some 37,000 rebels of various descriptions (including communists, Trotskyists, Muslims, and army mutineers) of whom an estimated 10,000 were Karens. The KNDO achieved a number of successes in 1949, and captured several important towns, including Mandalay, but a march on the capital Rangoon failed, and a government counter-offensive deprived the Karens of most of their gains. The initiative now passed to the government, and the revolt degenerated into sporadic guerrilla fighting. The capture of the KNDO stronghold of Papun in March 1955 marked the end of the Karens as a major threat, although rebel activity continued until the acceptance of a government amnesty in May 1980.

Indonesian occupation of East Timor 1975

Following the April 1974 revolution in Portugal, several political groups manoeuvred for power in the small Portuguese colony of East Timor. After a short civil war, the left-wing Frente Revolucionária Timorense de Libertação e Independência (Fretilin) proclaimed independence on 28 November 1975.

On 7 December, however, East Timor was invaded by Indonesian troops, who expelled Fretilin from the capital, Dili. Guerrilla fighting continued, even though East Timor was formally annexed by Indonesia on 14 August 1976, and Fretilin was able to survive repeated Indonesian offensives. Negotiations took place between Fretilin and the Indonesian authorities in March 1983, but fighting was renewed in August 1983, following the ambush of a group of Indonesian soldiers. Casualty figures on both sides are unknown.

East Asia

Chinese Civil War 1945-49

Following the defeat of Japan in 1945, the fragile alliance between the Chinese Communist Party and the nationalist Kuomintang rapidly collapsed, and by 1947 civil war once more raged in China.

The communist People's Liberation Army (PLA) had already won control of large areas during its guerrilla war against Japan, and its position was also strengthened by the occupation of key areas of Manchuria by the Soviet Army in August 1945.

Armed with captured Japanese weapons, the PLA outmanoeuvred and outfought the numerically superior and better equipped forces of Chiang Kai-shek's Kuomintang, and by the end of 1948 was in control of the whole of Manchuria. The Nationalists were unable to counter the relentless southward advance of the communist armies, to which vast numbers of Kuomintang troops defected, and on 1 October 1949, Mao Tse-tung proclaimed the foundation of a People's Republic in Peking. The war, which had cost millions of lives, was over.

The remnants of the Kuomintang retreated to the island of Taiwan, where they continued to dream of liberating the mainland, while Peking also maintained a claim to Taiwan and the Nationalist-occupied islands of Quemoy and Matsu. Both the latter were heavily shelled from the mainland during 1954, while Quemoy once more came under bombardment in 1958.

Tibet 1950-59
After the communists took power in Peking in 1949, they turned their attention to reasserting central control over Tibet, which had traditionally owed allegiance to the Chinese empire, but which had become semi-independent following the fall of the Manchu dynasty in 1911. Chinese troops entered Tibet in October 1950 and swept aside the tiny regular Tibetan Army. Peking negotiated a settlement which allowed it gradually to assert total central control over Tibet. Guerrilla resistance from nomadic Khamba tribesmen continued, however, and large-scale revolts in 1954 and 1959 indicated the degree of Tibetan opposition to the Chinese presence. The cost of this fighting was estimated at over 100,000 Tibetan dead, while thousands more were deported.

Sino-Soviet border clashes 1969
Following the Sino-Soviet split of the early 1960s, the previously close relationship between Moscow and Peking became violently hostile. Added to deep ideological differences were territorial disputes resulting from a number of treaties forced on China by Tsarist Russia during the 19th century. In March 1969, Chinese and Soviet border troops clashed over the possession of a disputed island in the Ussuri River. Fighting lasted for approximately 11 hours, and there were an estimated 100 casualties on either side. Between April and August 1969, there were a number of further incidents along the Sino-Soviet border, but both sides agreed to talks and tension was defused.

Korean War 1950-53
In 1945, Soviet and US zones of occupation were established in Korea following the defeat of Japan. These zones later developed into the communist Democratic People's Republic of Korea (DPRK) – led by Kim Il Sung – in the north, and the pro-Western Republic of Korea (ROK), led by Singman Rhee, in the south. Both sides claimed to be the sole legitimate government of Korea, and border clashes became regular in 1949 and early 1950.

On 25 June 1950, full-scale warfare erupted with the invasion of the south by the armed forces of the DPRK. In the absence of its Soviet delegate, the UN Security Council decided on armed intervention in support of the ROK, and on 7 July US General Douglas A. MacArthur – who had already been ordered by President Truman to assist South Korea with the US Eighth Army – was appointed commander-in-chief of UN forces in Korea.

The initial communist advance was rapid, and South Korean forces supported by US troops were soon bottled up in a small enclave around Pusan. On 15 September, however, MacArthur launched a daring amphibious landing at Inchon, and on 27 September UN forces retook the South Korean capital, Seoul. Despite a warning from China not to cross the 38th parallel into North Korea, MacArthur's troops continued to advance, and by late October were within 100km (62 miles) of the Chinese border. Consequently, Chinese troops moved into Korea to support the DPRK Army, and made their first contact with UN troops on 25 October. The tide of the war now swung back in favour of the communists. During the first half of January 1951, they recaptured Seoul and fought their way deep into South Korea.

By 25 January 1951, the communist advance had been halted, and UN forces began to push back towards the 38th parallel. The UN 'meatgrinder' tactics relied upon massive concentrations of firepower to smash communist opposition; the Chinese countered by employing massed assaults against UN positions. On 14 March the UN forces once more took Seoul, and on 31 March South Korean troops crossed the 38th parallel. MacArthur wished to pursue the offensive and extend the war with direct attacks on China, but on 11 April he was relieved of his command and replaced by General Matthew Ridgway.

A fresh communist offensive launched in late April was repulsed, leaving UN forces in control up to the 38th parallel by the end of May. Stalemate ensued, and peace negotiations began on 10 July 1951. It was not until 27 July 1953, however, that an armistice agreement was signed, and in the interim some costly battles took place, notably at Pork Chop Hill in April 1953. By the time the war finally came to an end, the UN forces had lost 118,515 dead, while North Korean dead numbered over 500,000 and China lost at least 900,000.

Huk insurgency in the Philippines 1946-54
In August 1946, peasant rebels – many of whom were former members of the wartime communist-led anti-Japanese guerrilla movement – were fighting against local landowners backed by the Philippine security forces and their own private armies. They were joined by a group of communists opposed to the newly-independent regime of President Manuel Roxas, and by 1950 the Hukbong Mapagpalaya ng Bayan (People's Liberation Army – known simply as the Huks), led by Luis Taruc was engaged in battalion-sized operations against government forces.

Huk successes were countered increasingly successfully after the appointment in September 1950 of Ramon Magsaysay as secretary for national defence. Magsaysay reorganised the armed forces and promoted a number of reforms in order to undermine peasant support for the Huks. The rebels were isolated and ruthlessly hunted down, and by 1954 the back of the rebellion had been broken. Some 9695 Huks had been killed, 1635 wounded and 4269 captured, while an estimated 15,866 had surrendered voluntarily.

Moro insurgency in the Philippines 1972-
The growing authoritarianism and centralism of the regime of President Ferdinand Marcos provoked widespread opposition in the Philippines, particularly after the introduction of martial law in September 1972. On the southern islands of Mindanao and the Sulu archipelago, Muslim separatists of the Moro National Liberation Front (MNLF) and its military wing, the Bangsa Moro Army, launched a guerrilla war to achieve total independence from Manila.

Allegedly backed by Libya and the neighbouring Malaysian state of Sabah, by 1973 the MNLF was in control of large areas of Cotabato Province and the Sulu islands, and its army of an estimated 50,000 men posed a serious threat to the Philippine security forces. By February 1974, the Moros were strong enough to capture the city of Jol for several days, but by 1975 Moro guerrilla activity had begun to decline and Marcos opened negotiations with the MNLF in order to end the war. Although Marcos' diplomatic offensive resulted in a withdrawal of Libyan support for the rebels, the Moros fought on, though their chances of gaining a separate Muslim state continued to decline as Christian settlers began to form a majority in many areas of the south.

The MNLF split into several factions, and many Moro guerrillas took advantage of government amnesty offers in order to surrender, but while the Moros alone were not strong enough to defeat Marcos, by the mid-1980s the president's position was becoming increasingly precarious as a result of urban opposition and a second Maoist-led rural insurgency.

New People's Army insurgency in the Philippines 1969-

The New People's Army (NPA), the military wing of the Maoist Communist Party of the Philippines (Marxist-Leninist), was formed in March 1969 as a result of a split with the pro-Moscow Communist Party. It began to operate in Tarlac Province in central Luzon, later transferring its main base to Isabela Province in the northeast of Luzon island. By 1971 the NPA had some 2000 men under arms, but as the Philippines security forces became more professional during the mid-1970s, the NPA suffered a series of reverses and was forced to reorganise.

By the early 1980s, however, the NPA had an estimated 7000-11,000 regular troops backed by thousands of part-time militia, and was operating in alliance with the MNLF as far south as Mindanao, where by 1985 it had become firmly entrenched.

Central America and the Caribbean

Cuban Revolutionary War 1956-59

On 2 December 1956, 81 men, led by Fidel Castro, landed on the Cuban coast near Niquero from the motor-boat *Granma*. Three days later, the small guerrilla band was dispersed in a clash with an army patrol, and only 22 survivors, including Castro, regrouped two weeks later in the Sierra Maestra, a rugged and remote mountain range in southern Cuba. Isolated, hungry and poorly equipped, the tiny rebel force nevertheless survived, and established a base area from which it began to conduct a guerrilla war against the dictatorial regime of the Cuban president, Fulgencio Batista.

On 28 May 1957, 80 guerrillas took part in a battle at El Uvero, and by the end of the year the rebels numbered some 200 men, who were able to move at will throughout Oriente Province. The urban network of Castro's 26th of July Movement provided a source of men and supplies, and carried out sabotage and bombings in the cities. A general strike called in February 1958 ended in defeat, but was followed by a declaration of total war by the rebels.

In March 1958, the United States halted arms supplies to Batista, who ordered a large-scale offensive against the guerrillas in the Sierra in May, during which some 11,000 government troops faced 300 rebels. After two months, the army was forced to retreat, having suffered heavy casualties and a major defeat. Castro now took the offensive, and launched two rebel columns on an invasion of the central provinces.

There were wholesale desertions and surrenders from Batista's corrupt and demoralised army, and although the rebels at no time numbered more than 1500 men, they were able to capture Las Villas by mid-October, and Placetas and Santa Clara in December. On 1 January 1959, Batista flew into exile, and that night the first rebel forces entered Havana, where Castro arrived on 8 January.

Bay of Pigs invasion 1961

US-backed Cuban exiles launched an invasion of Cuba on the morning of 17 April 1961. The day began with ineffectual attacks upon Cuban Air Force bases by exile-piloted B-26 bombers. In the Bay of Pigs, about 1300 Cuban exiles, organised in Brigade 2506, landed from vessels which had been escorted by the US Navy, but the beach-head was subjected to devastating attacks by Cuban aircraft, and the Castro regime swiftly mobilised against the invasion threat.

By the morning of 19 April, the invasion was already doomed to failure, and 1180 exiles were finally taken prisoner, after around 120 had been killed during the fighting. Cuban casualties are unknown.

US invasion of the Dominican Republic 1965

The overthrow of the right-wing junta by a military revolt in April 1965 led to civil war between junta supporters and proponents of a return to constitutional government. On 28 April, US Marines landed in the capital, Santo Domingo, ostensibly to protect American residents, but in fact with the wider aim of preventing a victory for the constitutional side, seen by Washington as subject to left-wing influence.

The disturbances continued, however, and following a decision by US President Lyndon Johnson on 29 April, the American contingent was reinforced with paratroopers and Marines. By late May, the US forces had grown to some 32,000 men, which resulted in a stalemate between the junta and rebel forces. The arrival of a Latin American peacekeeping force led to a reduction in the US presence, and in August both sides agreed to a compromise solution. Elections were held in June 1966, and by the late summer of that year, foreign military forces had been withdrawn. The conflict had resulted in the death of 1500 Dominicans and 24 US soldiers.

El Salvador-Honduras 'Football War' 1969

A dispute over the uncontrolled influx of immigrants from El Salvador into neighbouring Honduras during the 1960s inflamed national passions on both sides, and erupted into full-scale war after the Honduran national football team had been badly treated in El Salvador in 1969. The El Salvador Army crossed the border at three points on 14 July 1969, and advanced rapidly along the Pan American Highway, capturing the town of Ocotepeque.

Honduras immediately accepted an Organisation of American States (OAS) ceasefire proposal on the day of the invasion, but the refusal of El Salvador to comply led to fighting continuing until 29 July, when the OAS threatened economic sanctions against El Salvador, which it branded as the aggressor. El Salvador began to withdraw its troops from Honduras on the following day, and the operation was completed on 5 August. The war left some 3000-4000 dead, and forced over 100,000 refugees to flee Honduras for the safety of El Salvador. Relations between the two countries remained hostile.

Nicaragua's Sandinista revolution 1961-79

In July 1961, three students founded the Frente Sandinista de Liberación Nacional (FSLN), which embarked upon a guerrilla war against the regime of the Somoza family. The early stages of the insurgency were marked by the weakness of the Sandinistas, but following the massacre of several hundred demonstrators by Somoza's National Guard in January 1967, the insurrection grew rapidly, and guerrilla operations spread from isolated border regions to central Nicaragua.

The FSLN suffered a severe military defeat in August 1967, but continued to build a network of supporters amongst peasants, students and workers. Between 1970 and 1974, demonstrations and protests became common, particularly following the 1972 earthquake which devastated the capital, Managua. In December 1974, the FSLN took a number of hostages at a US embassy reception in Managua, and after a 60-hour siege the government was forced to accede to the rebels' demands. Martial law was declared, but an intensive counter-insurgency campaign failed to defeat the Sandinistas, who renewed their offensive in October 1977.

Rioting and a general strike in early 1978 showed the extent of FSLN support, and on 22 August Sandinistas occupied the presidential palace, successfully demanding a $500,000 ransom and the release of over 50 FSLN prisoners. Urban revolts were met by increased repression, but in May 1979, the Sandinistas launched a final offensive, which led to the capture of a string of Nicaraguan cities. A rising in Managua was crushed, but by 27 June the city was surrounded, and it fell to the FSLN after Somoza resigned and fled the country on 17 July. The war had cost an estimated 50,000 dead.

Contra insurgency in Nicaragua 1979-

Almost immediately after the Sandinista victory in 1979, former Somoza National Guardsmen began to regroup to carry on a guerrilla war against the new regime from bases in Honduras, while training camps were set up in Florida and Guatemala. They received extensive support from the United States, particularly after the inauguration of President Reagan in January 1981, and in March 1982 their attacks upon economic targets in Nicaragua led to the declaration of a state of emergency there.

Thanks to US support, the Contras were able to mount air attacks on targets inside Nicaragua, and carried out the mining of Nicaraguan harbours from US support ships. Nevertheless, they were unable to establish 'liberated zones' on Nicaraguan territory, and US pressure for the unification of the Honduras-based Fuerzas Democráticas Nicaraguenses (FDN) with the Alianza Revolucionaria Democrática (ARDE), which operated from bases in Costa Rica, was resisted by the ARDE leader, former Sandinista guerrilla Eden Pastora.

The Contras suffered a major set-back in June 1984, when the US Congress voted to halt all covert financial assistance to the rebels. The Sandinistas, meanwhile, were able to consolidate their regime and expanded their armed forces with aid from Cuba and the Soviet Union. An election held in November 1984, although boycotted by some opposition parties, confirmed popular support for the Sandinistas, and helped win them wider international backing in the continuing war against the Contras.

El Salvador Civil War 1972-

Decades of brutal exploitation of the peasantry and a long series of repressive military governments resulted in the formation of the Fuerzas Populares de Liberación-Farabundo Martí (FPL-FM) in 1972. Its guerrilla war was emulated by several other groups which emerged during the mid-1970s, including the radical christian democratic Ejército Revolucionario Popular (ERP), the Fuerzas Armadas de la Resistencia Nacional (FARN), and the Partido Revolucionario de los Trabajadores Centroamericano (PRTC).

The growing activity of right-wing death squads blocked any possibility of peaceful change, and following the massacre of a large number of peaceful demonstrators in San Salvador by the security forces on 22 January 1980, and the assassination of Archbishop Oscar Romero two months later, the opposition groups united to form the Frente Democrático Revolucionario (FDR), and in October the guerrilla groups joined together in the Frente Farabundo Martí de Liberación Nacional (FMLN).

Fighting intensified throughout 1980, and despite massively increased military aid to the government forces from the United States, the guerrillas controlled large areas of several provinces by mid-1981, and were able to mount a nationwide sabotage campaign against power supplies and communications.

Despite the election of the moderate Napoleón Duarte as president in May 1983, the security forces and death squads continued to prevent reforms, and the guerrilla war went on although in late 1984 Duarte opened negotiations with the guerrillas in an attempt to reach a peaceful solution to the conflict.

US invasion of Grenada 1983

The overthrow and murder of Grenadan Prime Minister Maurice Bishop by radical rivals within his own New Jewel Movement in October 1983 led to plans for an invasion to overthrow the new government by the United States and a number of conservative Caribbean states. The operation began early on the morning of 25 October, as US Navy SEALs (Sea-Air-Land teams) came ashore to secure the governor-general, Sir Paul Scoon.

Meanwhile, US Marines landed at Pearls airport, which they secured for use by American aircraft. The site of a new airport, under construction by Cuban workers at Point Salines, was attacked by US paratroopers who dropped onto their objective at around 0600 hours. They encountered heavy resistance from Cuban construction workers and Grenadan troops, and were forced to call in reinforcements and air support.

Having gained control of Point Salines, the US troops advanced towards the island's capital, St. George's, north of which Marines made an assault landing from the USS *Guam*. The town fell after heavy fighting and intensive US air strikes, but resistance continued for several days before full control of the island was established. The invasion cost US forces 18 dead, while 24 Cubans and 16 Grenadan troops were killed, as well as an unknown number of civilians.

South America

Bolivian left-wing insurgency 1966-67

On 3 November 1966, Ernesto 'Che' Guevara, formerly a leader of the Cuban revolution and a close colleague of Fidel Castro, arrived in Bolivia to begin a guerrilla campaign whose aim was to provoke US intervention and create a massive 'South American Vietnam' which would lead to a continent-wide revolution. From the beginning, however, Guevara was isolated from Bolivian left-wing groups, and his small band of guerrilla fighters found little support amongst the Bolivian peasants, who had recently benefited from a series of liberal land reforms, and who informed the authorities of the rebels' activities.

The first encounter with the Bolivian Army occurred on 23 March 1967 and, although a tactical success for the guerrillas, led to the discovery of their camp and the capture of vital supplies. From then on they were relentlessly hunted by the Bolivian security forces, trained and advised by US personnel. By late August, the guerrilla group had been divided, and on 8 October Guevara was captured near El Yuro. On the following day he was executed, and with the majority of his men killed or captured, the insurgency ended.

Uruguayan 'Tupamaros' insurgency 1968-72

The Movimiento de Liberación Nacional (MLN) was formed in Uruguay by Raul Sendic in 1963. Better known as the Tupamaros, the movement staged a series of flamboyant operations during the mid-1960s which won a great deal of publicity and support. Bank raids and kidnappings were used to finance the Tupamaros' campaign of urban guerrilla warfare, which became particularly intense after 1968.

The Tupamaros drew their activists largely from the Uruguayan middle-class, and their many supporters within the state apparatus provided them with valuable intelligence which gave them an important advantage over the security forces. The effect of their activities upon the hitherto stable, peaceful and relatively democratic Uruguayan society was to increase the importance of the military, which by 1970 was assuming the main role in the anti-Tupamaro counter-insurgency war. The Tupamaros turned to assassinations, and their kidnapping of a number of diplomats and a US police adviser led to a determined government response which began to turn the tide away from the guerrillas. Attempting to organise a rural insurgency, the Tupamaros became isolated and suffered heavy casualties.

In 1972, the government declared a state of 'internal war', and the Tupamaros were smashed by a campaign launched by the security forces and right-wing death squads, which rapidly gave the military effective control of the country. This was made total in February 1973, when a military coup overthrew the civilian government, and the last remnants of the Tupamaro network were ruthlessly destroyed.

Left-wing insurgency in Argentina 1970-78

During the early 1970s, a variety of Marxist and Peronist guerrilla groups became active in Argentina, including the Trotskyist Ejército Revolucionario del Pueblo (ERP), the Maoist Fuerzas Armadas de Liberación (FAL), and the Peronist Monteneros. Despite the return of Juan Perón as president of Argentina in June

1973, the Monteneros continued their guerrilla activities, although the ERP progressively became the most important force.

Following the death of Perón and the succession of his wife to the presidency in July 1974, the situation deteriorated, and right-wing death squads of the Alianza Anticommunista Argentina (AAA), mostly composed of off-duty members of the security forces, waged an undercover war against the insurgents.

In March 1976, a military coup marked the opening of what became known as the 'Dirty War', during which the AAA and the security forces were responsible for the arrest, murder or disappearance of thousands of people suspected of supporting the guerrillas. The government's counter-insurgency measures sharply reduced insurgent activity during 1977, and by the end of the following year the guerrilla threat had been smashed.

Falklands War 1982

In early 1982, the Argentinian military junta, led by President Leopoldo Galtieri, decided to resolve its long-standing dispute with Britain over sovereignty of the Falkland Islands by a resort to force. On 19 March, an initial probe was made when Argentinian scrap-dealers landed on the remote island of South Georgia. The main invasion of the Falklands occurred on 2 April, when the small British Marine garrison on the islands was overwhelmed by a massively superior Argentinian force.

Britain reacted immediately by despatching a strong Task Force to retake the islands. On 12 April, Britain declared a 200-mile (320km) Maritime Exclusion Zone around the Falklands, and on 25 April recaptured South Georgia. On 2 May, the British submarine HMS *Conqueror* sank the Argentinian cruiser *General Belgrano*, effectively excluding Argentinian Navy vessels from playing any further part in the conflict.

Arriving off the Falklands at the beginning of May, the British Task Force set out to weaken the Argentinian defences on the islands and to wear down Argentinian air power. The British efforts met with at least a measure of success, despite the loss of the destroyer HMS *Sheffield* to an Argentinian Exocet missile on 4 May. Although there were misgivings about the possible impact of Argentinian air power, 3 Commando Brigade began landing at San Carlos on 21 May. Naval vessels suffered heavily as waves of air strikes came in, but a beachhead was successfully established.

Advancing from San Carlos, British paratroopers took Goose Green and Darwin on 28 May. 3 Commando Brigade then moved across difficult terrain until they confronted the Argentinian defensive line around Port Stanley. There they awaited reinforcement from 5 Infantry Brigade, who arrived at San Carlos on 1 June. An Argentinian air attack at Fitzroy on 8 June killed 51 men aboard HMS *Sir Galahad*, but this did not delay the final offensive. On 11-12 June, Mount Harriet, Two Sisters and Mount Longdon fell to the British, and on the night of 13-14 June Wireless Ridge and Mount Tumbledown were captured. Facing inevitable defeat, the Argentinian forces in Port Stanley surrendered on 14 June. British losses in the campaign totalled 255 dead; Argentinian deaths were estimated at around 1000.

Africa

Revolt in Madagascar 1947

During the night of 29 March 1947, nationalist insurgents rose in revolt throughout the French-controlled island of Madagascar. Although poorly armed, they attacked army garrisons, sustaining large numbers of casualties. The rebels were dispersed in the capital, Tananarive, and a number of other centres, and were never able to control more than a sixth of the colony, mainly in the east coast region.

The French reacted vigorously, dispatching Foreign Legion units to quell the revolt. The insurgents were surrounded and isolated, and between April 1948 and the end of the year, a ruthless French counter-insurgency operation led to up to 90,000 rebel casualties. Tens of thousands of villagers were either killed in the fighting or died of hunger and exposure after fleeing to the safety of the forests. Although the insurgency was totally suppressed, France bowed to the strength of nationalist feeling in 1960 by granting full independence to Madagascar.

Mau Mau insurgency, Kenya 1952-60

Unrest amongst Kenya's Kikuyu tribe led to the introduction of a state of emergency by the British authorities in October 1952, and many nationalist leaders, including Jomo Kenyatta, were interned. Some 12,000 Kikuyu took to the bush, and Mau Mau guerrilla units became active, especially in the forests of the Aberdare mountain range. They were extremely poorly armed, however, and had no neighbouring 'safe haven' on foreign territory from which to operate. In addition, the mass internment of Kikuyu resulted in a collapse of Mau Mau organisation, and isolated groups were pursued by 'counter-gangs' of surrendered guerrillas who had gone over to the security forces. By 1956, the Mau Mau was virtually defunct, but the state of emergency lasted until January 1960, by which time over 10,000 alleged Mau Mau had been killed, as well as some 2400 civilians and members of the security forces. Kenyatta became prime minister of Kenya in June 1963, and president in December 1964, one year after independence.

Algerian War of Independence 1954-62

An outbreak of nationalist opposition to French colonial rule in Algeria in May 1945 resulted in the massacre of a number of European settlers (colons), for which the French Army and colons retaliated by killing thousands of Muslims. But it was only in October 1954 that the Front de Libération National (FLN) was formed to achieve full independence by armed struggle. The insurgency began with an unsuccessful national rising on 1 November 1954, but firm French counter-measures hit the FLN severely, and its network of military regions (wilayas) barely survived into the following year.

During 1956, the FLN network in the capital, Algiers, launched a terrorist campaign which became known as the Battle of Algiers. The city was put under the control of General Jacques Massu, whose paratroops succeeded in smashing the FLN organisation there with the aid of mass arrests and torture. By late 1957, the Battle of Algiers had been won by the French, and the French Army turned its attention to preventing the infiltration across the border of FLN forces based in Tunisia, which were organised into the regular formations of the Armée de Libération Nationale (ALN). A formidable barrier, known as the Morice Line, was constructed by the French along the border with Tunisia; consisting of an electrified fence, minefields and barbed-wire entanglements, it proved effective in greatly reducing the ability of the FLN to provide its wilayas with reinforcements or supplies.

During 1959-60, the Challe offensive, named after the French commander in Algeria, combined intensive counter-insurgency sweeps with the extensive use of air power to pursue and destroy the now isolated FLN guerrilla groups. Nevertheless, political pressures forced French President Charles de Gaulle to accept the need for a negotiated settlement and an independent Algeria – but as he moved towards an agreement with the FLN, he provoked violent opposition from the colons and sections of the French Army.

In early 1961, a right-wing terrorist group calling itself the Organisation de l'Armée Secrète (OAS) initiated a campaign of bombings and assassinations to prevent de Gaulle granting independence to Algeria. In April of that year, French generals opposed to de Gaulle attempted to mount a coup, basing themselves on the discontented armed forces in Algeria, but the revolt aborted due to the loyalty of the ordinary French conscripts and the determination of the president. The OAS continued to be active and narrowly failed to assassinate de Gaulle in September 1961, but several of its most important leaders were arrested in early 1962, and it could not prevent the achievement of Algerian independence on 3 July 1962.

Chad Civil War 1963-

The Front de Libération National du Tchad (Frolinat) was created in 1963 against a background of widespread peasant revolt. The guerrilla movement spread rapidly during 1967-68, and there was a general rising in the northern province of Tibesti. In September 1969, French troops arrived to support the black African government against the basically Arabic-speaking Muslim rebels.

French troops were withdrawn in December 1971, when the level of guerrilla activity had declined. The Chadian president, François Tombalbaye, sought to stabilise the situation by reaching an understanding with the Libyan leader, Colonel Muammar Gaddafi, who had been supporting the rebels. Libyan troops were permitted to occupy the disputed Aouzou Strip in the north of Chad, in return for cutting off aid to Frolinat.

In April 1975, Tombalbaye was overthrown by the Chadian chief of staff, General Malloum, and guerrilla activity soon broke out afresh, coordinated by Hissène Habré and Goukouni Oueddei. Libyan backing for the rebels grew rapidly, and Frolinat enjoyed increasing success. In early 1978, Malloum was forced to call for French military intervention to halt the deteriorating situation.

After indecisive fighting, in November 1979 Malloum tempted Habré and Oueddei into joining a Gouvernement d'Union Nationale de Transition (GUNT), but this coalition did not last. Fighting between supporters of Habré and Oueddei broke out in March 1980, and Habré was forced to flee the country. The French forces, now finding themselves supporting Oueddei – the man they had been deployed to oppose – withdrew in April 1980.

Habré returned to the offensive the following year at the head of the Forces Armées du Nord (FAN), and by April 1982 controlled an estimated one third of the country. On 7 June, Habré's troops captured N'Djamena, forcing Oueddei to flee to Libya where he set up a government-in-exile. On 24 June 1983, his army attacked Tibesti and captured the town of Faya Largeau. Habré appealed for support, receiving troops from Zaire and, in mid-August, another French expeditionary force (the third to be sent). The French troops deployed to the 'Red Line' on the 15th parallel, designed to stand between Oueddei's GUNT and Habré's FANT forces. In January 1984, after a Jaguar aircraft was shot down, the French pushed forward to the 16th parallel and a confrontation with Libyan forces was feared. In late 1984, however, France and Libya agreed on a mutual withdrawal of forces, which was soon implemented, although there were reports that Libya still occupied the Aouzou Strip.

Sudanese Civil War 1955-

Conflict between the dominant Arabic-speaking Muslim minority, living mainly in the north, and the black southern majority, both Christian and animist, led to a mutiny of black troops in 1955, shortly before independence was achieved on 1 January 1956. The mutiny was quelled, but the Sudanese government refused to consider southern calls for aid and greater autonomy, thereby creating the conditions for a persistent insurgency in the southern Equatoria Province.

In September 1963, the southern-based Sudan National African Union announced the formation of the Land Freedom Army as its military wing, under the command of Major-General Emilio Tafeng. During the following year, the Land Freedom Army, better known as the Anya-Nya, undertook its first large-scale assaults on government barracks, and the Sudanese Army responded by pursuing the rebels across the border into Zaire, Ethiopia and Uganda. The crisis in the south contributed to unrest in the north, and the military regime of General Ibrahim Abboud fell in November 1964. The fighting in the south continued, however, and the Anya-Nya greatly expanded its operations in the course of 1966, during a period of famine and general administrative collapse in the region.

In 1967, the rebels set up a Southern Sudan Provisional Government, which controlled almost all of Equatoria Province,

but the seizure of power in Khartoum in May 1969 by Colonel Gaafar Numeiri marked the turning of the tide against the southern guerrillas, and in February 1972 they concluded an agreement with the central government, under which the south received a large measure of autonomy. Some rebel forces continued to fight for complete independence, however, and the southern insurgency continued into the 1980s.

Congo crisis 1960-65

Within days of Belgium granting independence to the Congo on 30 June 1960, an army mutiny undermined the central government in Leopoldville (Kinshasa), and the mineral rich southern province of Katanga seceded under the leadership of Moise Tshombe. Some Belgian Army units were still in the country, and they were rapidly reinforced in order to secure the safe evacuation of Belgian civilians. On 14 July, the UN agreed to provide military assistance to the Congo, and on 12 August the first UN troops entered Katanga, where they took over some security functions from Belgian forces.

The prime minister of the Congo, Patrice Lumumba, sought aid from the Soviet Union to end the Katanga rebellion, and his troops attempted an invasion of the province. Its failure led to a virtual collapse of the central government, and in September Lumumba was arrested by the chief of staff of the Congolese Army, Colonel Joseph Mobutu. In November, Lumumba managed to escape, but he was recaptured and transferred to Katanga, where he was murdered in February 1961.

Following the death of Lumumba, one of his close supporters, Antoine Gizenga, established an alternative government in Stanleyville (Kisangani) which was recognised by the Soviet Union and China, but in August 1961, President Joseph Kasavubu was able to temporarily reunite the competing factions in a coalition government led by Cyrille Adoula, the aim of which was to end the Katanga secession with UN assistance. Tshombe, meanwhile, began to recruit white mercenaries to spearhead his own forces, but although these were initially successful against their poorly armed and trained Congolese opponents, when confronted by UN troops in late 1962 they were forced to give way, and Tshombe surrendered in January 1963.

The last UN troops withdrew from the Congo in June 1964, but in the following month Tshombe returned from exile to head a new central government, which found itself facing a widespread rebellion in the east and southwest, led by former supporters of Lumumba and Gizenga. The rebels captured Albertville (Kalémié) and Stanleyville, but backed by the US and Belgium, Tshombe collected a new mercenary force which routed the rebels. A conflict between Tshombe and President Kasavubu led to the seizure of power by Mobutu, however, in September 1965.

The Shifta War, Kenya 1963-68

When Somalia gained independence in 1960, it laid claim to large areas of territory belonging to its neighbours, including northeast Kenya, inhabited by nomadic tribesmen of Somali origin. As Kenyan independence approached in late 1963, the small but well-trained Kenyan Army was temporarily immobilised by a mutiny against its white senior officers, but after this was crushed with British assistance, Kenya turned to the task of countering the Shifta insurgency. Operating in vast semi-desert regions where control of wells was a key factor, the Shiftas relied on hit-and-run tactics, but were vulnerable to the aerial reconnaissance aircraft employed by the Kenyan security forces. The insurgency lasted until 1968, when the dispute was taken to the Organization of African Unity, which found in favour of Kenya.

Nigerian Civil War 1967-70

In January 1966, Major-General Ironsi, a senior Nigerian officer from the Ibo tribe – the dominant group in the Eastern Region – formed a military government following an unsuccessful attempt to seize power by a group of young Ibo officers. This provoked fears of Ibo domination among the largely Muslim population of the Northern Region, and on the night of 28-29 July 1966, Northern troops carried out a coup, during which large numbers of non-Northerners, particularly Ibos, were killed.

The new Nigerian leader, Lieutenant-Colonel (later Major-General) Yakubu Gowon, a Christian northerner, attempted to halt the widespread massacres of Ibos which continued into September, and hundreds of thousands of Ibo soldiers and civilians returned to their home region. The Ibo military governor of the Eastern Region, Lieutenant-Colonel Chukwuemeka Odemegwu Ojukwu, opposed Gowon's plan to introduce a new 12-state federal structure to replace the existing regions, and on 30 May 1967 declared the Eastern Region independent as the republic of Biafra.

On 9 July, the Federal Army began a cautious advance into the rebel region, and its early capture of a key oil terminal dissuaded the international oil corporations from supporting Ojukwu's mineral-rich breakaway state. The Biafran Army soon appeared to have seized the military initiative, however, and began a rapid drive westwards on the Federal capital, Lagos. This offensive ran out of steam in mid-August, and the Federal Army soon recaptured the lost ground. It advanced once more into Biafra, and captured the rebel capital, Enugu, on 4 October. Ojukwu transferred his headquarters to Umuahia, but several other Biafran towns were taken by the Federal Army before the end of 1967, and Gowon predicted an early Federal victory.

In February 1968, Biafran resistance stiffened, but was unable to prevent the fall of Onitsha in March and Port Harcourt in May. Federal air attacks and growing famine in Biafra generated public sympathy for the Biafran cause abroad, but Ojukwu's military position continued to deteriorate, and by mid-September 1968 the area controlled by his forces had shrunk to 100km by 50km (60 miles by 30 miles). The only remaining Biafran airfield, Uli, was under bombardment by Federal artillery. Gowon again predicted an early victory, but stiffened by mercenaries, the Biafrans managed to relieve the pressure on Uli and in October went over to the offensive, recapturing a number of small towns.

During early 1969, Federal air raids on Biafra were limited to military targets after international pressure. Umuahia fell to the Federal Army in late April, and Ojukwu moved his headquarters to Nkwerre. Although a Biafran counter-offensive inflicted a sharp defeat on the Federal Army in the south, and the Swedish-piloted Biafran Air Force carried out many bombing raids on Federal targets during May-October 1969, the Biafran position was increasingly hopeless, and in December the final Federal offensive was launched.

Biafran territory was rapidly split in two, leading to a sudden collapse in Biafran morale. Ojukwu fled into exile on 11 January 1970, and on the following day his forces surrendered. The war had cost an estimated 1 million lives, mostly due to starvation, but General Gowon's government appeared willing to make every effort to promote reconciliation and rebuild the shattered unity of the Nigerian nation.

Angolan War of Independence 1961-74

In January 1961, an insurrection broke out in northern Angola which was brutally suppressed by the Portuguese colonial authorities during the following month. On 4 February, the Marxist Movimento Popular de Libertação de Angola (MPLA) organised armed attacks in the capital, Luanda, which marked the beginning of a 14-year insurgency. On 15 March 1961, a further insurgency was launched by the Congo-based União das Populações de Angola (UPA) in northern Angola. The UPA, led by Holden Roberto, was strongly tribal, finding its support amongst the Bakongo people.

By late October 1961, the Portuguese had re-established control of northern Angola, and the UPA retreated to the Congo, where in 1962 it adopted the name of Frente Nacional de Libertação de Angola (FNLA). A third Angolan liberation movement was

formed when Roberto's 'foreign minister', Jonas Savimbi, broke away from FNLA to lead the União Nacional para a Independência Total de Angola (UNITA), which was based in the south amongst the Ovimbundu tribe.

During 1963-64, the MPLA unsuccessfully attempted to infiltrate the mineral-rich Cabinda enclave from bases in Congo-Brazzaville, but in 1964 transferred its main base to Zambia, from where it operated in the Moxico and Bié regions of eastern Angola. The sparse population and vegetation of this area assisted the Portuguese counter-insurgency campaign, and allowed them to employ their monopoly of air power to prevent deep MPLA penetration of Angola. Nevertheless, by the early 1970s, the Portuguese garrison in Angola had grown to some 60,000 troops, who, as in the rest of Lisbon's African empire, had largely lost the will to fight, and in many cases even showed a large degree of sympathy for the aims of their left-wing guerrilla opponents.

The long colonial wars fought by the Portuguese Army in Africa had dramatic political repercussions at home, where the left-wing Movimento das Forças Armadas staged a military coup on 25 April 1974, overthrowing the right-wing Caetano regime, and establishing a revolutionary government which rapidly moved towards granting independence to Portugal's colonies.

Guinea-Bissau War of Independence 1963-74

In 1956, the Partido Africano de Independência da Guiné e Cabo Verde (PAIGC) was founded by Amilcar Cabral, who began to prepare for a guerrilla war against the Portuguese after they repressed a dock strike in the capital, Bissau, in 1959. The main PAIGC base was in neighbouring Guinea-Conakry, and it was from there that the PAIGC launched its first military operations in January 1963, with attacks upon the towns of Buba, Tite and Fulacunda.

The small Portuguese garrison was soon forced onto the defensive, and by the end of the year the PAIGC claimed control of some 15 per cent of the colony. Guerrilla operations expanded throughout the late 1960s, and in 1967 the PAIGC began to operate from bases in Senegal. By 1971, the PAIGC had some 6000 men under arms, and administered 'liberated zones' comprising a claimed 80 per cent of the colony. The Portuguese were increasingly confined to the safety of their firebases, and in March 1973 the guerrillas for the first time challenged Portuguese control of the sky when they began to deploy Soviet-supplied SA-7 surface-to-air missiles.

In January of that year, however, Cabral was assassinated, and his brother Luiz assumed the leadership of the movement in 1974. The Portuguese revolution of April 1974 soon led to a negotiated Portuguese withdrawal from Guinea-Bissau, and the last troops left in October. An estimated 1875 Portuguese troops were killed in the war, as well as an unknown number of black auxiliaries, and anything from 6000 to 12,000 PAIGC guerrillas may have died.

Mozambique War of Independence 1964-74

The Frente de Libertação de Moçambique (FRELIMO) began its military campaign against Portuguese control in September 1964. Its operations were initially confined to the northeastern province of Cabo Delgado, and it encountered resistance to southward infiltration from Muslim tribes, but in 1967 it extended its activities to Niassa Province. In 1968, FRELIMO guerrillas became active in Tete Province, forcing the Portuguese to fortify heavily the area around the Cabora Bassa dam project.

In February 1969, the leader of FRELIMO, Eduardo Mondlane, was assassinated by a book-bomb, and was succeeded by Samora Machel. In spite of a vigorous counter-insurgency campaign against FRELIMO in the north during 1970, in Tete the Portuguese became increasingly passive, allowing FRELIMO to use the province as a jumping-off point for raids into neighbouring Rhodesia in cooperation with ZANU guerrillas, and for infiltration south and east into central Mozambique. By 1973, FRELIMO forces were active in Vila Pery and the Beira region, and the strategic Beira railway was increasingly coming under attack.

Fighting continued in spite of the April 1974 Portuguese revolution, but the guerrillas, now armed with Soviet SA-7 missiles, had penetrated Zambezia Province by July, and in September 1974 a negotiated settlement was reached, which led to full independence in June 1975.

Angolan Civil War 1975-

Angolan independence was scheduled for 11 November 1975, but in spite of an agreement to hand over power to an MPLA-FNLA-UNITA coalition, clashes between the three movements became increasingly serious. After fierce fighting in Luanda, the MPLA expelled the FNLA, which formed an alliance with UNITA, backed by South Africa, Zaire and the United States.

The MPLA had received large amounts of weapons from sympathetic Portuguese troops, and now turned to the Soviet Union and Cuba for support. In early October, a group of 480 Cuban instructors arrived in Angola. Stationed in the central provinces to train MPLA troops, they became involved in fighting with South African forces which invaded southern Angola in late October. On 7 November, the first 650 Cuban combat troops began to arrive in Luanda, and were immediately deployed to face an FNLA/Zairean invasion in the north. On 10 November, the invading column was routed and the FNLA virtually destroyed as an effective fighting force at Caxito.

On the same day, the Portuguese finally withdrew. All three rival movements proclaimed independence, but the MPLA enjoyed a decisive advantage in the continuing struggle for power; it controlled the capital, received growing amounts of Soviet military equipment, and had the backing of Cuban troops, who numbered an estimated 13,000 by early 1976. Meanwhile, the South African invasion column had reached a position some 320km (200 miles) from Luanda by late November, but unwillingness to risk a direct confrontation with the Cubans brought the South African advance to a halt.

Having smashed a final FNLA offensive, composed largely of British mercenaries, in December, the Cuban/MPLA forces swung south to face the South Africans, who began to withdraw. Their UNITA allies were left to suffer a number of serious defeats, which prompted Savimbi to re-adopt the guerrilla strategy he had pursued against the Portuguese.

The MPLA still relied upon the presence of a large contingent of Cuban troops for its security. UNITA continued to be active in the south, and by 1985 controlled large areas of the countryside, thanks in part to the continued support of South Africa, which on several occasions mounted large-scale raids into Angola from neighbouring Namibia against guerrilla bases of the Namibian liberation movement, SWAPO.

Post-independence conflict in Mozambique 1975-

Following independence, anti-FRELIMO guerrillas of the Resistançia Nacional Moçambicana (ReNaMo), backed by South Africa – and until 1980 by Rhodesia – carried out regular attacks, particularly against vital economic targets. An agreement signed by South Africa and Mozambique at the border town of Nkomati in March 1984 appeared to provide for the end of aid to ReNaMo by Pretoria, in return for a promise by Samora Machel to clamp down on the activities of the African National Congress (ANC), which had mounted a guerrilla campaign against South Africa from bases in Mozambique. However, despite the Nkomati accord, ReNaMo was still active in early 1985.

Incursions into Shaba, Zaire 1977-78

After the defeat of Moise Tshombe, former leader of the Katangan secessionist movement, by General Mobutu in the Congolese power struggle in 1965, members of the Katangan Gendarmerie loyal to Tshombe fled to Angola, where they fought for the Portuguese against the Angolan independence movements. In 1975, however, they changed sides to support the MPLA against

the FLNA forces of Mobutu's brother-in-law, Holden Roberto, in the Angolan Civil War.

After the MPLA victory in 1976, the Gendarmes organised themselves to launch attacks into Katanga, now renamed Shaba, against Mobutu's regime. Their first incursion, in March 1977, was repulsed, largely with the aid of Moroccan troops. A second incursion, in May 1978, led to the temporary capture of the important mining centre at Kolwezi, but French and Belgian paratroopers were flown in to retake the town.

The likelihood of further attacks was much reduced after the Angolan and Zairean governments reached agreement on non-interference in one another's internal affairs, and Angolan support for the Katangans was withdrawn.

Rhodesian War 1966-79

Within months of the Unilateral Declaration of Independence by the white Smith regime on 11 November 1965, guerrillas of the two Rhodesian black nationalist movements, the Zimbabwe African People's Union (ZAPU), led by Joshua Nkomo, and the Zimbabwe African National Union (ZANU), of which Robert Mugabe was later to assume the leadership, were operating from bases in Zambia against northern Rhodesia. Throughout the late 1960s these raids continued, but were a costly failure.

During the early 1970s, ZANU began to build up its military wing, the Zimbabwe African National Liberation Army (ZANLA), which from December 1972 staged operations into northeastern Rhodesia from FRELIMO-controlled areas of Mozambique. Rhodesia mounted an intensive counter-insurgency campaign, which by mid-1974 seemed to be turning in favour of the government forces, but the Portuguese revolution of April 1974 and the subsequent moves towards independence for Portugal's African colonies swung the balance back in favour of the guerrillas, who were now able to infiltrate along the whole length of Rhodesia's eastern border.

A brief ceasefire broke down, but splits weakened the nationalists, and Nkomo was involved in talks with Ian Smith. The war escalated during 1977, however, and soon spread throughout the whole country, with ZANLA forces active throughout eastern Rhodesia amongst the Shona tribe and Nkomo's Zimbabwe People's Revolutionary Army (ZIPRA) infiltrating the Matabele area in the west. In March 1978, Smith agreed to the creation of a coalition with black moderates, led by Bishop Abel Muzorewa, but the war continued, in spite of heavy guerrilla losses and Rhodesian attacks upon guerrilla bases in Mozambique, Zambia, Botswana and Angola.

Britain promoted a negotiated settlement, and at the Lancaster House conference in London during late 1979, an agreement was reached between the Smith-Muzorewa regime and Mugabe and Nkomo's Patriotic Front alliance, which led to a ceasefire on 28 December and full independence on 18 April 1980.

Elections held in early 1980 resulted in an overwhelming victory for Mugabe's ZANU faction of the Patriotic Front, and there were increasingly sharp clashes with Nkomo's ZAPU supporters, many of whom took to the bush once more to fight for a greater Matabele share in power. Mugabe reacted strongly, and his troops conducted a ruthless counter-insurgency campaign.

Namibian Liberation War 1966-

Namibia is a former German colony now administered by South Africa. In the early 1960s, the South West Africa People's Organisation (SWAPO) began to form a guerrilla army, the People's Liberation Army of Namibia (PLAN). Trained in black African and East European states, SWAPO guerrillas began to infiltrate through Portuguese-controlled Angola and the Caprivi Strip in northeast Namibia during late 1965, and the first clash with South African security forces occurred in August 1966.

Initially, the South Africans were able to contain the insurgency, even though it was widely supported by the majority Ovambo tribe. But the situation changed dramatically following the collapse of Portuguese control of Angola during 1974-75, which greatly improved SWAPO's position, allowing it to operate from bases in southern Angola. Large numbers of recruits flowed across the border to join SWAPO, and by 1978 it had an estimated 10,000 guerrillas, whose operations began to extend throughout Namibia.

SWAPO also gained wide international recognition, and in December 1976 the UN General Assembly voted to support its armed struggle against South African control. South Africa, on the other hand, remained determined to retain Namibia as a buffer against radical black African nationalism, and on repeated occasions invaded Angola to attack SWAPO bases, although under an agreement concluded with South Africa in February 1984, Angola appeared to have promised to restrain SWAPO infiltration across the Angolan-Namibian border in return for the withdrawal of South African troops from Angolan territory.

Eritrean insurgency 1961-

The former Italian colony of Eritrea was federated with neighbouring Ethiopia in 1952, and annexed by it in 1962, but already in September 1961, the Eritrean Liberation Front (ELF) had opened an armed independence struggle. During the 1960s, the ELF tied down large numbers of Ethiopian troops, but the Eritrean separatist movement was weakened by a number of splits and internal conflicts, which resulted in the formation of the more radical Eritrean People's Liberation Forces (EPLF) in 1970.

Nevertheless, the Eritrean insurgency became increasingly serious, and contributed to the downfall of Ethiopian Emperor Haile Selassie in 1974. His replacement by a left-wing military regime, the Derg, did not bring an end to the war in Eritrea, however, and a joint ELF-EPLF offensive was launched against the capital of Eritrea, Asmara, in January 1975. Although this was repelled, the Eritrean guerrillas extended their operations throughout 1975, and by May 1976 were strong enough to rout a mass Ethiopian peasant militia.

By December 1977, Ethiopian control of Eritrea was confined to Asmara and the Red Sea ports of Massawa and Assab, but a massive build-up of the Ethiopian armed forces, backed by the Soviet Union and Cuba, allowed the Derg to launch a successful offensive against the Eritrean separatists following the Ethiopian victory in the 1977-78 Ogaden War against Somalia. The Eritreans were forced to revert to guerrilla tactics, but retained control of much of the countryside, despite the Ethiopian recapture of most urban centres.

The insurgency continued into the 1980s, and along with similar guerrilla movements in several other Ethiopian provinces, including Tigre, presented a permanent challenge to central authority which the Derg was unable to suppress.

Ogaden War 1977-78

Somalia first laid claim to the Ethiopian Ogaden Province in 1960, and border clashes took place during 1964. But it was after the fall of Haile Selassie in 1974 that Somalia was tempted to exploit a period of Ethiopian weakness to seize the Ogaden by force. At first Somalia merely gave military aid to guerrillas of the West Somali Liberation Front (WSLF), which was formed in 1975. In May 1977, however, regular Somali troops were actively involved in support of a large-scale WSLF offensive in the Ogaden, and on 24 July the Somali Army launched an all-out invasion of the province. The Somali advance was rapid, and by 12 September Jijiga in northern Ogaden had fallen to Somali troops, leaving Harer as the last Ethiopian stronghold in the province. The suspension of US military aid to Somalia, and large-scale Soviet support for Ethiopia, gradually swung the balance away from Somalia, however, and the over-extended position of Somali forces in the Ogaden made them increasingly vulnerable.

The counter-offensive began on 3 February 1978, spearheaded by Cuban troops, and forced the Somalis to fall back on Jijiga in the Gara Marda Pass, but the town fell to the Ethiopians on 5 March after a Cuban armoured column had been successfully lifted by helicopter into the Somali rear. The Somalis were now forced into a headlong retreat, and the regular Somali Army was withdrawn from Ethiopian territory during mid-March.

Border clashes continued, however, and Somalia on several occasions alleged that Ethiopian aircraft had attacked Somali territory. Inside the Ogaden, a Cuban garrison remained stationed around Harer to deter a further Somali invasion, but guerrillas of the WSLF continued to be active in the sparsely populated region.

Tanzanian invasion of Uganda and its aftermath 1979-

As his regime became increasingly unstable, Ugandan dictator Idi Amin Dada was tempted to reinforce his position by a foreign adventure, and consequently launched an invasion of northern Tanzania in November 1978. His troops captured the Kagera salient in northern Tanzania, but by January 1979 had been thrown back across the border by the Tanzanian Army, which went over to the offensive in March, along with some 1000 troops of the anti-Amin Ugandan National Liberation Front (UNLF).

The Tanzanian invasion of Uganda progressed cautiously, but on 7 April Entebbe airport was attacked, and with its fall, Kampala itself came under siege. Some 2000 Libyan troops had been flown in to help in the defence of Kampala; they suffered heavy casualties before the city fell on 10 April. Amin's forces withdrew northwards, and by the end of April, Amin had fled into exile.

Supporters of former President Milton Obote staged a coup in May 1980, and Obote himself returned to power in December of that year. Anti-Obote groups turned to armed resistance, and in January 1982 formed the Ugandan Popular Front, which claimed to control most of the Ugandan countryside. In 1982, the 25,000-strong Tanzanian contingent which had supported Obote withdrew, and guerrilla attacks became increasingly regular, even in Kampala. The insurgency continued in 1985, and there were repeated allegations of brutality and massacres by the Ugandan Army in its attempts to impose control on the divided country.

Western Sahara 1976-

On 26 February 1976, Spain officially withdrew from its colony of Spanish Sahara. It had earlier concluded a secret agreement promising to hand over power to Polisario (Popular Front for the Liberation of Saguiet el Hamra and Rio de Oro), but following intense Moroccan pressure, including the 'Green March' by 350,000 unarmed Moroccans who crossed the border in November 1975, it allowed Morocco and Mauritania to partition the sparsely populated but phosphate-rich territory.

The occupation of the area by Morocco and Mauritania met with immediate resistance from Polisario, and the majority of the population of the former Spanish Sahara withdrew to refugee camps in Algeria, which provided support and bases for the Polisario guerrillas. The war placed an immense strain upon the relatively weak Mauritania, and following a military coup in July 1978, Mauritanian forces were withdrawn from the Western Sahara. The territory evacuated by the Mauritanians was rapidly occupied by Moroccan troops, however. The Moroccan forces adopted a strategy of attacking Polisario bases, while constructing a long, high rampart of sand in order to prevent Polisario infiltration. This fortification proved successful in diminishing Polisario attacks from the east, but did not prevent the wide-ranging operations of Polisario columns in the south.

Polisario established a government-in-exile of the Saharoui Arab Democratic Republic (SADR) in March 1976, and by November 1980 this had been recognised by 27 states. In February 1982, the SADR was admitted to the Organization of African Unity (OAU), although this proved an extremely contentious decision. By the mid-1980s, the situation in the Western Sahara appeared to have reached a military and diplomatic stalemate. The Moroccans were strong enough to defend their claim to the Western Sahara, particularly in the north, but the Polisario guerrillas seemed determined to fight on indefinitely.

WAR IN PEACE.